Empowering Women Through Microfinance in Developing Countries

Yahaya Alhassan
University of Sunderland in London, UK

Uzoechi Nwagbara
University of Sunderland in London, UK

A volume in the Advances in Finance, Accounting, and Economics (AFAE) Book Series

IGI Global
PUBLISHER of TIMELY KNOWLEDGE

Published in the United States of America by
IGI Global
Business Science Reference (an imprint of IGI Global)
701 E. Chocolate Avenue
Hershey PA, USA 17033
Tel: 717-533-8845
Fax: 717-533-8661
E-mail: cust@igi-global.com
Web site: http://www.igi-global.com

Library of Congress Cataloging-in-Publication Data

Names: Alhassan, Yahaya, 1971- editor. | Nwagbara, Uzoechi, editor.
Title: Empowering women through microfinance in developing countries / edited by Yahaya Alhassan, and Uzoechi Nwagbara.
Description: Hershey, PA : Business Science Reference, [2023] | Includes bibliographical references and index. | Summary: "This book addresses the lack of understanding about how microfinance can be used to empower women in developing countries. The insights provided in this book will be valuable for researchers, students, microfinance institutions, policymakers, state institutions, managers, non-governmental organizations, and financial institutions looking to expand their product portfolio and outreach. The book also provides policy directions and rethinking of practice in using microfinance as a strategy for eliminating barriers to women's empowerment in developing countries"-- Provided by publisher.
Identifiers: LCCN 2023023869 (print) | LCCN 2023023870 (ebook) | ISBN 9781668489796 (hardcover) | ISBN 9781668489802 (paperback) | ISBN 9781668489819 (ebook)
Subjects: LCSH: Microfinance--Social aspects--Developing countries. | Businesswomen--Developing countries. | Poor women--Employment--Developing countries. | Women--Developing countries--Economic conditions.
Classification: LCC HG178.33.D44 E45 2023 (print) | LCC HG178.33.D44 (ebook) | DDC 332.109172/4--dc23/eng/20230602
LC record available at https://lccn.loc.gov/2023023869
LC ebook record available at https://lccn.loc.gov/2023023870

This book is published in the IGI Global book series Advances in Finance, Accounting, and Economics (AFAE) (ISSN: 2327-5677; eISSN: 2327-5685)

British Cataloguing in Publication Data
A Cataloguing in Publication record for this book is available from the British Library.

Advances in Finance, Accounting, and Economics (AFAE) Book Series

Ahmed Driouchi
Al Akhawayn University, Morocco

ISSN:2327-5677
EISSN:2327-5685

Mission

In our changing economic and business environment, it is important to consider the financial changes occurring internationally as well as within individual organizations and business environments. Understanding these changes as well as the factors that influence them is crucial in preparing for our financial future and ensuring economic sustainability and growth.

The **Advances in Finance, Accounting, and Economics (AFAE)** book series aims to publish comprehensive and informative titles in all areas of economics and economic theory, finance, and accounting to assist in advancing the available knowledge and providing for further research development in these dynamic fields.

Coverage

- Economics Geography
- Auditing
- Economics of Intellectual Property Rights
- Finance and Accounting in SMEs
- Health Economics
- International Economics
- Banking
- Economic Theory
- Accounting information systems
- Development Economics

IGI Global is currently accepting manuscripts for publication within this series. To submit a proposal for a volume in this series, please contact our Acquisition Editors at Acquisitions@igi-global.com or visit: http://www.igi-global.com/publish/.

The Advances in Finance, Accounting, and Economics (AFAE) Book Series (ISSN 2327-5677) is published by IGI Global, 701 E. Chocolate Avenue, Hershey, PA 17033-1240, USA, www.igi-global.com. This series is composed of titles available for purchase individually; each title is edited to be contextually exclusive from any other title within the series. For pricing and ordering information please visit http://www.igi-global.com/book-series/advances-finance-accounting-economics/73685. Postmaster: Send all address changes to above address.

Titles in this Series

For a list of additional titles in this series, please visit: www.igi-global.com/book-series

The Importance of Entrepreneurship in Fostering Economic Progress
Mohammed El Amine Abdelli (University of Brest, France) Naima Bentouir (Ain Temouchent University, Algeria) and Esra Sipahi Döngül (Aksaray University, Trkey)
Business Science Reference • © 2023 • 205pp • H/C (ISBN: 9781668471272) • US $240.00

Circular Economy Implementation for Sustainability in the Built Environment
Nicoleta Cobîrzan (Technical University of Cluj-Napoca, Romania) Radu Muntean (Transilvania University of Braşov, Romania) and Raluca-Andreea Felseghi (Technical University of Cluj-Napoca, Roania)
Business Science Reference • © 2023 • 330pp • H/C (ISBN: 9781668482384) • US $250.00

Management, Technology, and Economic Growth in Smart and Sustainable Cities
Jorge A. Ruiz-Vanoye (Universidad Politécnica de Pachuca, Mexico)
Business Science Reference • © 2023 • 320pp • H/C (ISBN: 9798369303733) • US $240.00

Optimizing Energy Efficiency During a Global Energy Crisis
Meltem Okur Dinçsoy (Trakya University, Turkey) and Hamit Can (Trakya University, Turkey)
Business Science Reference • © 2023 • 408pp • H/C (ISBN: 9798369304006) • US $240.00

Theory and Practice of Illegitimate Finance
Abdul Rafay (University of Management and Technology, Pakistan)
Business Science Reference • © 2023 • 389pp • H/C (ISBN: 9798369311905) • US $295.00

The Sustainable Fintech Revolution Building a Greener Future for Finance
Kuldeep Singh (Faculty of Management Studies, CMS Business School, Jain University (Deemed), Bengaluru, India) Rebecca Abraham (Huizenga College of Business and Entrepreneurship, Nova Southeastern University, Fort Lauderdale, USA) and Prasanna Kolar (Koneru Lakshmaiah Education Foundation, India)
Business Science Reference • © 2023 • 358pp • H/C (ISBN: 9798369300084) • US $250.00

Sustainable Growth and Global Social Development in Competitive Economies
Andrei Jean Vasile (Petroleum-Gas University of Ploiesti, Romania & Romanian Academy, National Institute for Economic Research "Costin C. Kiriţescu", Romania) Mile Vasić (European Marketing and Management Association, Banja Luka, Bosnia and Herzegovina) and Predrag Vukovic (Institute of Agricultural Economics, Belgrade, Serbia)
Business Science Reference • © 2023 • 331pp • H/C (ISBN: 9781668488102) • US $250.00

IGI Global
PUBLISHER of TIMELY KNOWLEDGE

701 East Chocolate Avenue, Hershey, PA 17033, USA
Tel: 717-533-8845 x100 • Fax: 717-533-8661
E-Mail: cust@igi-global.com • www.igi-global.com

Table of Contents

Detailed Table of Contents

variables, namely: origin, development initiative, situation, intervening variables, intervention strategies, and outcomes. The communication dynamics model for women empowerment presented shows how the factors of success and failure lead to empowerment or no empowerment. There is also no empowerment when conditions are oppressive or too lenient.

This study examined the effect of credit access on women farmers' welfare through crop output in the Northern Region of Ghana. The impact of credit on welfare through output was examined using the conditional mixed process (CMP) model on 300 women farmers. Credit access, welfare, and output were estimated individually and also within a conditional mixed process (CMP) system for choice of appropriate estimation due to endogeneity. Age, household size, extension access, and membership of farmer-based organization (FBO) significantly influence farmers' choice of credit source while credit access, expenditure on inputs, years of farming, land size, and membership of FBO significantly impacts on crop output. Crop output and off-farm income significantly influence welfare of women farmers. Pairwise correlation of credit sources revealed that Village Savings and Loans Association (VSLA) and Susu sources are complementary, and farmers who accessed credit from VSLA also accessed credit from Susu (rotating savings and credit associations).

As households diversify their livelihoods, their credit demands will also be diversified. This creates competition among the livelihood activities pursued by farm households for credit and other productive resources. Whereas some households may be expanding the same livelihood activities to enjoy economies of scale (stepping up), others are expanding into other livelihood activities (stepping out). Better still, others are just maintaining their activities, levels of livelihood activities they engage in (hanging in). Whichever approach is adopted has specific implications for resource demands, allocation, and utilization. This chapter examines the gendered implications of livelihoods diversification for household credit demands and allocations using mixed methods. Most farm households in contemporary Ghana this chapter concludes are diversifying out of agriculture. The implication of this is that the number of households demanding credit for non-farm livelihood activities is increasing at the expense of farm livelihood activities.

This chapter explores the multifaceted linkages between microfinancing, financial inclusion, and women empowerment in India. It delves into the key mechanisms through which improved access to microfinancing and other financial services fosters women's economic, social, and political empowerment. The current study helps the financial regulators, government, and the banking industry to know the state of financial inclusion and to analyse the impact and effectiveness of the initiatives and measures taken by them on the empowerment of women in India. It is also providing in-depth knowledge to policy makers to review the existing policies regarding financial inclusion through microfinancing so as to have a substantial impact on women empowerment.

Women, who can benefit less from the resources in the world and have less access to opportunities, are more likely to face the problem of poverty. This study aims to question the role and effectiveness of micro-credit practices in empowering women and increasing their participation in the workforce in the province of Samsun. The method of the research is the survey method. The universe of the research includes women using micro-credit within the scope of the Turkish Grameen Microcredit Program in Samsun. In this context, 104 women who were registered in the Micro Credit Branch Directorate in Samsun were included in the study. According to research findings, the majority of the participants participated in the workforce thanks to microcredit, the use of microcredit is an important tool in increasing the income level of the household, and the use of microcredit increased women's self-confidence; however, the amount of microcredit allocated is not sufficient to meet the needs.

In today's globalized world, women are recognizing in the field of entrepreneurship. This study is on five central government finance schemes—Deendayal Antyodaya Yojana-National Urban Livelihoods Mission (DAY-NULM), Pradhan Mantri Employment Generation Programme (PMEGP), Dairy Entrepreneurship Development Scheme (DEDS), North East Industrial and Investment Promotion Policy (NEIIPP), and Scheme of Fund for Regeneration of Traditional Industries (SFURTI)—applicable in the state of Sikkim. The aim of the chapter is to analyze the year wise growth of women beneficiaries. The data has been collected from government websites, journals, and through 'Right to Information Act 2005'. The study is descriptive in nature. Microsoft excel has been used for data visualization. The results of study

Preface

Microfinance is an initiative that supports the poor and women, in particular, to improve their economic circumstance and living standards in an effective way (Kabeer, 1999). Specifically, microfinance from the prism of women is a catalyst for economic growth, effective resource for poverty alleviation, and women empowerment (World Bank, 2001). The disparities between male and female ratios are often not considered important, but in several areas of the world (especially in developing and emerging countries), women are provided less power, influence and importance when compared with men making them to have little control over their assets and political power (Garikipati, Johnson, Guérin, & Szafarz, 2017; Rahman, 2016). Additionally, women in more rigid, patriarchal societies are probable to experience a higher risk of domestic violence, economic impositions, and cultural maltreatment because economic empowerment challenges patriarchy and expedites social change in male-dominated societies with rigidly defined gender roles (Ajwani-Ramchandani, 2006).

In emerging economies, microfinance institutions (MFIs) and women empowerment is taken to be one of the most effective instruments for alleviating poverty, galvanising economic liberation and strengthening business development (Goetz & Gupta, 1996). Unquestionably, women are one of the most important facets of society and without their contribution to the economy as well as presence societies cannot improve (Fernando, 2006). Accordingly, this argument is given resonance in the penetrating study by Raji Ajwani-Ramchandani titled '*The Role of Microfinance in Women's Empowerment: A Comparative Study of Rural & Urban Groups in India*' as well as comparable texts. Consequently, this book follows in the footsteps of texts and studies that shed light on the interface between microfinance and women's empowerment, an often neglected and under-researched field, but from multiple perspectives that enrich the literature on this phenomenon.

This issue has created a huge gap in the literature, which rather foregrounds the ascendance of male-dominated discourse, which downplays the contributions of women in microfinance for development and empowerment (Garikipati, Johnson, Guérin, & Szafarz, 2017). Given the above research lacuna, *Empowering Women through Microfinance in Developing Nations* was conceptualised to not only address this gap but to shed light through a variegated perspectives – practice-based, scholarship-focused, and industry-led (Garikipati et al., 2017; García-Pérez, Fernández-Izquierdo & Muñoz-Torres, 2020). Business owners including women entrepreneurs seek microfinance for business development, expansion, and sustainability (Armendariz & Morduch, 2005). Recently, women's involvement in entrepreneurship through MFIs has been instrumental in socio-economic wellbeing of people, societal advancement, and poverty reduction (Ferdousi, 2015). It has been documented that about 916 MFIs globally, with an estimated $124 billion gross loan portfolio in 2018, where 80% of borrowers were women and 65% rural borrowers resulted in 140 million active borrowers (Alhassan & Nwagbara, 2021; García-Pérez et al., 2020).

In developing countries, virtually every business is male dominated causing women to suffer from discrimination, socio-economic dominance, and powerlessness personally and professionally. Also, financial segregation is more complicated for women in developing countries given the ascendency of corruption, illiteracy, weak institutions (including MFSs) and lax regulatory, financial environment (Ferdousi, 2015; Mazumder, 2015). In addressing the importance of financially excluded women in economic development and poverty reduction, MFIs have been institutionalised to help these women in establishing new entrepreneurial ventures (World Bank, 2001). Therefore, governments and non-government organizations waded in to provide subsidized loans for a better lifestyle of people, particularly women, and poverty alleviation. This process has precipitated addressing the issues of gender power imbalance, disempowering existing gender roles and rigid cultural practices that frustrate such interventions to empower women.

Women empowerment leads to increased participation in the workforce, increased voice in society, their increased capability to decide their economic state, and enhanced poverty reduction (Ajwani-Ramchandani, 2006; World Bank, 2001). Central to the philosophy of microfinance is empowering the poorest members of society, facilitating development, and enhancing capacity building (Alhassan & Nwagbara, 2021; World Commission of Environment and Development, WCED, 1997). As contended by Fernando (2006), globally, poverty is distributed unevenly (Bateman, 2011), and microfinance can be a catalyst in transforming the dynamics of women powerlessness and underdevelopment (James, 2018). Guided by the buoyancy of this debate, microfinance is institutionalised to alleviate poverty, enhance grassroots development, and increase women's participation in the economy as a method of not only empowering women but a technique of involving stakeholders to actualise sustainable rural development (Ferdousi, 2015).

Consequently, developing economies have made incredible effort in this regard; however, there is need to further investigate the impact of microfinance on rural women's development and in achieving the wider agenda of sustainable development as declared by the United Nations for social change, macroeconomic stability, and women's liberation in general (Mazumder, 2015). Microfinance is often touted as fundamental to social change and poverty alleviation (Cohen, 2018; Alhassan & Nwagbara, 2021; James, 2018), which are integral to achieving the ideals of Millennium Development Goals (MDGs) and lately Sustainable Development Goals (SDGs) (Alhassan & Nwagbara, 2022). Evidence on the effect of microfinance is mixed (Mazumder, 2015; García-Pérez et al., 2020). For example, some of the findings of Nawaz (2010) was that microfinance resulted in a moderate alleviation in poverty but did not reach many of the poorest potential recipients; however, other research concluded the opposite (Bateman, 2011). Similarly, Bateman (2011) reported that up to 5% of participants in three key microfinance institutions lifted their families out of poverty through microfinance within the context of Bangladesh.

1. THE CHALLENGES

Guided by the above logic, the nexus between microfinance and women's empowerment, power and socio-economic development cannot be over-emphasised. Also, the centrality of women's development, empowerment and liberation through microfinance is unquestionably crucial for realising the tenets and principles contained in the United Nation's SDGs (Ajwani-Ramchandani, 2006; UNDP, 2006).

The socio-economic, political, and cultural issues that microfinance confronts are palpably more complicated in emerging economies, as sketched in preceding sections, where there is rising poverty, high incidence of weak institutions, poor governance system, limited empowerment, rigid gender roles and for the foremost part leadership crisis (Mazumder, 2015; Nwagbara, 2014; Alhassan & Nwagbara, 2021). Accordingly, Nwagbara (2014) avers that unless these development, institutional and governance issues are addressed, developing nations would seemingly lag behind in the comity of nations thus negatively impacting women's empowerment, social transformation and genuine rise of female entrepreneurs for economic prosperity. The following are some of the challenges:

- The challenge of bettering the fortunes of women nationally and globally as ensconced in the SDGs and policy documents of countries around the world.
- The challenge of confronting pre-existing, rigid cultural practices that inhibit women from engaging in entrepreneurship and business venturing.
- The challenge of reinventing economies towards poverty eradication, social mobility, and urban/rural development.
- The challenge of creating and sustaining effective political, social, and economic institutions that can galvanise mobilisation of women's voice, power, and liberation in traditionally patriarchal societies.
- The challenge of establishing effective, financial institutions that regulate business financing/lending.
- The challenge of institutionalising effective corporate governance frameworks and financial policies and procedures that would encourage women's empowerment and sustainable finance.
- The challenge of establishing effective structures, instruments and institutions for responsibility, accountability and transparency given the spate of institutional voids (weak institutions) in developing nations.

Thus, this volume maintains that examining the interface between microfinance and women's empowerment could be one of the most effective methods of not only shedding light anew light on empowerment and microfinance but a way of responding to broader, global challenges that women face in society (Ajwani-Ramchandani, 2006). Consequently, microfinance is considered extremely important in reducing inequality, decreasing socio-economic disequilibrium, addressing injustice, mitigating risks associated with weak institutions, and developing microbusiness (James, 2018; Fernando, 2006). In the main, to the knowledge of the editors, the interface between microfinance and women's empowerment is still at an embryonic phase that is given less attention, under-researched and under-theorised, which foregrounds the conceptualisation of this volume!

2. SEARCHING FOR A SOLUTION

In searching from solution, *Empowering Women through Microfinance in Developing Nations* was conceived, which is in league with comparable texts and discourses on the subject matter of microfinance and women's empowerment, which is the mainstay of this book (Ajwani-Ramchandani, 2006). When compared to charity and related concepts, microfinance has a special ideological demand and is capable of transforming societies, addressing gender imbalance, triggering re-conceptualisation of men-women differences and changing socio-economic disparities in society (Mazumder, 2015). It is now taking a centre stage in strategies, methods, movements, policies, and practices that advance societal health, stakeholder relations and economic prosperity of nations (WCED, 1987). In a well-executed prior study,

Khursheed (2022) has awakened consciousness in rethinking the contributions of microfinance in women's empowerment, which finds continuation in related studies (see Ajwani-Ramchandani, 2006; Garikipati et al., S., 2017; Goetz, et al., 1996; Kabeer, 1999; Rahman, 2016; World Bank, 2001).

3. ORGANISATION OF THE BOOK

The book is organised into thirteen well-researched chapters. A brief description of each of the chapters is presented below:

This book begins with 'A Micro Financial Female Entrepreneurship Case From Turkey Kadama Women's Cooperative' brilliantly written by Ali Iskender, Beyza Hatirnaz, and Ahmet Istanbullu. It sheds new light on micro financial female entrepreneurship from the Turkish context. Similarly, Maybel Fernandez Vallado in Chapter 2 has brilliantly outlined and analysed communication dynamics of women in microfinance projects as a model for women empowerment. This is done from the prism of microfinance projects for poverty alleviation in the Philippines. In deepening this discourse, Hamna A Abdallah, Osman Tahidu Damba, Gideon Danso-Abbeam, Abdul-Razak Alhassan, and Issahaku Salifu have excellently contributed to this volume on the topic: 'Credit Access, Crop Output and Welfare of Women Farmers in the Northern Region of Ghana', which brings new vista to credit access could be instrumental in facilitating women's welfare and arguably empowerment within the Ghanaian context. Still on the Ghanaian context, Katherine Kaunza-Nu-Dem Millar, Abdul-Razak Alhassan, and Mamudu Abunga Akudugu have deftly broadened this horizon about microfinance and women's empowerment in Ghana through their well written piece: 'Gendered and Generational Analyses of Farm Households' Livelihood Diversification in Ghana: Implications for Credit Demands and Allocations' in Chapter 4.

Furthermore, in their thought-provoking piece, in Chapter 5, 'Impact of Financial Inclusion and Microfinancing on Women Empowerment in India: A Review', Richa Nangia, Rashmi Singel, Swati Shrivastava, Kshama Sharma, and Vijay Anand Dubey have investigated the phenomenon of microfinance more widely by using the methodology of a review of key literatures on the concept within the Indian context, which helps to give the book more contextualisation and depth. The Turkish context has been used by Bilgenur Sahbazoglu and Işıl Alkan to further drill down into the variegated context that this book delves into. This is operationalized leveraging the topic 'Microcredit Applications in Context of Empowering Women Case of Samsun Province, Turkey'. This was well executed with rigour and great insights furthering the dialectics of women's empowerment through microfinance. Also, Serdar Yener, Sinop, Aykut Arslan and Ayşegül Eda Kop have refreshingly used the topic 'Women Entrepreneurs in Turkey: The Empirical Analysis of Microcredit Applications and Economic Growth Relations' to further illustrate the Turkish context.

In taking forward the Indian context, Sunil Kumar and Soni Subedi wrote on the topic 'Microfinance Schemes for Women Entrepreneurship in India: A Case study of Sikkim State', which is a more contextualised portraiture of how microfinance initiatives can drive women entrepreneurship and development in India. Similarly, in their insightful chapter: 'The Role of Microfinance in Women Empowerment', Arohi Anand and Animesh Karn, precisely uncovers the interface between microfinance and women's empowerment in a rectilinear dimension, broadening insights into the Indian context. Leveraging the topic 'Processes, Challenges and Outcomes of the Self-Provision of Micro-Credit Schemes by Women's Group in Chókwè Region, Mozambique', Ndwa Ndwakhulu Stephen Tshishonga has brilliantly captured in bold relief the Mozambiquan context, which enriches the literature. This is further investigated by Peterson K

Ozili in his riveting chapter 'Women Financial Inclusion', which extends the confines of empowerment by taking into consideration the phenomenon of inclusion that is at the heartbeat of empowerment. From the angle of theoretical and conceptual development, Ndwa Ndwakhulu stephen Tshishonga uses his well captioned topic, 'Microfinancing for Women Economic Empowerment and Development: Conceptual and Theoretical Considerations' to enrich the theoretical contributions and dimensions of the volume. This conversation has been continued in 'The Role of Microfinance in Promoting Women's Empowerment: A Socioeconomic Approach' by Gertrude Amoakohene, which is penetrating and insightful.

Yahaya Alhassan
University of Sunderland in London, UK

Uzoechi Nwagbara
University of Sunderland in London, UK

REFERENCES

Ajwani-Ramchandani, R. (2006). *The Role of Microfinance in Women's Empowerment: A Comparative Study of Rural & Urban Groups in India*. Emerald Publishers.

Alhassan, Y., & Nwagbara, U. (2021). *Microfinance and Sustainable Development in Africa*. IGI Publishers.

Alhassan, Y., & Nwagbara, U. (2021). Institutions, Corruption and Microfinance Viability in Developing Countries: The Case of Ghana and Nigeria. *Economic Insights - Trends and Challenges, 10*(73), 61–70. doi:10.51865/EITC.2021.02.06

Alhassan, Y., & Nwagbara, U. (2022). *Transforming Economies through Microfinance in Developing Nations*. IGI Publishers.

Armendariz de, A. B., & Morduch, J. (2005). The Economics of Microfinance. MIT Press.

Bateman, M. (Ed.). (2011). Confronting Microfinance: Undermining Sustainable Development. Kumarian Press.

Cohen, S. (2018). *Transforming Social Action into Social Change: Improving Policy and Practice*. Routledge.

Ferdousi, F. (2015). Impact of microfinance on sustainable entrepreneurship development. *Development Studies Research*, *2*(1), 51–63. doi:10.1080/21665095.2015.1058718

Fernando, J. L. (Ed.). (2006). Microfinance: Perils and prospects. Routledge.

García-Pérez, I., Fernández-Izquierdo, M. A., & Muñoz-Torres, M. J. (2020). Microfinance Institutions Fostering Sustainable Development by Region. *Sustainability (Basel)*, *12*(7), 1–23. doi:10.3390u12072682

García-Pérez, I., Muñoz-Torres, M. J., & Fernández-Izquierdo, M. A. (2018). Microfinance institutions fostering sustainable development. *Sustainable Development (Bradford)*, *26*(6), 606–619. doi:10.1002d.1731

Garikipati, S., Johnson, S., Guérin, I., & Szafarz, A. (2017). Microfinance and gender: Issues, challenges and the road ahead. *The Journal of Development Studies*, *53*(5), 641–648. doi:10.1080/00220388.2016.1205736

Goetz, A. M., & Gupta, R. S. (1996). Who takes the credit? Gender, power, and control over loan use in rural credit programs in Bangladesh. *World Development*, *24*(1), 45–63. doi:10.1016/0305-750X(95)00124-U

Gueyie, J.-P. (2013). *Microfinance in Developing Countries Issues, Policies and Performance Evaluation*. Springer. doi:10.1057/9781137301925

James, V. (Ed.). (2018). Capacity Building for Sustainable Development. CABI.

Kabeer, N. (1999). Resources, Agency, Achievements: Reflections on the Measurement of Women's Empowerment. *Development and Change*, *30*(3), 435–464. doi:10.1111/1467-7660.00125

Mazumder, M. S. U. (2015). Role of Microfinance in Sustainable Development in Rural Bangladesh. *Sustainable Development (Bradford)*, *23*(6), 396–413. doi:10.1002d.1599

Milgram, B. L. (2005). From Margin to Mainstream: Microfinance, Women's Work and Social Change in the Philippines. *Urban Anthropology and Studies of Cultural Systems and World Economic Development*, *34*(4), 341–383.

Nwagbara, U. (2014). *Leading Sustainability in Nigeria: Problems, Processes and Prospects*. Lambert Academic Press.

Rahman, S. M. A. (2016). Leveraging ICTs for empowering women entrepreneurs in Bangladesh: A review of recent developments and way forward. *European Journal of Business and Social Sciences*, *5*, 1–15.

Spiegel, S. J. (2012). Microfinance services, poverty and artisanal mineworkers in Africa: In search of measures for empowering vulnerable groups. *Journal of International Development*, *24*(4), 485–517. doi:10.1002/jid.1781

United Nations Development Programme (UNDP). (2006). *Beyond scarcity: power, poverty and the global water crisis*. United Nations Development Programme.

Van Rooyen, C., Stewart, R., & de Wet, T. (2012). The Impact of Microfinance in Sub-Saharan Africa: A Systematic Review of the Evidence. *World Development*, *40*(11), 2249–2262. doi:10.1016/j.worlddev.2012.03.012

World Bank. (2001). *Engendering Development: Through Gender Equality in Rights, Resources, and Voice*. World Bank.

World Bank. (2018). *Poverty and Shared Prosperity 2018: Piecing Together the Poverty Puzzle*. World Bank.

World Commission of Environment and Development. (1997). *Our Common Future*. Oxford University Press.

Acknowledgment

Without the various effort made by all and sundry, this book would not have been possible, although, Drs Yahaya Alhassan and Uzoechi Nwagbara "fathered" the concept of the volume! Having said that, we wish to heartily thank and congratulate those who have been instrumental to the writing and production of this book.

First, without God the writing of this book would not have been possible. We thank Him for giving us the strength, knowledge and sound mind to execute this book project!

Second, we would also like to thank the members of the editorial and acquisition team of IGI for their professionalism, dedication, prop, and hard work during the production of this book. We want to say a big 'thank-you' to them, for the opportunity to co-edit this book. Particularly, we are indebted to Jocelynn Hessler, Managing Editor (Book Development); Jan Travers, Director of Intellectual Property & Contracts IGI Global; and Melissa Wagner; Vice President of Editorial, IGI Global.

Third, we are sincerely grateful to all the contributors – Ali Iskender, Beyza Hatirnaz, Ahmet İstanbullu, Maybel Fernandez Vallado, Hamna A Abdallah, Osman Tahidu Damba, Gideon Danso-Abbeam, Abdul-Razak Alhassan, Issahaku Salifu, Katherine Kaunza-Nu-Dem Millar, Mamudu Abunga Akudugu, Richa Nangia, Rashmi Singel, Swati Shrivastava, Kshama Sharma, Vijay Anand Dubey, Bilgenur Sahbazoglu, Işıl Alkan, Sunil Kumar, Soni Subedi, Ndwa Ndwakhulu stephen Tshishonga, Gertrude Amoakohene, Arohi Anand, Animesh Karn, Serdar Yener, Aykut Arslan, Ayşegül Eda KOP and Peterson K Ozili – for the spirit and sense of commitment shown.

Finally, our profound gratitude goes to our families for the time granted us to write this book!

Introduction

Microfinance is widely promoted as a key strategy for reducing poverty in developing countries across the world. The provision of microfinance has also been shown to be a viable strategy for microenterprise development in the developing world. In this regard, various books on the role of microfinance in reducing poverty and fostering microenterprises in developing countries have been written to aid our understanding. However, a huge amount of time and resources have recently been devoted by researchers and policy makers to understand how this concept can be used as a catalyst for women empowerment in developing countries. There is, therefore, no specific book that examines the influence of microfinance on women empowerment in developing countries. Undoubtedly, the use of microfinance as a strategy for improving the socio-economic wellbeing of beneficiaries in developing countries is growing. Yet, this microfinance experiment needs to be expanded with the view to specifically empower women in developing countries. Therefore, this book seeks to explore the influence of microfinance on women empowerment in developing countries. The book will not only shed light on the contribution of microfinance to the socio-economic well-being of women but will provide policy directions for using microfinance as a strategy for eliminating barriers to women empowerment in developing countries.

The role that microfinance institutions have played in women empowerment in developing countries is the focus of this book. Women empowerment is "an active, multi-dimensional process which enables women to realize their full identity and powers in all spheres of life" (Mandal, 2013). Varghese (2011) defines women empowerment as "a process whereby women become able to organize themselves to increase their own self-reliance, to assert their independent right to make choices and to control resources which will assist in challenging and eliminating their own subordination". The question therefore is "how can women be empowered?" Various studies (Mudaliar and Mathur, 2015; Asad, et al., 2020; Khursheed, et al. 2021) provide evidence of a positive relationship between provision of microfinance and the socio-economic wellbeing of women in developing countries. The work of Sanyal (2009) suggests that microfinance plays a pivotal role in fostering women's social capital and influence in society. Similarly, Aruna and Jyothirmayi (2011) have shown that microfinance has a significant impact on the economic and social status of women. This is because microfinance creates employment opportunities for unemployed women thus increasing the level of their income and productive capacity. Furthermore, the provision of microfinance has been shown to improve women's self-confidence and esteem. Kumar, et al. (2015) have also shown that women who receive microfinance have been found to be more independent and engaged in social and economic decision making in their communities. However, there is no specific book that explores how the provision of microfinance influence women empowerment in developing countries. To this end, this book hopes to examine the role of microfinance in empowering women in developing countries.

This book aims to examine and bring on board the various views and perspectives on the role of microfinance in empowering women in developing countries through industry experts, experienced researchers, and policymakers. The role of microfinance in empowering women in developing countries will be explored by these experts and contributors from different perspectives with the view to forming an opinion on the problems, processes, and prospects of using microfinance as a catalyst for women empowerment in the developing world. The book will focus on the nexus between microfinance and women empowerment in Asia, Africa, Middle East, Eastern Europe, and South America which have witnessed growing activities of microfinance institutions.

Theoretical and empirical insight to be provided in this book will be a priceless resource to researchers, students, microfinance institutions, policymakers, state institutions, managers and non-governmental organisations working in developing countries. This book is envisaged to also benefit financial institutions that are looking to expand their product portfolio and outreach. The book will offer great insight into theoretical, policy-oriented, and practical ways to address some of the challenges of using microfinance as a catalyst for empowering women in developing countries. Given the focus of this book on the nexus between microfinance and women empowerment, there will be a broadening of ideas on how the provision of microfinance can aid the empowerment of women in developing countries.

Yahaya Alhassan
University of Sunderland in London, UK

Uzoechi Nwagbara
University of Sunderland in London, UK

REFERENCES

Aruna, M., & Jyothirmayi, M. R. (2011). The role of microfinance in women empowerment: A study on the SHG bank linkage program in Hyderabad (Andhra Pradesh). *Indian Journal of Commerce and Management Studies*, *2*(4), 78–95.

Asad, A., Hameed, W. U., Irfan, M., Jiang, J., & Naveed, R. T. (2020). The contribution of microfinance institutes in women-empowerment and role of vulnerability. *Revista Argentina de Clínica Psicológica*, *29*, 223–238.

Khursheed, A., Khan, A. A., & Mustafa, F. (2021). Women's social empowerment and microfinance: A brief review of literature. *Journal of International Women's Studies*, *22*(5), 249–265.

Kumar, D., Hossain, A., & Gope, M. C. (2013). Role of micro credit program in empowering rural women in Bangladesh: A study on Grameen Bank Bangladesh Limited. *Asian Business Review*, *3*(4), 114–120. doi:10.18034/abr.v3i4.287

Mandal, R. K. (2013). Success Story of Self Help Groups without Financial Help: A Paradigm Shift of Women Empowerment. *Journal of Global Economy*, *9*(1), 29–40. doi:10.1956/jge.v9i1.275

Mudaliar, A., & Mathur, A. (2015). Women empowerment through microfinance. *International Journal of Arts, Humanities and Management Studies, 1*(2), 58-65.

Sanyal, P. (2009). From credit to collective action: The role of microfinance in promoting women's social capital and normative influence. *American Sociological Review, 74*(4), 529–550. doi:10.1177/000312240907400402

Varghese, T. (2011). Women empowerment in Oman: A study based on Women Empowerment Index. *Far East Journal of Psychology and Business*, *2*(2), 37–53.

Chapter 1
A Micro Financial Female Entrepreneurship Case From Turkey:
Kadama Women's Cooperative

Ali Iskender
Tourism Faculty, Atatürk University, Turkey

Beyza Hatirnaz
Akçakoca School of Tourism and Hotel Management, Turkey

Ahmet Istanbullu
https://orcid.org/0009-0008-0002-6100
Social Sciences Institute, Atatürk University, Turkey

ABSTRACT

In this study, the role of women's cooperatives in women's employment was examined. In this context, Kadama Women's Cooperative, which continues its activities in Erzurum province of Turkey, was determined as the sample group of the research. The research was prepared with a qualitative method and semi-structured interviews with Kadama officials. The data were written down and analyzed by content analysis. Kadama officials were asked questions about the activity areas of the cooperative, its role in women's employment, its studies and projects for training women for employment. Afterwards, the responses received from the participants were divided into specific themes. As a result of the research, it was concluded that Kadama Women's Cooperative conducted many studies on women's employment, nearly 1000 women took courses in the cooperative, the products produced by women at their homes or in the cooperative were sold and marketed via cooperative, and social and psychological support was provided to women within the cooperative.

DOI: 10.4018/978-1-6684-8979-6.ch001

INTRODUCTION

Economic growth, where human influence is high, is very important for countries (Arslan, 2020). The increase in women's participation in the workforce is one of the successes that caused social and economic changes by the 20th century (Schein, 2020). Although the participation of women in socio-economic life for Turkey dates back to the first years of the republic before many European countries, it is possible to say that there was a pause and a regression over time. Active participation of women in life and equal citizenship rights, which started with the right to vote and be elected, continued with women's active participation in education, employment and social life as a result of long discussions. Although there were important steps taken at that time, the fact that social perception transformations could not be achieved in the last 100 years caused women's employment in Turkey, women's economic independence, and their participation in social life to be kept in focus as a topic of discussion. The idea of sustainable development and the transformation of minds around sustainability have forced us to focus more on holistic planning, active participation in processes and equality. This paved the way for all regulations that could ensure the participation of all disadvantaged groups, especially women, in the economy and social life with equal rights in countries that adopt the idea of sustainability. Women's employment is an important factor for the sustainability of the economy and the continuity of growth (Şahin, 2022). While the female labor force increases in the developed countries depending on the level of education, this increase is slow in developing or less developed countries, but the rates are decreasing (Fallah et al., 2021).

The roles women had to obtain rarely in the early examples of socialization; and dominantly in developing and masculinizing social orders have caused their existence to be limited to household roles. These roles, which previously emerged as a division of labor within the household, spread over time to the social sphere; and it has not been possible for women to avoid taking on the maternal and recuperative household roles on their own. The placement of gender-based roles in social perceptions within the framework of the norms developed by the dominant systems has put women under the dominance of men, separating them from employment, education, art, philosophy, in other words, from all areas of social life. On the other hand, gender equality is among the main goals of sustainable development today. In addition to that, achieving economic growth is possible by ensuring gender equality in business life as well as in all areas of society (Korkmaz and Budak, 2022). The discriminatory behavior towards women in the workforce and the lack of adequate educational opportunities prevented women from turning to certain sectors and hindered growth in these sectors (Göcen, 2020).

Labor force participation in a region plays an important role for economic growth (Verdugo and Allègre, 2020). Particularly, the desire of developing countries to use the labor factor, which is the most important element of production, has made it necessary for women to participate in the workforce (Aksoy et al., 2019). In Turkiye, where nearly half of the population is women, women's participation in the workforce is important for development and growth (Türlüoğlu, 2018). The employment rate of women in Turkiye is lower than that of men. This situation stands as an obstacle to economic growth (Göcen, 2020). The existence of women in social life and in the economic system is not seen in the active area.

Associating all responsibilities of household duties with women, especially in traditional societies, is the most important internal obstacle to women's participation in employment by allocating additional time and energy. Similarly, the social perceptions associating women with the household and their interpretation as unpaid family workers, especially in the field of agriculture, are among the biggest external obstacles to women's participation in employment in developing and underdeveloped countries. With the sustainable development steps taken to ensure perceptual transformation, women's independence and economic choices have been increased. In Turkiye, although there is no legal prohibition, the thought towards women and the domestic responsibilities associated with women have prevented women from entering business life, and have also caused working women to end their business life (Umutlu and Öztürk, 2020). As in similar countries, traditional family structure hinders women's employment in Turkey (Aksoy et al., 2019). In other words, social perceptions and rules have limited women to domestic roles in a way that supports the general acceptance, and has greatly restricted their inclusion in socio-economic life. Although the lifestyles of individuals vary in both the eastern and western regions due to the diversity of the society in our country, with the development of the society in general, women's participation in the workforce has begun to undermine male supremacy in the context of the increased workforce (Beduk, 2005). Even if there are economic and social factors that prevent entrepreneurship, there are also organizations that provide support to women (Durukan, 2021). The double emphasis of the Sustainable Development Goals on both ensuring equality and ensuring gender equality has been instrumental in taking more precise and increasing steps that will support women's participation in socio-economic life, like all disadvantaged groups, and ensure positive discrimination. In countries like Turkey that fall under the category of developing countries and shape their development priorities around sustainability goals, all kinds of initiatives where women will gain their economic independence are supported in different ways. Especially in rural areas, there are cooperatives for women to achieve their economic independence and create a sustainable economy by uniting in line with the same goal by demonstrating their economic power (Yıldırım, 2020). With these supports, the labor force participation of women who want to be economically free and improve their economic situation has increased and they have even become entrepreneurs by establishing their own businesses (Beduk, 2005).

According to the Women in Statistics report of the Turkish Statistical Institute (2022), 49.9% of Turkiye's population is composed of women, while 50.1% is men. Although the population rates are so close to each other, the female employment rate is lower than the male employment rate (Yaman and Sarihan, 2021). In the Turkish Statistical Institute National Education Statistics Database and Household Labor Force Survey 2021 report, the employment and labor force participation rates of women and men in Turkiye are shown in Table 1.

Table 1. Indicators selected by gender, 2021

	Total	Men	Women
Illiterate population rate (25+ age)	%3,5	%1	%6,1
Higher education graduate population rate (25+ age)	%23	%25,1	%20,9
Employment rate (15+ age)	%45,2	%62,8	%28
Labor force participation rate (15+ age)	%51,4	%70,3	%32,8
Unemployment rate (15+ age)	%12	%10,7	%14,7

Source: Turkish Statistical Institute (2021), National Education Statistics Database - Household Labor Force Survey

As can be seen from the table above, while the labor force participation rate in the total population in Turkey was 51.4%, this rate was 70.3% for men of all men in population and 32.8% for women of all women in population. This imbalance in rates is one of the main motivations of the efforts to make women active in socio-economic life through cooperatives in rural areas. Cooperatives, which provide significant support for the products women produce within the scope of their skills or in the process of gaining the skills they can gain, are one of the important pillars of gender-based equality in rural development. Within the scope of the study, Kadama was considered as one of the cooperatives established in the rural areas of Turkey and playing an intermediary role in the transformation of women's labor into income, and its functioning was examined.

The Role of Education in Women's Employment

After the World War II, the increase in women's employment, which started with the agricultural sector, turned to the industrial sector with the industrial revolution. Today, thanks to the developing information and technology, the employment of women has also started to appear in the service sector. Migration from rural areas to the city, increase in women's education, decrease in agriculture supported the increase in the service sector (Dücan and Polat, 2017).

A U-shape has been observed in women's employment in Turkey. Firstly; While the unpaid employment of women on agricultural lands in the family was high, this situation declined with the expansion of the markets and the orientation of family-oriented production to the market, and finally, with the increase in technology and education, women's employment increased in the service sector (Tansel, 2002). "Studies show that education levels are not equally distributed between men and women, and the education level of individuals differs according to the development level, age and income levels of the countries (Erdoğan and Yaşar, 2018, p. 20)". People tend to the workforce according to their education level (Kavak, 1997). Women's participation in the workforce is not only important in terms of employment, their employment quality also reveals the place of women in the workforce (Sundari, 2020). The increase in education level allows women to participate in the workforce under better conditions and to have economic independence (Satı and Yılmaz, 2020). Since education is seen as a costly investment, it can be said that women are willing to join the workforce to meet their education expenses (Erdoğan and Yaşar, 2018). Low education levels of women also cause them to work more hours in labor-intensive sectors (Sati and Yılmaz, 2020).

As well as the growth need of the economy, there is a need for education in the qualified workforce as well. The education and skill capability received often appear as a criterion during the labor force participation phase. In addition, education stands out in terms of continuous development and sustainability of the economy (Pekel, 2019). "When girls who are deprived of education join the working life or have to earn an income, they cannot find the opportunity to participate in employment outside of certain occupational groups due to lack of education" (Öztürk and Karataş, 2020, p. 194).

According to the results of the Turkish Statistical Institute (2022) Women with Statistics report and the National Education Statistics Database, there has been an increase in the proportion of the population aged 25 and over who completed at least one education level between the years 2008-2021. This rate, which was 81.1% in 2008, became 92.1% in 2021. Considering the rates by gender, the rate of women, which was 72.6% in 2008, increased to 87.3% in 2021; the rate of men, 89.8% in 2008, and 97.1% in 2021. As can be understood from this result, the education level of women in Turkey continues at lower levels compared to men.

Factors Affecting Women's Employment

According to EU 2021 data, the rate of not seeking a job for women in the 25-54 age group who are out of the workforce is higher than men, but it has been determined that women have a 5.7% higher care responsibilities and a 2.9% higher rate of family reasons (Eurostat, 2022). While the female employment rate, which is less than the male employment rate in all European countries, was 67% in all European countries in the 20-64 age group in 2018, the highest female employment rate was 80% in Sweden, the lowest rate in Greece (49%) and Italy. (53%) (Eurostat, 2020). The fact that the female employment rate is almost the same in the socially developing Scandinavian countries and the less developed East Asian countries also reveals the importance of the perspective on women in society (Akgeyik, 2017).

Yılmaz and Zoğal (2015) emphasized that with the widespread employment of women, they can achieve economic independence and sustainability. The lower rate of female employment may have cultural, social or economic factors (Şahinoğlu and Ağırkaya, 2021). Wage inequality between men and women, as well as marital status of women, that is, being married with children or being single or widowed, are among the effects on women's participation or non-participation in employment (Kocabaş and Küçükbay, 2023). The status in which women are employed is as important as their rate of participation in employment. Although there is a developing industrial sector in Turkey, women are still employed as free family workers in the agricultural sector (Aksoy et al., 2019). According to the perception of society; It is thought that women with higher education levels should work in higher status in the society, and women with low education levels are more suitable for jobs such as cleaning and childcare (Öztürk and Karataş, 2020). According to the Women in Statistics report of the Turkish Statistical Institute (2022), the rate of female ambassadors in Turkey was 27.2%, the rate of female deputies was 17.3%, the rate of female professors was 33.2% and the number of women in managerial positions was 20.7%. According to the information obtained from the Labor Force Statistics report of the Turkish Statistical Institute (2023), the rate of employed people in the total population in Turkey was 48.4%, while this rate was 65.9% for men and 32.1% for women.

With thousands of years of social rules and perceptions, women have been limited to domestic roles with settled life and they have not been allowed to go out of these roles until recently. Among the gender-based social roles, women's roles, which were previously defined as child care and housekeeping, brought about their isolation from socio-economic life over time and their becoming completely dependent on men in the masculine world. Over time, all social rules, cultural transmissions, traditions, philosophical discourses and even religious teachings began to take shape around the power of men and the pacified existence and helplessness of women. In such an order, education, art and philosophy were shaped around men and women were tried to be isolated from these fields, and this caused women to participate in educational and cultural opportunities less than men. Women, who have been made dependent on men by being removed from economic life, have difficulties in accessing economic resources and obtaining economic independence (Şahinoğlu and Ağırkaya, 2021).

Especially in underdeveloped societies, the fact that household duties are still women's duties reduces women's entire lives to housework. The shortage of human capital experienced by women negatively affects their participation in the workforce (Beken, 2020). Although it is more in rural settlements than in urban settlements, family problems, religious belief or socio-cultural structure reduce the participation of women in the economy (Şahinoğlu and Ağırkaya, 2021).

Öztürk and Karataş (2020) determined the base situations that make women's employment difficult in their study as follows; educational inequality between men and women, prevailing thoughts that women should deal with chores such as housework and childcare, the opinion that women's productivity will be low where they will work because of their housework, the fact that women stay away from business life due to lower wages, the fact that men are more demanded in physically demanding jobs. As a solution, he argued that legal regulations that ensure equal opportunity between women and men and that women should be supported by necessary projects for their participation in employment.

It was mentioned in a similar study (Kocabaş and Küçükbay, 2023) that although women's employment increased, it was still at a lower level than male employment, and it was argued that this was caused by factors such as education level and fertility. They also stated that fertility and education level are related to each other and that women's employment will contribute to the growth of the country's economy. While the female employment rate of Turkey, which has many entrepreneurship and vocational courses for women's employment, is below that of European countries, the fact that the projects for women's employment within the country are not as high as the projects for men could not meet the demands in the EU accession process in terms of equality in opportunity for women and men (Cavlak and Akpinar, 2019).

Since women's employment has an important place in the economic sustainability of countries and women's employment is less than that of men, it should be supported by the countries (Durukan, 2021). In the first years of the republic, attempts to increase the place of women in socio-economic life slowed down and even regressed in the following periods. The issue of women's employment, which is one of the conditions of women's economic independence as a branch of gender equality, is one of the priority areas that Turkey should develop in the sustainable development process. Organizations such as the EU, UN and OECD have had an impact on bringing the issue of women's employment back to the agenda in Turkey again. Since 1990, studies on women's employment have accelerated (Yavuz Özgül, 2019). It was signed with the National Respectable Work Program agreement between Turkey and ILO (International Labor Organization) in 2009 in order to ensure equality between men and women and increase women's employment (Özmen, 2011). The increase in the education level of women has led them to turn to entrepreneurship and lead a more social life (Uyanık, 2020). Ever since, many public institutions and non-governmental organizations have been established to increase women's employment and entrepreneurship (Durukan, 2021).

The Foundation for the Evaluation of Women's Work (KEDV), one of the organizations in Turkey, has aimed to support women's collective efforts to create an egalitarian, inclusive and strong society, and has also adopted a vision of a society without inequality and poverty since 1986. KEDV carries out its activities through 3 main programs which are supporting women's organization and cooperatives against poverty around the common needs of grassroots women, encouraging women's leadership and economic empowerment in development and creating resilient societies, and strengthening the role of women in disaster and migration management (KEDV, 2023).

Another non-governmental organization established for the empowerment of women is the Women Entrepreneurs Support Association (KAGIDER). The aim of the association, which was established in Istanbul in 2002 is to empower women economically, politically and socially. KAGIDER, which acts with the public, private sector, many non-governmental organizations and its stakeholders and has more than 400 members, also advocates equality in opportunity for women and men. The "Supporting the Development of International Competitiveness" (UR-GE) Project planned by KAGIDER with the support of the Ministry of Commerce of the Republic of Turkey, was created with 11 KAGIDER membered companies from many sectors. With this project, it is aimed to gain and develop the foreign trade market competencies and export competencies of the participating companies. In addition, with the "Gender Sensitive Procurement and Investment" (GRPI) project of the United Nations Women's Unit (Un Women), it is aimed to raise awareness of private sector organizations to make purchases from women entrepreneurs and invest in women entrepreneurs (KAGİDER, 2023). To increase the competitive power of small and medium-sized enterprises in the market, to provide their technological equipment and to create economic empowerment are among the duties of the Small and Medium Enterprises Development and Support Administration (KOSGEB), which was established in 1990 with the aim of honesty, accessibility, respect, transparency, reliability, impartiality and innovation. Women's Business Development Centers (KİŞGEM) were opened in the provinces of Istanbul, Nevşehir, Kütahya, Çorum and Tekirdağ to support women entrepreneurs. KOSGEB, which provides 20% more support to women entrepreneurs than men, provides grant and loan support (Özyılmaz, 2016). In addition, KOSGEB provided a total of 1 billion 5 million 363 thousand 551 Turkish Liras to 55 thousand 46 businesses run by women between 2015-2019 (Uyanık, 2020).

Another organization that works for women's empowerment in society is the General Directorate of the Status of Women (KSGM), which continues its activities under the Ministry of Family and Social Services of the Turkish Republic and coordinates the activities related to women with other institutions such as the Ministry of National Education, Ministry of Health, Ministry of Agriculture (Özyılmaz, 2016). Projects such as "My Mother's Job is My Future Project", "Women's Empowerment Strategy and Action Plan" and "Engineer Girls of Turkey Project" are continued by the General Directorate (KSGM, 2023).

METHODOLOGY

In this study, Kadama Women's Cooperative, which was established and operated by Women serving in Erzurum, Turkey, was discussed. Kadama Women's Cooperative consists of Kadama Cafe where food products such as cakes and pies are served, Kadama Mansion where local delicacies are served, Kadama Green Yakutiye and Kadama Fruit Drying Facility, where women display and sell their products. Local cooperatives are important in terms of producing solutions to local needs and providing support for development by bringing qualified workforce to the economy especially in underdeveloped rural areas. Kadama also creates opportunities for women in Erzurum to combine their skills with education and cooperation, and creates opportunities for women to be included in socio-economic life. In this context, it is important to determine the mission and operating principles, to determine their multi-faceted contributions to gender equality, which is one of the key issues of sustainable development, to set an example for initiatives in different regions, and to create resources for possible initiatives in the same region. The main purpose of the research is to reveal the establishment and functioning systems of the Kadama Women's Cooperative. For this main purpose, sub-topics such as the effect of the cooperative on women, its effects on local life and family life, the role of women in the cooperative, their place in the sustainable rural development process and basic funding methods have been tried to be revealed within the scope of the research. The research shows the feature of a single case design developed to reveal the current situation of Kadama Women's Cooperative (Şimşek, Yıldırım, 2008).

Kadama Women's Cooperative was established by 7 women coming together for common purposes. The research group consists of 7 entrepreneur women. First of all, the director of Kadama Women's Cooperative was contacted and an appointment was made for an interview at a suitable time. Afterwards, an interview was held on 12 June 2023 with 4 women who were the architects of the establishment of the

Kadama Women's Cooperative. Two of the women participating in the research group are pharmacists, one is an art historian, and one is freelancer. Participants are 40 years old and older. In order to enable the participants to give detailed answers about the subjects to be informed, and to share their information and comments as widely as possible, the opinions of the participants were taken with a semi-structured interview form consisting of general questions.

A focus group meeting was held simultaneously with the participants in order to get different and/or complementary answers to the same questions together and to create an environment where different opinions can come together (Gülcan, 2021: 97). In order to increase the quality of the answers to be received, the interview was held in the cooperative where the participants felt comfortable and were ready in a chat environment.

Interview questions were formed in line with the main and sub-goals of the research. The statements in the interview form are as follows:

Table 2. Content of the semi-structured interview

Question	Related Goal
Could you please introduce yourself?	Defining participant profile
What is the main goal of Kadama?	Defining founding purposes of Kadama
What are the fields of activity of Kadama?	Defining practices related to founding purposes
What contributions can Kadama provide for women?	Defining support and benefits provided for women
Did you get or have you ever gotten any support from government?	Determining regional or/and national funding systems
What do you do socially responsible?	Determining diversity of benefits provided in developing process

During the interview, a voice recording was taken to increase the reliability of the data. The voice recordings were transcribed and the answers were classified and presented with explanations in order to reveal the existence and functioning of the cooperative.

FINDINGS

Founding Idea of Kadama Women's Cooperative

K4: The cooperative was formed with the aim of making women's labor visible and creating added value to a large extent. In this sense, both the participation of women in the economy, the diversification of their domestic roles, and the development and active maintenance of them in ways they can achieve their own independence constitute the basis of its establishment.

K2: We call The official incarnation of our journey on March 8, 2020, starting with the dream of a woman who contributes to the economy and builds the society, she gets stronger and stands up, as Kadama Women's Cooperative. Starting with only 7 women as a women's solidarity cooperative; we are currently a women's cooperative with nearly 40 partners, together with 100s of Erzurum women, aiming to add every handicraft product that women can make to the economy, from needle lace, raw linen, ehram to curd filling. This is a dream we all see at the same time. It is a dream that we all see as the common denominator. The story of a dream established to change the lives of thousands of women. We walk with them, develop together, learn together and grow together.

The goal of Kadama Women's Cooperative

K3: The cooperative remains loyal to its goals both to enable women to take an active role in economic life and to be self-sufficient, and to ensure the survival of handicraft products, one of the concrete cultural values in Erzurum, through women, and to create added value with this method. It is the aim of the Kadama Women's Cooperative to create an economy that fits the identities of women with low education and low income levels, starting with the best job, and bringing this together in a sustainable manner. In summary at this point; The main objective of the cooperative is to enable women to take an active role in sustainable development, to achieve economic independence and social equality.

K.1: Reproducing and embroidering the traditional products of Erzurum from the past to the future with needles, awls and rolling pins by completely reproducing the most beautiful examples of manual labor, and while doing this, involving women in employment is our main goals. Our aim is to serve all women in Erzurum, either as our employees, supporters or customers, actually to all women in Turkey, not only the ones in Erzurum. We are actually a collection of them. Kadama Women's Cooperative aims to have a buildingless factory that will have a say in social development by bringing women in the region together. In this respect, we aim to create a social development model. But of course, our primary premise is to open employment opportunities for women.

The Idea of the Kadama Women's Cooperative

K1: Kadama Women's Cooperative, which was established by women from Erzurum, plays an important role in women's employment in Erzurum. We came out as "if you don't exist, we are missing". In Erzurum women's denominator, all the stories of every woman living in Erzurum, about the production of this city, about the land, is our story.

The Mission of Kadama Women's Cooperative in Local Development

In parallel with its goals, the mission of the cooperative is presented as placing the existence of women, creativity, independence and the idea of equality in the local and sustainable development process; planning and practices are shaped within this framework;

K1: The Kadama Women's Cooperative will start with the best job they know, and will create a sustainable economy that suits their identities and thus will support them to continue their lives where they are. To date, we have provided nearly 400 women with half of the minimum wage to the economy of this city.

K2: We do our work for economically sustainable purposes. More than 1000 women have intermittently hired us now. They produce at home, produce here, in our kitchen, in our workshop, they give us what they bring from home. That way, but the woman will know that when I make 20 of these a month, she will get 10 lira per product. We're trying to find a sales guarantee.

K3: We contribute 586,000 TL per month to Erzurum's economy.

Kadama Women's Cooperative Employee and Member Profile

K3: Under the umbrella of women, many women from different lifestyles are members of the cooperative and offer support. This is one of the most important examples of the social respect for diversity, which is one of the most important and most difficult elements of sustainability, and the transition of the idea of diversity from diversity to life.

K1: We do not have any restrictions there, there are university graduates among the women here. There are deans, there are those who are illiterate. There is an 18 year old. There is someone who is 65 years old. This is a point where women come only with their female identity. There are those who come to be rehabilitated. There are people who come to contribute to the economy. There are those who come to maintain a unity. There are those who come to the women's story believing in the women's movement. In this sense, everyone comes to Kadama Women's Cooperative to get whatever they think.

K.2: Women socialize here every day.

Grants and Supports Received by Kadama Women's Cooperative

Kadama is a cooperative that has provided its investments with public support. The investments, which form the financial basis of today's continuity, have been provided with state supports.

K.1: We received two supports. We bought one for the resource of our drying facility within the framework of KOOP-DES (Support Program of Cooperatives) support of the ministry of commerce to cooperatives. We bought one of the benches you see here from KUDAKA (Northeast Anatolian Development Agency). The total support of both is 200.000 TL.

K4: Now look why the Kadama Women's Cooperative is actually accomplishing something incredible. I take great pleasure in saying this, which is the largest women's cooperative in the Eastern Anatolia region. Every woman here has a lot of work that she does with conviction in this sense. But can they be supported more as women's co-operatives? They really can. If we had this support, we could have gone much further. Because we have a fruit and vegetable drying facility. There is one mansion. There is this facility. We also have an artisan restaurant in Çaykara. We are a cooperative with many such businesses.

Kadama Women's Cooperative Target Market

K3: Kadama preferred digital channels for marketing and delivering products to consumers. the main reason for this is to increase the sales volume of the products and the area reached by reaching all parts of Turkey;

K4: We are at Trendyol now. We have just entered, but our aim is to sell the products of all women there. Now we are getting there, and it would be much easier if this export was supported. It's a little difficult, but we do it.

Steps for the Recognition of Kadama Women's Cooperative

In order to increase their awareness and credibility, Kadama has chosen and used both the social networks and promotion channels of the cooperatives, as well as the media and famous names as intermediaries.

K3: Within the scope of "Habitat Young Business International" women's empowerment through cooperatives, we came first in the world in a competition in which cooperatives in 65 countries were candidated. We talked about kadama live to 65 countries. In addition, there is a 10-page introductory magazine sharing that describes kadama in both Turkish and international languages, published in the international journal published with the Habitat UN. We have been featured in many local and national press. Doğan Haber, İhlas News Agency, Anadolu Agency, TV8, NTV, CNN, Beingurme, we took part in all of them. We hosted the "Buraların yabancısıyız (we are strangers around here)" program on Acun media and Exxen TV. We participated in the "Evdeki Mutluluk (happiness at home)" program with Vahe Kılıçarslan. We participated in the city cuisines program with Beingurme Asuman Kerkez.

The contribution of Kadama Women's Cooperative to the Survival of Traditional Products

Protection of cultural heritage and keeping it alive through women is one of the areas that the cooperative attaches importance to, as it is repeated in the target and mission.

In order to be successful in preserving cultural elements as they are and transferring them to future generations, it is made possible by women to open new areas of use for cultural elements whose usage areas have narrowed. The fact that they do not lose their essence with their updated usage areas is one of the points that the cooperative attaches importance and draws attention to. In this context, in addition to gender equality, social equality and development dimensions, the protection and survival of cultural elements have emerged over time as intermediate targets shaped around the main goal;

K1: After women come here, they are transformed into a completely different story. The woman makes it very interesting. We are trying to embrace everything that is about to be forgotten. It has both survival and economic purposes. We try to do all of these in our own way, encouraging adaptation to the present. Even though it is not used today, like the Ehram (a street dress entirely knitted from sheep's wool, used by women as outer clothing and covered in one piece), we diversify this product for different purposes and ensure that the product is used in daily life.

K2: We are working on the revival of the ehram and carnavas, which has been used very often in our history, and is now almost forgotten. These fabrics, which are used to protect from the cold, are produced on hand looms, remaining loyal to the old production method. The most important innovation here is to combine the texture of history with modern designs by combining this product, which is used to protect from the cold, with Seljuk motifs. On this road, which we say from inheritance to the future, we reveal the anonymous patterns revealed by our ancestors and put them into daily life. Our other innovative work on this subject is about product design and usage areas, and we turn these products, which are only used for covering, into products that can be used in many parts of daily life with our art historian Dear Serap.

K3: We have Çapana (a type of weaving) models attracting attention from Istanbul and Izmir

K1: Innovative products that can be bought, sold, applied, and produced, we do not think of changing the traditional part of such products without losing the respect of the products themselves. We don't change it, we adapt it to the point of how we use it today.

The Functioning of the Kadama Women's Cooperative

It is possible to define as getting amateur production processes to a professional level over time with a women cooperation by preserving the authentic features,

K1: Kadaman's own social responsibility. We work with flour, oil, yarn. Women transform these into such an added value. f you were to open a company now, you would bring in those who know best. We have no such obligation. Here, women are getting their best and we are getting better. Everyone has a contribution to offer, we look at it. Everyone has something to do. All the women you see and all the women you have not seen have a different story.

Product Variety of Kadama Women's Cooperative and Their Surviving Struggles

Erzurum cheese is produced with traditional methods and breakfast services are offered in an authentic atmosphere in certain areas. However, it has not been possible to ensure their active and systematic participation in tourism yet. If the needed support is provided, it is possible to potentially provide traditional gastronomic production and service delivery.

K.1: In fact, Erzurum's local breakfast is very extensive and special. We asked for a lot of support from the tourism guides, but we were undermined. We offer a very special breakfast in a very special setting. We asked so much support from the guides to promote it, but for now we couldn't. Gastronomy actually concerns all institutions closely. Erzurum is not a place that is monopolized by only a few, but I mean that this place should be paved. As we all know, France's cheese exports have a turnover of 3.3 billion dollars per year. The Netherlands is again 3.3 billion dollars.

K3: We have many kinds of cheese, but the people who said they would support us always let us down. In fact, if kadama had received enough support, it could have made more contributions to Erzurum.

Kadama Women's Cooperative Customer Satisfaction

One of the important issues to ensure continuity is the satisfaction of the target audience. In line with the explanations, the evaluation of the products and services offered by the cooperative, in which the preservation of authenticity, originality and tradition is one of the main objectives, contains clues in terms of continuing their existence.

K1: We have been on Trendyol for a month. Seller comments 10/10 We are on our way to becoming a tt in Trendyol.

K2: There are also good comments on Instagram. We are doing our job properly.

K3: There are people who come to us by chance. There are people who watch the live broadcast of Ms. Canan to 65 countries and then come from Spain, Mexico and Japan.

K4: I work in the mansion, the customers are very satisfied with the food. Especially the ladies spend their days there. No additives, so they prefer it.

The Effects of Kadama Women's Cooperative on Women's Social Life and Psychology

The fact that creativity and cooperation enter their lives shaped by daily routines and that they can develop themselves with people from similar or completely different lives also ensure that women and their close circles are psychologically affected positively. Socialization and participation in production bring a psychological relief of being useful, expressing themselves and producing to women and their related circles.

K4: We do not have time to get depressed here.

K1: Here, people reveal their own labor. People get away from their troubles and something good comes out.

K4: My son was obsessed with hygiene and he was constantly washing his hands. He is studying architecture. After coming here, his communication with people has been different. A monster who makes cakes has come out of him. He makes so delicious desserts that they are unbelievable.

K1: As we said over 800 products, we are open to all products in which women express themselves. The woman comes here for purely economic purposes, then she sees that she also embroiders. The spiritual side is very interesting. Never tell women that they can not do it, we learn every day.

K4: This place is addictive, we go home, but our heart is here.

K1: No Saturday, no Sunday. We are always here.

Kadama Gives Freedom to Women

Kadama provides women with the opportunity to take care of themselves and discover themselves, as well as economic freedom. It is seen that Kadama's most important achievements are that their daily lives, which are mostly spent at home and housework, turn into productivity and cooperation, and that they can provide economic freedom, social benefit and self-confidence from this production.

K1: Men are also very satisfied in this sense. Because the money is coming. It is a woman's business. The woman is happy. The most important message we will give is that "happy women, happy society".

K4: My husband says what did you do to my wife? There are some who say their wives want to come there even on the weekends.

K1: The woman is so productive... she just doesn't know what to produce. If the woman cannot express herself, it is a problem, but when the woman expresses herself here, the problem disappears. The woman, who has not been able to get her economic freedom and education or something, isolates herself from the society. She just gets into a mold with the TV and the phone. When a woman has the opportunity after an age, she hugs it with all her hands. This is the success of Kadama.

K3: Thanks to Kadama, the woman goes out at least every day. They are getting on the bus.

K2: Thanks to Kadama, the woman leaves the house and gets dressed. They dress properly and look after themselves.

K1: they also use time correctly. The women are programming their life. The real miracle of Kadama Women's Cooperative is that a woman can see herself where she never thought about herself. They meet their dreams here.

CONCLUSION

Kadama Women's Cooperative is an organization established in Erzurum province and takes its power from women. As a result of the interviews, it was understood that the cooperative provides services for the material and moral needs of women. The cooperative makes a great contribution to regional sustainable development goals in terms of women's participation in socio-economic life, supporting women's productivity and creativity, ensuring economic independence and social equality. Among the primary objectives of the cooperative are women's participation in employment, their qualification, vocational training and improving the quality of life. For these purposes, course programs are organized for women. After this course training, a certificate is given and women are employed. Kadama, which continues its activities in a city where women's employment is relatively low compared to other cities, makes a great contribution to the sustainable development process with this mission. The sole purpose of existence of kadama is not women's employment. Kadama sees the woman as a companion. Here, women feel themselves at home and socialize, contribute to production, and as a result, support their own family budgets. Some of the women who come to Kadama and participate in the production process are housewives. Thanks to Kadama, these housewives socialize, get away from the home environment and go to the work they love with great passion. In this way, they pass from the consumer dimension to the producer dimension. Kadama adds a new meaning to women's lives. Here, women transform from a woman who stays at home to a woman who is active in social life and economically free.

Kadama Women's Cooperative also offers women the opportunity to be better psychologically. Here, women also get the opportunity to get away from the stress they are exposed to at home or in their private life by keeping busy with a job. Similarly, it is possible to say that finding a space for self-expression and being able to put it into practice gives women a psychological relief and self-confidence. For this reason, women working in Kadama do their jobs with love and go to work with great enthusiasm. This contributes to women feeling better psychologically. The positive effects of this situation are also reflected in the family life of women. The husbands of these women also encourage their wives in this sense. At the same time, Kadama modernizes the fabric and weaving methods used traditionally in the past and presents them to the service of today's people. In this direction, it contributes to the survival of cultural heritage. In Kadama, local foods of Erzurum are produced and sold within the cooperative and online applications. Here, women also have the opportunity to establish their own businesses by turning their course training into a profession. Kadama offers women the opportunity to participate in the production process at home, allowing women to manage their business from home. Women also eliminate the problem of finding a market by selling the products they produce at home thanks to kadama.

It is seen that Kadama Women's Cooperative takes part in many television programs and international events and projects. Kadama is not content with the local and wants to show its influence all over Turkey. For this purpose, it has cooperated with many organizations and carried its target to the international dimension. Kadama and similar organizations are very important in terms of women's participation in production, education and social life, especially in places where women's employment is low. In this direction, the number of organizations working for women's employment should be increased. If necessary, these organizations should be supported financially by exempting them from practices such as taxes and VAT. The relations of these institutions with the public should be strengthened.

REFERENCES

Akgeyik, T. (2017). Türkiye'de kadınların işgücü piyasasına katılımını etkileyen faktörler: TÜİK verileri üzerine bir analiz. *Journal of Social Policy Conferences,* (70), 31-53.

Aksoy, N., Felek, Ş., Yayla, N., & Çeviş, İ. (2019). Türkiye'de Kadın İstihdamı ve Etkileyen Faktörler. *Journal of Management and Economics Research, 17*(3), 146–163.

Arslan, M. (2020). *Türkiye'de kadın istihdamı ve ekonomik büyüme arasındaki ilişki* (Publication Number 643103) [Master's thesis]. İstanbul Gelişim University, İstanbul. tez.yok.gov.tr

Bedük, A. (2005). Türkiye'de çalışan kadın ve kadın girişimciliği. *Elektronik Sosyal Bilimler Dergisi, 3*(12), 106–117.

Beken, N. (2020). Covid-19 pandemi sürecinde kadın istihdamı: Türkiye örneği. *Iğdır Üniversitesi Sosyal Bilimler Dergisi*, 47-74.

Cavlak, H., & Akpınar, İ. E. (2019). Türkiye-Avrupa Birliği katılım müzakereleri sürecinde sosyal politika ve istihdam projelerinde kadının yeri. *International Journal of Economics Administrative and Social Sciences, 2*(1), 40–58.

Dücan, E., & Polat, M. A. (2017). Kadın istihdamının ekonomik büyümeye etkisi: OECD ülkeleri için panel veri analizi. *Çukurova Üniversitesi Sosyal Bilimler Enstitüsü Dergisi, 26*(1), 155-170.

Durukan, L. (2021). Türkiye'de kadın girişimcilerin desteklenmesinde KOSGEB'in rolü. *Gazi İktisat ve İşletme Dergisi, 7*(1), 17–37.

Erdoğan, S., & Yaşar, S. (2018). Türkiye'de kadın istihdamının gelişimi: Konya-Karaman örneği. *Karamanoğlu Mehmetbey Üniversitesi Sosyal ve Ekonomik Araştırmalar Dergisi, 20*(34), 18–28.

Eurostat. (2020). *Women's Employment in the EU*. https://ec.europa.eu/eurostat/en/web/products-eurostat-news/-/edn-20200306-1

Eurostat. (2022). *More Women Than Men Outside the Labour Fource*. https://ec.europa.eu/eurostat/en/web/products-eurostat-news/-/ddn-20220622-1

Fallah, B., Bergolo, M., Saadeh, I., Abu Hashhash, A., & Hattawy, M. (2021). The Effect of Labour-Demand Shocks on Women's Participation in the Labor Force: Evidence from Palestine. *The Journal of Development Studies*, *57*(3), 400–416. doi:10.1080/00220388.2020.1806246

Göcen, S. (2020). Ekonomik Gelişme ve Kadın İş Gücü İstihdamı: Türkiye İçin Nedensellik İlişkisi İncelemesi. *Uluslararası İktisadi ve İdari İncelemeler Dergisi*, (29), 45–60.

Gülcan, C. (2021). Nitel Bir Veri Toplama Araci: Odak (Focus) Grup Tekniğinin Uygulanişi Ve Geçerliliği Üzerine Bir Çalişma. *Mersin Üniversitesi Sosyal Bilimler Enstitüsü Dergisi*, *4*(2), 94–109.

Kagider. (2023). *KAGİDER Hakkında*. https://kagider.org/tr/kurumsal/hakkimizda

Kavak, Y. (1997). Eğitim, İstihdam ve İşsizlik İlişkileri. *Hacettepe Üniversitesi Eğitim Fakültesi Dergisi*, *13*(13), 21–26.

Kedv. (2023). *KEDV Hakkında*. https://www.kedv.org.tr/kedv-hakkinda

Kocabaş, İ. Ü., & Küçükbay, F. (2023). Türkiye'de Kadınların İşgücüne Katılım Oranını Etkileyen Faktörlerin Ekonometrik Analizi. *Hak İş Uluslararası Emek ve Toplum Dergisi*, *12*(32), 29–51. doi:10.31199/hakisderg.1202393

Korkmaz, A. N., & Budak, S. (2022). Ekonomik (İktisadi) Kalkınma ve Kadın: Türkiye Örneği. *Mehmet Akif Ersoy Üniversitesi Uygulamalı Bilimler Dergisi*, *6*(1), 197–223. doi:10.31200/makuubd.1084496

Ksgm. (2023). *Projelerimiz*. https://www.aile.gov.tr/Ksgm/Faaliyetler/Projelerimiz/

Özmen, F. (2011). *Türkiye'de Kadın İşgücü İstihdamının Gelişiminde Mikro Kredi Uygulamaları* (Publication Number 286661) [Doctoral dissertation]. Celal Bayar University, Manisa. tez.yok.gov.tr

Öztürk, S., & Karataş, M. (2020). Türkiye'de Kadınların İstihdam Edilmelerini Zorlaştıran Faktörler. *Hak İş Uluslararası Emek ve Toplum Dergisi*, *9*(24), 180–204. doi:10.31199/hakisderg.747129

Özyılmaz, A. M. (2016). *Türkiye'de kadın girişimciliği ve girişimci kadınların karşılaştıkları sorunlar üzerine bir araştırma* (Publication Number 436702) [Master's thesis]. Hacı Bektaş Veli University, Nevşehir. tez.yok.gov.tr

Pekel, E. (2019). Eğitim ve İstihdam İlişkisinin Değerlendirilmesi. In *Cataloging-In-Publication Data* (p. 268). Internatinonal Balkan and Near Eastern Social Sciences Congress Series.

Şahin, D. K. (2022). Kadın İstihdamının Ekonomik Büyümeye Etkisi: Ampirik Bir Analiz. *Uluslararası Ekonomi ve Yenilik Dergisi*, *8*(2), 277–288. doi:10.20979/ueyd.1135131

Şahinoğlu, T., & Ağırkaya, M. B. (2021). Kadın İstihdamını Etkileyen Unsurlar ve Bu Unsurların Demografik Özelliklerle İlişkisi: Erzurum İli Örneği. *İktisadi İdari ve Siyasal Araştırmalar Dergisi, 6*(16), 398-421.

Satı, Z. E., & Yılmaz, B. O. (2020). Endüstri 4.0 ortamında değişen iş ve mesleklerin Türkiye'de kadın istihdamına etkileri. *Strategic Public Management Journal*, *6*(11), 54–76. doi:10.25069pmj.701685

Schein, A. (2020). Female labor force participation in Israel, 1955-2017. *Israel Affairs*, *26*(5), 635–649. doi:10.1080/13537121.2020.1806515

Sundari, S. (2020). Structural Changes and Quality of Women's Labour in India. *The Indian Journal of Labour Economics : the Quarterly Journal of the Indian Society of Labour Economics*, *63*(3), 689–717. doi:10.100741027-020-00245-2 PMID:33046952

Tansel, A. (2002). İktisadi kalkınma ve kadınların işgücüne katılımı: Türkiye'den zaman-serisi kanıtları ve illere göre yatay kesit kestirimleri. *ERC Workıng Papers in Economıcs,* (01/05T), 1-31.

Turkish Statistical Institute. (2021). *İstatistiklerle Kadın.* https://data.tuik.gov.tr/Bulten/Index?p=Istatistiklerle-Kadin-2022-49668

Turkish Statistical Institute. (2022). *İstatistiklerle Kadın.* https://data.tuik.gov.tr/Bulten/Index?p=Istatistiklerle-Kadin-2022-49668

Turkish Statistical Institute. (2023). *İşgücü İstatistikleri.* https://data.tuik.gov.tr/Bulten/Index?p=Isgucu-Istatistikleri-Nisan-2023-49373

Türlüoğlu, E. (2018). Kadın İstihdam ve Büyüme İlişkisi: Var Modeli Analizi. *Avrasya Sosyal ve Ekonomi Araştırmaları Dergisi*, *5*(9), 59–68.

Umutlu, S., & Öztürk, M. (2020). İş Yaşamında Kadın ve Karşılaştığı Sorunlar. *Süleyman Demirel Üniversitesi İktisadi ve İdari Bilimler Fakültesi Dergisi*, *25*(3), 297–306.

Uyanık, Ö. (2020). Türkiye'de Kadın Girişimciliğin Sosyal Hizmet Bağlamında İncelenmesi. *Toplumsal Politika Dergisi*, *1*(2), 134–154.

Verdugo, G., & Allègre, G. (2020). Labour force participation and job polarization: Evidence from Europe during the Great Recession. *Labour Economics*, *66*, 101881. doi:10.1016/j.labeco.2020.101881

Yaman, M., & Sarihan, N. Ö. (2021). Kadınlara Yönelik Yapılan Uygulamalarda Kalkınma Ajanslarının Önemi: Doğu Karadeniz Kalkınma Ajansı (Doka) Örneği. *Eskişehir Osmangazi Üniversitesi Sosyal Bilimler Dergisi*, *22*(1), 225–239. doi:10.17494/ogusbd.952814

Yavuz Özgül, S. (2019). *Kamu desteklerinden yararlanan kadın girişimciler: Ankara ili örneği* (Publication Number 555502) [Master's thesis]. Ankara Yıldırım Beyazıt University, Ankara. tez.yok.gov.tr

Yıldırım, A., & Şimşek, H. (2018). *Sosyal bilimlerde nitel araştırma yöntemleri.* Seçkin Yayıncılık.

Yıldırım, P. D. (2020). Kırsal Kalkınmada Kadın Kooperatiflerinin Rolü: Ahatlı Kadın Kooperatifi Örneği. *Erzurum Teknik Üniversitesi Sosyal Bilimler Enstitüsü Dergisi*, (11), 159–170. doi:10.29157/etusbe.2020.58

Yılmaz, M., & Zoğal, Y. (2015). Kadının işgücüne katılımının tarihsel gelişimi ve kadın istihdamını etkileyen faktörler: Türkiye ve Avrupa örneği. *Econ World*, *2015*, 1–25.

Chapter 2
Communication Dynamics of Women in Microfinance Projects as a Model for Women Empowerment:
Microfinance Projects for Poverty Alleviation in the Philippines

Maybel Fernandez Vallado
https://orcid.org/0009-0000-1039-1322
University of the Philippines, Visayas, Philippines

ABSTRACT

This chapter discusses the communication dynamics of women involved in microfinance projects that contribute to the success or failure of the projects in three cases. Specifically, the study (1) identifies the factors that lead to the success or failure of these projects, (2) identifies the MED (micro-enterprise development) lending methodology used in each case by presenting the key characteristics of the three cases, and (3) presents the communication dynamics of women involved in microfinance projects in the context of culture as a model for women empowerment. Using the paradigm model of the grounded theory approach to social science research, the study shows the relationship between and among different variables, namely: origin, development initiative, situation, intervening variables, intervention strategies, and outcomes. The communication dynamics model for women empowerment presented shows how the factors of success and failure lead to empowerment or no empowerment. There is also no empowerment when conditions are oppressive or too lenient.

DOI: 10.4018/978-1-6684-8979-6.ch002

INTRODUCTION

Despite advancements in Information, and Technology (ICT) and even in artificial intelligence (AI), poverty is still prevalent in most parts of the globe, the Philippines not being any different. People in Third World countries are in want of basic necessities of life that people in First World countries take for granted. Despite the promising prospects of the Philippines in the 1950s, it has remained poverty stricken.

The Philippine Statistics Authority (PSA) reports that poverty incidence among the population was estimated at 23.7 percent in the First Semester of 2021. Fisherfolk and farmers have the highest poverty incidences, where the proportion of poor families whose per capita income is not sufficient to meet basic food and non-food needs. The top three basic sectors with the highest number of poor population in 2021 were (a) individuals residing in rural areas, 13.67 million; (b) children, 10.46 million; and (c) women, 9.99 million (PSA, 2023).

Traditional notions of the role of women in the household or in the community have likewise added to this widening gap between the rich and the poor. Poverty alleviation projects involving women, geared towards the improvement of the quality of life of people are very minimal. Such efforts however, have not gone unnoticed. In fact, the World Bank (WB) has looked into the potential of women participation in development as a means to alleviate poverty in Third world countries (Fernandez, n.d., p. 159).

The author's concern for women sparked the interest for this research, not only because of the more disadvantaged group, but they also suffer from inequities. Women also comprise half of the world's population and constitute a huge reserve of human power that can be harnessed for sustainable development and alleviate poverty in the country. It is unfortunate that the vast potential of women remained untapped and underutilized.

Numerous innovations and development projects geared towards women have been implemented across various parts of the Philippines. It is unfortunate that very few of these have conducted analysis on its impact and implications not only on the environment but also on the members of their group.

Evaluation studies of development interventions have shown that many projects have very mixed, and in many cases, detrimental consequences to women. These interventions are often based on the "assumptions of women's 'inherent' responsibility for the care of the family and the household, and the nature of female-male economic and social relations, and appropriate notions of employment, economic activity and income, and many of these projects far from increasing women's welfare were actually undermining it" (WEMTOP, 1992, p. 3).

Data from the PSA (2016) show that women comprise about 25% of workers in the agricultural sector from 2007 to 2016. It may not accurately capture women's work in agriculture in the official data, as it is considered as extensions of their household tasks and therefore not reported as "work." Hence, women continue to be unaccounted for in agriculture work when in fact they continue to participate in unpaid family work in agriculture in larger numbers than that of men.

The PSA, in its 2019 List of Establishments, recorded 1,000,506 business enterprises operating in the country, with 99.5% (995,745) are Small and Medium Scale Enterprises (SMSEs). The Department of Trade and Industry recorded a total of 630,688 business name registration (new and renewal); 55.8% (352, 181) were women-owned/run (Department of Trade and Industry [DTI], 2019).

What Are the Property Relations Between Husbands and Wives in the Philippines?

In the Philippines, property relationships between husband and wife are governed (1) By marriage settlements executed before the marriage; (2) By provisions of this Code; and (3) By the local custom. (118) (Art. 74) The spouses may opt to agree to have "absolute community, conjugal partnership of gains, complete separation of property, or any other regime." If there is no marriage settlement, the system of absolute property is established. (119a) (Art. 75) Community property consists of all the property owned by the spouses at the time of the celebration of the marriage or acquired later (197a) (Art. 91) (Family Code, 1987).

This means that unless a prenuptial agreement has been duly notarized and legally in place, whatever properties and other obligations that both spouses have is conjugal and binding. Properties owned separately by both spouses prior to marriage, remain their sole properties, unless otherwise declared as community property as well.

Both spouses jointly own the community property, but if there is a disagreement on administration of the property, the husband's decision shall prevail. If a spouse is incapacitated, the other may assume sole powers of administration. (Art. 96) Either spouse may dispose by will of his or her interest in the community property (Art. 97) Neither spouse may donate any community property without the consent of the other. However, either spouse may, without the consent of the other, make moderate donations from the community property for charity or on occasion of family rejoicing or family distress. (Art. 98) The absolute community ends: (1) Upon the death of either spouse; (2) When there is a decree of legal separation; (3) When the marriage is annulled or declared void; or (4) In case of judicial separation of property during the marriage under Articles 134 to 138 (175 a) (Art. 99) (Family Code, 1987).

The laws of marriage and property in the Philippines favors the innocent spouse. If the aggrieved is the husband, then even the care of their young children will be given to the father (Family Code, 1987).

Women are regarded as equal to men in the Philippine constitution. "Women have the legal right to enter contracts, own property, and choose their place of residence. Article 16: Marriage and family - Women have equal rights with men in matters related to marriage and family relations. Articles 17-24: The Committee on the Elimination of Discrimination against Women (CEDAW) and reporting procedures." Likewise, according to Article 13: Economic and social life - "Women have equal rights to family benefits, financial credit, and participation in recreational activities" (Philippine Commission on Women [PCW], n.d.).

Microfinance as a Tool for the Fight Against Poverty

In the 1990s, microfinance was a "booming" method of poverty alleviation in the Philippines. In fact, many institutions from different sectors of society, from non-government organizations, cooperatives, religious organizations and even private companies, were involved in microfinance projects.

Brief History of Grameen Bank

As a "Banker to the Poorest of the Poor," Professor Muhammad Yunus established the Grameen Bank in Bangladesh in 1983. He believed that credit was a fundamental human right and he wanted to help poor people escape from poverty. His idea was to provide loans on terms suitable to them and to teach them sound financial principles to help themselves.

At the start, Dr. Yunus provided personal loans of small amounts of money to poor basket weavers in Bangladesh in the mid-70s. The Grameen Bank had become a world movement to eradicate poverty through microfinance. Grameen Bank Replication Projects operate in more than 100 countries worldwide, including the Philippines (NobelPrize.org, 2023).

Association for Social Advancement (ASA)

Culture being dynamic and relative to its location, Philippine micro-credit practitioners faced problems of delinquency, high cost of administration, and lack of institutional funds to sustain their microfinance operation. Not known to all, another institution in Bangladesh challenged the traditional notion of doing microfinance. Due to its adaptability to the changing times, the institution's exponential growth was indeed phenomenal. From 150 branches, it grew to 600 branches in less than seven years. This institution is known as the Association for Social Advancement or ASA. This acronym means "hope" (in Bangla).

ASA is recognized as one of the most effective microfinance institutions in the world in terms of cost effectiveness, simplicity and adaptability because it can easily be replicated for fast expansion. The key elements in the success of this organization are not "written in stones" but one that changes along with the times. Principles are timeless, but their applicability depends on its contextual application. ASA has mastered this key element that keeps an institution relevant and effective (AD Alvarez, 1999, 2001). Thus, it emphasizes that change is necessary for growth and encourages people to adapt to new ideas and innovations to improve their service to their clients.

Microfinance in the Philippines

A few institutions in the Philippines ventured into micro-credit, in the mid-80s. They studied Grameen, replicated (if not copied it) and experienced relative success. The Pulo grameen banking method or Grameen Bank Replication Project (GBRP) in Banga, Aklan, Philippines was one of several other Centers of the Cooperative Rural Bank of Aklan (CRBA) was successfully given credit to poor families in the communities in the provinces of Aklan and Antique. It reversed conventional banking practice by removing the need for collateral and created a banking system based on mutual trust, accountability, participation and creativity. By lending to women, profits were used to improve the family's quality of life, and led to a rise in the women's status. It provided the poor a vehicle for self-employment and a proven path that led families out of poverty to sustainable enterprise development and self-reliance.

Significance of the Research

This Chapter is an offshoot of the author's initial study on the grameen method of banking in Aklan, specifically, the CRBA. It is an initial attempt to bring to fore probable communication and cultural implications development project may bring about for women, and its benefits and especially their social and economic significance. Initial investigations have shown positive results in terms of its viability in terms of economic and social development thrusts and it was with curiosity and a strong determination to help in the poverty alleviation efforts in the Philippines that the researcher embarked on this ambitious undertaking.

This research is a pioneering work on the study of the dynamics of communication of women involved in microfinance projects in the Philippines. It also serves as a model for women empowerment while identifying the factors of success and failure in these projects. The important contribution of women is highlighted here as necessary for poverty alleviation initiatives to be sustainable. The three cases reveal nuances of different MED methodologies that can help development workers and would be partners in MED initiatives to validate and to improve on their services to clients. This study likewise serves as a policy beacon on what to do in organizations involving women in microfinance projects. This is an important initiative that illustrates the need for a holistic approach for development efforts to be sustainable. Culture requires communication and communication affects all aspects of culture. People communicate and interact in various capacities and microfinance projects are seen as a potential tool for alleviating poverty in the land.

The study is also a breakthrough in communication in terms of innovating the Grameen method of banking in the context of Philippine culture. It is a huge step in concretizing development efforts to mobilize people to be partners and co-laborers in the development process. This underscores the important role of women in this development initiative, and the need of a communication dynamics model that would cut across cultures and different situations. It emphasizes the need for new modes of thinking and acting to answer poverty alleviation problems and a concerted effort to realize a genuine move towards sustainable development, especially in the countryside.

This dissertation also stresses the need for partnerships in order for development to be sustainable. Men and women, families and communities, and the government and non-government organizations, as well as people's organizations should work together for people to realize development and uplift their standards of living.

The problem of poverty has been a constant plague that has beset the nation for centuries. The clamor for government support for the poor still echoes everywhere, even in the countryside. Though there have been numerous efforts at providing help for the poor, they have not been taught self-reliance and others have merely lined their own pockets instead and left the people in utter helplessness and hopelessness. Very few have actually succeeded in taking concrete steps to help alleviate poverty in our country. Ironically, it is not the government that has had many successful projects for the poor in the area of micro-enterprise development. People believe it is the government's obligation to help the poor so most of the time they think of these projects as "dole outs," thus, these projects were not sustained.

It is good however, that there are non-government organizations and people's organizations that genuinely care for other people. The bank workers here in the study have a heart for the people and believe that there is strength in groups and families.

The researcher looked into the communication dynamics in microfinance projects involving women and underscored the important role that they played in this development initiative to help in the alleviation of poverty in the Philippines. The task was overwhelming, but it is with hopeful expectation that this developmental paradigm will be a useful instrument to critically look into development projects that may cause more harm than good to the country and the people (Fernandez, 2003).

Objectives of the Study

This Chapter looks into the communication dynamics of women involved in microfinance projects (in the context of culture) that contribute to its failure and success, specifically, a) to identify factors that lead to the success or failure of these microfinance projects; b) to identify the basic MED lending methodology used in each case by presenting the key characteristics of the three cases; and, c) to illustrate the communication dynamics of women involved in microfinance projects in the context of culture as a model for women empowerment.

At the end of the research, a communication dynamics model for women involved in microfinance projects was presented. Different combinations of interactions were noted in the three cases studied. The similarities and differences revealed that communication is culture and culture uses communication in all aspects of people's interactions. The way of life, or culture - the dynamics of communication - of women involved in microfinance projects were looked into, as well as the factors for its success or failure. This model illustrated how communication interactions (both verbal and non-verbal behavior) led to empowerment or no empowerment.

REVIEW OF RELATED LITERATURE

In the Introduction, we talked about property relations between husband and wife in the Philippines; microfinance as a tool for the fight against poverty - how Grameen bank, the Association for Social Advancement (ASA) and microfinance started in the Philippines; and the significance and objectives of the research.

Now, let's look at the Related Literature on the status of MFIs and various lending projects for the poor in the Philippines.

Studies on microfinance in the Philippines were made over the years, however, there was no specific study which focused on communication dynamics in microfinance projects that led to women empowerment and as a tool for poverty alleviation in the Philippines.

Seibel et. al (1997) showed that the Philippines tremendously lagged behind many Asian countries and urban poverty declined from 26% to 29%; but rural poverty stagnated at a much higher rate of 55% and 54% respectively, between 1991 to 1994. Numerous lending programs were instituted, but their impact remained insignificant and their viability were undermined. A vast number of NGOs and self-help groups tried to fill the void, yet institutions that possess the capacity for substantial outreach to the poor lacked the focus, while those that focus on the poor lack the capacity. Policymakers in the Philippines relied more on government intervention and credit channeling than the self-reliant intermediation of market oriented microfinance institutions (MFIs), despite liberalization efforts. Seven MFIs were selected from the Philippines and analyzed in terms of outreach to the poor, resource mobilization, viability and sustainability, six credit NGOs and one cooperative rural bank. This was in the framework of a wider UNDP-supported program of the Asian Pacific Development Centre in Kuala Lumpur on *Microfinance for the Poor in Asia-Pacific*. All but one of the MFIs were found to be donor-driven and subsidy-dependent, though they did adhere to market interest rates. Only the cooperative bank, which applied both the conventional individual and Grameen-type group-group technology was analyzed in greater detail. It was found to be operationally and self-sufficient financially, yet showed little capacity for dynamic growth. While its Grameen-type group technology multiplied the bank's outreach and was profitable, it added very little to the overall profits that management considered its termination. One recommendation that stood out from the case studies: transform credit non-government organizations (NGOs) into formal financial institutions that rely on their own internal resources and stop using them as credit channels and to cover their costs from the margin.

The Grameen Bank in Bangladesh has become widely known worldwide for successfully providing credit to the poor. However, not all Grameen Bank Replications Projects in other parts of the globe have been successful. Siebel (1999) in another study on "Banking with Very Poor Women" tried to answer the question: "Is there really an infallible solution that works everywhere, and is outreach to the poor compatible with sustainability?"

The Center for Agriculture and Rural Development (CARD), a Grameen Bank replicator in the Philippines had set itself firmly on this path of becoming a sustainable, formal sector rural bank, the first credit NGO to do so in the Philippines. From 1993 to June 1999, CARD's all-female outreach soared from 1,711 to 26,369 and its operational self-sufficiency ratio increased from 0.46 to 1.09. By June 1999, CARD's loan portfolio reached $2.7 million, with a repayment rate of 99.9 percent and its financial self-sufficiency ratio was 0.85. The main lesson to be learned from CARD's success is that Grameen-type MFIs have the potential to be sustainable and increase their outreach. CARD's social capital included: (a) good Grameen practices, (1) high moral commitment of the leaders, (2) based on values instilled through training; (3) peer control – to preclude adverse selection and moral hazard; and, (4) strict credit discipline; (b) innovative adaptations to suit the Philippine context, (1) adoption of rural bank status under the supervision of the Central Bank of the Philippines; (2) encouraging voluntary savings; (3) provision of differentiated, profit-making loan and insurance products; and, (4) increasing clientele to include poor and non-poor depositors, while adhering to its mission of lending to poor women only (Siebel, 1999).

Although written in French, another study entitled "Rural finance in Bangladesh and the Philippines" provided a very original and worthwhile econometric analysis on the field of microfinance/rural finance. Using trivariate probit analysis on the drivers of different types of credit constraints (productive vs nonproductive vs productive & nonproductive credit constraints) with Maximum Likelihood equations and program files impact of participation to a group/ a financial group/ a non-financial group on credit constraints (Philippines - Chapter 2) - duration analysis of microfinance performance behavior on Bangladesh (Chapter 3) - conditional impact of participation in productive vs nonproductive groups (Chapter 5). The study contributed to the understanding of the rural financial market in developing countries with a specific focus on the role of groups/social networks given microfinance successes in providing sustainable financial services to the poor have largely been attributed to the use of credit groups. Beyond the participation in microcredit groups, participation in structured groups of all sorts attracted development practitioners' attention as a privileged means for the poor to accumulate a specific form of capital, namely social capital. The analysis was based on two countries that differ greatly in their rural credit market: Bangladesh and the Philippines. While microfinance was overwhelming the rural credit market in Bangladesh, it was almost absent in the Philippines. This difference in the structure of the credit market motivated the two research areas of the study, in which the microeconometric approach was privileged. The first area explored the determinants of microfinance repayment performance in Bangladesh using both analysis of repayment probabilities and analysis of duration of repayment delays. The second research area was devoted to credit constraints in the Philippines. The range and determinants of credit constraints were analyzed in the first step. The rationale behind membership in different types of groups and the possibility for group membership to relax credit constraints were then studied (Godquin, 2006).

Tahir and Tahrim (2013) explained in their study that there were limited studies on the efficiency of microfinance institutions (MFIs) in the ASEAN (Association of Southeast Asian Nations) and to their knowledge, there had been no research done to compare the MFIs in ASEAN using Data Development Analysis (DEA). Their study on efficiency was significant and contributed to existing literature. The purpose was to examine and compare the efficiency levels of MFIs in the five countries in ASEAN, namely, Indonesia, the Philippines, Vietnam, Cambodia and Laos from 2008 to 2011. DEA was employed in this study, with the production approach. Results suggested that microfinance institutions in Vietnam were relatively more efficient than their counterparts with efficiency levels of 87.6% in 2008 and 2009, 90.8% in 2010 and 91.35 in 2011. Microfinance institutions in Laos were found to be least efficient (45% in 2008, 43.8% in 2009, 60.8% in 2010 and 62.5% in 2011). Further the results suggested that during the period of study it was found that pure technical efficiency was lower than the degree of scale efficiency for Indonesia, Cambodia, Philippines, and Vietnam, which implied that during the period of study, the microfinance institutions had been inefficient in controlling their costs rather than operating at the wrong scale. In contrast, in Laos, pure technical efficiency was higher than scale efficiency, which indicated that microfinance institutions in Laos were operating at the wrong scale of operation rather than producing below production. The results implied that improvements were suggested especially in reducing excessive use of inputs.

Ojone (2023) examined the importance of religion to microfinance banks using Christian based microfinance banks as a model. This research wanted to ascertain the extent to which the microfinance bank has impacted the lives of the people targeted towards the active poor; and to determine the significance of religion to the operations of the bank. The study adopted Max Weber's theory of religious economy, which hinged on the role of Christianity in the management of economic organizations. The research instruments used were oral interview, participatory observation and relevant literature and the data was properly analyzed and discussed. The study observed that the microfinance banks have a religious influence based on its operations or services such as savings, deposits, loans and asset acquisition. The research also identified the religious importance of the bank which was evident in premised trust, manifestation of charity, biblical context of usury, and it inculcated Christian teachings and inventiveness. However, there were some challenges identified with the bank which are peculiar to the microfinance system of operation and these include abuse, limitation of scope, Central Bank directives, difficulty in monitoring and competition. These have in no way reduced the efficiency of the bank in some areas. Therefore, microfinance banks have contributed to national economic development and were achieved due to its religious importance, despite the challenges. This work proved that religion had not lost its relevance and it was not only a spiritual reality but a social phenomenon as well. It was an important tool that helped various economic institutions in society to function well. The study recommended more of religious teachings to be inculcated into microfinance banks to have a growing and sustainable microfinance industry and also brought to the limelight the religious importance of microfinance banks which could serve as a springboard for further research. The increase in disparity between the rich and the poor even in this age of globalization, has seen a rise in new and popular poverty-fighting strategies in the past decades. Microfinance banks have been providing small loans to help poor entrepreneurs to start or grow their small businesses. Previous studies on microfinance banks were mostly about its economic, sociological and psychological perspectives and little attention was paid on its religious importance.

The Grameen method of banking, the use of microfinance for sustainable development, and the importance of groups and religion, have been discussed in the studies mentioned above. However, it lacks the comprehensive discussion of looking into culture - the communication dynamics in microfinance that empowers women which is discussed comprehensively in this Chapter. The same Conceptual Framework in this study can be used in future studies on microfinance projects to determine if women are empowered or not.

METHODOLOGY

In the Related Literature Review section, we looked into the status of MFIs and various lending projects for the poor in the Philippines, Bangladesh and other members of ASEAN.

Here, we will discuss how the research was undertaken using the Grounded Theory Approach to qualitative research; using the case study method; and ethnographic descriptions with (1) informal/key informant interviewing, and (2) collection of life histories; and the Centrifugal vs Centripetal effects of media in society.

The Grounded Theory

The main method used in this Chapter is the Grounded Theory Approach. As a qualitative research, because of the amount of data it is a challenge to make sense of the information and identify patterns and construct a framework to reveal the essence of the data.

Glasser and Strauss developed the Grounded theory. Its systematic procedures and techniques of analysis enable the researcher to develop research that is significant, compatible with theory-observation, generalizable, reproducible, precise, uses rigor, and verification. Though the procedures are designed to give the analytical process of precision and rigor, another important element is creativity (Strauss and Corbin, 1990, p. 31).

Subcategories are linked to a category in a set of relationships. These relationships are, namely, *origin, development initiative, situation, intervening variables, intervention strategies,* and *outcomes.*

Triangulation was used in recording and collecting information. Qualitative information on demographics were gathered from the members and the key characteristics of MED methodologies, consisting of the following clients, group characteristics, role of groups, credit officer relation to client, loan appraisal, loan characteristics, guarantee mechanisms, savings policies and other development services were taken from Waterfield and Duval (1996, p. 94). This was the basis for the identification of the MED lending methodology of the three cases. Qualitative research was employed on communication dynamics of women involved in microfinance projects that contributed to its success and failure through the case study method and ethnographic descriptions (Fernandez, 2002, p. 162).

The Case Study Method

Using the case study method, the researcher identified at first, two groups of women involved in microfinance projects. One group is relatively well established and the second is a new organization. The third case came as a consequence of the second group that became a failure.

The case study as an empirical inquiry investigates a contemporary phenomenon, specifically, the development initiative on - *communication dynamics of women in microfinance projects that contribute to its success and failure* - within its real-life context, especially when the boundaries between phenomenon and context are not clearly evident. Microfinance serves as a tool for poverty alleviation and women empowerment. The case study method was used to deliberately uncover contextual conditions - believing that these are highly pertinent to the phenomenon under study.

Ethnographic Descriptions

Using ethnographic description (Jocano, 1997, p. 13), an approach that focuses on detailed or "thick descriptions" of life-ways, the dynamics of communication of women involved in microfinance projects in the three cases were studied. This is particularly true with respect to their conduct of meetings and transactions with the Bank/Community Workers, Loan Officers, Account Officer or the Executive Director of the Organizations. The aim is to record as much information as possible about the communication dynamics of women involved in microfinance projects that contribute to its success and failure, and to discover new insights into the dynamics of relating with the organizations that help them.

The basic techniques used were, namely, (1) informal/key informant interviewing, and (2) collection of life histories.

The informal/key informant interviewing involved asking a number of previously prepared and unprepared questions. These people included the project Assistant, the Center Chief and group members of Barangay Pulo, Grameen Bank Replication Project in Banga Aklan, the Account Officer, Convenor and member of the Lanton Christian Savers in GSC, and Executive Director, LO/CO and member of the *Malipayon* Group in Bacolod City.

The life history of some of the members were highlighted as sample cases. The researcher made use of indigenous methods for collecting information. These include namely, (1) *pagmamasid* (observation); (2) *pakikiramdam* (feeling your way through); (3) *pakikilahok* (participation); (4) *pagtatanong-tanong* (interview); (5) *pakikipag-usap* (conversation); and, (6) *sama-samang talakayan* (focused group discussion or FGD).

The researcher made use of a combination of approaches described by Patton (1990) in doing the interview, namely (1) informal conversational approach; (2) interview guide; and, (3) standardized, open-ended approach.

Since conversation is a human exchange based on openness and trust, rapport was first established with the key informant(s)/interviewee(s). This was achieved when the interviewee did not feel tense or restricted, neither was the researcher rigid, straight-laced or overly dependent on a predetermined set of questions. The interviews were done casually and were merely built on the answers exchanged.

The researcher had a list of issues and questions in mind. One, it was important to establish what their situations were prior to joining the group and receiving credit for their microfinance projects. Second, the researcher had to identify the factors of success and failure in the projects. This was done by carefully analyzing their reasons for being better off than they were before or if there was no apparent change in their lifestyles at all. The list of questions aided the researcher in setting the direction of the interview. Questions were clarified and things unfamiliar to the researcher were also discussed. For instance, there were a lot of developmental terminologies that the researcher had to ask for clarifications. Certain norms of behavior were likewise learned. One does not ask for anything from the members. When they insist on giving something, they express their thanks and simply ask for water if they know that the water supply comes from a reliable source. Community Workers know that these people are poor and would not want to take advantage of their generosity.

The researcher also had to be ready for new areas, insights and perspectives. There were times when the interviewee herself would divulge information quite different from what the researcher expected, and this in turn enriched the information elicited. Some predetermined questions would then seem irrelevant and a new line of thinking initiated by the interviewee was pursued. This was especially true in Katuwang. The researcher was surprised to know that according to AD, the Executive Director, "microfinance is successful if it is not for profit."

Purposive sampling was done in identifying the cases for the study. Purposive sampling was likewise employed in choosing the key informant(s)/interviewee(s) for the case histories and FGD participants. The need for a contact person in each center was also a major consideration. There was close coordination with the PA in CRBA, whom the researcher befriended while doing a paper for one of the requirements of a course in 1998. The researcher was able to gather the data needed even with limited visits to the center meetings. Timing was of vital importance because meetings were set only once a week and in some cases, these were moved to a later date. The GRBP in Barangay Pulo was suggested by the PA who was more knowledgeable about the area and her clients. The Center Chief was kind enough to accommodate the researcher in their home during her visits and was able to gain valuable insights for the research.

The center in GSC was chosen on the basis of all its members being female. The Executive Director (ED) of DALSAKA is a good friend of the researcher so she was also able to stay at their office-home in Gensanville, GSC.

The third area in Bacolod, was referred to by a friend that the researcher met during a meeting. The case history in that area was based on the fact that the key informant/interviewee already received her first credit from Katuwang (KRCI). The researcher was able to attend the group meeting and conducted FGD with the members. Since it was fairly new, only two members had been given credit and the interviewee mentioned here is one of them.

Centrifugal vs. Centripetal Effects of Media and Society

The Centrifugal versus Centripetal Effects of Media and Society was the basis for the Communication Dynamics Model for women empowerment. According to Carey (1969) and McQuail (1987), though the relevant value positions of general societal effects of mass communication are complex and the alternative effects even more so, two basic dimensions summarize and capture many questions in dispute. These two dimensions are positive versus negative valuation and centrifugal versus centripetal tendencies, illustrated in Figure 1. Societal effects are either positively valued and the media viewed optimistically or are disliked and media viewed with pessimism.

The second dimension refers to the dual or alternative effects from mass media. Though it may be liberating, the latter can have an effect on society that causes dispersal and fragmentation (centrifugal effect). On the other hand, the media can strengthen social bonds and social control (the centripetal effect), towards integration and unity of culture and society (McQuail & Windahl, 1993, pp. 129-130).

The illustration in Figure 2 (Fernandez, 2002, p. 163) simply meant that the *origin* or event and situation that led to the development initiative is **poverty alleviation.** The *development initiative* in the study was "Communication dynamics of women involved in microfinance projects that contribute to its success and failure". This referred to the main idea, situation, happening about which a set of intervention strategies was directed at managing or handling or to which the set was related. The *situation* presented the specific set of characteristics that pertain to a development initiative that was the location of happenings or events about it, along a dimensional range. Situation also meant the set of conditions within which the intervention strategies were done to carry out, manage and handle a specific development initiative. The situation included the following: intensity, duration, location and obtained help. The three cases mentioned in the study had women who lived in communities among the poor. There was prolonged poverty in the area with usurpers prevalent. The locations were rural areas, government settlement areas, and squatter areas in the Visayas and Mindanao. Women obtained help from a relatively well-established microfinance institution with a good track record and one relatively new microfinance institution.

Figure 1. Centrifugal/centripetal model: Four images of societal effect from mass media

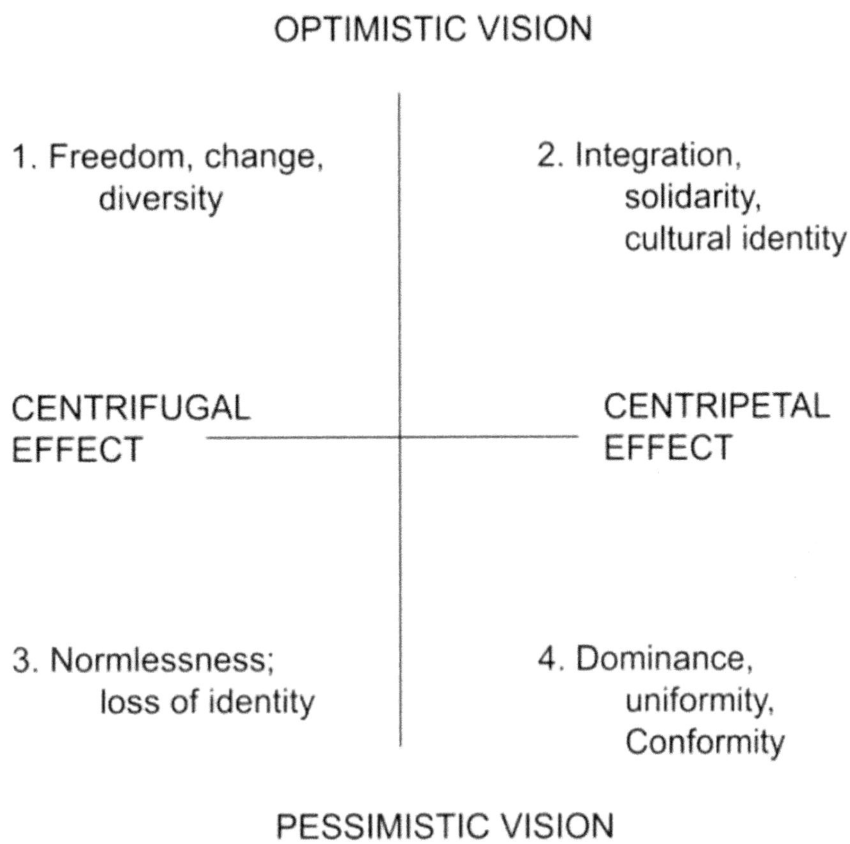

The *intervening variables* were general conditions bearing upon intervention strategies. These situations or conditions included: key characteristics, time, space, culture, economic status, technological status, career, history and individual biography.

Grounded Theory here was an action/interaction-method of theory building. These intervention strategies were directed at managing, handling, carrying out, and responding to a development initiative, as it existed in a situation. The interaction component referred to self as well as other interactions. Intervention strategies had certain dimensions: 1) It was a process. It could be observed over time, in terms of consequences or in terms of movement; 2) the intervention strategies was goal-oriented and has purpose - as an action or to manage a phenomenon; 3) It was also as important to look into failed intervention strategies; 4) Intervening variables that either helped or hindered intervention strategies must also be looked into.

Here, three cases were presented, namely, 1) Pulo Grameen Bank Replication Project, CRBA; 2) Lanton Christian Savers, DALSAKA; and 3) Group Malipayon, Katuwang. Over a period of two years from May 2001- August 2003, the researcher attended several center meetings to study the communication dynamics of women involved in microfinance projects. The key characteristics of the three cases and MED lending methodology used in each case were identified.

Figure 2. Conceptual framework of the grounded theory approach to communication dynamics of women involved in microfinance projects

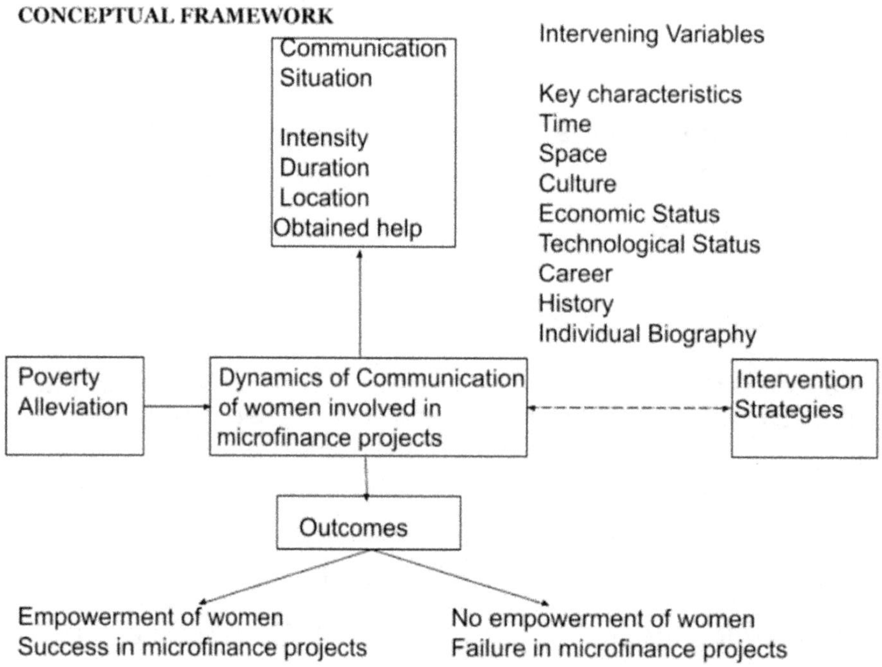

Intervention strategies done to handle a development initiative have certain *outcomes* or results. These may be actual or potential and may happen in the present or the future, the results of which may become part of the situation (or intervening variables) affecting the next set of intervention strategies occuring in a sequence. Whatever outcomes of intervention strategies now become part of future situations. In this particular study, the outcome was a successful or failed intervention strategy that resulted in the success or failure of the microfinance projects and a communication dynamics model for women empowerment or no empowerment, accordingly.

RESULTS

Previously, we discussed how the research was undertaken using the Grounded Theory Approach to qualitative research, using the case study method, and ethnographic descriptions with (1) informal/key informant interviewing, and (2) collection of life histories.

Now, we will discuss the three organizations that provided microfinance to the poor (1) Pulo Grameen Bank Replication Project, CRBA; (2) Lanton Christian Savers, DALSAKA; and, (3) Malipayon Group, Katuwang (KRCI). These organizations were studied over a period of two years from May 2001 - August 2003.

Poverty alleviation was the *origin* or the event and *situation* that led to the development initiative. The *development initiative* in this study is " Communication dynamics of women involved in microfinance projects that contributed to its success and failure."

Intervention strategies were made by the three organizations that provided microfinance to the poor. These are, namely, (1) Pulo Grameen Bank Replication Project, CRBA; (2) Lanton Christian Savers, DALSAKA; and, (3) Malipayon Group, Katuwang. Over a period of two years from May 2001 - August 2003, the researcher attended several center meetings to study the communication dynamics of women involved in microfinance projects. The key characteristics of the three cases and MED (Micro-Enterprise Development) lending methodology used in each case were likewise identified.

Under conditions where the communication dynamics involving women in poor communities with prolonged poverty in the area and usurpers were prevalent in rural areas and government settlements in the Visayas and Mindanao and the obtained help was from GBRP, SIVAP/SIKAP & Katuwang, Resource, Inc. then: In Barangay Pulo, Banga, Aklan (CRBA, Visayas), (a) Credit is unavailable to the poor without collateral, but, is made available to the GBRP (Grameen Bank Replication Project); and, (b) Women are not usually given credit, but in GBRP the women are the ones given credit for microfinance; (2) In SIVAP/SIKAP DALSAKA, General Santos City, South Cotabato (Mindanao, Philippines), Members usually belong to a Church community; and (3) In Katuwang (KRCI) in Bacolod City, Negros Occidental, Credit is given to family/households with women representation.

Intervening variables include the following: (1) My 2001 - August 2003; (2) grameen banking method in Barangay Pulo, Banga, Aklan (Visayas) is Case 1; Lanton Christian Savers, SIKAP/SIVAP DALSAKA, General Santos City (GSC), South Cotabato (Mindanao) is Case 2; and, Group *Malipayon*, Barangay 3, Purok Lubi, Bacolod City Negros Occidental (Visayas) is Case 3; (3) No religious/cultural affiliation for Case 1 & Case 3 and born again Christian for Case 2; (4) All three cases come from poor families, with Case 2 having other economic means; (5) Highly Educated (College level and College graduates) for Case 1, and Educated (Elementary and High School Level and Graduates) Case 2 and Case 3, (6) No collateral needed for Case 1 and savings is a requirement before loan is processed in Case 2 and Savings is part of the methodology in Case 1 and Case 3; (7) Values education - CGT (Compulsory Group Training) and GRT (Group Retention Test) for Case 1; Six months savings for Case 2; and Accessible savings for Case 3.

Intervention strategies done to handle this development initiative had certain *outcomes* or results. In this particular study, the outcome was either a successful or failed intervention strategy that resulted in success or failure of the microfinance projects and a communication dynamics model for women empowerment or no empowerment, accordingly.

A. The Story of Grameen Bank Replication Project (GBRP) in Brgy. Pulo, Banga Aklan (Visayas)

Pulo Grameen Bank Replication Project, CRBA

Barangay Pulo was a sparsely populated area in Banga, Aklan. The rough road leading to the Barangay Pulo GBRP Center was located at the home of the Center Chief (CC). The Center was made of light building materials, made of bamboo, and nipa for the roof. According to the Project Assistant (PA), the group decided to build a center in order to have a permanent meeting place for the group. They used to go from one house to another, even as far as a three kilometer trek up a hill, just to reach the other member's house to another, even as far as a three kilometer trek up a hill, just to reach the other member's house. The CC recalled that even when the PA was already seven months pregnant, she would still go to the meeting place, even if she had to walk some three kilometers to reach the place.

The Members

The members were mostly High School graduates, a handful of College level and College graduates.

According to the PA, there were problems at the initial stages of implementation of the program in the area. Later, when the credibility and reliability of the organization was established, people in the community became interested to join.

Political Aspect

During Center meetings, the CC was never absent or late since meetings were held in their home. Meetings were held on time, with some members arriving two hours before the meeting.

The CC expressed disappointment regarding non-payment of dues. Members were repeatedly reminded about agreements among the group and appealed to their sense of responsibility and abiding by what was agreed upon.

Policies on attendance were made by the members themselves. Women were given space to express themselves and decide - the democratic leadership style of the CC enabled the members to be part of the decision-making process, communicated problems encountered and presented possible solutions.

Social Aspect

Prospective members were required to form groups of five and these groups were joined together to form a center. Prior to membership, they were required to undergo a CGT and GRT.

Attendance was checked by the Secretary and the Meeting was called to order by the CC after the excuse letters were read to the group.

Meetings were also social activities for the members so they also updated each other on the latest happenings in the area and sold some of their home-made goods. At first, the husbands were apprehensive about their wives joining GBRP saying it was a waste of time. Lucita Cahilig recalls what her husband told her during the CGT: "'You keep going back and forth for nothing.' I told him (husband) that I started this, so I'm finishing it."

The PA invited the husbands to join the Christmas Party and allowed them to see what their wives were doing and made them part of the program. They became more open afterwards.

Economic Aspect

When asked if the Grameen helped them, they answered: *"Oo nakatulong sa amin lalo na yung sa mga bata, nag-aaral na ng high school, kaya malaki-laki yung tulong sa amin ng Grameen. Unti-unting na naming nababayaran yung mga utng namin. Tapos ngayon parang medyo maluwag-luwag na kami ngayon.* (Yes, this really helped especially for the children, they are studying high school and Grameen is a big help. Little by little we are able to pay our debts. And now things are much better)" - Nancy Halasan

Nancy Intano on the other hand had this to say: *"Bale yung Gameen, nakakatulong sa amin kahit papaano may pagkukunan kami ng pang allowance nila pang-araw-araw kaya siguro kung wala itong Grameen, bale ang dami naming utang sa tao, kahit tuition na lang ng mga bata, kaya nakatulong itong Grameen sa amin.* (Grameen really helps us somehow because we have a source for their everyday allowance. Perhaps without Grameen we would have so many debts from people, even just for the tuition of the children.)"

"Magmula pumasok ako sa Grameen, yung bahay ko... pwede nang itulak. Ngayon hindi na kasi kongkreto na ang kalahati. (Since I joined Grameen, my house, if pushed, will fall. Today, half of it is made of concrete.)" - Martina Sarandoni

Teresita Cahilig tells: *"Nakabulig naman ang Grameen sa amin dahil nakakatulong naman sa eskwela ko sa College at nakapagawa naman ako ng bahay na kahit ganito lang. Tapos nakakatulong naman pag may sakit kami.* (Grameen has helped with my College education and to build a house. It has also helped when we are sick.)" Veronica Izcasenza also reiterates: *"Pero pag-entra ko sa Grameen, abu gid ana nga nabulig. Napaeskwela ako sa akon mga unga.* (When I entered grameen, it helped me a lot. I was able to send my children to school.)"

They had not been required collateral to join the group, however, loan credits were given one at a time. If a member of the group failed to pay their debt, the other members would in turn, be unable to receive credit.

Penalties were imposed for non-payment of dues, absenteeism, having no excuse letters. The money collected was pooled into the Group Savings that was to be used for emergency purposes.

The PA mentioned that they also had death benefits.

Religious Aspect

Meetings began with a prayer.

Education Aspect

The members then recited their pledge together:

Sampung Pangako ng mga Kaanib (Ten Pledges of the Member): Pangako (Pledges/Promises) "...We shall educate our children and ensure that we earn to pay for their education. We shall look after our health. We should pay our debts on time so people will trust us. At all times, we shall always be ready to help each other. If anyone is in difficulty, we shall help him or her. May God help us fulfill these vows."

This was adapted from the Sixteen Decisions of Grameen bank, memorizing these pledges was part of the CGT and the questions during the GRT, necessary to the process of becoming a member. It was a very trying time for all of them and they were glad that they made it.

Update on the Grameen Bank Replication Project of CRBA

In 2000, the Cooperative Development Authority considered the CRBA as one of the most successful cooperative rural banks in the country (Philippine News Agency, 2008). After a few years of flourishing existence, the CRBA was prohibited from doing business in the Philippines. "The PDIC (Philippine

Deposit Insurance Corporation) took over the COOPERATIVE RURAL BANK OF AKLAN, INC., and its branches, assets, records and affairs on January 30, 2008." (PDIC, 2008). The PDIC is an authorized agency of the Banko Sentral ng Pilipinas (Central Bank of the Philippines). PDIC is a government instrumentality created in 1963 by virtue of Republic Act 3591, as amended to insure the deposits of all banks. The PDIC exists to protect depositors by providing deposit insurance coverage for the depositing public to help promote financial stability.

In 2007, the National Bureau of Investigation (NBI) probed the operation of the said bank (CRBA) and filed malversation of fund charges against several executives of the bank. The cases are still ongoing in the court.

B. The Story of DALSAKA's SIKAP-Pilipinas in General Santos City (Mindanao)

Dalan sa Kalambuan Foundation, Inc.

Dalan sa Kalambuan Foundation, Inc., or DALSAKA, is a Non-Government Organization (NGO) based in General Santos City, Southeast of the island of Mindanao, south of the Philippines. Their program SIVAP-Pilipinas (Savings and Investment for a Values-based Alleviation of Poverty)/ SIKAP-Pilipinas (*Sama-samang Impok para sa Kapayapaan at Pag-unlad*) is a micro-lending project for underprivileged women and indigenous people groups (IPs). This project began in late 2000, and by January 2002, they had 58 existing centers from the initial 7 Pilot centers established.

DALSAKA's vision is to improve the quality of life of ethnic, underprivileged communities through holistic endeavors. "Kalambuan" is a Cebuano word used to mean growth, prosperity or progress. While most of the founders of the organization are Professors at Mindanao State University (MSU) Fatima Campus, General Santos City, it is envisioned to be multi-sector and multidisciplinary in character.

It is noteworthy to say that the Financial Center (FC) in Lanton was the "only casualty." From DALSAKA's beginnings of seven (7) pilot centers of SIVAP/SIKAP-Pilipinas launched, it has grown to 58 budding SIKAP centers as of January 2002.

Lanton Christian Savers

Lanton is located in the outskirts of GSC. The dirt road leading to the Church where the women met is a few kilometers from the main highway. The place is a relocation site situated in a government property, where the residents are given a 400 square meter lot to build their homes.

The Members

Lanton Christian Savers (LCS), whose host church is Southern Baptist, is located in Lanton, Apopong, GSC. The program was presented on November 4, 2000, and was organized on November 26, 2000. There were 26 members, and the values and banking hour was held every Wednesday at 6pm.

The women in the center were mainly elementary and high school graduates. They have one thing in common, and that is "having debts." they have been used to borrowing money from usurpers who charge exorbitant interest. It is not uncommon that these poor women are forced to borrow from "5-6" (20% interest) which buries them deeper in debt. There were even times that they had to borrow money to pay for previous debts.

Political Aspect

During the meeting, the members themselves discussed the policies and Carol, the ED of DALSAKA was the facilitator. They discussed the pros and cons of certain policies and they came to agreement through mutual consensus.

The SIKAP/SIVAP program of DALSAKA practices participative governance - as subjects of their own development. Unlike the usual top-down communication processes in organizations, it uses the bottom-up approach, allowing the members to formulate their own policies. This method ensures strict compliance of center rules because the members themselves are part of the planning, organizing, controlling and monitoring the use of resources.

Policies and rules were formulated and agreed upon by the members, however, they did not follow them. The Convenor (which is equivalent to the Center Chief in the grameen banking method) had many things to do and did not follow up on her members. The *laissez-faire* leadership style was followed. There was no peer pressure on the members and they were not obliged to attend meetings. There was no responsibility and no accountability among the members.

The AO tried several times to meet with the members of the group, but since the group leader was busy and the members were likewise busy earning a living, they were unable to continue with the program.

Economic Aspect

Emphasizing the value of savings, the members were required to build the habit of saving for six months. The collections were done on a weekly basis, during the values and banking hour (on business hour) that the members themselves set. One of the values formations that DALSAKA would like to instill in the members of the FC is the importance of saving. The money they have saved may be transferred to the Capital Share of the members and their loans may be double the amount of money saved. DALSAKA's interest rate is two percent (2%) per month - one percent (1%) goes to DALSAKA, from their counterpart loan, and the other one percent (1%) goes back to the center. Eventually, this village banking system will graduate to form a Cooperative.

Social Aspect

The ED and AO also invested in the group's capital build-up by saving in the group's fund to earn their trust, which they gave during the weekly values education and banking hour.

The members of the centers were mostly members of a particular Church that DALSAKA approached to teach this village banking method. In time however, other members of the community were encouraged to participate and to be part of this initiative. The role of DALSAKA is to help the people save and to be self-reliant and to eventually do away with borrowings.

Though not totally different from the Grameen Bank of five women in a group, having 4-6 groups in a center; it was replaced by the FC, composed of 15 to 45 members, or less, depending on the number of Church members willing to participate.

There was minimal to no participation from most of the members. Eventually, in August 2001, almost a year after the first meeting that the researcher attended, the FC no longer met. The members were in inactive status, with an accumulated group savings of more than eight thousand pesos.

Religious Aspect

There was a problem where most of the members were part of and the pastor of the Church in Lanton was on leave for a month. Although the AO visited the group regularly, the members did not attend the meeting.

Education Aspect

Using the Vela Approach to learning in adult education to facilitate, the ED, asked questions to guide and help the members of the center to come up with their own policies. The people's knowledge was brought out - their community wisdom, experiences and learning. They participated and communicated their ideas in an open environment - sharing the same interest, relying on credibility and trust.

The members were also taught values education by illustrating the amount of money one saved if he/she quit smoking or stopped buying soft drinks.

Values formation through the six months savings prior to the release of credit was also part of their education.

Update on Dalan sa Kalambuan (DALSAKA)

The Dalan sa Kalambuan (DALSAKA) still have an office in General Santos City, but details about the program and their operations are hard to find. Currently, there is no presence of DALSAKA online, apart from their address and telephone number. The researcher also was unable to contact the previous ED who has been living in the US for more than a decade now.

C. The Story of Katuwang (KRCI) in Bacolod City, Negros Occidental

Malipayon Group

The *Malipayon* group regularly met near Barangay 3 Hall in Bacolod City; and was accessible by jeep and trisikad (bicycle-driven carriage)near the member's homes. The meeting was held at the compound of a member's house, one of several doors to a small apartment-type building. Depending on the availability, the garage-like structure was one of several places they go to transact business.

The Members

At the time of the research, the group was new with eleven all women members, only four had been given credit. Two of the women were already making loan repayments for their first loan cycle.

The ED of Katuwang explained they required at least six weeks of getting to know the client before they released the loan. The members have experienced joining other credit institutions, where rates were very high and unreasonable.

Political Aspect

The ED explained their clients were mostly women (with household membership) since women were easier to deal with. There was no leader, since there was no group needed to be a member of KRCI. Everyone was free to choose the kind of project they wanted to go into. Members were treated individually.

Economic Aspect

Repayment loans were affordable. When a member was asked if the payment scheme was difficult for her, Marissa answered:

Kung negosyo may ka, di naman problema… Kung wala ka negosyo, wala kuhaan sang imo weekly na balayran. Pero kung adlaw-adlaw, may negosyo ka naman, matiyog lang. Luwas kung magstop ka. (If you have a business, it is not a problem, unless you don't have a source for your weekly payment. But if you have a daily business, it will just continue. Unless you stop.)

Savings was accessible to members. They were able to withdraw their money anytime in case of an emergency. One member also encouraged her daughter to save with Katuwang. According to Marissa, *"My daughter also saves [in Katuwang]. She has an RTW [ready-to-wear] business, and what she receives as payment, she saves."*

The MED lending methodology was individual lending, where every member was accountable to herself. They needed two cosigners to guarantee the loan. Savings earned a relatively high interest of 9 percent per annum and it was accessible.

The ED thought of the "pouch system" where the LO/CO placed the amount received from the members in a bag. Like the market vendor's long apron with huge and deep pockets, to ensure that *"Nobody loses cash, even if they don't count the money."*

Social Aspect

The household membership with women representation had no group pressure because credit extended to clients/members was given on an individual basis.

According to the ED:

Wala kaming group, as individual… Gagawin namin, individual collection, in one area. Ito and ASA style, collection center lang. At kung magbi-business advice kami, dito na rin. Kaya kung na-detect namin, halimbawa magaling na yung community worker nila, madali nang ma-detect kung may problema, na hindi ma-describe o mapag-usapan dito sa marami, we go to their house. (We don't have a group. We meet them individually. That is ASA style, just a collection center. We also do business advice there. When the community worker knows them well and there is a problem that cannot be described or discussed in front of others, we go to their house.)

The members began to arrive one by one for weekly transactions. They were quiet at first. When they were all there, the researcher and the ED were introduced. The CO collected the payment of members, listed it in his ledger and recorded the payment and savings in their individual passbooks. While waiting for their turn, other members asked about the happenings in the community and talked in smaller groups of three while the others merely listened and waited for their turn.

Some brought their children to the group assembly to pay for their loans and gave additional money for savings.

The group leader of the LO/CO did an over the shoulder, "spot check auditing" everyday while he made the rounds. This minimized if not eliminated errors that would jeopardize the program. Katuwang was problem-solution oriented and tried to adapt to new ways of doing things to make things simpler for the staff. In the words of the ED "If the staff is happy, then that is success. He explained:

The common mistake of NGOs in the Philippines is to copy in toto. They are not effective. What you copy are the principles. You need to squeeze the principles to make it a concentrate that you would mix. For example, in ASA, Bangladesh 'sit-down approach'. If you don't pay, I will not leave your porch until you pay your debt. That is the ASA, the reason behind is immediate action. That is the principle behind it. If there is a default [in payment], there should be immediate action.

The Community Worker (CO/LO) did not ask for any favor from the members of the group and paid for the food served to him.

Initial loans were usually small, amounting to Php 2,000 ($ 40), enabling them to pay easily. The auditor carefully explained the reason why the amount to be given was less than what the member applied for and the member readily agreed with a smile. Katuwang tried to simplify everything, from the forms they used to their accounting system. The loan application was also a blank check and the voucher for the release of the money. Credit was released in the afternoon at the Office. The Office became a miniature bank and the CO gave money to the client/member, congratulated her and counted the money meticulously. She then explained that she would visit her microfinance project within the week while she went about her business. There was warmth and pleasantness and the client/member thanked the CW and smiled. The Cashier likewise inquired a bit more about the client/member and was affectionate, and this made the client/member feel at ease. The value of the individual was given primary importance and the membership survey was done personally by the CW, doing house to house calls in the morning.

Religious Aspect

The CO/LO and other members of Katuwang lived the Christian tenet of "Love your neighbor as yourself." They went the extra mile and expected nothing in return.

According to AD Alvarez: "In Corinthians, 'What good is it if you can explain if you do not have love? *Yung pa and sinasabi kong unique po sa isang Christian organization. Hindi sya kalinya ng secular organizations. Meron tayong deeper reason why we do it. Yung system, mine-measure pa rin namin sa Biblical perspective.* (That's what makes Christian organizations unique. It is not in line with secular organizations. We have a deeper reason why we do it. We measure the system with a Biblical perspective.) *It might work, but not everything that works is Biblical. Not everything that is lawful is Biblical... In the same principle, the way we facilitate microfinance, we're trying. It's a goal to reach that level. Nakita mo yung corporate objective namin, di ba? Kaunahan, yun talaga ang pinakamahalaga:* (Did you see our corporate objective? The first is the most important): *'To glorify God.' Pero, nakabutang dun* (But we also put), *excellent microfinance. Market driven kami. Compare mo kami sa existing microfinance sa city, pinakamarketable. Kasi katapat naming six months, kami four months.* (We are market driven. Comparing us to other microfinance institutions in the city, we are the most marketable. We offer four months, others six months.) *People would like that. Four months loan term - 15 weeks.*"

Education Aspect

Katuwang did not have a direct educational program component. But the accessible savings component was one way of sharing the value of preparing for emergencies and being good stewards of meager resources. According to the ED "Savings can create 'values formation'." Future plans included providing for training needs of their clients.

Update on Katuwang (KRCI)

Katuwang Resource Center, Inc. (KRCI) is still a viable MED organization for alleviating poverty. Their website is no longer available, but their services remain and their commitment to serve the community is intact. The former Executive Officer is now a farmer in Cebu, but he continues to serve the community through sharing technology and innovations for farmers for sustainable development. As of September 22, 2023, Katuwang has 1,279 members/clients and is still growing. They have financed a total of 2,219 livelihoods amounting to a total of 7.8 Million Pesos ($156,000), with a recovery rate of 93.18%. The regular member's savings balance is Php 464,172 Pesos ($ 9,283.44). According to KRCI: "the entrepreneurial poor that we have reached is already 84,000+ families in Negros Island Philippines." (Katuwang Resource Center Incorporated, n.d.)

The Current Status of the MED Projects in the Philippines: MCPI

The Microfinance Council of the Philippines, Inc. (MCPI) evolved out of the USAID-funded project entitled "Developing Standards for Microfinance Projects" (DSMP) that started in mid-1996 and continued until the end of 1999. MFIs, part of DSMP, formed an association or network - MCPI, registered in the Securities and Exchange Commission (SEC) as a non-stock corporation in June 1999. As of December 2021, MCPI has 66 institutions - 55 regular members and 11 support institutions with 33 regular non-government organization members; 12 banks; 7 corporations; and two (20 regional networks). MCPI members account for between 80-90% of total active outreach of the microfinance sector in the Philippines. (MCPI, n.d.)

DISCUSSION

The Key Characteristics of Basic MED Lending Methodologies (adapted from Waterfield and Duval, p. 94), as shown in Table 1, described the basic principles of the organization's clients, group characteristics, role of groups, the credit officer's relation to client, loan appraisal procedure, loan characteristics, guarantee mechanisms, savings policies and other development services are illustrated. The Katuwang Resource Center Inc. (Katuwang), was an example of Individual Lending; the Cooperative Rural Bank of Aklan, with the Pulo Grameen Bank Replication Project (GBRP) used the Grameen Banking method; the Dalan sa Kalambuan, Inc. or DALSAKA used the Village Banking method as shown in Table 2.

Modifying and applying this to the current study, the results showed that:

Table 1. Key characteristics of basic MED lending methodologies

Principles	Individual Lending	Grameen Banking	Village Banking
Clients	Individual business often above poverty line	Individual members of groups of people often below poverty line	Groups of people usually well above poverty line
Group Characteristics	None	✓ Self selected small sub-groups of 5 federated into larger "center of 20 to 40 people" ✓ Required attendance at weekly meetings	✓ Self selected groups of 15 to 50 people ✓ Democratic control ✓ Administrative self-sufficiency ✓ Independence ✓ Regular Meetings
Role of Groups	None	✓ Approve members ✓ Approve loans ✓ Social support desired	Groups establish bylaws and policies
Credit Officer Relation to Client	Very close relationship with individualized attention	Relatively close	Distant
Loan Appraisal	Based on careful viability analysis	Group involved in loan appraisal	✓ Group loans processed by agent ✓ Individual loans analyzed by group
Loan Characteristics	Loans adapted to client needs	✓ Limited to range of loan conditions ✓ Rotating access to credit ✓ Various types of loans	✓ Group loan is aggregate of individual loans ✓ Loans disbursed in cycles ✓ Rigid loan conditions
Guarantee Mechanisms	Collateral and/or cosigners	✓ Mutual agreement of all loans ✓ Emergency and other savings fund	✓ Peer pressure from group ✓ Group savings and partial guarantee ✓ No guarantee on individual loans
Savings Policies	Savings is often not essential	Savings is mandatory part of methodology	Savins is essential part of methodology
Other Development Services	Business training available for free often through partnering organizations	✓ Sometimes education package based in *16 Decisions* ✓ Training on Basics of MED program ✓ Minimal business training	✓ Training in Basics of MED program ✓ Sometimes health education or literacy training

(Waterfield and Duval, p. 94)

Katuwang Resource Center, Inc.

There was no leader (in a group) since clients were dealt with individually. They were usually below the poverty line. There was no distinct characteristic and no role of groups (since there were no groups needed to become a member). The Credit Officer relation was a very close relationship and they are given individualized attention. Loan appraisal was based on careful viability analysis. Loans were adapted to client needs. Guarantee mechanisms were ensured by two co-makers or cosigners who were also members of the household. Savings policies were favorable because of accessible savings to create 'values formation'. Other development services included business training, which was available without fees through partnering organizations.

Table 2. Key characteristics of Katuwang Resource Center, Inc.; Pulo Grameen Bank Replication Project, CRBA; and SIKAP/SIVAP DALSAKA

Principles	Katuwang Resource Center, Inc.	Pulo, Grameen Bank Replication Project CRBA	SIKAP/SIVAP DALSAKA
Leadership Style	Democratic Leadership	Democratic/Autocratic Leadership	Democratic/ *Laissez-faire* Leadership
Clients	Individual business below poverty line	Individual members of groups of people often well below poverty line	Groups of people usually above poverty line
Group Characteristics	None	✓ Self-selected small sub-groups of 5 federated into larger "center of 20 to 40 people" ✓ Required attendance at weekly meetings	✓ Self-selected groups of 15 to 50 people ✓ Democratic control ✓ Administrative self-sufficiency ✓ Independence ✓ Regular meetings
Role of Groups	None	✓ Approve members ✓ Approve loans ✓ Social Support desired	Groups establish bylaws and policies
Credit Officer Relation to Client	Very close relationship with individualized attention	Relatively close	Relatively close
Loan Appraisal	Based on careful viability analysis	Group involved in loan appraisal	✓ Group loans processed by agent ✓ Individual loans analyzed by group
Loan Characteristics	Loans adapted to client needs	✓ Limited to range of loans conditions ✓ Rotating access to credit ✓ Various types of loans	✓ Group loan is aggregate of individual loans ✓ Loans disbursed in cycles ✓ Rigid loan conditions
Guarantee Mechanisms	Cosigners	✓ Mutual guarantee of all loans ✓ Emergency and other savings fund	✓ Peer pressure from group ✓ Group savings and partial guarantee ✓ No guarantees on individual loans
Savings Policies	Accessible savings to create values formation	Savings is mandatory part of methodology	Savings is essential part of methodology
Other Development Services	Business training available without fees through partnering organizations	✓ Sometimes education package based in *Sampung (10) Pangako ng Kasapi* ✓ Training on Basics of MED program ✓ Minimal business training ✓ Death benefits	✓ Values Education & Banking Hour ✓ Training in Basics of MED program ✓ Sometimes health education or literacy training

Pulo, Grameen Bank Replication Project, CRBA

The leadership style in this case was usually democratic, although there were instances when the autocratic leadership style was used to enforce policies. Clients were individual members of groups of people often well below the poverty line. The group characteristics were as follows: (1) self-selected small sub-groups of 5 members, federated into a larger "center" of 20 to 40 people; and, (2) required attendance in weekly meetings. Role of groups included, (a) approving members, (b) approving loans; and, (c) social support was desired. The Credit Officer's relation to the Client was relatively close. The group was also involved in loan appraisal. Loan characteristics had (1) a limited range of loan conditions; (2) rotating access to credit; (3) various types of loans. Guarantee mechanisms included (a) mutual guarantee of all loans; and, (b) emergency and other savings funds. Savings was a mandatory part of the methodology. Other development services were (1) sometimes an education package based on *Sixteen Decisions* (modified into *Sampung [10] Pangako ng Kasapi)*; (2) training of Basics of MED program; (3) minimal business training; and, (4) death benefits.

SIKAP/SIVAP DALSAKA

The leadership style in SIVAP/SIKAP DALSAKA was predominantly democratic, however, in the case of the Lanton Christian Savers, *laissez-faire* leadership style. Clients were usually groups of people above the poverty line. Group characteristics were (1) self-selected groups of 15-50 people; (2) had democratic control; (3) was administratively self-sufficient; (4) independent; and, (5) had regular meetings. Role of the group was to establish bylaws and principles. The Credit Officer relation to Client was relatively close. The Credit Officer or Loan Officer (CO/LO or agent) processed the group loans, while individual loans were analyzed by the group. Loan characteristics were (a) group loan was aggregate of individual loans; (b) loans were disbursed in cycles; and, (c) had rigid loan conditions. Guarantee mechanisms included: (1) peer pressure from group; (2) group savings and partial guarantee; and, (3) no guarantees on individual loans. Savings was also an essential part of the methodology. Other development services offered were (a) 'Values education' and banking hour; (b) training on the basics of MED (Micro-Enterprise Development) program; and, (c) sometimes health education or literacy training.

Identifying Factors of Success and Failure in Microfinance Projects

Using the Paradigm Model of the Grounded Theory Approach to social science research, the study showed the relationship between and among different variables. Subcategories were linked to a category in a set of relationships. These relationships were *origin, development, initiative, situation, intervening variables, intervention strategies,* and *outcomes.*

Factors of success and failure were identified as *outcomes* of action and interaction of the different variables. As a consequence, the *situation, intervening variables* and *intervention strategies* affecting the *development initiative* which was the dynamics of communication of women involved in microfinance projects whose *origin* was poverty alleviation, led to a model of women empowerment.

The Communication Dynamics in Microfinance Projects for Women Empowerment from the Centrifugal versus Centripetal Effects of Media in Society (McQuail and Windahl, 1993, p. 129) is shown in Figure 3.

As the Model indicated, the first two quadrants (upper portion, 1 & 2) led to empowerment and the last two quadrants (lower portions, 3 & 4) did not empower the women. The centripetal effect was seen on the right quadrant (2& 4) and moved towards the centrifugal effects on the left quadrants (1 & 3). This meant that communication dynamics that empower women worked best in freedom, change, diversity, integration, solidarity and cultural identity. Too much freedom led to normlessness and loss of identity, and likewise, too many restrictions led to dominance, uniformity and conformity, meaning, no empowerment.

Figure 3. Communication dynamics on microfinance projects for women empowerment model

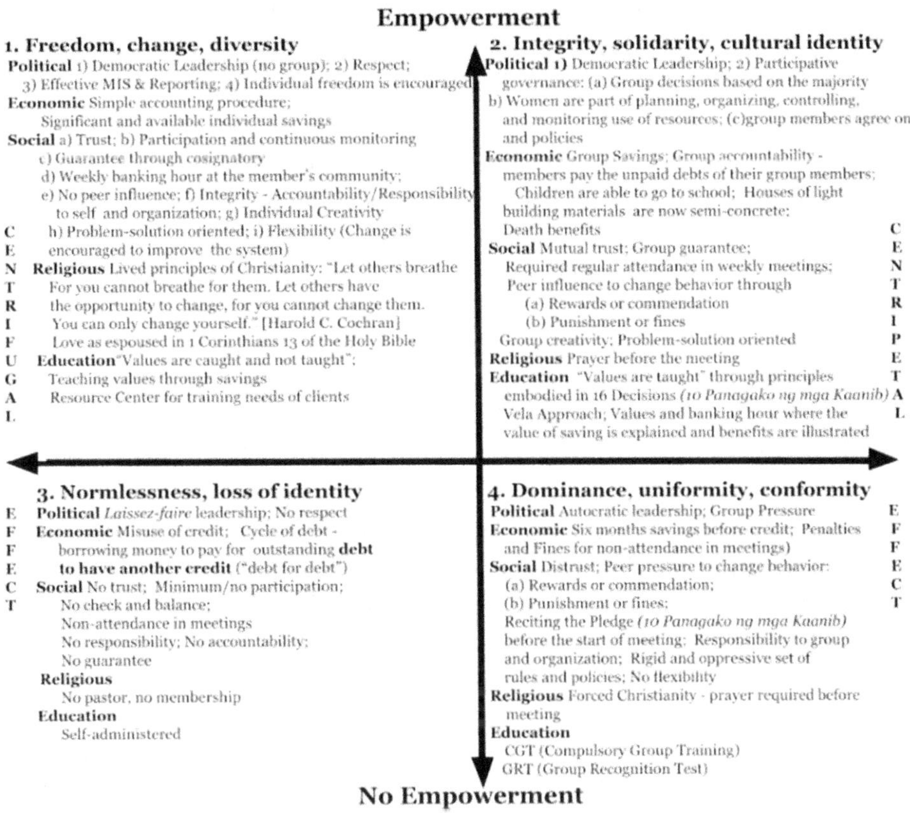

The Katuwang (KRCI) as an individual MED lending method, can be illustrated with the first (1) quadrant of the Model. Women were empowered through freedom, change and diversity that was encouraged. Communication dynamics in the political aspect included (1) the absence of a leader (no group); (2) respect; (3) effective MIS (management information system) and reporting; and (4) individual freedom to express views was encouraged. In the economic aspect, they had to make use of simple accounting procedures to be understood and there was significant and available individual savings for the members to use. The social aspect were (a) trust; (b) participation and continuous monitoring; (c)guarantee through co-makers or co-signatories; (d) weekly banking hour at the member's community; (e) no peer influence; (f) integrity - accountability/responsibility to self and to the organization; (g) individual creativity; (h) problem-solution oriented; and, (i) flexibility - change is encouraged to improve the system. In the religious aspect, they practiced the lived principle of Christianity - Love as espoused in 1 Corinthians 13 of the Holy Bible. On the extreme however, Katuwang at times provided too much freedom and the effect was normlessness and loss of identity as depicted in the third (3) quadrant. There was non-attendance in meetings, no participation and non-repayment of dues and hence, the misuse of credit and the "default" of the members/clients and accounts for the almost seven (7) percent loss of investments for Katuwang.

The SIKAP/SIVAP DALSALA, as an example of village banking method, was represented in the second and third quadrants (2 & 3). The second quadrant also empowered women. Integration, solidarity and cultural identity were encouraged. In the political aspect, the leadership style was democratic. There was participative governance, meaning, (1) group decisions were based on the majority; (2) women were part of planning, organizing, controlling, and monitoring the use of resources; and, (3) group members agreed on rules and policies. In the economic aspect, the following principles were followed: (a) group savings; (b) group accountability - members pay the unpaid debts of their group members; (c) children were able to go to school; (d) houses of light building materials were now semi-concrete. In the social aspect, they agree on the following: (1) mutual trust; (2) group guarantee; (3) required regular attendance in weekly meetings; (4) peer influence to change behavior through: (a) rewards or commendation; and (b) punishment or fines; (5) group creativity; (6) problem-solution oriented. In the religious aspect, they practiced praying before the meeting. In the education aspect, (1) "Values are taught" through principles embodied in the 16 Decisions [*Sampung (10) Pangako ng Kaanib*]; (2) Vela Approach; and, (3) Values and banking hour where the value of saving was explained and benefits were illustrated.

The Grameen bank method in Barangay Pulo, Banga, Aklan under the CRBA predominantly depicted the communication dynamics in the second and fourth quadrants (2 & 4). There was empowerment when integration, solidarity and cultural identity were encouraged. Like the SIKAP/SIVAP, it also empowered women. In the political aspect, the leadership style was democratic. There was participative governance, meaning, (1) group decisions were based on the majority; (2) women were part of planning, organizing, controlling and monitoring the use of resources; and (3) group members agreed on rules and policies. In the economic aspect, the following were followed: (a) group savings; (b) group accountability - members paid the unpaid debts of their group members; (c)children were able to go to school; d) houses of light building materials were now semi-concrete; (e) they also had death benefits - all the members gave 10 pesos each. In the social aspect, they agreed on the following: (1) mutual trust; (2) group guarantee; (3) required regular attendance in weekly meetings; (4) peer influence to change behavior through: (a) rewards or commendation; and, (b) punishment or fines; (5) group creativity; (6) problem-solution oriented. In the religious aspect, they practiced having prayer before the meeting. In the education aspect, (1) "Values are taught" through principles embodied in the 16 Decisions [*Sampung (10) Pangako ng Kaanib*]; and accessible savings is also a value formation principle. However, there were instances when the extreme was espoused as depicted in the fourth quadrant where dominance, uniformity and conformity were imposed on the group and there was no empowerment.

The third (3) quadrant depicted normlessness and loss of identity. This meant there was no empowerment. This happened in the case of Lanton Christian Savers of SIKAP/SIVAP, DALSAKA in Lanton, General Santos City, South Cotabato. The political aspect showed that *laissez-faire* leadership style was practiced. There was no respect for the leader and its members. In the economic aspect, there was (1) misuse of credit, and (2) cycle of debt - borrowing money to pay for outstanding debt to have another release in credit ("debt for debt"). In the social aspect, (a) no trust; (b) minimal/no participation; (c) no check and balance; (d) non-attendance in meetings; (e) no responsibility; (f) no accountability; (g) no guarantee. In the religious aspect, when there was no pastor, or spiritual adviser, there was no membership, education was self-administered.

The fourth (4) quadrant, which did not empower women, showed dominance, uniformity and conformity in the group. As mentioned earlier, at times, the grameen method, adopted by the Barangay Pulo, in Banga, under the CRBA had a tendency to use this. In such cases, the political aspect was an autocratic leadership style with group pressure. In the economic aspect, there was (1) distrust; (2) peer pressure to change behavior through rewards and punishment; (3) a need to recite the Pledge *(Sampung Pangako ng Kaanib)* before the start of the meeting; (4) responsibility to group and the organization; (5) Rigid and oppressive set of rules and policies; (6) no flexibility. In the religious aspect, the practice of forced Christianity was observed - the members were required to pray before the meeting starts. In the education aspect, the organization requires CGT (Compulsory Group Training) and the GRT (Group Recognition Test) prior to membership.

The three cases revealed that communication dynamics that led to empowerment also led to success of the microfinance projects or a successful intervention of the development initiative. Consequently, the converse, communication dynamics that did not lead to empowerment also led to the failure of the microfinance project or the failed intervention of the development initiative as an outcome.

It can be said that the three organizations were successful in providing an improved quality of life for the women, thus empowering them. The failure of the Lanton Christian Savers of SIKAP/SIVAP DALSAKA was a consequence of a *laissez-faire* leadership style, no participation, no trust, no significant savings, etc. as shown in the fourth quadrant of the model (Figure 3). The opposite, which can be seen in the first and second quadrants, empowered the women and led to the success of the other groups of women involved in microfinance projects.

The Pulo Grameen Bank Replication Project was both liberating and restricting. Certain aspects of the communication dynamics had both led to empowerment and no empowerment. This was also true in the two other cases. All three cases indicated that communication was truly dynamic and that the three MED lending methodologies led to empowerment or no empowerment.

The Communication Dynamics Model indicated that when the women were successful in implementing their microfinance projects, their way of life improved, they were empowered, and poverty was alleviated. On the other hand, when their microfinance project failed, the women also did not improve their way of life, they were not empowered and remained in poverty.

CONCLUSION

In the Results section, we discussed how the three organizations provided microfinance to the poor: (1) Pulo Grameen Bank Replication Project, CRBA used the Grameen method of banking; (2) Lanton Christian Savers, DALSAKA was an example of Village Banking method; and, (3) Malipayon Group, Katuwang (KRCI) was an example of Individual Lending method.

The important contribution of women in sustainable development in microfinance projects cannot be overlooked. They are essential in ensuring that these projects are impacting their families and changing communities. Women have the power to help alleviate poverty in the land. Their full potential and vast reservoir of creativity and innovative ideas have been proven in many successful microfinance projects over many years. Whether as an individual lending, group lending or Grameen bank lending method, women have been empowered and helped increase their family income.

This chapter on the communication dynamics of women in microfinance projects in the Philippines, presented a model for women empowerment and identified factors of success and failure in microfinance projects. The essential contribution of women in the alleviation of poverty through microfinance was explained here and considered as a breakthrough in communication in terms of innovating the Grameen banking method, ASA and in the context of Philippine culture.

The *democratic leadership* was the best style to empower women involved in microfinance projects since it encouraged freedom, change, depicted by diversity as well as integration, solidarity and cultural identity which leads to empowerment.

In contrast, the *laissez-faire leadership* often led to normlessness and loss of identity and did not empower women. Likewise, *autocratic leadership* led to dominance, uniformity, and conformity also failed to empower the women. Communication dynamics that empowered women worked best in freedom, change, diversity, integration, solidarity and cultural identity. Having too much freedom however, led to normlessness and loss of identity. Moreover, too many restrictions led to dominance, uniformity and conformity, meaning, no empowerment.

The three case studies were successful in providing an improved quality of life for women at the time the research was conducted. Women were empowered through freedom in deciding what microfinance project to be involved in. Women empowerment was also encouraged through participative decision-making processes - problems were discussed and decisions were consulted. The women were part of the planning, management and control of resources.

Success in the microfinance projects enabled women to have increased credit and thereby improved their status in life and gained access to more resources. Concrete examples: a) children were able to go to school; b) they were able to have home improvements, and houses made of light building materials were later made of semi-concrete structure. More credit also enabled the women to have more microfinance projects. Creativity was enhanced and more ways to simplify things and improve services were encouraged. Death benefits were also given to members, as was the case of the grameen banking method of CRBA.

Failure in the implementation of the microfinance projects meant no empowerment for the women. When conditions were oppressive or too lenient, there was also no empowerment for the women.

As an update, the Grameen Bank Replication Project in Aklan ended when the CRBA closed on 30 June 2008. The National Bureau of Investigation also filed malversation of fund charges against several executives of the bank in 2007. Next, DALSAKA in General Santos City in Mindanao, has no presence online, with only their address and telephone number available. Finally, the KRCI (Katuwang) have reached 84,000+ entrepreneurial poor families in Negros Island, Philippines as of 2023.

As of December 2021, the Microfinance Council of the Philippines (MCPI) has grown to 66 institutions, which include 55 regular members and 11 support institutions with 33 regular non-government microfinance organization members; with 12 banks; 7 corporations; 1 finance company and two regional networks. This is between 80-90% of total active outreach of the microfinance sector in the Philippines.

The proposed Model for the communication dynamics of women involved in microfinance projects that lead to the success or failure of the projects also leads to women empowerment or no empowerment. This study is an important contribution to the study of MFIs. Microfinance projects will continue to be a viable method of alleviating poverty and providing credit to the poorest of the poor and empowering women in the process. With a democratic leadership style, freedom to choose the microfinance projects that the women will implement, an open and encouraging communication dynamics that empower women, success of these projects are possible. Whether individual, group or Grameen lending method, what matters is allowing the women freedom and access to resources to improve their way of life, the situation in their community, and eventually alleviate poverty in the land.

REFERENCES

Alvarez, A. D. (1998, July) *Transformational development program.* Kabalikat Para sa Maunlad na Buhay (KMBI - A Microfinance NGO). Unpublished Manuscript.

Alvarez, A. D. (1999, October). *Microfinance: An alternative tool in the fight against poverty. An Introduction to Microfinance.* Unpublished Paper.

Alvarez, A. D. (2001, June 8) *Katuwang Resource Center, Inc.* (2nd ed.). Concept Paper.

Department of Agrarian Reform (DAR). (2016). https://www.dar.gov.ph/

Department of Trade and Industry. (2019) *2019 MSME Statistics*. https://www.dti.gov.ph/resources/msme-statistics/

Family Code of the Philippines. (1987). *Property relations between husband and wife.* Executive Order No. 209.

Fernandez, M. R. (2002). Dynamics of communication of women involved in microfinance projects. *Danyag. Journal of the Humanities and Social Sciences, 7*(2), 161–172.

Fernandez, M. R. (2003, October). *Dynamics of communication of women involved in microfinance projects: A model for women empowerment* [Unpublished Dissertation]. College of Mass Communication, University of the Philippines, Diliman.

Godquin, M. (2006). Finance rurale au Bangladesh et aux Philippines [Rural finance in Bangladesh and the Philippines]. In *Economies et finances.* Université Panthéon-Sorbonne - Paris I.

Grameen Bank. (1986). *Grameen bank: A bank for the poor.* Dhaka: Grameen Bank Grameen Foundation. https://grameenfoundation.org/

Jocano, F. L. (1997). *Filipino value system: A cultural definition.* PUNLAD Research House, Inc.

Katuwang Resource Center, Inc. (KRCI). (n.d.). *Microfinance*. https://www.katuwang.com/services/microfinance

MCPI Regular Members. (2002-2023). *Microfinance Council of the Philippines*. https://microfinance-council.org/regular-members/

McQuail, D., & Widahl, S. (1993). Communication models for the study of mass communications (2nd ed.). Longman Singapore Publishers (Pto.) Ltd.

NobelPrize.org. (2023). Muhammad Yunus - Biographical. *The Nobel Peace Prize 2006.* Nobel Prize Outreach AB 2023. https://www.nobelprize.org/prizes/peace/2006/yunus/biographical/

Ojone, J. E. (2023). Religious importance of microfinance bank: A Christian perspective. *International Journal of Scientific and Management Research, 6*(7), 50-70. doi:10.37502/IJSMR.2023.6704

Patton, M. Q. (1990). *Qualitative evaluation methods*. SAGE Publications.

Philippine Commission on Women. (n.d.-a). *Agriculture, fisheries and forestry.* https://pcw.gov.ph/agriculture-fisheries-and-forestry/

Philippine Commission on Women. (n.d.-b). *Micro, small and medium enterprises (MSMEs) development.* https://pcw.gov.ph/micro-small-and-medium-enterprises-development/

Philippine Commission on Women. (n.d.-c). *Mission and Vision*. https://pcw.gov.ph/mission-and-vision/

Philippine Deposit Insurance Corporation (PDIC). (2008). *Bulletin No. 2008-02*. Philippine Deposit Corporation Official Website. pdic.gov.ph

Philippine News Agency (PNA). (2008, February 1). *PDIC takes over four branches of CRBA Banks.* Iloilo City, Philippines. pdic.gov.ph

Philippine Statistics Authority. (2016). psa.gov.ph

Philippine Statistics Authority. (2023, March 24). *Press Release 2023-119. HomePoverty Statistics*. psa.gov.ph

Press Kit. (2003, April 25-27). *1st Community Press Summit.* Kalibo, Aklan and Boracay.

Seibel, H. D. (1999, August). Banking with very poor women: Outreach and sustainability of CARD-Rural Bank, a Grameen Innovator in the Philippines. *The Journal of Microfinance, 1*(1), 117–130.

Seibel, H. D., Llanto, G. M., Garcia, E., & Callanta, R. (1997). *Microfinance in the Philippines: An assessment of viability, sustainability and outreach among Grameen replicators.* Working Paper/ University of Cologne, Development Research Center, No. 1997, 4. http://hdl.handle.net/10419/23667

Strauss, A., & Corbin, J. (1990). *Basics of qualitative research: Grounded theory procedures and techniques*. SAGE Publications, Inc.

Tahir, I. M., & Tahrim, S. N. C. (2013, October) Efficiency analysis of microfinance institutions in ASEAN: A DEA approach. *Business Management Dynamics, 3*(4), 13-23. www.bmdynamics.com

Waterfield, C., & Duval, A. (1996). *Care savings and credit sourcebook.* CARE.

Women's Enterprise Management Training Outreach Program for Asia (WEPTOP). (1992, August). *Pilot Project, Revised Draft Project Document for the Philippines*. Author.

Yunus, M. (1992). *Grameen Bank Replication Project in Bangladesh: A Poverty Focused Rural Development Programme*. Grameen Bank.

KEY TERMS AND DEFINITIONS

Account Officer: Bank worker directly involved with the clients; collects payments and dues and assists clients (refers to *Community Officer/Credit Officer/Project Assistant*).

Accountability: Self-group pressure to influence behavior.

Appreciative Inquiry: A capacity building process that begins by: (a) valuing the organizations or community and the culture in which it is embedded; (b) learning about the organization or community, its relationships and its environment; and (c) discovering the building upon existing strengths.

ASA: Acronym for Association for Social Advancement which in Bangla means "hope."

Client: People who avail of credit from microfinance organizations such as CRBA, DALSAKA and Katuwang, (refers to *member*) to be used for microfinance projects.

Communication: Verbal and nonverbal exchange of signs and messages to share meaning with others.

Community Officer/Credit Officer (CO/LO): Bank worker directly involved with the clients - collects payments and dues and assists clients (refers to *Project Assistant*).

Creativity: Use of appropriate media and innovative ideas to improve service to clients.

Credibility: Trustworthiness.

Credit: Money lent to members of the GBRP, DALSAKA or Katuwang for microfinance projects.

Credit Institutions: Lending institutions such as GBRP, DALSAKA or Katuwang that provide credit or loan to be used for microfinance projects of clients or members (refers to *MED lending organizations*).

Culture: Total way of life of people which includes: political, social, economic, religious, and education.

DALSAKA (Dalan sa Kalambuan, Inc.): An organization in General Santos City (GSC) that extend credit to marginalized communities; roughly translated, it means "road to progress."

Development: Increased purchasing power of an individual, and improved way of life (i.e. more material things at her disposal).

Development Initiative: Refers to the main idea, situation, happening about which a set of intervention strategies is directed at managing or handling or to which the set is related (also refers to the *phenomenon*).

Dynamics of Communication: Whole communication process of exchanging verbal or non-verbal signs, symbols and messages to share meaning in the context of culture; action/interaction and transaction between and among members/clients, bank workers or AOs/COs/LOs.

ED: Executive Director, heads the operations and management of the organization.

Empowerment: These are manifested in three ways: a) person has self-confidence to be heard; b) person is given space to express herself; c) others listen and give room for the person to speak and act. These can be evident in the improved way of life in terms of political, economic, social, religious and educational aspects, namely, 1) women are able to express themselves freely; 2) they are part of the planning, management and control of resources; 3) they have increased purchasing power; 4) their children are able to go to school and, 5) they are able to afford home improvements and increased credit; 6) they are able to pray and worship God freely and not forcibly; and, 7) they are also able to participate in the conduct of organization in policy formulations and attendance in trainings.

Flexibility: Adaptability to the changing times.

Grameen: Means "village" in Bangla.

Grameen Bank: "Village bank" established by Prof. Yunus in Bangladesh that has been replicated worldwide; it provides credit to the poor without need for collateral.

Grameen Bank Replication Projet (GBRP): Application of the Grameen Bank method/technology outside Bangladesh.

Intervening Variables: Are general conditions being upon intervention strategies. These conditions include key characteristics, time, space, culture, economic status, technological status, career, history and individual biography (refers to *intervening conditions*).

Intervention Strategies: Grounded theory is an action/interaction-oriented method of theory building. These intervention strategies are directed at managing, handling, carrying out, and responding to a development initiative, as it exists in a situation. The interaction component refers to self as well as other interaction. It has certain dimensions: 1) It is a process. It can be observed over time, in terms of consequences or in terms of movement; 2) the intervention strategies is goal-oriented and has a purpose - as an action or to manage a phenomenon; 3) It is also as important to look into failed intervention strategies; 4) Intervening variables that either help or hinder intervention strategies must be looked into (refers to *action/interaction strategies*).

Katuwang: Filipino word meaning "helpmate."

Katuwang Resource Center, Inc.: A Christian organization that provide credit to marginalized communities.

Lived Christianity: Showing Christian tenet of "love thy neighbor" by words, thoughts, and deeds.

Loan Officer (LO): Also refers to the Account Officer, Account Executive, Bank Worker or Community Loan Officer or Extension Worker (refers to *Community Officer*).

Marginalized Community: Landless poor that engage in small business an often neglected in the economic world that results to the movement in the o called "underground economy" and these micro-entrepreneurs resort to high interest credit of banks, money lenders, loan sharks, and credit unions since they have no alternative source.

Micro-Enterprise Development (MED) Lending Organizations: Organizations such as the (1) Cooperative Rural Bank of Aklan (CRBA); (2) Dalan sa Kalambuan (DALSAKA); and, (3) Katuwang Resource Center, Inc. that extend credit to marginalized communities without collateral to help in the alleviation of poverty (refers to *credit institutions*).

Microfinance: "Small monetary infusion" provided as an additional capital for small and medium scale enterprise production that will increase income or returns (refers to *credit*).

Microfinance Projects: Small business ventures engaged in by women to improve their quality of life.

Mutual Trust: Achievement of social consensus.

Origin: The event and situation that lead to the development initiative (refers to *causal conditions*).

Outcomes: Actual or potential results that may happen in the present or the future that may become part of the situation (or intervening variables) affecting the next set of intervention strategies occurring in a sequence. Whatever outcomes of intervention strategies now to handle a development initiative may become part of future situation (refers to *consequences*).

Participation: Sharing of interests through attendance in meetings and payment of loans.

Poverty Alleviation: The upliftment of social and economic status of an individual in society.

Project Assistants/Bank Workers: Partners in the Grameen rural microfinance, who facilitate the loans and payment of members' dues (refers to *AO, CO/LO*).

Public Decisions/Pledges: Public declaration to abide by the philosophy and principles of Grameen Bank.

Respect: Honoring the person's decision-making capabilities and judgment.

Situation: Presents the specific set of characteristics that pertain to a development initiative that is the location of happenings or events about it, along a dimensional range. Situation also means the set of conditions within which the intervention strategies are done to carry out, manage and handle specific development initiatives. The situation includes the following: intensity, duration, location, and obtained help (refers to *context*).

Trust: Respect for the person and belief in his ability to keep his word or abide by his decisions or pledge.

Vela Approach: An approach to adult education adopted by DALSAKA, using Appreciative Inquiry (AI) that was developed in the mid-1970s by David Cooperide and his colleagues in the Department of Organizational Behavior at the Weatherhead School of Management, Case Western Research University., Cleveland, Ohio, USA.

Chapter 3
Credit Access, Crop Output, and Welfare of Women Farmers in the Northern Region of Ghana

Hamna A. Abdallah
University for Development Studies, Tamale, Ghana

Osman Tahidu Damba
University for Development Studies, Tamale, Ghana

Gideon Danso-Abbeam
University for Development Studies, Tamale, Ghana

Abdul-Razak Alhassan
University of Surrey, UK

Issahaku Salifu
Birmingham City University, UK

ABSTRACT

This study examined the effect of credit access on women farmers' welfare through crop output in the Northern Region of Ghana. The impact of credit on welfare through output was examined using the conditional mixed process (CMP) model on 300 women farmers. Credit access, welfare, and output were estimated individually and also within a conditional mixed process (CMP) system for choice of appropriate estimation due to endogeneity. Age, household size, extension access, and membership of farmer-based organization (FBO) significantly influence farmers' choice of credit source while credit access, expenditure on inputs, years of farming, land size, and membership of FBO significantly impacts on crop output. Crop output and off-farm income significantly influence welfare of women farmers. Pairwise correlation of credit sources revealed that Village Savings and Loans Association (VSLA) and Susu sources are complementary, and farmers who accessed credit from VSLA also accessed credit from Susu (rotating savings and credit associations).

DOI: 10.4018/978-1-6684-8979-6.ch003

1.0 INTRODUCTION

The current climate change effect has further exposed smallholder farmers to low yield and productivity. The most affected are women with low access to factors of production. To women who have access to the factors of production, cost of these factors are beyond their reach due to the lack of access and or inadequate access to finance including credit. Women constitute about 95% of those engaged in agro processing and 85% of those in food distribution (WAG, 2014).

Majority of household incomes of rural dwellers hinges on agriculture with women accounting for above 40% of the total labour force. Women in rural areas cultivate basically to meet household needs and sell the surplus to the markets. In some cultures, the division of labour is strict and hence women are required to handle household chores while men bring in the financial resources for household needs. Sanginga and Bervinson (2015), noted that crops that are mostly cultivated by women in Sub Saharan Africa (SSA) include oilseeds and legumes (cowpeas, soybean and groundnuts) due to the social, economic, and environmental benefits of these crops added to its ability to address food security needs. Notwithstanding the critical roles played by women in the cultivation of these oilseeds and legumes, empirical evidence points out that there is a gap between men and women concerning farm yield in Africa. This emanates from the gender differences that continue to exist in respect of access to productive resources such as land, livestock, labour, extension, financial services, and technology (Muriithi et al., 2018).

Gender inequality remains a critical issue in Ghana in particular, and Sub-Saharan Africa (SSA) in general. This is as a result of the norms and traditions that do not allow men and women to have equal access to production resources. Manda et al., (2016) indicated that cultural rules and customs hamper women's capacity to take over farmlands and as a result, add to widening gender gaps in the quality and size of farmland. But it is known that reducing gender inequality is a step in the right direction as it adds to agricultural growth and achieving food and dietary security. However, for productivity to increase in the agriculture sector in most countries in SSA, not only do we need equality in access to production resources, but also there is the need to consider access to finance as a booster of productivity (Sekyi, 2017).

Also, according to the IISD, (2015), for a country to move from subsistence to commercial agricultural production, there is the need to pay attention to finance which will boost growth in the sector. Hussain and Thapa (2015) also affirmed that one of the significant challenges facing smallholder farmers, especially those in developing countries in their day-to-day farming activities is access to credit. However, in developing countries where the majority depend on agriculture, financing for investment is scarce (IFC, 2013).

One of the main channels of reaching a drastic decline in poverty and improving farmers' welfare is to increase agriculture productivity through technology adoption, and this is tied to financing. It is evident that there is a direct positive association between credit access and agricultural output, and one of the solutions to agricultural financing is easy access to credit (Obisesan & Akinlade 2013). Making credit available to rural households has been noted as an essential instrument that can alleviate poverty among poor rural families. Sekyi (2017) indicated that improving access to financial services is a crucial step to reducing poverty and improving development outcomes by enabling the rural poor to smoothing their consumption and cope with risk. Credit access is necessary for increasing the ability of households to cater for expenses such as the purchase and use of improved agricultural inputs and the achievement of food security (IFPRI, 2002; Sekyi, 2017). There are two primary sources of credit in Ghana, the formal and the informal sources. The formal sources of credit comprise of banks, and the registered financial institutions and the informal sources include self-help groups such as "susu groups", Rotating Savings and Credit Association (ROSCA), Village Savings and Loans Association (VSLA) and other unstructured agents like money lenders, family and friends, among others. Despite these sources of credit, majority of farmers in Ghana still face inadequate access to credit (Owusu and Antwi, 2010) and this is due to the constraints which either limits the farmer's ability to obtain the loan or the adequacy of a loan facility.

Considering such comparatively high levels of poverty in the north, the role of credit access and participation among women farmers cannot be underestimated. However, women's simultaneous access to the various sources of credit and the factors influencing women's decision to access credit from different sources have not been adequately explored. Moreover, whether access to credit does have an impact on farm productivity and translate into welfare gains has also not be sufficiently assessed. This study adds up to the body of knowledge in two unique ways: (1) it models the joint decision of women to access credit from diverse sources and (2) the impact of credit access on productivity, and its subsequent effects on welfare.

2.0 LITERATURE REVIEW

Access to Credit and Agricultural Output Relationship

Farmers' access to financing, whether formal or informal, is critical to increasing agricultural output and improving farmer welfare. According to Carter and Weibe (1990), farmers require both ex-ante and ex-post access to credit in order to maximize crop yield production. On the one hand, Carter and Weibe (1990) argue that ex-ante capital is required to finance significant crop output production expenditures such as buy inputs and labour costs, which must be paid in advance (ex-ante) before crop yield production can be realized. However, when there is no insurance, as is commonly the situation for farmers in low-income agrarian economies like Ghana, ex-post capital access is critical. Ex-post access to capital is thus critical for the year-to-year stabilization of farmer household spending in the event of annual fluctuations in production.

Access to credit, according to Awotide et al. (2015), may not have a direct impact on productivity, but it may have a positive and significant indirect impact through its positive influence on agricultural technology adoption, increased capital for farm investment, hired labour, and farmer household welfare through better health care and nutrition. Furthermore, according to Feder et al. (1990), credit allows farmers to meet the cash needs induced by the production cycle that characterizes agriculture; land preparation, planting, cultivation, and harvesting are typically done over a period of several months during which very little cash revenue is earned, while expenditure on materials, purchased inputs, and consumption must be made in cash. As a result, access to credit, or the lack thereof, may have an impact on farm productivity since farmers who are bound by capital limitations tend to use lower levels of inputs in their production activities than those who are not, and this has an impact on crop yield production (Awotide et al., 2015; Petrick, 2004). The fact that inputs are transformed into outputs with significant time lags strongly influences agricultural crop output production (Awotide et al., 2015; Conning and Udry, 2005), forcing rural household farmers to balance their budgets during the season when input purchases and consumption are high, and revenue is low. The budget balance by farmers within the year might become a limitation to agricultural crop output production due to a lack of or limited access to finance. As and when liquidity is a binding restriction, a farmer's input amounts and combinations may diverge from optimal levels, limiting optimal output or consumption options. According to economic theory, farmers with constrained capital would employ lower levels and combinations of inputs than those whose production activities are not constrained by capital limitations (Freeman et al., 1998). As a result, access to finance may improve rural poor farmer households' propensity to adopt new technology, raising both mean income levels and income riskiness (Rosenzweig and Binswanger, 1993; Carter, 1984).For example, there is empirical evidence that good planting material improves cassava productivity and enhances varietal yield stability, and the type of planting material plays a significant role in determining the quantity of roots at harvest, Feder and Umali (1993) and Cornejo and McBride (2002) highlight access to credit as a key determinant of adoption of most agricultural innovations in their reviews of factors that affect technology adoption. It is thought that access to credit encourages the adoption of riskier agricultural technologies by easing the liquidity constraint and increasing the risk-bearing capacity of farmer households.

As a result, with the option of borrowing, a household can forego risk-reducing but inefficient income diversification measures in favor of riskier but more efficient investments (Eswaran and Kotwal, 1990). Lack of access to credit is seen as a barrier to the adoption of modern farming techniques such as herbicides, insecticides, inorganic fertilizers, tractors, proper spacing, planting date, and tillage (Nweke et al., 2002). Despite this, numerous findings in the literature (Iyanda et al., 2014) have pointed to the enormous importance of adoption of these technologies in increasing productivity, eradicating poverty, improve economic welfare, and achieving food security in developing nations. More crucially, according to Freeman et al. (1998), farmers' access to finance is critical in that it can help them get closer to their potential levels of input utilization when capital is not a restriction, resulting in higher levels of crop output production per farm and productivity, given fixed resources like land. This means that credit's marginal contribution brings input levels closer to optimal levels, boosting output and productivity, and hence improving farmer welfare (Feder et al., 1990). Furthermore, credit is regarded as a vital tool for smoothing consumption and stimulating output, particularly for disadvantaged households Conning and Udry, 2005; Armendariz and Morduch, 2005). This means that farmer households with no or limited savings can use loans to meet their financial demands for agricultural inputs, particularly those that are critical for weed, insect, and disease control as well as productive investments. Furthermore, having easy access to loans allows farmers and businesspeople to diversify their businesses by making new investments.

Many developing countries' rural areas are practically devoid of traditional banking institutions, which regard smallholders as high-risk, high-cost consumers (Mpuga, 2010; Sakyi et al., 2020). However, informal loan markets are quite active, and rural farmers prefer them (Yuan & Gao, 2012). Sector failures coordinated by adverse selection and moral hazard are a prevalent aspect of the loan market in emerging economies (Besley, 1994). Costly imprecise information, hazards, and market segmentation are key reasons of these failures in Africa (Atieno, 2001). Credit rationing is a common symptom of market failure and has been studied extensively in the credit demand literature (Abu et al., 2016). As a result, a number of empirical studies (Adegboye & Iweriebor, 2018; Akudugu, 2016; Sekyi et al., 2017) have been conducted to better understand the essential elements that determine credit access. Education, age, nonfarm business equipment, multiple crop production, and group participation are the elements impacting farmers' access to finance, according to Sakyi et al. (2020).

Another branch of the literature looks at credit sources to see whether there's any indication that farmers get credit from different places (Abu et al., 2016; Sekyi et al., 2014). The third branch of credit literature consists of research that are conditional on credit access and investigate the impact of credit on certain variables. Nkegbe (2018), for example, looked at the impact of credit on farmers' technical efficiency, whereas Akudugu (2016) looked at the impact of credit on agricultural production. Agricultural development in Ghana has a number of problems, the most significant of which are capital limits and uninsured risks (Karlan et al., 2014). Agriculture is found to be subject to climatic, natural, and biological hazards (Nunoo & Acheampong, 2014), and the insufficient supply of agricultural finance is a result of the high risk in agriculture (Nunoo & Acheampong, 2014).

The literature demonstrates the usefulness of agricultural insurance as a risk management strategy (Karlan et al., 2014). Agricultural insurance programs and initiatives in Ghana are mostly aimed at providing insurance products to farmers to manage their risks. Few efforts target the insurance of financial institutions (Sakyi et al., 2020). The focus on farmers is also skewed to the provision of index-based insurance (Lence, 2015). The first attempt at introducing agricultural insurance started in 2009 under a research project that piloted a small weather index insurance initiative in northern Ghana by the Innovation for Poverty Action (Karlan et al., 2014). However, the first formalized and broad-based insurance scheme was initiated by the German Development Cooperation in 2011 (Nunoo & Acheampong, 2014).

Farmers can prepare fields early, buy raw materials early, and pay for labor costs throughout the production process if they have access to capital. Access to money also enables farmers to deliver crop output to marketing centers on time, as well as providing storage facilities for crop output that will be sold later, thereby boosting farmer welfare. As a result, there is a link between access to money, crop output production, and farmer welfare. Feder et al. (1990) argue that farmers would have to keep cash reserves in the absence of credit markets in order to facilitate production and consumption in the following farming cycle and that access to credit makes it possible for farmers to consume more and use more purchased inputs, so improving their well-being.

3.0 MATERIAL AND METHODS

Sampling Techniques and Data Collection

A multi-stage sampling technique involving purposive and simple random sampling was used for this study. Purposive sampling technique was used to select the two study areas, that is, Savelugu Municipal and Karaga district in Northern Ghana due to the high level of female farmers in these areas. Five communities were selected through simple random sampling from each district. Out of the five communities, a total of 30 respondents were selected from each community through a simple random sampling. This means the study covered about 150 respondents in each study area making a total sample size of 300.

The sample size was calculated using the following Cochran's (1977) sample size determination formula:

$$n = \frac{z^2 p\left(1-p\right)}{d^2} \tag{1}$$

Where n= the required sample size, z= the confidence level at 95% (standard value of 1.96), p= estimated population percentage under study (90%) and d^2= margin of error at 3.4% (standard value of 0.034). Since according to the GSS (2021), an estimated average of 90% of households across the two selected districts (Savelugu and Karaga) in the Northern Region are farm households, the population percentage used in this computation is 90%. Therefore, assuming a margin of error of 3.4% and the total estimated population percentage of 90% or 0.90 on farming and credit access, the formula above computed a sample size of 299 farm households. But with reference to Cohen's (1992) arguments of statistical accuracy of high sample size, 300 questionnaires were administered. Statistically, the sample size is large enough to study and generalize about the population.

Sources and Type of Data

Data was primarily sourced from smallholder women farmers through semi-structured questionnaire. This was administered through face-to-face interviews. Data on the socio-demographic factors such as age, household size, level of education, off-farm income; Farm factors also included farming experience and farm size and in relation to institutional factors, extension access, and member of farmer-based organization were obtained.

Theoretical Framework

The decision of people to access credit or not depends on the satisfaction one derives from making that decision which falls under the theory of utility maximization. An individual farmer's decision to participate or not in any credit scheme depends on the level of satisfaction the farmer derives from either participating or not.

The theoretical framework adopted for the study was based on the random utility model, as specified by Greene (2003) as detailed below.

Assuming (U_1) and (U_0) are the utilities one drives accessing credit or not respectively, the linear random model for the utility (U_1) derived from one's decision to have credit is expressed as a function of independent or explanatory variables X_i and it is given by:

$$U_1 = X_i\beta_1^* + \mu_1 \tag{2}$$

On the other hand, the utility (U_0) one derives for not accessing credit is given as:

$$U_0 = X_i\beta_0^* + \mu_0 \tag{3}$$

Where X_i is explanatory or independent variables (such as educational level, age, income, marital, religion etc), β_1 and β_0 are parameters for decision to join or not to access credit respectively, μ_1 and μ_0 are error terms for deciding to or not to access credit respectively. According to Gujarati (2006), the error terms in the above equations are assumed to be normally independently and identically distributed. For an individual to make the decision to access credit, the expected utility derived from accessing credit must be greater than the expected utility derived for not accessing credit thus $E(U_1)>E(U_0)$.

The probability of participating in credit is given by:

$$P\left(U = 1 \middle| X\right) = P\left[\left(X_i\beta_1^* + \mu_1\right) > \left(X_i\beta_0^* + \mu_0\right)\right] \tag{4}$$

$$P\left(U = 1 \middle| X\right) = P\left[\left(X_i \beta_1^* + \mu_1\right) - \left(X_i \beta_0^* + \mu_0\right) > 0 \middle| X\right] \tag{5}$$

$$P\left(U = 1 \middle| X\right) = P\left[X_i\left(\beta_1^* - \beta_0^*\right) + \left(\mu_1 - \mu_0\right) > 0 \middle| X\right] \tag{6}$$

$$P\left(U = 1 \middle| X\right) = P\left[\left(\beta^* X_i + \mu^*\right) > 0 \middle| X\right] \tag{7}$$

$$P\left(U = 1 \middle| X\right) = F\left(\beta_0 + \beta_1 X_1 + \beta_2 X_2 + \ldots\ldots + \beta_n X_n\right) \tag{8}$$

Where P is a probability function, $\mu^* = \mu_1 - \mu_0$ is a random term, $\beta^* = \beta_1 - \beta_2$ is a vector of unknown parameters and F is the cumulative distribution function of μ^*. The ^{d}istribution of "*F*" depends on the distribution of the error term, μ^*. Given that the effect of X which is a vector of explanatory variables on the response probabilities (Y) can be estimated using a binary probit model as stated below.

$$Y_i = \left(\beta_0 + \beta_1 X_{1i} + \ldots\ldots + \beta_{ni} X_{ni} + \mu_i\right) \tag{9}$$

Model Specification

This section presents the approaches applied for empirical estimation in the study. These are the multivariate model, the endogenous switching regression model and the conditional mixed process.

The Multivariate Probit Model

A farmer's decision to participate in a particular credit source is discrete in nature and calls for a choice model. Univariate logit and probit models are not appropriate in this case, since they may generate biased estimates because these methods assume the independence of error terms of the different credit sources. Whereas a farmer may participate in different credit sources and the decision to participate in one source could be influenced by the decisions to participate in other sources. Therefore, a multivariate probit model introduced by Ashford and Snowden (1970) is appropriate. This model allows for the interrelationships among various credit sources, that is, the potential correlation among the unobserved disturbances in the participation equation. Ignoring such issues leads to biased and inefficient estimates (Greene, 2003; Wooldridge, 2002).

The multivariate probit model (MVP) is a popular classic model for studying binary responses of multiple entities. In a single-equation statistical model, information on women farmers` participation in a source of credit does not alter the likelihood of her participating in another source of credit. However, the MVP approach simultaneously models the influence of the set of explanatory variables on each of the different practices, while allowing for the potential correlation between unobserved disturbances, as well as the relationship between the adoptions of different practices (Belderbos et al., 2004). One source of correlation may be complementarities (positive correlation) and substitutability (negative correlation) between different practices (Ibid). Failure to capture unobserved factors and interrelationships among adoption decisions regarding different practices will lead to bias and inefficient estimates (Greene, 2008).

The observed outcome of a credit participation can be modeled following random utility formulation. Consider the ith farmer (i=1,…,N) facing a decision on whether or not to participate in available source of credit s (s = 1,……, N). Let U_0 represent the benefits to the farmer from not participating in any form of credit, and let U_k represent the benefit of participating in the kth source of credit: (k= V,S,F) denoting choice of VSLA (V), Susu (S), and Family and friends (F). The farmer decides to participate in the kth source if $Y_{isk}^{*} = U_k^{*} - U_0 > 0$. The net benefit Y_{isk}^{*} that the farmer derives from the kth source is a latent variable determined by observed household demographic characteristics X_{is}, and unobserved characteristics u_{is}:

$$Y_{isk}^{*} = X_{is}'\beta_k + \mu_{is} \quad (k=V,S,F) \tag{10}$$

Using the indicator function, the unobserved preferences in equation (1) translate into observed binary outcome equation for each choice as follows:

$$Y_k = \begin{cases} 1\, if\, Y_{isk}^{*} > 0 \\ 0, otherwise \end{cases} \quad (K=V,S,F) \tag{11}$$

In the multivariate model, where participation in the various sources of credit is feasible, the error terms jointly follow a multivariate normal distribution (MVN) with zero conditional mean and variance normalized to unity (for identification of parameters) where (μ_v,μ_s,μ_F)~ MVN(0,Ω) and the symmetric covariance matrix Ω is given by.

$$\Omega = \begin{bmatrix} 1 & \rho_{VS} & \rho_{VF} \\ \rho_{SV} & 1 & \rho_{SF} \\ \rho_{FV} & \rho_{FS} & 1 \end{bmatrix} \tag{12}$$

Particular interest are the off-diagonal element in the covariance matrix, which represent the unobserved correlation between the stochastic components of the various sources of credit. On the basis of this assumption, equation (3.12) gives an MVP model that jointly represents the decision to access credit from a particular source. The off- diagonal element allows for correlation across the error terms of several latent equations representing unobserved characteristics that affects the choice of alternative sources of credit.

Empirically, the general model for access to credit for each of the various sources in a system of equations can be specified as:

$$Y_{ik} = \beta_0 + \sum_{i=1}^{m}\beta_{ik}S_{ik} + \sum_{i=1}^{m}\beta_{ik}F_{ik} + \sum_{i=1}^{m}\beta_{ik}I_{ik} + \varepsilon_i \tag{13}$$

$\forall i$=1…m regressors.

Econometric Framework and Estimation Strategy

The empirical challenge in impact assessment using observational studies is establishing a suitable counterfactual against which the impact can be measured because of self-selection problems. To accurately measure the impact of credit on crop output of farm households, decision to access credit should be randomly assigned so that the effect of observable and unobservable characteristics between the treatment and comparison groups is the same, and the effect is attributable entirely to the treatment. However, when the treatment groups are not randomly assigned, credit access decisions are likely to be influenced both by unobservable (e.g., managerial skills and motivation) and observable heterogeneity that may be correlated to the outcome of interest.

Econometric approaches to deal with selection bias in cross sectional data include Propensity Score Matching (PSM), Generalized Propensity Score (GPS) matching in a continuous treatment framework, Instrumental Variable (IV) approaches and Endogenous Switching Regression (ESR). PSM only controls observed heterogeneity while IV can also control unobserved heterogeneity. The traditional IV treatment effect models with one selection and outcome equation assumes that the impact can be represented as a simple parallel shift with respect to the outcome variable. The endogenous switching regression (ESR) framework relaxes this assumption by estimating two separate equations (one for those with access to credit and one for those without access to credit) along with the selection equation (e.g., Kassie et al., 2008; Di Falco et al., 2011; Kabunga et al., 2012). In this research work, a binary ESR treatment effects approach was adopted to reduce the selection bias by controlling for both observed and unobserved heterogeneity despite its distributional (trivariate normal distribution) and exclusion restriction assumptions. The GPS is an extension of the binary PSM methods for the case of continuous treatment impact assessment (for details see Hirano and Imbens, 2004). Unlike the ESR and PSM, the focus is on assessing the heterogeneity of treatment effects arising from different treatment levels. It uses the same assumptions as in the standard PSM methods, including selection into different credit access based on a set of observed covariates.

Impact Evaluation Framework: Endogenous Switching Regression Model (ESR)

The research examines the impact of women farmers' access to credit on crop output. Many past studies have attempted to measure the impact of credit on some outcomes by estimating a supply and production functions separately for those with access to and without access to credit and then compare the two estimates. However, this approach implicitly assumes that all farmers are identical with respect to those with and without access to credit which serves as its weakness. Also, there is the problem of endogeneity which may arise because of the nature of access to credit. This is because access to credit is either voluntary or some farmers are in better position to have access to credit than others. The decision to access credit or not is voluntary and may be based on individual self-selection and farmers who access credit may have decided based on expected benefit. For example, well-to-do, educated, or productive farmers may choose to access credit and if not controlled for may lead to endogeneity and one way of accounting for such endogeneity is by estimating a simultaneous equation model (Hausman, 1983). More importantly the ESR is adopted specifically to correct for any possible sample bias (Lee, 1978; Madalla, 1983; Freeman et al., 1998).

In the ESR model framework, we estimate a two-stage estimation procedure simultaneously. The first stage is the factors that influence credit access and the second, the impact of credit access on crop output which is the outcome variable is specified for two regimes of those with access to credit and those without access to credit as.

Regime 1(With access): $Y_{i1} = X_{i1}\beta_1 + \varepsilon_{i1}\ if\ C_i = 1$ (14)

Regime 2(Without access): $Y_{i2} = X_{i2}\beta_2 + \varepsilon_{i2}\ if\ C_i = 0$ (15)

Where Y_{i1} and Y_{i2} are outcome variables for those with and without access to credit respectively; X_{i1} and X_{i2} are unobserved characteristics; β_1 and β_2 are vector of parameters to be estimated and ε_{i1}, ε_{i2}, and μ_i are the error terms assumed to have a trivariate normal distribution, with zero mean and non-singular covariance matrix expressed as

$$\sum = \begin{bmatrix} \sigma_1^2 & \sigma_{12} & \sigma_{1\mu} \\ \sigma_{12} & \sigma_2^2 & \sigma_{2\mu} \\ \sigma_{1\mu} & \sigma_{2\mu} & \sigma_\mu^2 \end{bmatrix} \quad (16)$$

Where σ_1^2 and σ_2^2 are variance of error terms, ε_{i1} and ε_{i2}. σ_μ^2 is the variance of the error term, μ_i and σ_{12}, $\sigma_{1\mu}$ and $\sigma_{2\mu}$; are the covariance of, ε_{i1} and ε_{i2}, ε_{i1} and μ_i and ε_{i2} and μ_i *respectively*. The term σ_μ^2 is assumed to be 1 because γ is estimable only up to scale factor (Maddala, 1983).

Because the error terms in equation are conditioned on the sample selection criterion and have non-zero expected values, estimating β_1 and β_2 with Ordinary Least Squares will suffer from sample selection bias yielding inconsistent estimates (Lee, 1977; Maddala, 1983).

The structure of the ESR model allows for an overlap of the selection and outcome equation but for identification purposes, at least one variable in the selection equation should not be included in the outcome equation. A valid instrument is expected to influence credit access and not crop output.

In this study, distance to district capital is hypothesized to affect credit access and not crop output and as such is considered as a valid and relevant instrument.

To account for selectivity bias, the variables X_{i1} and X_{i2} account for only observed factors. However, the ESR model is able to address selection bias due to unobserved factors within the framework of omitted variable problem. Following Heckman (1970) the inverse mills ratio from the selection equation (λ_{i1} and λ_{i2}) for those with and without credit respectively and the covariance terms $\delta_{1\varepsilon}$, $\delta_{2\varepsilon}$ are plugged into the above equations and specified as.

$$Y_{i1} = X_{i1}\beta_1 + \delta_{1\varepsilon}\lambda_1 + \vartheta_{i1}\ if\ C_i = 1 \quad (17)$$

$$Y_{i2} = X_{i2}\beta_2 + \delta_{2\varepsilon}\lambda_2 + \vartheta_{i2}\ if\ C_i = 0 \quad (18)$$

Where selectivity term λ_{i1} and λ_{i2} correct for selection bias from unobserved factors and ϑ_{i1} and ϑ_{i2} are the error terms with conditional zero means.

It is argued that the two-stage approach is disadvantaged in the sense that it generates residuals that are heteroskedastic and cannot be used to obtain standard errors that are consistent without adjustment (Lokshin and Sajaia, 2004). They, therefore, proposed an FMLA which can efficiently estimate the outcome and selection equation simultaneously where the FIML method was estimated using the movestay command available in the STATA statistical software. The FIML method has been adopted by Alene and Manyong (2007) and Asfaw (2010) among many others. The FIML method simultaneously estimates the probit equation and the regression equation to yield consistent standard errors. The log likelihood function for the ESR is specified as.

$$\ln L\left(\beta_1,\beta_2,\sigma_1^2,\sigma_2^2,\sigma_{1\mu},\sigma_{2\mu}\right)=\sum_{i=1}^{n}\left[\ln\left\{F\left(\frac{\gamma Z_i+\rho_1\varepsilon_{1i}/\sigma_1}{\sqrt{1-\rho_1^2}}\right)\right\}+\ln\left\{f\left(\frac{\varepsilon_{1i}/\sigma_1}{\sigma_1}\right)\right\}\right]$$
$$+\left(1-I_i\right)\left[\ln\left\{1-F\left(\frac{\gamma Z_i+\rho_2\varepsilon_{2i}/\sigma_2}{\sqrt{1-\rho_2^2}}\right)\right\}+\ln\left\{f\left(\frac{\varepsilon_{1i}/\sigma_1}{\sigma_1}\right)\right\}\right] \quad (19)$$

Where F is a cumulative normal distribution function, f is a normal density distribution function, $\rho_1 = \sigma_{1\mu}/\sigma_\mu\sigma_1$ is the correlation coefficient between ε_{i1} and μ_i, and $\rho_2 = \sigma_{2\mu}/\sigma_\mu\sigma_2$ is the correlation coefficient between ε_{i2} and μ_i. Only the values of Y, Y_{i1} and Y_{i2} is actually observed for any given household depending on the regime the household is, credit access or not. Therefore σ_{12} does not occur in the likelihood function and it is not estimable.

To examine the impact of credit access on crop output, we compare the expected output of those who had access credit with the expected outcome of the counterfactual (those without credit had access to credit). This is express below as.

$$E\left(Y_{i1}/C=1\right)=X_{i1}\beta_1-\delta_{1\varepsilon}\lambda_1 \quad (20)$$

$$E\left(Y_{i2}/C=1\right)=X_{i2}\beta_2-\delta_{2\varepsilon}\lambda_1 \quad (21)$$

The difference between

$$ATT=E\left(Y_{i1}/C=1\right)-E\left(Y_{i2}/C=1\right) \quad (22)$$

We can also compare the expected output of those who did not have access to credit with its counterfactual (those with credit if they did not have access). This is expressed below as

$$E\left(Y_{i2}/C=0\right) \quad (23)$$

$$E\left(Y_{i1}/C=0\right) \quad (23)$$

The difference gives us the ATU

$$ATT = E\left(Y_{i2} / C = 0\right) - E\left(Y_{i1} / C = 0\right) \tag{24}$$

The empirical equation of the ESRM to be estimated is the credit demand function, which is a Probit regression and a crop-output function. Access to credit decision equation is specified as:

Credit access (Access=1, 0=Otherwise) = f (Age, Hhgender, Educ, Hhsize, Extaccess, Famlabour, Memberfbo, Distance)

Creditaccess=β_0+ β_1Age + β_2Hhgender+ β_3Educ+ β_4Extaccess+ β_5Farmlabour+ β_6MemberFBO+ β_7Distance+μ (25)

The dependent variable is binary thus taking the value of 1 if the farmer has access to credit and 0 otherwise. The separate value of output function for the farmers that have access to credit and those that did not have access to credit was also specified. This was followed by an output model expressed as:

Ln (Output) = f (Age, Hhgender, Educ, Hhsize, Extaccess, Famlabour, Memberfbo)

Ln (Output) =β_0+ β_1Age + β_2Hhgender+ β_3Educ+ β_4Extaccess+ β_5Farmlabour+ β_6MemberFBO+ β_7Distance+μ (26)

Where ln is a natural logarithm, value of output is the total output multiplied by price per bag of each crop as at the time of the research. It is important to note that all crops were measured in bags.

Conditional Mixed Process

In terms of the effect of credit participation and agricultural output on the welfare of women farmers, the study applied the conditional recursive process framework. This process consists of three structural models in the study: access to credit model, crop output model and welfare model. Access to credit is a discrete model and hence a farmer either has access to credit or not. The crop output and welfare model are continuous models measured as a value of output per crop and welfare as expenditure per capita. It is possible to analytically model these structural models as a stand-alone using single equation estimation techniques comprising of credit access model estimated by using a probit or logit while crop output and welfare can be estimated using ordinary least square. However, this study proposed a system approach known as the conditional mixed process (CMP) as proposed by Roodman (2011). The CMP framework is built primarily on a Seemingly Unrelated Regression (SUR) and thus allows mixing and building different models in multi equations (Roodman, 2011). The CMP framework employs the Maximum Likelihood Estimation (MLE) technique and assumes joint modelling of two or more equations while permitting correlation between error terms across the equations. The major advantage of this system of estimation is that it produces precise parameter estimates.

$$y_1^* = \theta_1 + \varepsilon_1 \tag{27}$$

$$y_2^* = \theta_2 + \varepsilon_2 \quad (28)$$

$$y_3^* = \theta_3 + \varepsilon_3 \quad (29)$$

$$\theta_1 = \beta_1 X, \qquad \theta_2 - \beta_2 X, \qquad \theta_3 = \beta_3 X_3$$

$$y = g\left(y^*\right) = \left(1\left\{y_1^* > 0\right\}, 1\left\{y_2^* > 0\right\}, y_3^*\right)$$

$$\in = \left(\varepsilon_1, \varepsilon_2, \varepsilon_3\right) \sim \mathrm{N}\left(0, \Sigma\right)$$

$$\sum \begin{bmatrix} 1 & \rho & \sigma_{13} \\ \rho & 1 & \sigma_{23} \\ \sigma_{31} & \sigma_{32} & \sigma_{33} \end{bmatrix}$$

Where credit access=y_1, Crop output=y_2 and Welfare= y_3
Let's assume y_i= $(0,0,y_{i3})$ is observed, then the likelihood function can be specified as:

$$L_i\left(\beta_1, \beta_2, \beta_3, \Sigma; y_i \middle| x_i = \int_{-\infty}^{-\theta_1} \int_{-\infty}^{-\theta_2} \varphi_j \left\{\left(\varepsilon_1, \varepsilon_2, y_{i3} - \theta_{i3}\right)' ; \Sigma\right\} d\varepsilon_1 d\varepsilon_2\right) \quad (30)$$

According to Roodman (2011), this function is impossible to directly estimate using standard functions in statistical software. To directly estimate, we have to factor $\varphi_j \left\{\left(\varepsilon_1, \varepsilon_2, y_{i3} - \theta_{13}\right); \Sigma\right\}$ into probability distribution functions, ε_1,ε_2|ε_3 and ε_3. The formula for then conditional distribution of a normal distribution leads to the factoring:

$$\varphi j \left\{\left(\varepsilon_1, \varepsilon_2, \varepsilon_3\right); \Sigma\right\} = \left[\varphi_1 \left(\varepsilon_1 - \frac{\sigma_{13}}{\sigma_{33}} \varepsilon_3; 1 - \frac{\sigma_{13}\sigma_{31}}{\sigma_{33}}\right) \varphi_2 \left(\varepsilon_2 - \frac{\sigma_{23}}{\sigma_{33}} \varepsilon_3; 1 - \frac{\sigma_{23}\sigma_{32}}{\sigma_{33}}\right)\right] \left(y_{i3} - \theta_{i3}; \sigma_{33}\right) \quad (31)$$

Substituting this into equation (3.26) yields:

$$L_i\left(\beta_1, \beta_2, \beta_3, \Sigma; y_i \middle| x_i\right) = \int_{-\infty}^{-\theta 1} \int_{-\infty}^{-\theta 2} \left[\begin{matrix} \varphi_1 \left\{\varepsilon_1 - \frac{\sigma_{13}}{\sigma_{33}} \left(y_{i3} - \theta_{i3}\right); 1 - \frac{\sigma_{13}\sigma_{31}}{\sigma_{33}}\right\} \\ \varphi_2 \left\{\varepsilon_2 - \frac{\sigma_{23}}{\sigma_{33}} \left(y_{i3} - \theta_{i3}\right); 1 - \frac{\sigma_{23}\sigma_{32}}{\sigma_{33}}\right\} d\varepsilon_1 d\varepsilon_2 \end{matrix}\right] \left(y_{i3} - \theta_{i3}; \sigma_{33}\right)$$

$$= \varphi\left(y_{i3} - \theta_{i3}; \sigma_{33}\right) \int_{-\infty}^{-\theta 1} \int_{-\infty}^{-\theta 2} \varphi_1 \begin{bmatrix} \varphi_1 \left\{ \varepsilon_1 - \frac{\sigma_{13}}{\sigma_{33}}\left(y_{i3} - \theta_{i3}\right); 1 - \frac{\sigma_{13}\sigma_{31}}{\sigma_{33}} \right\} \\ \phi_2 \left\{ \varepsilon_2 - \frac{\sigma_{23}}{\sigma_{33}}\left(y_{i3} - \theta_{i3}\right); 1 - \frac{\sigma_{23}\sigma_{32}}{\sigma_{33}} \right\} d\varepsilon_1 d\varepsilon_2 \end{bmatrix} \tag{32}$$

$$= \varphi\left(y_{i3} - \theta_{i3}; \sigma_{33}\right) \begin{bmatrix} \varphi_1 \left\{ -\theta_1 - \frac{\sigma_{13}}{\sigma_{33}}\left(y_{i3} - \theta_{i3}\right); 1 - \frac{\sigma_{13}\sigma_{31}}{\sigma_{33}} \right\} \\ \phi_2 \left\{ -\theta_2 - \frac{\sigma_{23}}{\sigma_{33}}\left(y_{i3} - \theta_{i3}\right); 1 - \frac{\sigma_{23}\sigma_{32}}{\sigma_{33}} \right\} \end{bmatrix}$$

In estimating the effect of credit and agricultural productivity on welfare, there is the tendency of the problem of endogeneity since the exogenous variables are bound to be endogenous. A recursive system will be taken into consideration likely influence of the unobserved factors which can jointly impact credit access, crop output and welfare leading to three (3) equations.

The first equation describes credit access as a binary choice that is 1 if a farmer has access and 0 otherwise with its associated independent variables.

The second equation describes crop output which depends on credit and other independent variables while the third equation describes welfare which is also dependent on credit, output and other independent variables. The empirical model is specified as

$$C = \alpha_0 + \alpha_2 x_i + \mu_i \tag{33}$$

Where C is the propensity to access credit.

$$\begin{aligned} Credit\ Access = \alpha_0 + \alpha_1 Age + \alpha_2 HHH + \alpha_3 Yrsedu + \alpha_4 Dep \\ + \alpha_5 Mrst + \alpha_6 HHS + \alpha_7 LandS + \alpha_8 Ext + \alpha_9 FBO + \mu_1 \end{aligned} \tag{34}$$

However, C is unobserved and what we observe instead is the following:

$$C = \begin{cases} 1\ if\, C > 0 \\ 0\ if\, C \leq 0 \end{cases} \tag{35}$$

C= credit access, x_i is a vector of independent variables that can affect credit access and u_i represents the unobserved variation.

In the second equation we try to find out the effect of credit access on crop output.

$Y = \alpha_0 + \alpha_1 C + \alpha_2 x_1 + \mu_i$ (36).

$$Output = \alpha_0 + \alpha_1 CA + \alpha_2 ExpInput + \alpha_3 Yrsfarm + \alpha_4 LandS + \alpha_5 FamLab + \mu_2 \quad (37)$$

From the above, Y= crop output, C = credit access, x_i is a vector of independent variables that can affect crop output and μi is the error term.

The third equation jointly estimate the effect of credit and output on welfare

$$W = \alpha_0 + \alpha_1 C + \alpha_2 Y + \alpha_3 x_i + \mu_i \quad (38)$$

Where W= welfare, C= credit access, Y= crop output and μ_i is the error term.

$$Percapitaexp = \alpha_0 + \alpha_1 Credit + \alpha_2 Output + a_3 OffFarmI + \alpha_4 HH + \mu_3 \quad (39)$$

Based on literature, factors influencing credit access and its effect on output and welfare are explained in Table 3.1 in terms of the means of measurement as well as the *a prior* expectations. These factors are used in establishing the hypothesis of the study.

Data Analysis

Both descriptive and inferential analysis were used. The proportions of farmers in the district and the sources of credit to farmers in the district were analyzed using frequencies and percentages. Econometric models were also used in analyzing the data. The determinants of access to credit from the identified informal sources of credit in the district were analyzed using multivariate probit model. The effect of access to credit on agricultural productivity of credit beneficiary farm households in the districts was analyzed using the endogenous switching regression model and the effect of credit on agricultural productivity and welfare was analyzes using the conditional mixed process (CMP).

4.0 RESULTS AND DISCUSSIONS

Socio-Demographic Characteristics of Women Farmers in the Savelugu-Nanton Municipality

The average age of a farmer was 41 years with a minimum of 19 years and a maximum of 82 years. The majority of the farmers were within the age bracket of 19-40 years and 81 years and above constituted 0.33 percent. Generally, 56.33 percent were within the economically active age group which represents a potential for agriculture in the Savelugu and Karaga districts of the Northern region of Ghana. The average household size was 14 with a minimum of 2 and a maximum of 41 members while the average land size was 2.04 hectares. Farm size ranged between 0.2 hectares and 6 hectares with 79.33 percent cultivating 2 hectares and below.

Out of the 300 women farmers interviewed, majority (85.33 percent) were married while 2 percent were single, 3.67 percent were divorced, while 9 percent were widows. This indicates that majority of women farmers engaged in agricultural activities are married. This may be due to the physical, psychological, and emotional support they get from their spouses (Bammeke, 2003). Furthermore, majority of the women farmers (86.67 percent) have never been to school. However, 10 percent had primary education, 2 percent had Junior High School (JHS) education, while 0.67 percent attained Senior High School (SHS) education. This reflects the situation in Ghana where about 62.5 percent of the population in the Northern region are not literate in any language (GSS, 2013).

This phenomenon has a greater negative impact on the productivity of women farmers, especially in the uptake, adoption and utilization of new and improved technology. Each farmer belongs to one of the dominant religions in Ghana. However, majority (96.67 percent) were Muslims, and the remaining 3.33 percent were Christians. In terms of access to land for farm activities, the majority (56 percent) received their lands from their husbands, 23.7 percent were gifts, 13.7 percent was by inheritance, 3.6 percent was by outright purchases while 3 percent acquired through renting. This indicates that women do not own lands and confirms the role of a long-held tradition on land tenure and ownership in Northern Ghana. From the Table, 65.33 percent and 46 percent respectively had access to credit and extension services while a few (18.33 percent) belonged to farmer-based organizations.

Credit Status of Respondents

The credit status of the women farmers in the study area as shown in Table 1 below indicates that majority (65.33 percent) do not have access to credit in the study area. This confirms that access to credit is still a challenge in Savelugu and Karaga in Northern Ghana largely attributed to the risky nature of agriculture.

Pairwise Correlation of Farmers' Sources of Credit

The pairwise correlation depicts whether pairs of credit sources are substitutes, complementary, or do not affect each other in their choices. From Table 2, results indicate that the estimated correlation coefficients are statistically significant in two of the sources of credit. Out of these two sources, one has a positive sign while the other has a negative sign. Since the correlation between Village Savings and Loans Association (VSLA) and susu is positive, it means that the two sources are complementary with a correlation coefficient of 0.8069 or 80.69 percent. The association of family and friends and VSLA is statistically significant but negative, implying that the two sources are substitutes with a correlation coefficient of -0.2971 or 29.71 percent.

Determinants of Women Farmers' Access to Credit

Results from the Multivariate probit model on the determinants of women farmers access to credit in the Savelugu and Karaga districts as presented in Table 3 indicates that age, dependence, household size, land size, expenditure on input and distance to district capital influenced access to credit. The results are confirmed by the significance of the Wald test and confirms the hypothesis that all the regression coefficients in each equation are jointly equal to zero is rejected. This means that exogenous variables within each model significantly explain the endogenous variable. Moreover, a statistically significant likelihood ratio test of 28.2529 of the null hypothesis that the covariance of the error terms across equations are not correlated is also rejected. The correlation among the error terms justifies the use of the multivariate probit model which allows the interrelationship among the various sources and hence leading to unbiased and efficient estimates.

Findings from the study revealed that as women farmers increase in age, the likelihood of participating in VSLA increases but negatively influences access to credit from family and friends (F & F). This was statistically significant at 1%. Thus, older farmers are more likely to access credit from VSLA but less likely to access credit from F&F. VSLA has been promoted in rural areas as an alternative to meeting the credit needs of farmers (Dawuni, Mabe, & Tahidu 2021). This finding is attributed to the already low-income level of family and friends making it difficult to rely on them for farm credit. However, women farmers borrow more from VSLA because the group give them the sense of belongingness and the chance to interact with others which makes comfortable. This however contradicts the findings of the World Bank Global Financial Development Report (2014) which reported that adults in developing countries are three times more likely to borrow from family and friends than formal financial institutions.

The number of dependents was found to have a negative effect on VSLA and Susu but a positive effect on F&F. This was significant at 5%, 1%, and 5%, respectively. That is, the higher the number of dependents, the more income the farmer spends in taking care of these people hence less income will be available to participate in VSLA and Susu contributions. Because VSLA and Susu require regular contribution, the high expenditure may not permit them to contribute regularly and hence the negative sign. The positive sign for F&F is attributed to the flexibility nature of these sources of credit. A farmer with more dependents is likely to source credit from family and friends since their expenditure is likely to increase coupled with less income due to daily expenditures. This is in line with a study conducted by Pew (2016) who asserted that lower income households commonly borrow money from family and friends to take care of their daily expenses such as medication. The estimated coefficient of household size for both VSLA and Susu had a positive sign and significant at 10% and 5%, respectively. This indicates that an increase in household size enhances a farmer's likelihood of accessing credit from VSLA and Susu. This is attributed to the availability and low interest rate charged on VSLA and Susu credits relative to F&F which will be woefully inadequate or not available at all.

Also, land size showed a negative effect on access to credit from Susu at 1% significant level indicating a 1 acre increase in the size of woman's farm will lead to a decrease in the likelihood of accessing credit from Susu. This may be attributed to the low amount made available by Susu merchants which makes farmers switch to other sources of credit where they are likely to get more credit.

Expenditure on inputs (amount invested in the farm) showed a positive effect on farmer's access to credit from Susu, and statistically significant at 10%. This means that an increase in the amount of money spent on farm inputs which is assumed to increase output, increases a farmer's access to credit from Susu. This is attributed to expected yields from the large application of farm inputs and Susu merchants hope of quick repayment of credit borrowed by women farmers.

Furthermore, distance to district capital negatively influenced women farmers access to credit and highly significant at 1%. This means that a 1-kilometer increase in the distance of a farmer to the district capital to access credit led to a reduced likelihood of farmer accessing credit from that source. Farmers therefore prefer to access informal credit sources such as Susu, VSLA and Family and Friends which are closer to them than to go to the district capital to access formal credit sources from the bank. The proximity of the farmer to the source of credit is one of the most important factors that determines a household's access to credit. Women farmers are often reluctant to access credit from far located vendors. Also, the cost of transportation could be a major deterrent to poor households (Hussien, 2007).

Effect of Credit Access on Crop Output

This section presents the empirical evaluation of the impact assessment. The basic impact model adopted is the ESRM capable of controlling all possible biases in the results.

The results of the estimation are presented in Table 4. The results of the estimates are presented in three parts. The first part consists of the Probit model estimates of the determinants of access to credit, the second part being the output of those farmers with access to credit and thirdly, the output of farmers without access to credit.

The result of the Probit model revealed that extension access, members of FBO, are positive and statistically significant in determining farmers' access to credit. However, the coefficient of household size and distance to district capital was statistically significant but negative.

The coefficient of the second stage estimates of the switching regression model for the crop output are shown in the third and fifth column of Table 4 of the crop output regression among farmers who have access to credit and those without access to credit, respectively. With respect to output, age has a positive coefficient and was statistically significant for those with and without access to credit. This implies that farmer experience in terms of age has the potential of positively influencing farm output. This could be since as the farmer grows older in farming, the experience gained increases and she is able to efficiently maximize output given a certain number of inputs.

Similarly, household size was statistically significant and positive for the output of farmers with and without credit. This implies that the larger the household size, the more the farmer is endowed with family labour to increase farm size leading to an increase in crop output. As more people from the household are used as farm labour, the farmer will not incur an explicit cost of hiring labour from outside, thus reducing the cost of production and increasing output.

Also, extension access is significant and has a positive effect on output of farmers without access to credit. Farmers who have access to extension services can improve their level of technology and have exposure to new methods of farming. This has the potential of raising the farmer`s level of productivity. This is consistent with the findings of Hussien (2007).

The correlation coefficients rho_1 and rho_2 was negative and positive respectively, but are statistically significant only for the correlation between access choice equation and crop output of farmers with access to credit. Since rho_1 was negative and statistically significantly different from zero, the model suggests that farmers who choose to acquire credit have lower output than a farmer chosen by chance from the sample otherwise would have gotten. Individual farmers without access to credit are not better or worse than a chanced farmer. This means that, women farmers with above average output are more likely to access credit and indicates positive selection bias due to unobserved factors and therefore justified the use of the ESR. The likelihood ratio test for joint independence of the three equations was statistically significant implying that these three models are not jointly independent and should not be estimated separately. This means that selection bias due to unobserved factors occurred in the credit access equation hence the use of the model like the ESR which account for both observable and unobservable factors is appropriate for the study.

Table 5 revealed the mean Average Treatment effect on the Treated (ATT) to -0.4854 and the t-test of the ATT was statistically significantly different from zero. This implies that those farmers that have access to credit have lower crop output than those that did not have access to credit.

Effect of Credit and Crop Output on Welfare

The CMP framework consists of three equations. The first equation consists of the effects of farm characteristics on credit access; the second consists of the effects of credit on crop output and the third equation consist of the joint effect of credit access and crop output on welfare.

Effect of Farm Characteristics and Other Factors on Credit Access

The age of a farmer in the results was found to be negatively significant at 10% on access to credit. For every additional unit increase in the age of a farmer, all other things being equal decreases the probability of the farmer accessing credit by 0.04. This finding is in line with that of Mpuga, 2010 who maintained that access to credit decreases with increase in age. However, this finding is contrary to Tang et al. (2010) who proved that old farmers are more likely to borrow than younger farmers.

Household size was significant but negative at 1% on access to access to credit. The implication is that farm households with fewer members per house have a higher probability of accessing credit. For every additional member added to a farm household decreases the probability of a farmer accessing credit by 0.017. This study confirms the findings of Tang et al, (2010) who maintained that there is a negative correlation between household size and access to credit. That is larger household size tends to spend huge portion of credit on the livelihood of the family, particularly children and the elderly. The results also conform to a study conducted by Danso-Abbeam et al. (2014). The study found out that increasing household size lowers the probability of accessing credit. This however contradicts the findings of Weber & Mushof (2012) who found household size to be an increasing function of the probability of accessing credit.

Extension access was positive and significant at 1% on access to credit. This implies that farmers who have access to extension service have 0.119 probability of accessing credit than their counterparts who do not have access to extension service. This is in line with (Sanusi and Adedeji, 2010; Muhongayirea et al., 2013; Anang and Amikuzuno, 2015) who found that access to extension services increases farmers access to credit since extension agents help link farmer groups to credit sources.

Farmers who join FBO have a higher probability of accessing credit since most of them join for financial service. From the findings, members of FBO were positively significant at 1% on access to credit. That is farmers who belong to FBO have 0.245 probability of accessing credit than their counterparts who do not belong to any FBO. This is consistent with the findings of Akudugu (2012) who found that membership of social groups was positive and statistically significant at 1% and that farmers who join these social groups have a higher probability of demanding credit from rural banks.

Effect of Credit on Crop Output

The second stage of the equation in the CMP model estimates the effect of credit on crop output. Out of five variables in the equation, all were found to be statistically significant influence on crop output. The variables include credit access, expenditure on inputs, years of farming, land size and member of FBO.

From the estimates, credit access was surprisingly revealed to be statistically significant and negative at 1%. This implies that farmers who have access to credit decrease their output by GH¢1.136 holding other factors constant. This could be because most of the farmers spent little of the credit on their farms and the rest on household needs leading to diversion of credit. This result is in line with Kocher, (1977) findings that credit has no effect on farm output and also Selasi et al. (2017) findings of low contribution of credit to maize output.

The results from the Table above revealed that the influence of expenditure on inputs on output was positive and statistically significant at 1%. In other words, for every increase in expenditure on inputs in the farm, increases crop output by Ghc 0.09. This could be since the more a farmer invests in purchasing inputs such as farm equipment and fertilizer needed to enhance productivity, the more they are likely to get from their farms. Years of farming (experience) in the study reveals a positive value and was statistically significant at 10%. The results show that farmers with more experience in farming reported Ghc 0.070 increase in output. This implies that though women farmers may not have access to credit as they grow older, their long experience in farming still have a significant effect on their output. They can utilize resources more efficiently and be productive hence increase output. Land size was reported to be positive and statistically significant at 10%. In other words, for every hectare, an increase in crop land size leads to a Ghc 0.096 increase in crop output. Valerio (2014) confirmed the importance of land in productivity in Philippines by observing that land is an important resource in increasing rice productivity. Family labour had a positive and significant influence on output suggesting that farmers who use family labour are likely to have higher output than those who do not. One of the major elements of agricultural production is whether family labour is available as it provides ready labour to support household farm production. From the empirical results, family labour was revealed to be positive and statistically significant at 5%. That is, any increase in available family labour results in Ghc 0.246 increment in crop output (Table 4.8 above). Economic intuition is that migration of youth from the study area to major cities in the country reduces availability of family labour for agricultural activities, crop output and overall economic wellbeing of farm households. Banerjee *et al.* (2014) confirmed that lower yields of farmers are mainly associated with availability of family labour.

Effect of Credit Access and Crop Output on Welfare

The third stage equation of the CMP model estimates the effect of credit access on crop output and welfare (measured in per capita expenditure). The estimated coefficient of output on per capita expenditure was statistically significant at the one percent level. A kilogram increase in output will lead to Ghc 61.4419 decrease in per capita expenditure. The findings revealed an inverse relationship between crop output and per capita expenditure. This implies that farmers with low output spend more as compared to those with high output. Expenditure made by farmers in the study was basically on food. Thus, farmers with low output spent more on food to augment what they have to cater for their household. However, farmers with high output spent less on food since they had enough for household consumption.

Off farm income had a positive impact on welfare of farmers and significant at 1%. This implies that as the farmer earns income from farm activities, it increases the farmers' welfare by Ghc 0.214. Off-farm work is a form of diversification which enhances income mobilization and household risk reduction. Most farmers often reinvest their off-farm income into their farm activities to generate more income and hence the positive influence on welfare. This finding is not in isolation since it supports the findings of Osarfo et al. (2016) who found out that engagement in off farm activities lead to improved income and food security.

Household size had a negative impact on welfare and was statistically significant at (1%). This is an indication that an additional person to a household decreases welfare by Ghc 5.862. Larger number of household members exerts pressure on household assets/ resources, and this makes it more difficult for household to meet their basic need such as adequate nutrition and housing as well as education of their children which tend to reinforce poverty. These findings are in line with Gardiner & Miller (2006) and Ukoha et al. (2007) who observed that larger households have higher poverty and hence lower welfare.

5.0 CONCLUSION

Improving the production capacity of agriculture in developing countries like Ghana through productivity increase is a significant policy goal, particularly in Ghana where agriculture represents a key sector in the economy. The majority of the farmers are within the economically active age group, cultivating an average of 2.04 ha of farmland, most of which belong to their husbands.

Sources of credit among women farmers comprise of Village Savings and Loans Associations, susu as well as Family and Friends. However, there is over reliance on Village Savings and Loans Association and Family and Friends, and these constitute informal sources of credit. This implies that majority of women farmers within the study area rely more on informal sources of credit since they do not own physical assets to be used as collateral.

Extension access significantly and positively contributes to crop output relative to women farmers without access to credit.

Age and household size significantly influence credit access negatively while extension access and membership of famer-based organization significantly affect credit access positively. Access to credit does not guarantee an increase in crop output since women farmers with access to credit surprisingly had lower crop output than those without credit. However, expenditure on inputs (amount invested on the farm) leads to an increase in crop output and welfare. Hence, agriculture development interventions must not only be output targeting but instead, include welfare enhancement.

REFERENCES

Akudugu, M. A. (2012). Estimation of Determinants of Credit Demand by Rural Banks in Ghana's Upper East Region. *Asian Journal of Agriculture and Rural Development*, *2*(2), 189–200.

Alene, A., & Manyong, V. M. (2007). The Effect of Education on Agricultural Productivity under Traditional and Improved Technology in Northern Nigeria: An Endogenous Switching Regression Analysis. *Empirical Economics*, *32*(1), 141–159. doi:10.100700181-006-0076-3

Anang, B. T., & Amikuzuno, J. (2015). Factors Influencing Pesticide Use in Smallholder Rice Production in Northern Ghana. *Agriculture, Forestry and Fisheries*, *4*(2), 77–82. doi:10.11648/j.aff.20150402.19

Armendariz, B. A., & Morduch, J. (2005). *The Economics of Microfinance*. MIT Press.

Asfaw, S. (2010). *Estimating Welfare Effect of Modern Agricultural Technologies: A Micro-Perspective from Tanzania and Ethiopia International Crops Research Institute for the Semi-Arid Tropics*. ICRISAT.

Bammeke, T. O. A. (2003). *Accessibility and Utilization of Agricultural Information in the Economic Empowerment of Women Farmers in South Western Nigeria*. University of Ibadan.

Belderbos, R., Carree, M., Diederen, B., Lokshin, B., & Veugelers, R. (2004). Heterogeneity in R&D Co-operation Strategies. *International Journal of Industrial Organization*, *22*(8-9), 1237–1263. doi:10.1016/j.ijindorg.2004.08.001

Cochran, W. G. (1977). The Estimation of Sample Size. *Sampling Techniques*, *3*, 72–90.

Cohen, J. (1992). Statistical Power Analysis. *Current Directions in Psychological Science*, *1*(3), 98–101. doi:10.1111/1467-8721.ep10768783

Conning, J., & Udry, C. (2005). *Rural Financial Markets in Developing Countries, Economic Growth Centre*. Yale University, and Centre Discussion Paper No. 914.

Cornejo, J., & McBride, W. (2002). *Adoption of Bioengineered Crops*. Agricultural Economics Report No. 810. Academic Press.

Danso-Abbeam, G., Ansah, I. G. K., & Ehiakpor, D. S. (2014). Microfinance and Micro-Small-Medium Scale Enterprises (MSME's) in Kasoa Municipality, Ghana. *British Journal of Economics, Management and Trade*, *4*(12), 1939–1956.

Dawuni, P., Mabe, F. N., & Tahidu, O. D. (2021). Effects of Village Savings and Loan Association on Agricultural Value Productivity in Northern Region of Ghana. *Agricultural Finance Review*, *81*(5), 657–674. doi:10.1108/AFR-02-2020-0024

Di Falco, S., Veronesi, M., & Yesuf, M. (2011). Does Adaptation to Climate Change Provide Food Security? A Micro-Perspective from Ethiopia. *American Journal of Agricultural Economics*, *93*(3), 829–846. doi:10.1093/ajae/aar006

Eswaran, M., & Kotwal, A. (1990). Implications of Credit Constraints for Risk Behavior. Oxford Economic Papers. *New Series*, *42*(2), 473–482.

Feder, G., Lau, L. J., Lin, J. Y., & Luo, X. (1990). The Relationship Between Credit and Productivity in Chinese Agriculture: A Microeconomic Model of Disequilibrium. *American Journal of Agricultural Economics*, *72*(5), 1151–1157. doi:10.2307/1242524

Feder, G., & Umali, D. L. (1993). The Adoption of Agricultural Innovations: A Review. *Technological Forecasting and Social Change*, *43*(3-4), 215–239. doi:10.1016/0040-1625(93)90053-A

Freeman, H. A., Simeon, K. E., & Jabar, M. A. (1998). Credit Constraints and Smallholder Dairy Production in the East African highlands: Application of a Switching Regression Model. *Agricultural Economics*, *19*(1-2), 33–44. doi:10.1111/j.1574-0862.1998.tb00512.x

Gardiner, K., & Miller, J. (2006). How Low-Paid Employees Avoid Poverty: An Analysis by Family Type and Household Structure. *Journal of Social Policy*, *35*(3), 351–369. doi:10.1017/S0047279406009822

Ghana Statistical Service (2021). *2021 Population and Housing Census - Regional Analytical Report-Northern Region Census Report*. Author.

Greene, W. H. (2003). *Econometric analysis*. Pearson Education India.

Greene, W. H. (2008). *Econometric Analysis* (6th ed.). Pearson.

Gujarati, D. M. (2006). *Essentials of Econometrics* (3rd ed.). McGraw Hill International.

Hausman, J. A. (1983). Specification and Estimation of Simultaneous Equation Models. In Z. Griliches & M. Intriligator (Eds.), *Handbook of econometrics*. North Holland Press. doi:10.1016/S1573-4412(83)01011-9

Hirano, K., & Imbens, G. W. (2004). The Propensity score with Continuous Treatments. Applied Bayesian Modeling and Causal Inference from incomplete-data. *Perspectives, 226164*, 73–84.

Hussain, A., & Thapa, G. B. (2015). Fungibility of Smallholder Agricultural Credit: Empirical Evidence from Pakistan. *European Journal of Development Research*.

Iyanda, J. O., Afolami, C. A., Obayelu, A. E., & Ladebo, O. J. (2014). Social Capital and Access to Credit among Cassava Farming Households in Ogun State, Nigeria. *Journal of Agriculture and Environmental Sciences*, *3*(2), 175–196.

Kabunga, N. S., Dubois, T., & Qaim, M. (2012). Yield effects of tissue culture Bananas in Kenya: Accounting for selection bias and the role of complementary inputs. *Journal of Agricultural Economics*, *62*(2), 444–464. doi:10.1111/j.1477-9552.2012.00337.x

Kassie, M., Pender, J., Yesuf, M., Kohlin, G., Bluffstone, R., & Mulugeta, E. (2008). Estimating Returns to Soil Conservation Adoption in the Northern Ethiopian Highlands. *Agricultural Economics*, *38*(2), 213–232. doi:10.1111/j.1574-0862.2008.00295.x

Kazi, S., Raza, B., & Al-Jalaly, S. Z. (2015). Rural Women's Access to Credit and Extension: A Strategy for Change. *Pakistan Development Review*, *34*(4), 753–765.

Kocher, A. (1997). An Empirical Investigation of Rationing Constraints in Rural Credit Markets in Indian. *Journal of Development Economics*, *53*(2), 339–371. doi:10.1016/S0304-3878(97)00020-5

Lee, L. (1978). Unionism and Wage Rates: A simultaneous Equation Model with Qualitative and Limited Dependent Variables. *International Economic Review*, *19*(2), 415–433. doi:10.2307/2526310

Lokshin, M., & Sajaia, Z. (2004). Maximum Likelihood Estimation of Endogenous Switching Regression Models. *The Stata Journal*, *4*(3), 282–289. doi:10.1177/1536867X0400400306

Maddala, G. (1983). *Limited Dependent and Qualitative Variables in Econometrics*. Cambridge University Press. doi:10.1017/CBO9780511810176

Manda, J., Alene, A. D., Gardebroek, C., Kassie, M., & Tembo, G. (2016). Adoption and impacts of sustainable agricultural practices on maize yields and incomes: Evidence from Rural Zambia. *Journal of Agricultural Economics*, *67*(1), 130–153. doi:10.1111/1477-9552.12127

Mpuga, P. (2010). Constraints in Access to and Demand for Rural Credit: Evidence from Uganda. *African Development Review, 22*(1), 115–148. doi:10.1111/j.1467-8268.2009.00230.x

Muhongayirea, W., Hitayezub, P., Mbatiac, O. L., & Mukoya-Wangiad, S. M. (2013). Determinants of Farmers' Participation in Formal Credit Market in Rural Rwanda. *Journal of Agricultural Science, 4*(2), 87–94.

Muriithi, P., Horner, D., Pemberton, L., & Wao, H. (2018). Factors influencing Research Collaborations in Kenyan Universities. *Research Policy, 47*(1), 88–97. doi:10.1016/j.respol.2017.10.002

Nweke, F. L., Spencer, D. S. C., & Lynam, J. K. (2002). *The Cassava Transformation*. Michigan State University Press.

Nyangena, W., & Köhlin, G. (2008). *Estimating Returns to Soil and Water Conservation Investments: An Application to Crop Yield in Kenya*. Environment for Development Discussion Paper Series, EfD DP 08-32.

Obisesan, A. A., & Akinlade, R. J. (2013). Credit constraints and Poverty among Nigerian farming Households. *Agricultural Journal, 8*(2), 94–100.

Osarfo, D., Senadza, B., & Nketiah-Amponsah, E. (2016). *The Impact of Nonfarm Activities on Rural Farm Household Income and Food Security in the Upper East and Upper West Regions of Ghana*. Academic Press.

Owusu-Antwi, G., & Antwi, J. (2010). The Analysis of the Rural Credit Market in Ghana. *The International Business & Economics Research Journal, 9*(8). doi:10.19030/iber.v9i8.611

Petrick, M. (2004). Farm investment, credit rationing, and governmentally promoted credit access in Poland: A cross-sectional analysis. *Food Policy, 29*(3), 275–294. doi:10.1016/j.foodpol.2004.05.002

Roodman, D. (2011). Fitting Fully Observed Recursive Mixed-Process Models with CMP. *The Stata Journal, 11*(2), 159–206. doi:10.1177/1536867X1101100202

Sakyi, S., Abu, B. M., & Nkegbe, P. K. (2020). Effects of farm credit access on agricultural commercialization in Ghana: Empirical evidence from the northern Savannah ecological zone. *African Development Review, 32*(2), 150–162. doi:10.1111/1467-8268.12424

Sanginga, N., & Bergvinson, D. (2014). *Oilseeds and Cowpeas*. Background Paper.

Sanusi, W., & Adedeji, I. (2010). A Probit Analysis of Accessibility of Small Scale Farmers to Formal Source of Credit in Ogbomoso Zone, Oyo State, Nigeria. *Agricultura Tropica et Subtropica, 43*(1), 49–53.

Sekyi, S. (2017). Rural households' credit access and loan amount in Wa Municipality, Ghana. *International Journal of Economics and Financial Issues, 7*(1), 506–514.

Selase, A. E., Xinhai, L., & Worlanyo, A. S. (2017). Combination Effects of Opportunity International Savings and Loans Credit Facility on Maize Production and Health: Evidence of Techiman Municipality in Ghana. *Agriculture Science Food Research Journal, 8*, 196.

Tang, S., Guan, Z., & Jin, S. (2010). Formal and Informal Credit Markets and Rural Credit Demand in China. *Agricultural & Applied Economics Association, CAES, & WAEA Joint Annual Meeting*, 1–26.

Ukoha, O., Mejeha, R., & Nte, I. (2007). Determinants of Farmers' Welfare in Ebonyi State, Nigeria. *Pakistan Journal of Social Sciences*, *4*(3), 351–354.

Weber, R., & Musshoff, O. (2012). *Microfinance for Agricultural Firms-Credit Access and Loan Repayment in Tanzania.* Paper presented at the EAAE Seminar, Dublin, Ireland. www.Nyu.edu/classes/nagler/quant1/Probit1-post.pdf

Wooldridge, J. M. (2002). *Econometric Analysis of Cross Section and Panel Data.* MIT Press.

APPENDIX

Table 1. Credit status of respondents

Credit Status	With Credit	Without Credit	Total
Frequency	104	196	300
Percentage	34.67	65.33	100

Source: Field Data (2019).

Table 2. Pairwise correlation of farmers sources of credit

Source of Credit Correlation Coefficient Standard Error		
'VSLA' and 'Susu'	0.8069***	0.1368
'F&F' and 'VSLA'	-0.2971***	0.0905
'F&F' and 'Susu'	-0.1160	0.1264

Note: ***, ** and * represent1%, 5% and 10% level of significance respectively.
Source: Field Data (2019).

Table 3. Determinants of farmers' choice of sources of credit from a multivariate probit model

Variable	VSLA	Susu	Family and Friends
Age	0.0184***	0.0127	-0.0259***
	(0.0071)	(0.0130)	(0.0077)
Head of household	-0.4365	0.9791	0.9456
	(0.7111)	(0.9862)	(0.6680)
No of Dependents	-0.0746 **	-0.1201*	0.0742**
	(0.0370)	(0.0725)	(0.0367)
Marital Status	0.2960	-0.3291	-0.3211
	(0.3779)	(0.5133)	(0.3593)
Household Size	0.0365*	0.0761**	-0.0215***
	(0.0210)	(0.0352)	(0.0210)
Land Size	-0.1504	-0.9368***	0.0480
	(0.1006)	(0.3075)	(0.1031)
Expenditure on inputs	0.0005	0.0032*	-0.0002
	(0.0006)	(0.0014)	(0.0006)
Distance	-0.0951***	-0.2735***	-0.0849***
	(0.0298)	(0.0985)	(0.0296)
Number of obs	300	300	300
Wald chi2(24)	64.7		
Prob > chi2	0.000		
Log likelihood	-376.7536		

Note: ***, ** & * are significance at 1%, 5% & 10%, respectively
Source: Field Data (2023).

Table 4. FIML estimates of the endogenous switching regression model

Variable	Selection		With Credit		Without Credit	
	Coefficient	Std. Error	Coefficient	Std. Error	Coefficient	Std. Error
Constant	1.3181***	0.3813	5.9306***	0.2823	5.2278***	0.5435
Age	-0.0116	0.0074	0.0147**	0.0059	0.0208***	0.0063
Household gender	0.2601	0.2788	-0.2126	0.2090	-0.0895	0.2237
Education	-0.0315	0.0362	0.0177	0.0289	0.0223	0.0342
Household size	-0.0333**	0.0138	0.0248**	0.0112	0.0243**	0.0139
Extension access	0.3168*	0.1666	-0.1325	0.1315	0.3947*	0.1799
Family labour	0.0218	0.0297	-0.0372	0.0240	0.0035	0.0264
Member of FBO	0.8981***	0.1954	-0.2030	0.1457	0.1405	0.2850
Distance	-0.0933***	0.0284				
/lns1	-0.0764	0.0926				
/lns2	-0.4320	0.0755				
/r1	-1.0553	0.3550				
/r2	0.0920	0.5198				
sigma_1	0.9264	0.0858				
sigma_2	0.6492	0.0490				
rho_1	-0.7839	0.1369				
rho_2	0.0917	0.5154				
LR test of indep. Eqns.: LR chi2(8) = 23.23 Prob > chi2 = 0.0031						

Note: ***, ** and * are statistically significant at 1%, 5% & 10% respectively
Source: Field Data (2023).

Table 5. One-sample t-test

	With Credit	Without Credit	ATT	t-Value
Value of output	6.734	7.220	-0.485***	13.462
Variable	**Obs**	**Mean**	**Std. Err.**	**Std. Dev**
ATT	300	-0.4854	0.0361	0.6245

Source: Author's computation, 2023

Table 6. Estimated coefficients of the effects of credit and crop output on welfare of women farmers-conditional mixed process

Variables	CMP Estimation		Marginal Effect	
	Coefficient	Std. Error	Coefficient	Std. Error
Equation 1 (Credit Access)				
Age	-0.0115*	0.0055	-0.0353*	0.0166
Household head	0.0511	0.5627	0.0157	0.1729
Years of education	-0.0792	0.0285	-0.0243	0.0875
No of Dependents	-0.0997	0.0312	-0.0306	0.0960
Marital Status	-0.0938	0.3037	-0.0288	0.0933
Household size	-0.0555***	0.0184	-0.0171***	0.0546
Land size	-0.0540	0.0832	-0.0166	0.0255
Extension access	0.3885***	0.1280	0.1194***	0.0386
Member of FBO	0.7978***	0.1809	0.2452***	0.0515
Constant	1.5391**	0.6855		
Equation 2				
logvoutput				
Credit access	-1.1361***	0.1407		
Expenditure on input	0.0877***	0.0265		
Years of farming	0.0701*	0.0395		
Land size	0.0964*	0.0534		
Family labour	0.2456**	0.0987		
Constant	6.3780***	0.1374		
Equation 3				
percapitaexp				
logvoutput	-61.4419***	15.66166		
off farm income	0.21433***	0.0463		
Household size	-5.5688***	0.5294		
Constant	496.3887***	97.6408		
ln	-0.1729***	0.0557		
ln	4.419596***	0.0917364		
atanh	4.4196***	0.0917		
atanh	0.0147182	0.0792101		
atanh	0.8733***	0.1445		
	0.8412595	0.0468353		
	0.0147	0.0792		
	0.7030269	0.0730579		
	0.5827	0.1289		
	0.5246076	0.0934593		

Note: ***, ** & *are statistically significance at 1%, 5% and 10% respectively
Source: Author's computation, 2023.

Chapter 4
Gendered and Generational Analyses of Farm Households' Livelihood Diversification in Ghana:
Implications for Credit Demands and Allocations

Katherine Kaunza-Nu Dem Millar
University for Development Studies, Tamale, Ghana

Abdul-Razak Alhassan
University of Surrey, UK

Mamudu Abunga Akudugu
https://orcid.org/0000-0003-3191-721X
University for Development Studies, Tamale, Ghana

ABSTRACT

As households diversify their livelihoods, their credit demands will also be diversified. This creates competition among the livelihood activities pursued by farm households for credit and other productive resources. Whereas some households may be expanding the same livelihood activities to enjoy economies of scale (stepping up), others are expanding into other livelihood activities (stepping out). Better still, others are just maintaining their activities, levels of livelihood activities they engage in (hanging in). Whichever approach is adopted has specific implications for resource demands, allocation, and utilization. This chapter examines the gendered implications of livelihoods diversification for household credit demands and allocations using mixed methods. Most farm households in contemporary Ghana this chapter concludes are diversifying out of agriculture. The implication of this is that the number of households demanding credit for non-farm livelihood activities is increasing at the expense of farm livelihood activities.

DOI: 10.4018/978-1-6684-8979-6.ch004

INTRODUCTION

Rural livelihood diversifications are warranted by different aspirations and objectives of farm households and may be looked at in two ways. It could be diversification into different activities within the same sector (vertical diversification) or into different sectors (horizontal diversification). In the case of vertical diversification, farm households may diversify their livelihood to include different farm livelihood activities. This may include the production of exotic or local crops varieties; food or cash crops using modern or traditional technologies or rearing of improved or local livestock breeds. With regards to the horizontal diversification, farm households may diversify into non-farm livelihood activities such as petty trading and craftsmanship among others. This categorization of rural livelihood diversification is consistent with Ellis (2000) who observed that the issue of livelihood diversification in rural development context usually has to do with either the need for farm changes in the mix of agricultural activities or of the desirability of developing rural-based non-farm industries.

According to Dorward (2009) and Deogharia (2018), the main focus of diversification is to decrease livelihood vulnerability and increase livelihood productivity. This is achieved by changing farm livelihood activities with increasing importance of non-farm activities and this involves three main dimensions (ibid). The first dimension is termed as "hanging in" which involves using strategies that are concerned with maintaining and protecting current levels of wealth and welfare in the face of threats of stresses and shocks. The second dimension is termed as the "stepping up" in which individuals employ strategies that seek to expand the scale, or productivity of existing assets and activities. The third and final dimension in Dorward's view is referred to as "stepping out" which is concerned with adopting strategies geared towards the accumulation of assets to allow investments or switches into new activities and assets. This implies that the dimension of diversification a given household adopts depends on its abilities in terms of resource endowments and needs.

Evidence in the empirical literature reveals that many rural farm households in Africa and Ghana for that matter are diversifying outside agriculture as a main source of livelihood (see for instance Ellis 1998, Bryceson 1999, Ellis 2000, Barretta, Reardon et al. 2001, Bryceson 2002, Hilson 2002, Niehof 2004, Banchirigah 2006, Ellis 2006, Iiyama 2006, Banchirigah 2008, Demurger, Fournier et al. 2010, Haggblade, Hazell et al. 2010, Motsholapheko, Kgathi et al. 2011, Chavas and Falco 2012, Hilson and Garforth 2012, Salayo, Perez et al. 2012). According to Ellis (2000) and Hilson and Garforth (2012) among others, households diversify outside agriculture in order to deal with seasonality in agricultural production, risks, labor market dynamics, credit market failures and also as a coping mechanism. A growing body of literature suggests that artisanal small scale mining is one of the major non-farm livelihood activities that rural Africans and Ghanaians for that matter diversify into (see for instance Banchirigah 2006, Banchirigah 2008, Hilson 2009, Banchirigah and Hilson 2010, Bryceson and Jonsson 2010, Hilson 2010, Hilson and Garforth 2012). Seasonality and household needs also influence household diversification decisions.

Irrespective of the type of diversification or reason for diversifying, the basic reality is that it affects resource allocation. In this regard, the struggle to secure a livelihood in the face of adverse socio-economic and politico-cultural circumstances by rural farm households determines which livelihood activity they demand and allocate resources to. As households diversify their livelihoods, their credit demands will also be diversified. This creates competition among the livelihood activities pursued by farm households for credit and other productive resources. One might expect that farm households demand credit to finance their livelihood activities based on their relative importance and contribution to household welfare. The higher the contribution of a livelihood activity, be it farm or non-farm to the welfare of a farm household, the higher the likelihood that the household will demand credit to finance it. However, it is not clear in the literature if these assertions are true. It is therefore important to find out if livelihood diversification among farm households affects their credit demand dynamics.

Credit demands of rural farm households represent the amounts they request from formal and informal lenders to finance their livelihood activities. These credit demands are largely not met (Akudugu 2012, Zerai and Rani 2012) as most households always receive less than they ask for (Quaye 2008, Akudugu 2010). Borrowers considered not to be credit worthy and representing high risk of default are rationed out of the formal credit markets (Schindler 2010). Similar situations are reported across Sub-Saharan Africa including Kenya (Atieno 2001, Kibaara 2006, Mwangi and Sichei 2011) and Nigeria (Rahji and Fakayode 2009) among others. In fact, in their study, Turvey, He et al. (2012) estimated the credit demands of 897 farm households in the Shaanxi and Gansu provinces of China and concluded that there is heterogeneity in the credit demands of farm households. This must be taken into consideration in developing tailor-made financial intermediations that are context specific to farmers and farm households across different regions of the world. This is of great concern given that credit is placed at the center as one of the critical factors in the drive towards the green revolution agenda in Ghana in particular and Africa at large as captured in the AGRA framework.

According to IFAD (2003), only 8 percent of small clients, particularly the poor in Ghana are able to access financial services delivered by the formal financial market. The implication of this is that about 92 percent of the poor in Ghana, the majority of who are engaged in agriculture for their livelihoods do not patronize credit from the formal credit market. This is worrisome given that initiatives such as establishment of rural and community banks as well as liberalization of the financial market were implemented in Ghana to ensure that the poor, particularly rural people get adequate access to formal credit and other financial services. Yet over two decades after the implementation of these policy initiatives, widespread inadequate access to financial services, particularly credit by rural households is reported across Ghana.

The issue of limited access to credit by actors in the agricultural sector in Ghana is severest among rural farm households in the poverty endemic areas of the country such as Upper West, Upper East and Northern Regions with poverty levels of 88 per cent, 83 per cent and 63 per cent respectively against the national average of about 29 per cent (Ghana Statistical Service 2008). For instance, Akudugu (2010) reported in his study that only 21 per cent of rural farm households in the Upper East Region have access to formal financial services, particularly credit and savings facilities for their farming activities. In a related study, Quaye (2008) reports that only 19 per cent, 14 per cent and 11 per cent of rural farm households in the Upper West, Northern and Upper East Regions of Ghana respectively have access to formal credit for their farming activities. Similar findings of limited access to credit for farming purposes by rural households have been reported from other empirical studies in Ghana (see for instance Al-hassan and Sagre 2006, Ayamga, Sarpong et al. 2006, Ntifo-Siaw and Bosompem 2008, Akudugu, Egyir et al. 2009, and 2009). At the national level, Demirgüç-Kunt and Klapper (2012) reported that only 20 per cent of adult Ghanaians are included in the formal financial sector.

The limited access to credit is made worse by the mission drift phenomenon of Microfinance Institutions (MFIs) originally setup to serve the financial needs of the poor, majority of who are in rural areas where agriculture remains the main source of livelihood. These institutions have overtime drifted away from their poor customers and the financing of farming. As reported by Alhassan et al. (2023), MFIs have not appropriately met their dual expectation of pursuing both financial and social objectives resulting in the lack of attainment of the double bottom line or convergence. So, they are unable to meet the welfare needs of the poor while maintaining commercial viability. There has also been an over focus on access to formal credit markets, particularly the banks by farm households without considering the informal credit markets. Farm households' credit demands and access from the informal financial market is not adequately considered in many empirical studies. The relationship between credit demands from formal and informal credit markets in meeting credit needs of farm households is not established. This chapter therefore focuses on exploring how livelihoods diversification of farm households is shaping their demands for credit from formal and informal sources. This chapter illustrates the interrelationships between livelihoods diversification, credit demands from formal and informal sources and the allocations thereof.

The Methodology

To examine the trends of households' credit demands for farm and non-farm livelihood activities, narratives and descriptive statistics are used. Two main techniques integrated at two different levels are used to examine how the diversification decisions of farm households in Ghana are shaping and determining their demands for credit for farm and non-farm livelihood activities. The first technique and level employed was the use of personal narratives to establish the trends of farm households' credit demands for farm and non-farm livelihood activities. This was done using key informant interviews and focus group discussions. The key informants were people deemed to be knowledgeable in livelihood diversification as well as credit demands of farm households and included influential farmers, entrepreneurs, formal and informal lenders and policy makers. Key informants and participants of focus group discussions were asked to describe by assigning scores, the trends of households' dependence on farm and non-farm livelihood activities as well as credit demands for such activities. They were also tasked to identify and describe the possible inter and intra-household as well as community and district characteristics that determine the trends observed. Participants were asked to assess the trends of their dependence on farm and non-farm livelihood activities. They were further tasked to identify and describe the possible inter- and intra-household as well as community characteristics responsible for the trends observed.

Participants were tasked to use a score of 100 to demonstrate the patterns of their dependence on livelihood activities in terms of farm and non-farm production. They assigned the scores in such a way as to depict increasing; decreasing; or no changing patterns of dependence on the different livelihood activities. They were further asked to indicate whether or not they demanded credit for financing of farm and non-farm livelihood activities over period of ten (10) years (2013 – 2022). The aim of this was to establish the trends of households demanding credit for livelihood activities in the selected farming communities. Those that said they demanded credit were asked to indicate the credit market from which they demanded the credit and also whether or not they were successful in their credit demands as well as indicate whether the credit was used for farm, non-farm or both livelihood activities and the relative allocations thereof. To determine the relationships between the trends in dependence on farm and non-farm livelihood activities, the credit demands for farm and non-farm livelihood activities and the credit demands by farm households, the results were presented by gender, generation, geographical location and the wealth class that one belongs to. In all, 24 key informants were interviewed and 36 focus group discussions with each group making up of 6 participants giving a total of 216 participants.

Trends in Dependence on Farm and Non-Farm Livelihood Activities

Farm households in contemporary Ghana engage in different livelihood activities in order to survive. This means that their livelihoods are diversified. As observed by Ellis (2000), rural dwellers engage in a mix of farm activities and/or rural-based non-farm industries so as to guarantee survival. The essence of this according to Dorward (2009) is to decrease livelihood vulnerability and increase livelihood productivity which could be achieved by changing farm livelihood activities with increasing importance of non-farm activities. The finding of households engaging in diversified livelihood activities is further corroborated by evidence in the empirical literature that many rural farm households in Africa and Ghana for that matter are diversifying outside agriculture as a main source of livelihood (see for instance Ellis, 1998; Bryceson, 1999; Hillson, 2020; Osumanu, 2020; Ellis, 2000; Barretta et al., 2001, Bryceson, 2002; Hilson, 2002; Niehof, 2004; Banchirigah, 2006; Ellis, 2006; Iiyama, 2006; Banchirigah, 2008; Demurger et al., 2010; Haggblade et al., 2010; Motsholapheko et al., 2011; Chavas & Falco, 2012; Hilson & Garforth, 2012; Salayo et al., 2012; Baffour-Kyei et al., 2021).

Ellis (2000) and Hilson and Garforth (2012) reported in their studies that households diversify outside agriculture in order to deal with among other things seasonality in agricultural production, risks, labor market dynamics, credit market failures and also as a coping mechanism. In the specific case of Ghana, it has been reported that households, especially in rural areas of the country are diversifying out of agriculture partly due to general stagnation in crop productivity (Akudugu et al., 2013) exacerbated by climate change(Akudugu & Alhassan 2012; Akudugu et al., 2012). One of the major non-farm livelihood activities that rural Africans and Ghanaians for that matter diversify into as captured in the empirical literature is small scale mining (see for instance Baffour-Kyei et al., 2021; Hilson, 2020; Osumanu, 2020; Banchirigah, 2006; Banchirigah, 2008; Hilson, 2009; Banchirigah & Hilson, 2010; Bryceson & Jonsson, 2010; Hilson, 2010; Hilson & Garforth, 2012).

The compositions of farm households' livelihood activities have been changing in recent times and the changes in the composition of livelihood strategies are largely in favor of the non-farm sector. The dependence of farm households on farm livelihood activities are on the decline and that of non-farm livelihood activities is on the increase. These changing patterns of dependence on farm and non-farm livelihood activities engaged in by farm households can be attributed to a number of factors, prominent among which are climate change, population growth, and low returns from farming.

It is common these to hear farmers indicate that they are gradually moving away from agriculture because of factors such as unpredictability of the rains. They argue that rainfall patterns have become highly unreliable. There is either too much rain or too little rain that is not enough to support crop production. Incidence of drought and floods occurring within single cropping seasons are now being experienced, which used not to be the case. The result is that crop yields become very low. The decreasing dependence on agriculture as a livelihood strategy has also been attributed to the youth of today being interested in getting money quick, which is not possible in agriculture. So, because of that most of them are abandoning farming for other activities such as trading and skills acquisitions such as hairdressing, dress making, carpentry, mechanics, masonry, or even formal education to become teachers, nurses and what have you. The dependence of men and women as well as old and young people across the three main ecological zones of Ghana (Coastal, Forest and Savannah) on agriculture as a source of livelihood is on the decline (Figure 1). For example, the level of dependence of women on agriculture as a source of livelihood reduced from 56% in 2014 to 25% in 2022 with a corresponding increase on non-farm livelihood activities from 60% in 2013 to 75% in 2022 (Figure 1). Similar trends are observed for men and of course for the old and the youth.

Figure 1. Farm and non-farm dependence by gender and generation (n=216)
Source: Field Data, 2023

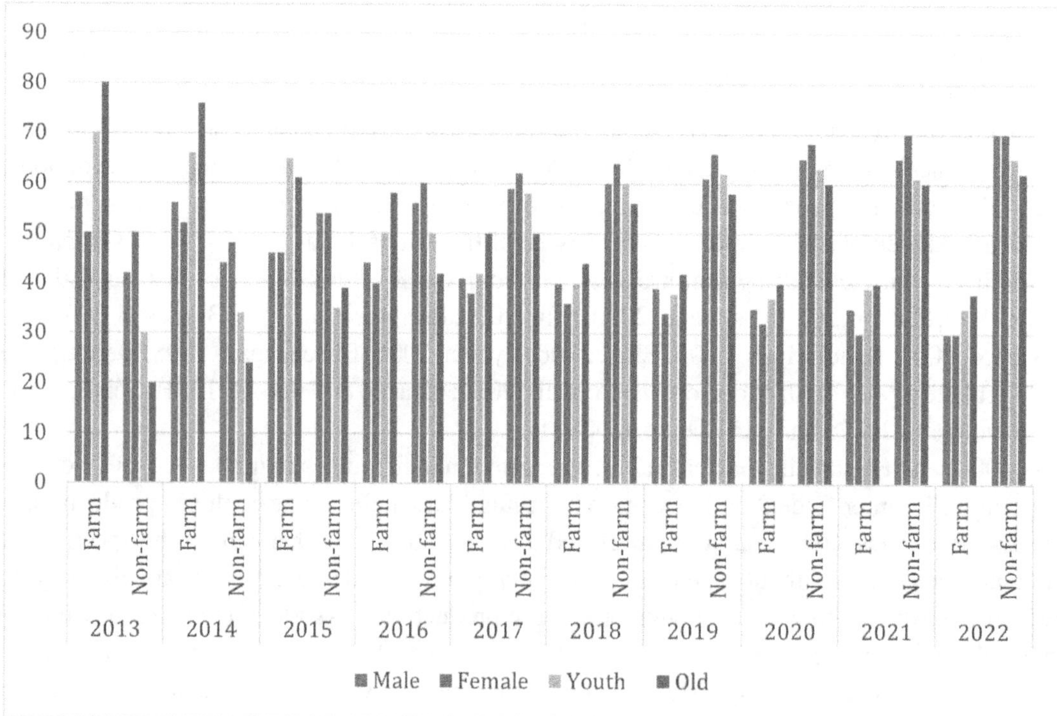

Figure 2. Farm and non-farm dependence by location and wealth classes (n=216)
Source: Field Data, 2023

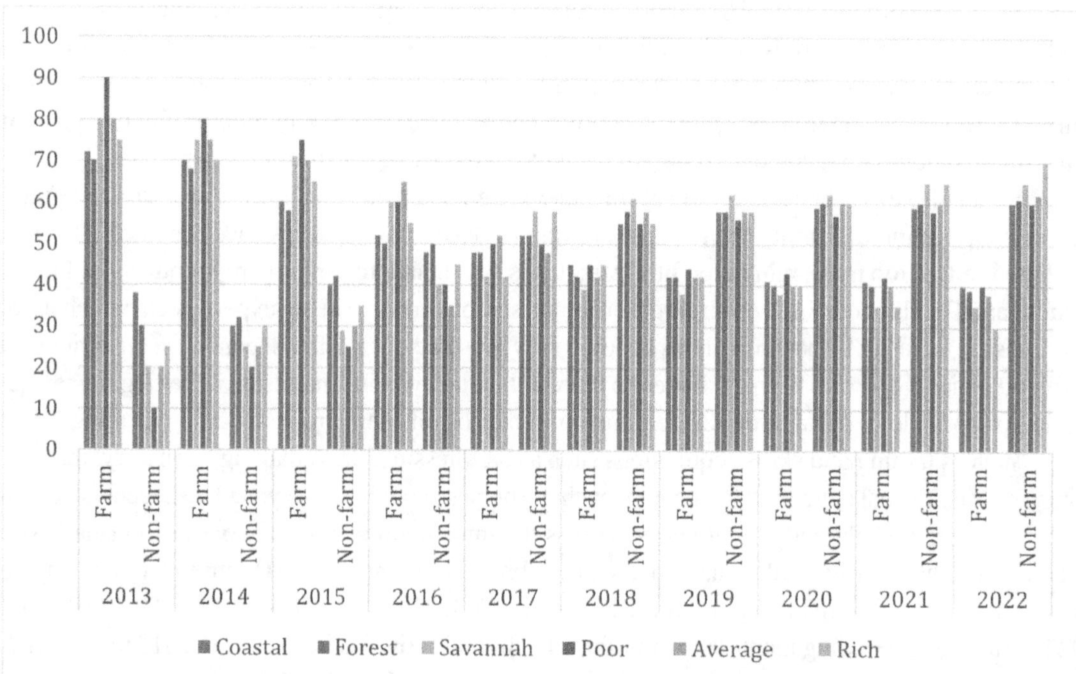

We further examined the trends across the different geographical locations and wealth classes. Similar trends of reducing dependence on agriculture was observed across the different categories (Figure 2).

It has also been noted across Africa and Ghana for that matter that a number of people start with farming and when they get the initial capital, they move away into the non-farm sector. For example, some young people go into cocoa or other cash crop farming as a start and when they get the money, they abandon the cocoa farms to go into trading or transport business. In the opinion of others, the reason for decreasing trends of importance of agriculture is because policymakers are not serious with the sector. For those who argue this way, agriculture cannot be attractive when the policymakers allow agricultural imports to flood the country. In the specific case of Ghana, some farmers had to stop poultry production because of the imported poultry products, which even appear cheaper than the locally produced poultry products. Similar stories have been reported in the rice and maize subsectors. A number of rice and maize farmers have stopped producing because the imported rice and maize do not allow them to get market for their produce. The commonest question that many farmers and other agricultural commodity value chains actors continue to ask is, how can Africa and Ghana in particular that are operating agrarian economies attach no importance to the agricultural sector? Governments of African nation states subventions to institutions mandated to oversee agricultural production have drastically reduced in real terms. The Maputo Declaration that required all nation states to allocate at least 10% of their total expenditures to the agricultural sector has not been met.

There is a negative relationship between farm households' dependence on farm livelihood activities and non-farm livelihood activities. The implication of this is that farm livelihood activities are being replaced with non-farm livelihood activities across Ghana. Households across the different ecological zones of Ghana have different levels of resource endowments. For those households that are adequately endowed, they do not need to seek external resources in the form of credit to be able to pursue their livelihood activities. On the other hand, resource constrained households have to rely on external sources to be able to carry out their production activities. For example, Akudugu (2014) reported that 13 out of the 18 case study household heads representing about 72 percent said they demanded credit from formal and informal sources to finance their livelihood activities in 2007, which reduced to 56 per cent by 2011. One of the explanations given for this trend as reported by the author was that in 2007, there were adverse climatic conditions including floods and droughts. This was particularly severe in the northern part of the country where there was the occurrence of double tragedy of droughts and floods within the same year. This led to some farmers not being able to repay the credit they took during the 2007 cropping season and hence reduction in demand in 2008. Some of them even abandoned farming activities for non-farming activities and this resulted in the reduction of number of households demanding credit for farm livelihood activities in the proceeding year. Following this was an increase in demand for credit for farming purposes in 2009, which the participating household heads attributed to some interventions by government to support flood affected households and communities to undertake farming. They therefore demanded credit in order to take full advantage of these interventions, hence the increase. Unfortunately, some of the interventions promised by government to alleviate the sufferings of victims of floods were not fulfilled in 2009 and this left a number of households that demanded credit in debt. The failure might have been due to change in government in 2009. For instance, subsidized fertilizers by government arrived late. Thus, money borrowed to buy fertilizer was diverted into unintended uses. This led to less or no farm produce to sell to be able to repay the loans. This however, increased to about 56 percent in 2011 and this increment was also attributed to the fact that they had more interventions from government and NGOs to help them farm.

Trends in Credit Demands for Farm and Non-Farm Livelihood Activities

Credit demand is the amount of money a farm household requests from lenders in the formal and informal credit markets. Trend of credit demands in the context of this chapter is defined as the amount farm households have been requesting from formal and informal lenders over a given period. Thus, farm households across Ghana demand credit to finance their farm and non-farm livelihood activities. The trend in demand for credit for farm and non-farm livelihood activities (Figure 3) is similar to that of livelihoods diversification by men and women; old and young people across the different ecological zones of Ghana (Figure 1) as well as the poor, average and rich (Figure 2).

On the other hand, the number of people demanding credit for non-farm livelihood activities across the sampled communities is reported to be on the increase. This is attributed to the fact that many farm households are moving away from agriculture due to issues of climate change and low productivity (Akudugu, et al., 2012; 2013; Blattner, 2020; Wegren, 2021). For instance, in 2013, only 2 out of the 36 (6%) key informants demanded credit for non-farm livelihood activities and this figure increased steadily to 15 (42%) in 2022. Overall, as illustrated in Figure 3, more households are demanding credit for non-farm livelihood activities. In particular, the number of women demanding credit for non-farm livelihood activities such as petty trading increased from 35% in 2013 to about double (70%) in 2022 (Figure 3). Comparatively, their demand for credit for farm livelihood activities decreased from 65% in 2013 to 30% in 2022. Similar trends are observed for men, youth and the old (Figure 3).

Figure 3. Credit demands for farm and non-farm livelihoods activities (n=36)
Source: Field Data, 2023

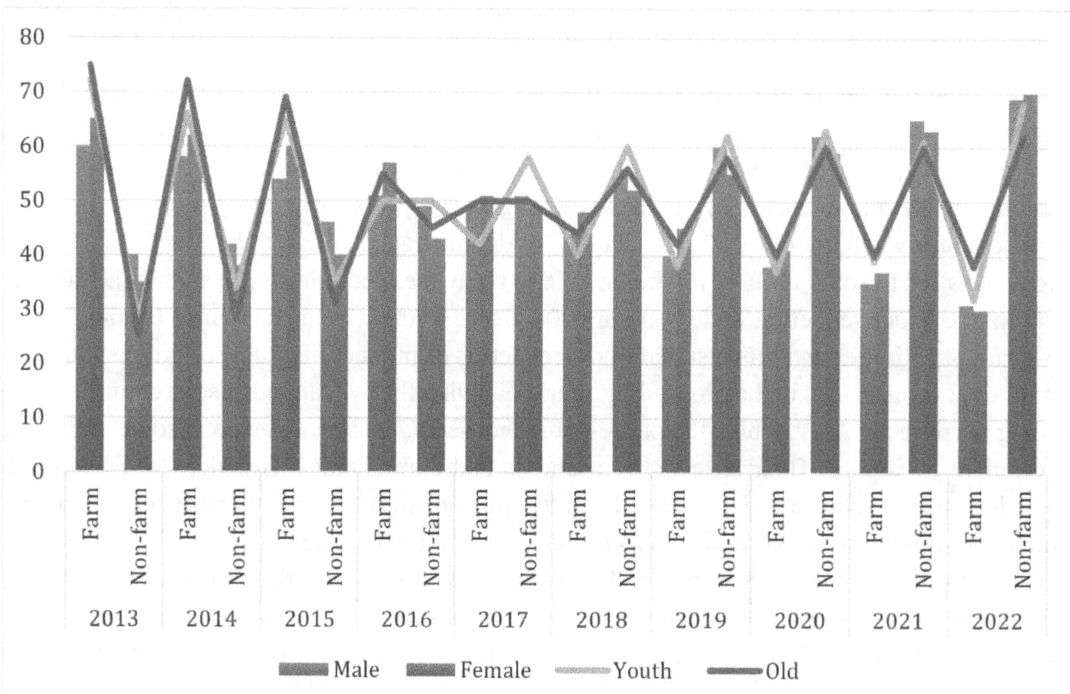

The proportions of household credit demands allocated to farm and non-farm livelihood activities over the years have been changing. Akudugu (2014) reports that the amount of household credit demands allocated to the financing of farm livelihood activities continues to assume a downward trend and that for non-farm livelihood activities is moving upwards (Figure 3). In fact, in the coastal zone, the proportion of credit allocated to the farm livelihood activities reduced from 72% in 2013 to 40% in 2022 whilst that of the non-farm livelihood activities increased from 38% to 61% in 2022 (Figure 4). Similarly, in the forest zone 70% of credit demanded in 2013 was allocated to farm livelihood activities and this decreased to 39% in 2022 compared to the non-farm livelihood activities which increased from 30% in 2013 to 61% in 2022 (Figure 4). In the savannah zone, the results indicate similar trends in reduction of credit allocation to farm livelihood activities and increase in that of non-farm livelihood activities over the period (Figure 4). A number of reasons were given for the observed trends in reduction in credit allocations to farm livelihood activities in favour of non-farm livelihood activities including the fact that most lenders in the formal financial sector prefer to grant credit for non-farm activities. According to some of the research participants many people demand credit for non-farm livelihood activities because of the low risks associated with that sector. In the agricultural sector, less credit is demanded due largely to the unfavorable natural weather conditions, which have become very unreliable these days.

Figure 4. Farm and non-farm credit demands across zones & wealth class (n = 216)
Source: Field Data, 2023

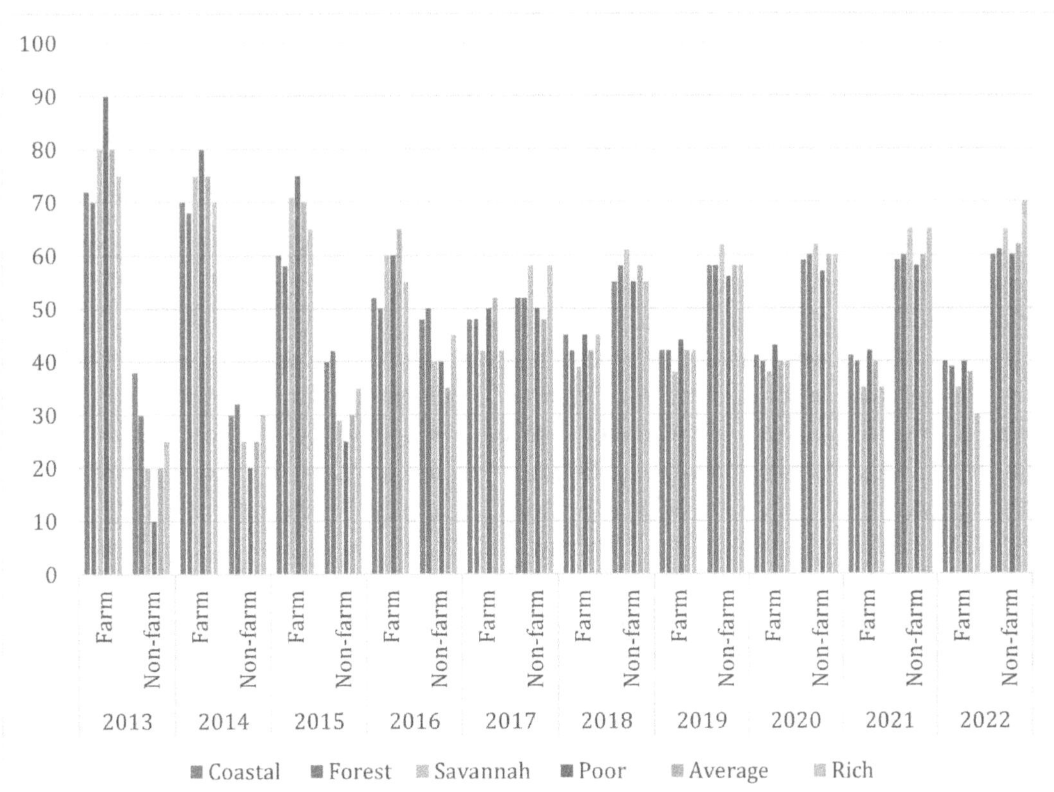

"If one goes and takes credit to cultivate maize for instance, there are so many possibilities that can occur. First, the crop may fail because of drought, flood or both. … Second, the crop may do well with good yields, but the problem is that one may not be able to sell the produce at good prices because in general, the better the yields, the more likelihood of gluts in agricultural produce markets, which will push prices low and the vice versa". This makes repayment difficult, and borrowers may not be able to get credit in the future for same purposes. On the other hand, if the credit is put into petty trading, the risks are less. ...".

The situation is not different when examined across the different wealth classes. The demands for credit for farm and non-farm livelihood activities have been fluctuating over time across the different wealth classes. Specifically, whereas 9 in every 10 poor households that demanded credit in 2013 allocated it to agricultural activities, this drastically reduced to 4 out of every 10 poor households in 2022. On the other hand, only one out of every ten poor people who had access to credit allocated it to non-farm livelihood activities in 2013 compared to six out of every ten poor people doing same in 2022. Similar trends are observed for both the average and rich households demanding credit for farm and non-farm livelihood purposes (Figure 5). These trends have been observed in earlier empirical studies focusing more on the complimentary of formal and informal credit (Awunyo-Vitor & Abankwah 2012). This clearly demonstrates that most borrowing farm households in recent times seek credit more for non-farm livelihood activities at the expense of farm livelihood activities. This view was clearly supported by research participants who noted that because of the risk averse nature of banks and other financial institutions in lending to agriculture, many do not even contemplate borrowing for farming activities. This is exacerbated by climate change that has significantly increased the risk of crop failures that makes it more difficult for farmers to repay loans if used for farming.

CONCLUSION

Most farm households in contemporary Ghana are diversifying out of agriculture. The dependence of farm households on agriculture as the main source of livelihood is on the decline. On the other hand, their dependence on non-agriculture activities as the main source of livelihoods is on the upward trajectory. Some of the reasons for this trend include the fact that farmers are finding ways of coping with the climate change menace and other risks inherent in agricultural production. As a result, most farm households are diversifying their resources including credit to cover a wider range of livelihood activities. This has greatly influenced their demands for credit to finance farm and non-farm livelihood activities. Increasingly a smaller number of farm households are demanding credit to finance farm livelihood activities compared to the number of farm households demanding credit for non-farm livelihood activities. The implication of this is that the number of households demanding credit for non-farm livelihood activities is increasing at the expense of farm livelihood activities. This is further supported by the fact that the credit demands for non-farm livelihood activities continue to move upward with that of the farm sector generally declining. Apparently, there is a negative relationship between credit demands for farm livelihood activities and non-farm livelihood activities. It is concluded that more farm households in rural Ghana are increasingly demanding credit from the informal financial market to finance non-farm livelihood activities at the expense of farm livelihood activities. On the basis of the conclusion, it is recommended that financial intermediation interventions targeting farming communities in Ghana and elsewhere appreciate the fact that livelihoods are being diversified in these areas. This is critical in ensuring that the long-standing practice of focusing interventions that target farming communities largely on the farm sector will no longer be a beneficial approach.

REFERENCES

Akudugu, M. A. (2010). Assessment of access to financial capital by rural people in Ghana: The case of the Upper East Region. *Savings and Development*, *34*(2), 169–189.

Akudugu, M. A. (2012). Estimation of the determinants of credit demand by farmers and supply by Rural Banks in Ghana's Upper East Region. *Asian Journal of Agriculture and Rural Development*, *2*(2), 179–190.

Akudugu, M. A. (2014). *Farm Credit and Agricultural Productivity in Ghana* [PhD Thesis]. School of Agriculture, Policy and Development, University of Reading, Reading, UK.

Akudugu, M. A., & Alhassan, A.-R. (2012). The climate change menace, food security, livelihoods and social safety in northern Ghana. *International Journal of Sustainable Development and World Policy*, *1*(3), 80–95.

Akudugu, M. A., Dittoh, S., & Mahama, E. S. (2012). The Implications of Climate Change on Food Security and Rural Livelihoods: Experiences from Northern Ghana. *Journal of Environment and Earth Science*, *2*(3), 21–29.

Akudugu, M. A., Egyir, I. S., & Akwasi, M.-B. (2009). Access to credit from rural banks in Ghana: The case of women farmers in the Upper East Region. *Ghana Journal of Development Studies*, *6*(2), 142–167.

Akudugu, M. A., Egyir, I. S., & Akwasi, M.-B. (2009). Women farmers' access to credit from rural banks in Ghana. *Agricultural Finance Review*, *69*(3), 284–299. doi:10.1108/00021460911002671

Akudugu, M. A., Garforth, C. J., & Dorward, P. (2013). Improvement in Crop Production in Ghana: Is it due to Area Expansion or Increased Productivity? *Developing Country Studies*, *3*(1), 176–186.

Al-hassan, S., & Sagre, B. (2006). Microcredit and poverty alleviation: An analysis of the performance of women in microcredit activities in the Kassena/Nankana District of Ghana. *Ghana Journal of Development Studies*, *3*(2), 41–56.

Alhassan, A.-R., Akudugu, M. A., & Akuriba, M. A. (2023). The Double Bottom Line in Microfinance: Implications for the Performance Measurement Practices of Microfinance Institutions. In Y. Alhassan & U. Nwangbara (Eds.), *Transforming Economies Through Microfinance in Developing Nations*. IGI Global. doi:10.4018/978-1-6684-5647-7.ch002

Atieno, R. (2001). *Formal and informal institutions' lending policies and access to credit by small-scale enterprises in Kenya: An empirical assessment*. African Economic Research Consortium Research Paper 111.

Awunyo-Vitor, D., & Abankwah, V. (2012). Substitutes or complements: Formal and informal credit demand by maize farmers in Ashanti and Brong Ahafo Regions of Ghana. *Journal of Agricultural Science*, *7*(1), 1–13.

Ayamga, M., Sarpong, D. B., & Asuming-Brempong, S. (2006). Factors influencing the decision to participate in microcredit programmes: An illustration for Northern Ghana. *Ghana Journal of Development Studies*, *3*(2), 57–65.

Baffour-Kyei, V., Mensah, A., Owusu, V., & Horlu, G. S. A. K. (2021). Artisanal Small-Scale Mining and Livelihood Assets in Rural Southern Ghana. *Resources Policy*, *71*, 101988. doi:10.1016/j.resourpol.2021.101988

Banchirigah, S. M. (2006). How have reforms fuelled the expansion of artisanal mining? Evidence from Sub-Saharan Africa. *Resources Policy*, *31*(3), 165–171. doi:10.1016/j.resourpol.2006.12.001

Banchirigah, S. M. (2008). Challenges with eradicating illegal mining in Ghana: A perspective from the grassroots. *Resources Policy*, *33*(1), 29–38. doi:10.1016/j.resourpol.2007.11.001

Banchirigah, S. M., & Hilson, G. (2010). De-agrarianization, re-agrarianization and local economic development: Re-orienting livelihoods in African artisanal mining communities. *Policy Sciences*, *43*(2), 157–180. doi:10.100711077-009-9091-5

Barretta, C. B., Reardon, T., & Webb, P. (2001). Nonfarm income diversification and household livelihood strategies in rural Africa: Concepts, dynamics, and policy implications. *Food Policy*, *26*(4), 315–331. doi:10.1016/S0306-9192(01)00014-8

Blattner, C. E. (2020). Just Transition for Agriculture? A Critical Step in Tackling Climate Change. *Journal of Agriculture, Food Systems, and Community Development*, *9*(3), 53–58. doi:10.5304/jafscd.2020.093.006

Bryceson, D. F. (1999). *Sub-Saharan Africa betwixt and between: Rural livelihood practices and policies.* Afrika-Studiecentrum (Leiden University) Working Paper 43.

Bryceson, D. F. (2002). The Scramble in Africa: Reorienting Rural Livelihoods. *World Development*, *30*(5), 725–739. doi:10.1016/S0305-750X(02)00006-2

Bryceson, D. F., & Jonsson, J. B. (2010). Gold digging careers in rural Africa: Small-scale miners' livelihood choices. *World Development*, *38*(3), 379–392. doi:10.1016/j.worlddev.2009.09.003

Chavas, J.-P., & Falco, S. D. (2012). On the role of risk versus economies of scope in farm diversification with an application to Ethiopian farms. *Journal of Agricultural Economics*, *63*(1), 25–55. doi:10.1111/j.1477-9552.2011.00319.x

Demirgüç-Kunt, A., & Klapper, L. (2012). *Financial inclusion in Africa: An Overview.* World Bank Policy Research Working Paper WPS No. 6088.

Demurger, S., Fournier, M., & Yang, W. (2010). Rural households' decisions towards income diversification: Evidence from a township in northern China. *China Economic Review*, *21*, 32–44. doi:10.1016/j.chieco.2010.05.007

Deogharia, P. C. (2018). Diversification of Agriculture: A Review. *Journal of Economic and Social Development*, *14*(1), 46–59.

Dorward, A. (2009). Integrating contested aspirations, processes and policy: Development as hanging in, stepping up and stepping out. *Development Policy Review*, *27*(2), 131–146. doi:10.1111/j.1467-7679.2009.00439.x

Ellis, F. (1998). Household strategies and rural livelihood diversification'. *The Journal of Development Studies*, *35*(1), 1–38. doi:10.1080/00220389808422553

Ellis, F. (2000). The determinants of rural livelihood diversification in developing countries. *Journal of Agricultural Economics*, *51*(2), 289–302. doi:10.1111/j.1477-9552.2000.tb01229.x

Ellis, F. (2000). *Rural Livelihoods and Diversity in Developing Countries*. Oxford University Press.

Ellis, F. (2006). Agrarian change and rising vulnerability in rural sub-Saharan Africa. *New Political Economy*, *11*(3), 387–397. doi:10.1080/13563460600841025

Ghana Statistical Service. (2008). *Ghana Living Standards Survey*. Report Number 5. Government of Ghana.

Haggblade, S., Hazell, P., & Reardon, T. (2010). The rural non-farm economy: Prospects for growth and poverty reduction. *World Development*, *38*(10), 1429–1441. doi:10.1016/j.worlddev.2009.06.008

Hilson, G. (2002). The environmental impact of small-scale gold mining in Ghana: Identifying problems and possible solution. *The Geographical Journal*, *168*(1), 57–72. doi:10.1111/1475-4959.00038

Hilson, G. (2009). Small-scale mining, poverty and economic development in sub-Saharan Africa: An overview. *Resources Policy*, *34*(1-2), 1–5. doi:10.1016/j.resourpol.2008.12.001

Hilson, G. (2010). Once a miner, always a miner: Poverty and livelihood diversification in Akwatia, Ghana. *Journal of Rural Studies*, *26*(3), 296–307. doi:10.1016/j.jrurstud.2010.01.002

Hilson, G. (2020). Formalization Bubbles: A Blueprint for Sustainable Artisanal and Small-Scale Mining (ASM) in Sub-Saharan Africa. *The Extractive Industries and Society*, *7*(4), 1624–1638. doi:10.1016/j.exis.2020.11.001

Hilson, G., & Garforth, C. (2012). 'Agricultural poverty' and the expansion of artisal mining in Sub-Saharan Africa: Experiences from Southwest Mali and Southeast Ghana. *Population Research and Policy Review*, *31*(2).

IFAD. (2003). *Ghana: Women's access to formal financial services*. Retrieved from https://www.ifad.org/gender/learning/sector/finance/42.htm

Iiyama, M. (2006). *Livelihoods diversification patterns among households and their implications on poverty and resource use: A case study from a Kerio River Basin Community*. LUCID Working Paper Series 51.

Kibaara, B. (2006). *Rural Financial Services in Kenya: What is Working and Why*. Tegemeo Working paper (25).

Motsholapheko, M. R., Kgathi, D. L., & Vanderpost, C. (2011). Rural livelihoods and household adaptation to extreme flooding in the Okavango Delta, Botswana. *Physics and Chemistry of the Earth*, *36*, 984–995. doi:10.1016/j.pce.2011.08.004

Mwangi, I. W., & Sichei, M. M. (2011). Determinants of access to credit by individuals in Kenya: A comparative analysis of the Kenya National FinAccess Surveys of 2006 and 2009. *European Journal of Business and Management*, *3*(3), 206–226.

Niehof, A. (2004). The significance of diversification for rural livelihood systems. *Food Policy*, *29*(4), 321–338. doi:10.1016/j.foodpol.2004.07.009

Ntifo-Siaw & Bosompem. (2008). *Microfinance as Poverty Alleviation Tool: Case Study of Social Investment Fund Interventions in the Central Region – Ghana*. Governance and Sustainable Development. Marcel Hughes Publicity Group.

Osumanu, I. K. (2020). Small-Scale Mining and Livelihood Dynamics in North-Eastern Ghana: Sustaining Rural Livelihoods in a Changing Environment. *Progress in Development Studies*, *20*(3), 208–222. doi:10.1177/1464993420934223

Quaye, W. (2008). Food Security Situation in Northern Ghana, Coping Strategies and Related Constraints. *African Journal of Agricultural Research*, *3*(5), 334–342.

Rahji, M. A. Y., & Fakayode, S. B. (2009). A multinomial logit analysis of agricultural credit rationing by commercial banks in Nigeria. *International Research Journal of Finance and Economics*, (24), 90–100.

Salayo, N. D., Perez, M. L., Garces, L. R., & Pido, M. D. (2012). Mariculture development and livelihood diversification in the Philippines. *Marine Policy*, *36*(4), 867–881. doi:10.1016/j.marpol.2011.12.003

Schindler, K. (2010). Credit for what? Informal credit as a coping strategy of market women in northern Ghana. *The Journal of Development Studies*, *46*(2), 234–253. doi:10.1080/00220380903002905

Turvey, C. G., He, G., Ma, J., Kong, R., & Meagher, P. (2012). Farm credit and credit demand elasticities in Shaanxi and Gansu. *China Economic Review*, *23*(4), 1020–1035. doi:10.1016/j.chieco.2012.05.004

Wegren, S. K. (2021). Vulnerabilities in Russian Agriculture to Climate Change. *Sustainable Development Research*, *3*(1), 2021. doi:10.30560dr.v3n1p1

Zerai, B., & Rani, L. (2012). Is there a tradeoff between outreach and sustainability of microfinance institutions? Evidence from Indian Microfinance Institutions (MFIs). *European Journal of Business and Management*, *4*(2), 90–98.

Chapter 5
Impact of Financial Inclusion and Microfinancing on Women Empowerment in India: A Review

Richa Nangia
https://orcid.org/0000-0002-6128-8648
K.R. Mangalam University, India

Rashmi Singel
Manav Rachna International Institute of Research Studies, India

Swati Shrivastava
https://orcid.org/0000-0003-2122-6837
Sushant University, India

K. Shama Sharma
K.R. Mangalam University, India

Vijay Anand Dubey
Sushant University, India

ABSTRACT

This chapter explores the multifaceted linkages between microfinancing, financial inclusion, and women empowerment in India. It delves into the key mechanisms through which improved access to microfinancing and other financial services fosters women's economic, social, and political empowerment. The current study helps the financial regulators, government, and the banking industry to know the state of financial inclusion and to analyse the impact and effectiveness of the initiatives and measures taken by them on the empowerment of women in India. It is also providing in-depth knowledge to policy makers to review the existing policies regarding financial inclusion through microfinancing so as to have a substantial impact on women empowerment.

DOI: 10.4018/978-1-6684-8979-6.ch005

INTRODUCTION

Indian economy is the one of the largest and fastest growing economy in the world. It is expected that between 2012 and 2014 Indian economy will become 3rd largest in the world by overtaking economy of Japan. The tremendous growth has coincided with better overall performance. Indian entrepreneurs have registered noticeable global presence not only in IT or ITES and knowledge process services but also in world class manufacturing capabilities. Main drivers of Indian economic growth are domestic consumption, service sector, high tech capital intensive industry, human capital, natural resources and so on.

As a catalyst to economic development, the financial system plays a role of intermediation in the mobilization and allocation of savings for productive activities in the economy. While crossing of Indian GDP to over a trillion dollar mark was an important milestone back in 2007, the robust health of Indian financial institutions during the global recession of 2008 was noteworthy when banks and financial institutions across US and Europe were tumbling down. For sustainable economic growth, it is important that all segments of the society get to participate in this growth process and basic utilities like financial services are made available to the excluded ones through Financial Inclusion.

The financial inclusion through microfinancing can be both a catalyst and barometer of women empowerment. With access to micro credit through various microfinancing schemes women do have an opportunity for social and economic empowerment.

Presently 8.16 crore rural women across India have been mobilized into more than 74.98 lakh self-help groups under the DAY-NRLM (Deendayal Antyodaya Yojana – National Rural Livelihoods Mission)) umbrella (PIB,2022). Some 3.9 million rural women are mobilized in 40,000 SHG are in the state of Haryana itself (according to the NRLM portal).

As defined by RBI, Financial Inclusion is the process of ensuring access to appropriate financial products and services needed by all sections of the society in general and vulnerable groups such as weaker sections and low income groups in particular at an affordable cost in a fair and transparent manner by mainstream institutional players.

Microfinancing through financial inclusion has emerged as a critical tool for empowering women in India. Microfinance, characterized by the provision of small loans, savings, and other financial services to low-income individuals and marginalized communities, has gained prominence in India as an effective means of financial inclusion. The country has made significant strides in enhancing microfinancing and financial inclusion over the past decade, with various initiatives and policy reforms. Women may build wealth, generate income, manage financial risks, and participate fully in the economy with the help of financial inclusion.

"Financial inclusion is a key element of social inclusion, particularly useful in combating poverty and income inequality by opening blocked advancement opportunities for disadvantaged segments of the population" (Omar, M.A. & Inaba, K. 2020). But various authors and economists in advanced economies, consider Financial Inclusion in a broader prospect and include access to services such as no-frills bank account, check-in account, micro-credit, savings products, remittances & payment services, insurance, healthcare, mortgage, financial advisory services, entrepreneurial credit, pension for old age etc. to excluded groups and people such as marginal farmers, landless labour, workers in unorganized sector, urban slum dwellers, migrants, ethnic minorities and other socially excluded groups, with a purpose to provide equitable opportunities to every individual to avail the facility of formal channels for better life, better living and better income. "One Study draw attention to some issues such as optimal financial inclusion, extreme financial inclusion, how financial inclusion can transmit systemic risk to the formal financial sector, and whether financial inclusion and exclusion are pro-cyclical with changes in the economic cycle" (Ozili et al. 2020).

As per RBI "Financial inclusion has been defined as "the process of ensuring access to financial services, timely and adequate credit for vulnerable groups such as weaker sections and low-income groups at an affordable cost". (Dr C Rangarajan, RBI, 2008). According to RBI, availability of banking services means availability of following 6 products:

- Basic "No-Frills" Account with overdraft facility.
- Remittance product for Electronic Benefit Transfer (EBT) and other remittances.
- Pure saving product either a recurring or a variable recurring deposit.
- Entrepreneurial Credit such as General Credit Card (GCC) and Kissan Credit Card (KCC).
- Micro Insurance (life and non-life).
- Micro Pension

In recent years Government of India has taken various steps and initiatives for the economic, social-psychological, and political empowerment of rural women. One of the most important initiatives taken by the Indian Government is Deendayal Antyodaya Yojana - National Rural Livelihood Mission (DAY-NRLM) which mobilizes women into self-help groups (SHG). The scheme aims to reach out to poor rural women and link them to sustainable livelihood opportunities, nurturing them until they come out of poverty and enjoy a decent quality of life. Microfinance institutions (MFIs) have also played a crucial role in extending financial services to those who were previously excluded from the formal banking system. By adopting innovative delivery models, such as self-help groups (SHGs) and village-based banking, MFIs have reached remote and economically disadvantaged areas, including regions where women's financial participation was historically limited.

Access to microfinance has enabled women to engage in income-generating activities and entrepreneurial ventures. With access to small loans and savings products, women have ventured into micro-enterprises, agriculture, and crafts, enhancing household income and financial resilience. Microfinance has not only created employment opportunities for women but has also empowered them to become employers, leading to a ripple effect of economic growth within their communities.

IDENTIFICATION OF THE PROBLEM

In India, RBI used the term 'Financial Inclusion' for the first time in a policy document in 2005 and started undertaking Financial Inclusion initiatives in a mission mode through a combination of strategies ranging from provision of new products, relaxation of regulatory guidelines and other supportive measures to achieve sustainable and scalable Financial Inclusion.

Despite all the efforts of RBI, progress in this direction is far from satisfactory. According to RBI, Indian banking industry has been able to penetrate just half of the population. Out of over 6,00,000 Villages in country, only about 30,000, or just 5% have a commercial bank branch. Just about 55% of the population across the country have deposit accounts and 9% have credit accounts with banks. The proportion of people having any kind of life insurance cover is as low as 20% and the proportion having non-life insurance is an awfully low 9.6%. People having debit cards comprise only 18% and those having credit cards are a marginal 2%. A significant percentage of saving accounts is lying dormant and less than 10% of the 'No-Frills Accounts' are active.

In India, focused attention on Financial Inclusion started in 2005. A series of initiatives and programmes have been launched by the Reserve Bank of India to bring more and more people into the fold of formal financial institutions. As the impact of financial inclusion and microfinancing on women empowerment is taken in the strategic mode very recently but very limited researches have been conducted in this area.

The problem of financial inclusion and microfinancing has significant implications for women's empowerment. Here's an overview of how these issues intersect and impact each other:

1. **Financial Inclusion:** Financial inclusion refers to the accessibility and usage of a wide range of financial services, including savings, credit, insurance, and payment services. Many women, particularly in developing countries, face barriers to accessing these services due to factors such as lack of documentation, limited financial literacy, cultural norms, and restrictive regulations.

Impact on Women:

Limited Access to Capital: Without access to formal financial services, women often struggle to secure loans and credit, hindering their ability to start or expand businesses.

Vulnerability: Financially excluded women are more susceptible to economic shocks and hardships, as they lack safety nets like insurance and savings.

Limited Economic Opportunities: Financial exclusion constrains women's participation in economic activities and limits their potential to generate income and build assets.

2. **Microfinancing:** Microfinance involves providing small loans, savings, and other financial services to low-income individuals, often marginalized or underserved populations, who lack access to traditional banking systems. Microfinancing aims to alleviate poverty, create economic opportunities, and promote financial inclusion.

Impact on Women:

Empowerment: Microfinancing can empower women by giving them the means to invest in income-generating activities, start businesses, and contribute to household finances.

Skill Development: Microfinance institutions often provide financial education and training, enhancing women's financial literacy and management skills.

Social Impact: When women have access to microfinancing, they can contribute to poverty reduction and community development, positively impacting their families and societies.

Women Empowerment: Empowerment refers to the process by which women gain the knowledge, skills, resources, and agency to make informed decisions, exercise control over their lives, and participate actively in social, economic, and political spheres.

Microfinancing and Empowerment

Economic Independence: Microfinancing allows women to generate income, reduce financial dependence, and contribute to household decision-making.

Decision-Making Power: Increased economic participation can lead to greater influence in household and community decisions, enhancing women's roles and status.

Confidence and Leadership: Successful engagement with microfinancing can boost women's self-confidence and encourage them to take on leadership roles in their communities.

Challenges and Considerations: While financial inclusion and microfinancing hold promise for women's empowerment, several challenges need to be addressed:

Gender Bias: Financial institutions may exhibit gender bias in lending practices and terms, limiting women's access to fair and appropriate services.

Repayment Pressures: Microfinance loans can sometimes lead to over-indebtedness and repayment pressures, affecting women's well-being.

Holistic Approach: Empowerment requires more than just access to financial services; it also involves addressing social norms, education, and legal barriers.

In conclusion, the problem of financial inclusion and the potential of microfinancing play crucial roles in women's empowerment. Addressing these challenges requires a comprehensive approach that includes financial education, gender-sensitive policies, and efforts to promote women's economic participation and leadership.

Objectives of the Study

- To study the evolution of Financial Inclusion and initiatives taken by various agencies for better Financial Inclusion in India.
- To understand the impact of financial inclusion and microfinancing on women empowerment.

Research Methodology

In this research secondary data has been collected to present a comprehensive study on financial inclusion and microfinancing with respect to women empowerment. The research was carried out depending on secondary sources which require no direct contact to gather information and is effectively based newspapers, business journals, books and periodicals, bank reports etc.

REVIEW OF LITERATURE

a) Financial Inclusion and Women Empowerment

The authors want to explain about the Impact of Financial Inclusion on Women Empowerment with special reference to Ranchi District. The objective of current research paper is to examine the present state of women's engagement in banking and financial operations which will lead to women empowerment. 13 questionnaires were constructed to assess the knowledge of various financial schemes, subsidies, and services offered by the Government of India to 150 rural women from Ranchi District. The result of the study shows that women have a high level of interest in financial and banking services, financial inclusion has low but positive impact on women empowerment and there is a long way to go, illiteracy, reliance, and lack of awareness among women remain barriers to empower them (Chaudhary & Rinki, 2022).

The authors have critically analysed the impact of social and economic dimensions on women empowerment through financial inclusion in rural India. Primary and Secondary data has been taken into consideration for the study. Women respondents from the Gujarat state of India by a simple random sampling method and applied a logistic regression approach to identify the relationship between the need of a bank account (determinant of financial inclusion) as a dependent variable and social and economic dimensions of women empowerment such as earning status, participation in financial decision-making, recipient of social welfare schemes and perception towards the safety of saving as independent variables have been taken. The results of this study show that earning status, participation in financial decision-making at household level and recipient of social welfare schemes by women have a significant impact on women empowerment through financial inclusion (Pal et al, 2022).

The fifth Sustainable Development Goal on gender equality's aim of the economic empowerment of women depends on financial inclusion. One in five Indian women do not have access to a bank account. Even though the nation's financial inclusion initiatives have raised the proportion of women with access to bank accounts, there are still significant inequalities in account usage and access to savings and loans. For a variety of reasons, women continue to have difficulty obtaining financial services. For example, they are more likely to live distance from a bank branch, lack a mobile phone, or require assistance to open and efficiently operate a bank account. This article investigates the barriers and analyzes the gender gaps in financial inclusion in India (Sunaina Kumar, 2022).

Women's ability to manage their finances appears to have been disproportionately harmed by the COVID-19 disaster. In truth, there is still a gender gap in women's economic participation in the finance industry. In this study, the effect of digital financial inclusion on Saudi Arabia's COVID-19 epidemic and women's economic empowerment is compared. The research investigates the association between economic women's empowerment and digital financial inclusion using data gathered from the Global Financial Inclusion Database for 2017 and 2021 and ordered probit models. Findings suggest that after the epidemic, using digital banking services has grown even more important. The findings show that women today make more economic decisions than they did prior to the epidemic because they have access to a variety of digital financial services that may influence their decisions (Mabrouk et al, 2023).

Despite making up half of the population, there is status discrimination when it comes to birth, education, health, employment rights, and pay. In India, women's empowerment has made remarkable strides during the previous ten years. In spite of the fact that women make up about half of the population in India, authors still see that they lack power there. Accelerating economic progress requires empowering the female population. However, a 2018 assessment by the World Economic Forum placed India 139th out of 144 nations in terms of economic participation, with a 66% gender gap. The nation's poor financial inclusion, particularly in rural areas, is one of the causes of this gap's oncoming development. This paper contends about the importance of financial inclusion, Financial Inclusion Schemes, different initiatives are taken by RBI and Government, etc. towards women empowerment in India (Bobillapati & Bathula, 2022).

The current study reveals that, generally speaking, the influence of financial inclusion on women's empowerment is favourable. According to the study, greater financial inclusion will benefit women by enabling them to recognize their strengths and abilities, which make them powerful and dominant. Only with the correct education, awareness, and freedom to express oneself are such abilities capable of being developed and improved in the proper manner. The findings show that gender discrimination has a detrimental effect on women's empowerment while financial development, the gender parity index, and women's employment have positive effects. The report emphasizes that to promote women's emancipation in emerging nations. Governments and politicians need to thoroughly examine and reevaluate what the best financial inclusion policies are that will contribute to increasing women's empowerment in the nation (Arshad, A., 2023).

b) Microfinancing and Women Empowerment

Microfinance is widely seen as supporting the uplift of the most vulnerable rural poor groups. It is viewed as a way to reduce credit-based poverty by promoting financial inclusion. India also experiences this. NABARD designed the self-help group bank linkage program (SHG-BLP) in India as a trial initiative in 1992. In order to connect the informal and organized financial sectors, the initiative was mainstreamed in 1996. Through SHG-BLP, a registered participant in the Deendayal Antyodaya Yojana-National Rural Livelihoods Mission, microfinance services are made available in Assam. The epicentre of Operation SHG-BLP is in Central Assam. This setting inspires us to investigate SHG-BLP's role in the social and financial inclusion of the disadvantaged rural residents of central Assam. Financial inclusion index and social exclusion index are two self-developed indices (Maity S., 2023).

Microfinance, which is made feasible by financial inclusion across all society sectors, is one technique for fostering economic growth in the country. Financial inclusion requires the expansion of banking or financial services at a reasonable cost to provide a sizable section of society's most vulnerable groups with a financial safety net for survival as well as social empowerment. According to the 2011 census, women make up 48.53 percent of the population overall in India, yet due to their financial dependence, the majority of women are denied chances and rights. Through the analysis of prior research, survey data, and the development of a hypothetical model, this study explores how financial inclusion and microfinance might empower women. Lack of trust in a person is one of the biggest obstacles to inclusion (Haritha et al, 2023).

The project's goal was to advance our understanding of institutional barriers to microfinance, financial inclusion, and financial development by utilizing Mauritania as a case study. Authors employed a mixed method approach, which incorporates expert's interviews and secondary data analysis. First, a logit model with dummy independent variables was used to look into the variables that affect households' access to credit. The key benefit of this model is that it avoids confusing effects by looking at how all of the variables are related to one another. According to research, men and women in Mauritania have equal access to financial services, but those who work in the public sector, have greater levels of education, and have smaller families have easier access to credit. Second, we discovered that the various regions of Mauritania can be divided into four quadrants—attractive, industrious, moderate, and resource-constrained—based on unemployment, income, literacy, financial inclusion, and population density—into two main dimensions. Authors anticipated that countries with low populations would have less access to loans. Contrary to expectations, we discovered that individuals in low-density areas within a nation have a better likelihood of obtaining credit. Third, we identified the main issues that Mauritania's microfinance sector is facing and offered solutions based on an expert interview. External validity was constrained, as it is in most case studies (Bouasria et al, 2020).

c) Financial Inclusion and Microfinancing

Sachin Joseph in his article has opined that the limitations of traditional banking can be overcome by putting in to practice innovative products, strategies and channels that have easy accessibility and reach among those sections of the society, who have been ignored by the formal banking system. Leveraging technology for Financial Inclusion by using innovative methods such as Business Correspondent (BC) Model With Hand Held Devices, Hand Held Devices Operated Through Smart Cards and Bio Metric Scanner, Mobile Banking, Information Technology - Telecom Platform, UID - (Unique Identification Number), Technological tie-up between Banks and Microfinance Institutions, ICT (Information and Communication Technologies) for Rural Connectivity, Pre-printed Security Stickers and SMS Based Authentication on a real time basis, OMR Based Automated form Processing System, Online form Tracking System, Micro-Finance Institutions as Non-Banking Financial.

Companies, CSP (Customer Service Points) Cum Training Institutes, Banking Vans & Mobile ATMs, KIOSK Banking, Innovative Business Facilitation Centres like bus stand, Railway station, Network of Large Retail Outlets, Interactive Voice Response Systems (IVRS), Television Based Financial Inclusion, Lottery Based Savings Accounts, Micro Payments and Remittance System, Sub Saving A/C etc. will help in achieving the aim of Financial Inclusion more profitably (Joseph Sachin, 2011).

According to Goyal, Government of India and RBI have to go a long way to reach their goal of Financial Inclusion. The assorted cultural and economic status of Indian states demands a special and distinct treatment in the case of each state. In North-east region specifically, the transaction costs are a major issue. Then the region's basic features of peculiar topography, sparse and scattered population, difficult terrain with transport bottlenecks and poor law and order condition in some areas pose a challenge to branch expansion. According to him, the branch expansion efforts require a proper linkage between the formal institutions like banks and community-based organizations such as Self help Groups (SHGs) and Non-Government Organisations (NGOs). This will help overcome the basic problems faced by the formal institutions i.e., asymmetric information and the associated ills. He suggested that besides stimulating demand for appropriate banking services among financially excluded groups, other actions such as assessment of the suitability of the existing financial products for the farmers/poor, adoption of suitable mechanisms to address the risk faced by farmers and other poor, and development of need-based financial instruments to promote economically viable activities, will also prove very helpful (Goyal Chandan, 2008).

In a study the author has highlighted that scaling up access to finance for India's poor presents a formidable development challenge. This study based on primary research suggests key interventions and intermediations to speed up the process of Financial Inclusion, and thereby poverty alleviation. Apart from providing key recommendations in the form of roadmap to speed up the process of Financial Inclusion, the study also sought to determine the viability and cost-effectiveness of the Business Correspondent (BC) model and has identified several options to make the model viable (Kochhar Sameer, 2009).

A reportjointly produced by Department of Financial Services, Department of Economic Affairs, and Department of Post and Invest India Economic Foundation (IIEF) stated that India Post is the largest and most credible outreach infrastructure in the country. It has several decades of experience in delivering bank accounts and payments across the country, especially to the poor. India Post is already in the process of reinventing itself and has implemented several innovative products. A combination of the India Post outreach and credibility, with its extensive experience in delivering savings accounts and payments on a pan-India basis can serve as a critical building block for broad-based Financial Inclusion. This report recommended that India Post harnesses the rapid Information Technology and telecom capacity expansion to deliver three basic integrated products to every Indian citizen viz, a savings account hosted on a lightweight banking platform, a broad based payments network and a competitive mechanism to deliver micro-loans to the poor.

Rao in his research article has sought to find out the understanding of Financial Inclusion by ground level operating functionaries of banks. He also tried to find out whether Top-down structure (by following instructions from RBI, Government) or Bottom-up approach (through educating and encouraging bankers at the ground level) is effective for better understanding of Financial Inclusion by ground level operating functionaries of banks. For his study he used secondary data based on speeches, statistical information from RBI and other banks, NABARD, various Government agencies and primary data on the basis of feedback gathered from 26 experienced bank officials from rural and semi-urban branches from 13 states in India. According to him, if concepts of Financial Inclusion reach the operating functionaries in the right spirit, banks can achieve real Financial Inclusion. He concluded that, there is an urgent need for bottom-up approach in driving the Financial Inclusion movement in the coming days (Rao Nageswara, 2010).

Mr Bihari conducted a study in which he attempted to measure Financial Inclusion through an index based on three parameters: banking penetration (BP), availability of the banking services (BS) and usage of the banking system (BU). He stated that a lot of research work has been done on how to increase Financial Inclusion but very less importance is given on how to measure the extent of Financial Inclusion across economies. In his study, he attempted to bridge this gap by proposing an Index of Financial Inclusion (IFI). The IFI is a multi-dimensional index that captures information on various dimensions of Financial Inclusion in one single digit between 0 and 1, where 0 denotes complete financial exclusion and 1indicates complete Financial Inclusion in an economy. On the basis of his study, he concluded that Financial Inclusion is very low in India (Bihari Chandra Suresh, 2011).

Janmejaya and Aggarwal have an opinion that India is at a tipping point where a few positive steps on the part of government and financial service providers can lead to a breakthrough by converting Financial Inclusion (from being a mere obligation) into a real opportunity. This requires a deep understanding of customers need and innovative collaboration cross industry business initiatives to reduce the cost of service delivery (Sinha Janmejaya & Aggarwal Neeraj, 2011).

Authors have critically analyzed SHG-bank linkage program to assess its contribution towards Financial Inclusion and removing the disparities prevailing in various regions of the country. In their study they have found that the scheduled commercial banks have played a crucial role in the growth and advancement in urban areas but in the context of the rural area these banks have not lived up to the expectations. Share of smaller credit in the total credit disbursed by the scheduled commercial banks has been decreased to a very insignificant proportion. Rural areas and rural people are still deprived and discriminated in the context of Financial Inclusion and growth. Regional distribution of the banking system shows the inclination of banking facilities towards the Southern and Northern regions. According to them microfinance promoted through the SHG-bank linkage program has performed well in bridging the gap in financial network and spreading banking facilities to the poor in rural and urban areas but the benefit of this program have not remain equally distributed in all regions of country (Pokhriyal A.K & Ghildiyal Vipin, 2011).

According to Madhavi, finance is one of the critical inputs for growth and development of the MSMEs. They need credit support not only for running the enterprise and operational requirements but also for diversification, modernization/up gradation of facilities, capacity expansion, etc. Inadequate access to credit is a major problem facing micro, small and medium enterprises. Generally, such enterprises operate on tight budgets, often financed through owner's own contribution, loans from friends and relatives and some bank credit.

They are often unable to procure adequate financial resources for the purchase of machinery, equipment and raw materials as well as for meeting day-to-day expenses. This is because, on account of their low goodwill and little fixed investment, they find it difficult to borrow at reasonable interest rates. As a result, they have to depend largely on internal resources.

In respect of MSMEs, the problem of credit becomes all the more serious whenever any difficult situation occurs such as a large order, rejection of consignment, inordinate delay in payment, etc. Sometimes they have to close down their operations due to shortage of funds. Also, there is little or no scope for expansion and growth due to dearth of capital. Hence, economies of scale are not available. Recognizing the importance of easy and adequate availability of credit for ensuring sustainable growth of the MSME sector, the government has undertaken several measures. The need of the hour is to ensure that these measures benefit the segment they have been designed for (Lokhande A Madhavi, 2011).

This paper looks at an overview of financial inclusion globally and in Africa discusses the impact of ICT on reaching individuals who were otherwise financially excluded, mainly through mobile payments. Trend analysis shows a faster growth in mobile telephone subscription than financial inclusion through mobile financial services. This paper also discusses the opportunity costs of possible ICT both at microeconomics and macroeconomic level and concludes with possible recommendations for policy in leveraging ICT for increase financial inclusion (Lapukeni, A. F., 2015).

The aim of this study is to analyse the research advances made in the field of financial inclusion and the main lines of investigation currently being addressed by means of a bibliometric analysis. Among the scientific community, there is growing interest in this study area. The most assiduous in this respect are SA Asongu (the most productive author), Enterprise Development and Microfinance (the journal that has published the most articles in this field), Makerere University, Uganda (the most productive institution) and India (the country where most recent studies have taken place). Foreseeably inspiring future research, there is currently great interest in developing a more accessible financial system, especially through the use of digital money (Fintech) as an instrument to promote financial inclusion. For all this, a line of research is proposed that also includes the proposals from the 2030 Agenda for Sustainable Development and its 17 Sustainable Development Goals (Gálvez-Sánchez et al, 2013).

The importance of long-term financial inclusion in achieving energy efficiency is widely acknowledged. It is critical for an economy to obtain low-carbon energy sources. From 2004 to 2019, this study attempts to integrate financial inclusion as a primary defining feature of efficient energy, as well as the influence of economic growth, environmental-related technology, and the human capital index for RCEP countries. For co-integration reasons, the Westerlund error correction co-integration test is utilized, while the augmented mean group (AMG) approach is used for short-run and long-run analysis, and the dynamic ordinary least square (DOLS) test is used to confirm the model's robustness. Financial inclusion has a favorable impact on renewable energy efficiency and ensures low energy sources for RCEP countries, according to the findings. Furthermore, the importance of economic growth, environmental-related innovation, and human capital in achieving energy efficiency cannot be overstated. Furthermore, in the short-run, the Dumitrescu & Hurlin (Economic Modelling, 29(4), 1450–1460, 2012) panel heterogeneous non-causality test underscores causal bi-directional relationship among these variables) (Omar, M.A. & Inaba, K. 2020).

The role of sustainable financial inclusion is seen as central to achieving energy efficiency. This is very important to obtain low carbon energy sources for the economy. This study attempts to integrate economic inclusion as a key determinant of energy efficiency with the role of economic growth, environmental technologies and human capital index in RCEP countries from 2004 to 2019. The Westerlund error correction cointegration test is used for cointegration, while the AMG method is used for short- and long-term analysis, and the dynamic ordinary least squares (DOLS) test is used to ensure model robustness. The results show that financial inclusion has a positive effect on the efficiency of renewable energy and provides low energy sources for RCEP economies. In addition, the role of economic growth, environmental innovations and human capital are also important to achieve energy efficiency. In addition, in the short term, the panel heterogeneous non-causality test of Dumitrescu & Hurlin (2012) reveals a causal two-way relationship between these variables. Based on these observations, decision-makers ensure the improvement of the financial system and promote financial inclusion to increase energy efficiency and improve the standard of living of their citizens (Xiajing Dai et al, 2022).

This article provides a comprehensive review of recent evidence on financial inclusion from all regions of the world. It identifies emerging themes in the financial inclusion literature and some of the controversies surrounding financial inclusion in policy circles. In particular, I focus on some issues such as optimal financial inclusion, extreme financial inclusion, how financial inclusion can transfer systemic risk to the formal financial sector, and whether financial inclusion and exclusion are procyclical with changes in the business cycle. The main findings of this review show that financial inclusion affects and is affected by the level of financial innovation, poverty, financial stability, economic situation, financial literacy and regulatory framework, which varies from country to country. Finally, the questions addressed in this paper open several avenues for future research (Ozili et al. 2020).

According to UNCDF report, In the 2030 Sustainable Development Goals, financial inclusion is highlighted as a key enabler of other development goals, with targets in eight of the seventeen goals. SDG 1 is about ending poverty; SDG 2 is about ending hunger, achieving food security, and promoting sustainable agriculture; SDG 3 is about promoting health and well-being; SDG 5 is about gender equality and women's economic empowerment; SDG 8 is about promoting economic growth and jobs; SDG 9 is about supporting industry, innovation, and infrastructure; and SDG 10 is about reducing inequality. Furthermore, there is an implied role for increased financial inclusion in SDG 17 on improving the means of implementation, which can boost growth by increasing savings mobilization for investment and consumption.

Financial inclusion approaches have been shown in academic studies to help overall economic growth and the achievement of larger development goals. According to a recent analysis by the McKinsey Global Institute, digital finance alone could benefit billions of people by fostering inclusive growth that adds $3.7 trillion to emerging economies' GDP within a decade. According to the findings of a long-term impact study on Kenya's M-PESA mobile money service, mobile money has lifted as many as 194,000 households out of poverty, accounting for 2% of the country's population, and has been effective in improving the economic lives of poor women and members of female-headed households. Financial inclusion is also showing signs of making financial institutions and economies more stable, as well as mobilizing domestic resources.

CONCLUSION

Financial inclusion in India has made significant progress in recent years. Microfinance has emerged as a powerful tool for financial inclusion and women empowerment in India. By specifically targeting women as beneficiaries, microfinance institutions have contributed to the economic, social, and political empowerment of women. The availability of financial resources and services has unlocked women's potential as change-makers, leading to greater gender equality and inclusive development. Going forward, continued efforts to strengthen microfinance initiatives and address associated challenges will be critical in sustaining and amplifying the positive impact on women's lives and the overall growth of the nation.

Microfinance initiatives have contributed significantly to women's social empowerment by improving their decision-making abilities within the family and community. As women gain economic independence, they gain a stronger voice in household matters and community affairs. Additionally, microfinance interventions often include capacity-building programs, fostering financial literacy and leadership skills among women, thereby enhancing their social standing.

This paper provides a comprehensive review of the recent evidence on financial inclusion, microfinancing and women empowerment from all regions of the World. It identifies the emerging themes in the microfinancing as a tool of financial inclusion and driver of women empowerment literature as well as some challenges in policy circles regarding financial inclusion through microfinancing. In particular, I draw attention to some issues such as optimal financial inclusion, extreme financial inclusion, how financial inclusion can transmit systemic risk to the formal financial sector, and whether financial inclusion and exclusion are pro-cyclical with changes in the economic cycle. The key findings in this review indicate that microfinancial inclusion affects, and is influenced by, the level of financial innovation, poverty levels, the stability of the financial sector, the state of the economy, financial literacy, and regulatory frameworks which differ across countries. Finally, the issues discussed in this paper open up several avenues for future research.

REFERENCES

Arshad, A. (2023). Nexus between financial inclusion and women empowerment: Evidence from developing countries. *Gender in Management, 38*(4), 561–580. doi:10.1108/GM-04-2022-0125

Bouasria, M., Ashta, A., & Ratsimalahelo, Z. (2020). Bottlenecks to Financial Development, Financial Inclusion, and Microfinance: A Case Study of Mauritania. *Journal of Risk and Financial Management, 13*(10), 239. . doi:10.3390/jrfm13100239

Chandan Kumar Goyal. (2008). *Financial Inclusion in the North-eastern Region of India with Special Reference to Assam.* The ICFAI University Press.

Chandra, B. S. (2011). Growth through Financial inclusion in India. *Journal of International Business Ethics, 4*(1), 2011.

Chaudhary & Kumari. (2022). Impact of Financial Inclusion on Women Empowerment: A Case Study of Ranchi District. *International Journal for Research in Applied Science & Engineering Technology, 10*(8), 1388-1398. doi:10.22214/ijraset.2022.46423

Dai, X., Qian, S., & Zhang, J. (2022). *Sustainable financial inclusion as a source of green environment? Evidence from selected regional comprehensive economic partnership countries.* Economic Research-Ekonomska Istraživanja., doi:10.1080/1331677X.2022.2035244

Gálvez-Sánchez, F.J., Lara-Rubio, J., Verdú-Jóver, A.J., & Meseguer-Sánchez, V. (2013) Research Advances on Financial Inclusion: A Bibliometric Analysis. *Sustainability, 13*, 3156. doi:10.3390/su13063156

Haritha, M., & Prasad Reddy, A. (2023). *Microfinance, Financial Inclusion & Women Empowerment.* https://ssrn.com/abstract=4399783

Janmejaya, S., & Neeraj, A. (2011). *Financial Inclusion: From Obligation to Opportunity*. Boston Consulting Group Publications.

Kumar, S. (2022). *Financial Inclusion of Women: Current Evidence from India. ORF Issue Brief No. 600*. Observer Research Foundation.

Mabrouk, F., Bousrih, J., Elhaj, M., Binsuwadan, J., & Alofaysan, H. (2023). Empowering Women through Digital Financial Inclusion: Comparative Study before and after COVID-19. *Sustainability (Basel), 15*(12), 9154. doi:10.3390u15129154

Madhavi, A. L. (2011). Financial Inclusion: Options for Micro, Small and Medium Enterprises. Synergy, 9(2).

Maity, S. (2023). Financial inclusion also leads to social inclusion—Myth or reality? Evidences from self-help groups led microfinance of Assam. *Journal of Innovation and Entrepreneurship*, *12*(1), 42. doi:10.118613731-023-00307-x

McKinsey Global Institute Report. (2023). https://www.mckinsey.com/featured-insights/sustainable-inclusive-growth/future-of-america/financial-inclusion-and-sustainable-inclusive-growth-in-action

Nageswara Rao, N. D. S. V. (2010). Financial Inclusion –Banker's Perspective. Bank Quest, 81(4).

Omar, M. A., & Inaba, K. (2020). Does financial inclusion reduce poverty and income inequality in developing countries? A panel data analysis. *Journal of Economic Structures*, *9*(1), 37. doi:10.118640008-020-00214-4

Ozili, P. K. (2020). Financial Inclusion Research around the World: A Review. Advance online publication. doi:10.2139srn.3515515

Pal, M., Gupta, H., & Joshi, Y. C. (2022). Social and economic empowerment of women through financial inclusion: Empirical evidence from India. *Equality, Diversity and Inclusion*, *41*(2), 294–305. doi:10.1108/EDI-04-2021-0113

Pokhriyal, A. K., & Ghildiyal, V. (2011). Progress of Microfinance and Financial Inclusion: A Critical Analysis of SHG-Bank Linkage Program in India. *International Journal of Economics and Finance*, *3*(2). doi:10.5539/ijef.v3n2p255

Report of Expert Committee on Harnessing the India Post Network for Financial Inclusion. (2010, June 16). Department of Financial Services, Department of Economic Affairs, Department of Post and Invest India Economic Foundation (IIEF).

Sachin, J. (2011). Financial Inclusion: Involving the Uninvolved through Product, Channel and Marketing Innovations. Bank Quest, 82(2).

Sameer, K. (2009). Speeding Financial Inclusion. Academic Foundation in Association With Skoch Foundation.

Shanthi & Padmaja. (2022). Financial Inclusion and Women Empowerment in India-An Overview. *International Journal of Creative Research Thoughts, 10*(2), d30-d33.

The UNCDF Report. (2023). https://www.uncdf.org/financial-inclusion-and-the-sdgs

Chapter 6
Microcredit Applications in the Context of Empowering Women:
Case of Samsun Province, Turkey

Bilgenur Sahbazoglu
Ondokuz Mayıs University, Turkey

Işıl Alkan
Faculty of Economics and Administrative Sciences, Ondokuz Mayıs University, Turkey

ABSTRACT

Women, who can benefit less from the resources in the world and have less access to opportunities, are more likely to face the problem of poverty. This study aims to question the role and effectiveness of micro-credit practices in empowering women and increasing their participation in the workforce in the province of Samsun. The method of the research is the survey method. The universe of the research includes women using micro-credit within the scope of the Turkish Grameen Microcredit Program in Samsun. In this context, 104 women who were registered in the Micro Credit Branch Directorate in Samsun were included in the study. According to research findings, the majority of the participants participated in the workforce thanks to microcredit, the use of microcredit is an important tool in increasing the income level of the household, and the use of microcredit increased women's self-confidence; however, the amount of microcredit allocated is not sufficient to meet the needs.

INTRODUCTION

As many international statistics reveal, women benefit less from opportunities and resources in the world. This situation causes women to be impoverished, hence women's poverty becomes permanent. Therefore, empowering women and increasing their participation in the labour force is an important step to be taken against women's poverty. Microcredit practices are practices that pave the way for women's empowerment and aim to increase women's participation in the workforce. The main purpose of microcredit is to ensure the inclusion of poor women who are not in employment in the labour force and to support

DOI: 10.4018/978-1-6684-8979-6.ch006

relevant women in breaking the vicious circle of poverty. The foundation of microcredit practice was laid by economics professor Muhammed Yunus in Bangladesh initially. The microcredit application, which was implemented in the 1970s, had positive repercussions all over the world and determined the fate of millions of people. Microcredit applications, which started in Bangladesh, are applied not only in Bangladesh but also in many countries such as the USA, China, South Africa and France. Mentioned practices, which have become widespread in the world since the 1980s, started to be implemented in Turkey in the 2000s. Microcredit activities in Turkey have been implemented with the Grameen Bank Microcredit Program (TGMP) since 2003. It has been observed that related applications have become widespread rapidly in Turkey since the relevant date.

This study aims to question the role and effectiveness of microcredit practices in the empowerment of women and increasing their participation in the workforce specific to Samsun province in Turkey. For this purpose, female poverty was discussed and female labour force participation in Turkey was examined as a beginning. Afterwards, concepts of microcredit and microfinance are investigated, and the development of microcredit in the world and in Turkey is explained. The third and the fourth sections reveal the method, scope and limitations, research gap and findings related to the field research. The study ends with the conclusion part, where the findings are summarized, evaluations and recommendations regarding microcredit applications are developed.

1. FEMALE POVERTY AND FEMALE LABOUR FORCE PARTICIPATION IN TURKEY

Poverty is a multidimensional phenomenon with many different definitions in the literature. Gender has been ignored in various definitions of poverty, and the situation of women within the scope of combating poverty has been inadequately addressed in the relevant definitions. There is a difference between female poverty and male poverty as female poverty is an issue that needs different solutions. The segment where female poverty is most visible is the group in which the head of the household is female. Besides the female heads of household, other victim groups are those living in rural areas, asylum seekers or refugees, ethnic minority, disabled and elderly women (Alptekin, 2014, pp. 16-17).

Although there were significant increases in the female labour force participation rates towards the end of the 20th century, this period was also known as a period in which the economic situation of women compared to men gradually deteriorated. Diane Pearce first explained this process with the concept of "feminization of poverty" as women constitute two-thirds of the poor in America in 1978. The separation of home and work place as a result of the capitalist structure of production caused men's increasing presence in public sphere and women's increasing presence in private sphere, and this seperation brought the feminization of poverty (Ulutaş, 2009, pp.2-3).

Although the causes of women's poverty are diverse and vary from region to region in the world, they can be classified under certain categories. Gender inequality, lack of education, employment problems, household inequalities and social exclusion are the categories to be addressed. According to the United Nations' 2022 projections, women and girls are at greater risk of extreme poverty. According to the related organization, as of 2022, 372 million adult men and boys in the world are in the grip of extreme poverty, while 388 million women and girls are struggling with the related problem. More than three-quarters (about 84%) of the world's extremely poor women and girls live on two continents. These continents are Sub-Saharan Africa (63%) and Central and Southern Asia (21%) (UN, 2022). According to a report on poverty and gender, published by the United Nations in 2018, poverty is more valid for women in the world. According to the related report, while the male poverty rate is 12.3%, the female poverty rate is 12.8%. In addition, poverty is a phenomenon that includes mostly women living in rural areas, 20.2% of women living in urban areas and 79.8% of women living in rural areas are poor. Therefore, women living in rural areas are more disadvantaged all over the world concerning poverty (UN, 2018). Barriers to women's access to property in rural areas, the fact that they do not even have the right to own land in some countries, the limited land scale even when they own land, inequalities in access to the means of production, discriminatory practices in accessing both formal and agricultural education, and unpaid status of female labour impoverish women in rural areas (Alkan, 2018, pp. 47-53).

The rigidity of gender roles and the patriarchal system in Turkey are among the main causes of women's poverty. The fact that women are not considered equal to men causes women to have a secondary status in family life, business life and education process, and also causes them to be excluded from management and decision-making processes. Exclusion and secondary status cause women to become more impoverished and powerless than men. The inadequacy of women's participation in economic life in Turkey significantly exacerbates women's poverty. When the general characteristics of female employment in Turkey is investigated, it is seen that the participation in the labour force is low, women are left out of the labour market especially in cities and the wage levels of women who cannot benefit enough from education opportunities are quite low (Şener, 2009, p.7).

Female labour force participation in Turkey has been below the world average since the past. The regulations implemented since the establishment of the republic in Turkey aimed to strengthen the place of women in society and working life. With the republican era in Turkey, important steps have been taken to increase the status of women in society and working life. Since the 1980s, Turkey has chosen an export-based growth strategy that emphasizes the free market economy. In the process of adaptation to the free market, the field of activity of the public economy was narrowed and a large part of the public enterprises were transferred to the private sector by making privatizations. Implementation of export-based growth strategies and structural adjustment programs subsequent to 1980's brought important opportunities for the female workforce, as well as problems. For example; while female labour force participation and employment rates have increased in many countries within the process, the same increases have not been seen in Turkey (Toksöz, 2007, p.1).

Table 1 presents the development of female labour force participation and employment in Turkey since 1990. As can be seen, Turkey has not made any progress regarding the indicators. Some economic, social and cultural factors are among the reasons for this situation in Turkey. Initially, export-led growth policies adopted in Turkey since the 1980s did not create a positive effect on the employment creation capacity, and the rate of increase in the manufacturing industry declined considerably after 1989 (Onaran, 2003). On the other hand, the small scale of foreign capital investments in the country exhibited limited demand for female labor and the agricultural policies followed in the relevant period reduced the population working in agriculture. The primary goal in agriculture has been to increase productivity and competition, and in this context, supports given to products, subsidies given to farmers and price support practices have been abandoned. As a result of these practices, agricultural employment decreased and since non-agricultural employment was not at a level to compensate for the decrease, female employment rates declined. On the other hand, the patriarchal structure that dominates the society expected women to fulfill their responsibilities regarding the home first, caused the woman to be deprived of educational opportunities and prevented women from entering the working life (Toksöz, 2007, pp. 2-28).

Table 1. Main labour ındicators of females in Turkey

Years	Female Labour Force Participation Rate (%)	Female Employment Rate
1990	34.1	31.2
1995	30.9	28.7
2000	26.6	24.9
2005	23.3	20.7
2010	27.6	24
2015	28.8	25.6
2020	30.8	26.2
2021	32.8	28

Source: TUIK (2022a)

Informal work is one of the factors that impact on female labour force participation in Turkey and this type of work cause the labour force participation rate to be lower among women, especially in urban areas (Karabıyık, 2012, p.246). One of the reasons for the low female labour force participation rate in Turkey is urbanization. The labour force participation rate of women living in cities is lower than women living in rural areas. Migration from rural areas to cities affects the labour force participation rate, and the low level of education of women and the fact that they are considered as unskilled labour limit their employment in urban areas (Ata, 2006, p. 19). When female labour force participation rates are analyzed by considering marital status, it is seen that generally divorced women have high labour force participation rates. Generally, the inability of women to receive adequate alimony as a result of divorce puts women in economic distress. This problem is especially felt in cities where living costs are higher, and thıs situation increases the participation of divorced women in the workforce in cities (Özer&Biçerli, 2003, p.70). The inadequacy of public nurseries in Turkey and the expensiveness of private nurseries are other important factors that prevent women from entering working life. It is observed that women are forced to stay in the status of housewife because their wages are insufficient to cover the cost of childcare (Eyüboğlu et al., 2000, p.150).

2. THE DEVELOPMENT OF MICRO-CREDIT APPLICATIONS IN THE WORLD AND IN TURKEY

Although the terms “microcredit” and “microfinance” are often used interchangeably, there are fundamental differences between them. Microfinance refers to the sustainable provision of banking services to micro-entrepreneurs and low-income people who do not have access to financial services in general, it targets the poor or the extreme poor. Briefly, microfinance is banking for the poor. On the other hand, microcredit is one of the microfinance services and it is the most important one. The reason why these two concepts are so intertwined is that microfinance applications started with the provision of micro-credit service (Özmen, 2011, p.87).

There are various definitions of microfinance and microcredit, which emerged in 1974 to combat poverty. It is possible to summarize these definitions as follows:

Microfinance is the name given to financial services offered for small businesses and entrepreneurs who have difficulties in accessing banking and similar services. (TGMP, 2020)

Microfinance is the provision of loans, savings, insurance, transfer services and other financial services to low-income people. (Seymen, 2011, p. 50)

Microcredits are generally loans given by microfinance institutions to entrepreneurs who want to start their own business or to small businesses operating informally to purchase raw materials and materials and to meet their working capital needs. The reason why these loans are called micro is due to the fact that their amounts are much smaller than the loans given by banks and other financial institutions. (Ateş & Öğütoğulları, 2012, p. 35)

Microcredit is a type of traditional loan service that provides low amount loans to people who cannot guarantee loan repayment due to poverty-related reasons. Entrepreneurs who receive loans are called "micro-entrepreneurs". The reason for this is that the scope of the system and the amount of loans given are very modest figures. (Fidan & Yeşil, 2014, p. 255)

When the historical development of microcredit is examined, it is observed that this practice first emerged in the 1970s. The whole story began in the village of Cobra, near the University of Chittagong, Mohammed Yunus' own university. Yunus defined the village of Cobra as his university and the people of Cobra as his teachers. He sought a solution to the situation of women like Safiye Begüm, one of the poor people she met in this village. Safiye Begüm is a 21-year-old mother of 3 children who earns her living by making bamboo stools. She borrows the materials for the bamboo stools from the intermediary and sells the stools to the same broker and pays her debt. She earns only 2 cents from this business. Muhammad Yunus understood that people in this situation are facing a great deal of exploitation. (Yunus, 1997, pp.15-19). Muhammed Yunus thought that people in the position of Safiye Begüm would earn more income if their capital was sufficient to buy the material. Although poor people have various skills, they cannot use loans from commercial banks with suitable interest rates because they do not have collateral, and they have to borrow higher interest rates from intermediaries (Apaydın, 2015, p.36). Muhammed Yunus identified 42 people like Safiye Begüm with his students in the village of Cobra. These people stated that the capital required for the beginning was 27 dollars, and Yunus first loaned this amount to the villagers himself. Thus, in 1976, the microcredit application started in the village of Cobra. Providing much more advantageous loans than intermediaries and usurers and the increase in the incomes of the poor reveal the success of the microcredit application. With this loan, women have increased their income from 2 cents a day to $1.25 by selling their products. With this example, the importance of providing access to credit to people who do not have savings and sufficient capital for the beginning has been revealed (Kabakçı, 2012, p.101). With the institutionalization of this system, Muhammed Yunus aimed to help poor people in rural areas, get rid of moneylenders and make a living by their own means. He believed that this economic development would be on a regional scale (Şahin, 2015). For this purpose, the project was named "Grameen", which means "rural" or "village" in the local language. He opened the first branch of Grameen Bank in 1979. And the boundaries of the project have developed to include cities outside of Bangladesh (Akkul, 2011, p.42). When Grameen Bank was first opened, it continued its activities with 500 micro-entrepreneurs. Then, these microcredit activities, which started in a small village of Bangladesh, started to grow rapidly and while the applications were operating in different regions of the country, they managed to attract attention throughout the world (Şahin, 2015, p.1). The microcredit system implemented in the 1980s eliminated the idea that such practices, which financed the poor, would fail. The people who financed from these programs were mostly women and showed much better repayment performance than people who got loans from other commercial banks. With this performance, microfinance institutions were able to attract savings, commercial loans and investment capital. Thus, microfinance institutions have shown that the state and social aid institutions can survive without financial support (Özmen, 2011, p.92). As a result, while 42 people were given 27 dollars in 1976, 2.3 billion dollars were allocated to 2.3 million families in 1998. In the period from 1997 to 2005, it was aimed to reach 100 million families worldwide. Thus, with Grameen programs, access was provided to the whole world from Ecuador to Eritrea, from the Lotofen Islands in the Arctic Circle to Papua-New Guinea (Yunus, 1997, p.25).

The Asian continent, and especially Bangladesh, is in an important position as it hosts the beginning of the microcredit application. The microcredit system, which started to be implemented in Bangladesh in 1976, started to spread in the surrounding countries in a short time. In many Asian countries such as India, Nepal, Sri Lanka, Pakistan and Indonesia, few problems have been encountered in the implementation of Grameen-type loan schemes. Since four-fifths of the world's poor live in Asia, this program has played an important role in reducing poverty. The example given to the fact that no problem has been encountered in the implementation of microcredit in Asian countries is India. Even within the strict caste system in India, the Grameen Bank Micro Credit Program could find a place for itself (Yunus, 1997, pp. 227-228). Latin America is among the continents with the longest history in terms of sustainable service in microfinance. Competition among institutions providing microfinance services in Latin America is at a high level. Due to the extreme competition situation, interest rates in some countries have been significantly reduced. For example, interest rates in Bolivia, which were 50% in the 1990s, decreased to 20% in 2004 due to excessive competition between institutions (Gökyay, 2008, p.60). Although microfinance institutions in the African continent provide limited services, these institutions have high transaction costs when compared to other regions. A very small portion of the population in the African continent has a bank account, and even in South Africa, one of the most developed countries of the African continent, close to fifty percent of the population has a bank account. In French-speaking African countries, there are cooperative-type microfinance institutions that serve hundreds of thousands of people. In Portuguese and English-speaking African countries, microcredit institutions mostly formed by non-governmental organizations provide service besides microfinance institutions organized in cooperative type (Çolakoğlu, 2016, pp.57-58). In many European Union states, micro-credit programs are implemented in different ways and incentives are created with innovative approaches in order to provide the poor people with the qualifications to make and implement economic decisions (Sürücü&Bahar, 2015, p. 67).

Although the microcredit system, which has been actively used by the World Bank to reduce poverty since 1990, is considered a new practice in Turkey compared to other countries, its history is based on the Ottoman Empire as a system of thought. "Money Foundations" established during the Ottoman Empire is the foundation that forms the basis of today's micro-credit program. Foundations established like this have supported small tradesmen and entrepreneurs with their small-scale loans. In the Republican period, the cash needed by small tradesmen was met by institutions such as credit unions, cooperatives and trust funds (Serinikli, 2016, p.603). The Foundation for the Support of Women's Work (KEDV), which started its activities in Istanbul between 1995 and 1997 to support women's economic activities, established MAYA as a subsidiary of the foundation. MAYA Micro Economic Support Enterprise started to give loans to women in June 2002 as Turkey's first microfinance institution. Headquartered in Istanbul, MAYA started its work in Kocaeli, one of the provinces most affected by the 1999 earthquake. The first loan was given in Kocaeli in 2002 and then MAYA started its activities in Istanbul in 2003, Düzce in 2004 and Sakarya in 2005 (Baltacı, 2011, p.86). The operation of the MAYA program is as follows; MAYA officers identify the people in need of loans, and women in need can apply for loans with the promotions made by members who have used loans before. The women who decide to use the loan and the field staff fill out the application form after providing guidance on the process of obtaining the loan. The loan is approved between 4 and 7 days and 3 weeks after the approval of the loans, the field officers visit the borrowers and check whether the loan is used in accordance with its purpose. Loan repayments are made through banks and branches do not make cash transactions (Haspolat, 2010, p.116).

Turkey Grameen Microcredit Program (TGMP) officially started its activities in Turkey as a pilot application in the Southeastern Anatolia Region. On 11 June 2003 Prof. Dr. Muhammed Yunus and Prof. Dr. Aziz Akgül; on behalf of Muhammed Yunus and Turkish Waste Prevention Foundation (TİSVA), signed the Grameen microcredit model to be implemented in Turkey. This application, which started as a pilot project in Diyarbakır, was implemented with 130 million USD allocated by the Prime Ministry and 500 million USD given by the World Bank. The main purpose of the non-profit TGMP is to provide microcredit to entrepreneurs and especially women in line with the program to eradicate poverty. The target audience of TGMP is the female population trying to live below the poverty line in rural or urban areas. Those who want to take advantage of this loan should establish a group consisting of five women living in the same neighborhood or village (Aydın, 2012, pp.103-104). There are 37,907 micro-entrepreneurs in Turkey who received microcredit as of April 2022. TGMP has distributed a total of 1,301,634,942 TL micro loans in the country until 2022. TGMP currently continues its activities with 95 branches in 65 provinces with the funds obtained from public institutions and organizations, donors and bank loans (TGMP, 2022).

3. RESEARCH AREA AND RESEARCH METHOD

The research area is Samsun Province, which is the gateway of the Black Sea Region to Anatolia and makes a significant contribution to the regional economy. The economic life in Samsun has developed in the axis of agriculture, animal husbandry, industry and service sectors. In recent years, the energy sector has also been added to mentioned sectors. In 2020, 64.3% of the gross product is obtained from the service sector, 22.1% from the industrial sector and 13.6% from the agriculture sector (KTB, 2022). The population of Samsun province is 1,371,274 according to the results of the 2021 Address Based Population Registration System. There are 17 districts in total, including the center, in Samsun. The per capita gross domestic product value of Samsun province is below the Turkey average. While the per capita gross domestic product value in Turkey was 60,525 TL in 2020, it was 41,395 TL in Samsun (TUIK, 2022).

The method used in collecting the data regarding the research is the survey method. Survey is a research method that is used for both quantitative and qualitative measurements and analyzes and is conducted in oral and written form in order to obtain information from individuals about their attitudes and thoughts on certain issues (Arıkan, 2018, p. 98).

The questionnaire prepared for this research consists three parts that are mainly based on closed-ended questions. The survey was conducted in Ilkadım, Atakum, Bafra and Tekkeköy districts of Samsun province.

3.1. Sample Selection, Scope, and Limitations

The universe of the research includes women using micro-credit within the scope of the Turkish Grameen Microcredit Program in Samsun. The total number of participants registered in Samsun Micro Credit Branch Directorate is 400 as of October 2020. The surveys were carried out by the researcher in the company of Micro Credit Branch officers during a 5-month period covering the period of May-September 2021. The researcher attended the central meetings organized by the Branch for micro-credit users and completed the surveys by conducting face-to-face interviews. The permission was obtained from the Ondokuz Mayıs University Ethics Committee for the survey.

In the study, the following formula was used to reveal the size of the sample size (Akbulut &Yılız, 1999, p. 8).

$$n=\frac{NPQZ^2}{(N-1)d^2+NPQZ^2}$$

In the formula; n refers to sample mass size, N refers to population size (number of micro-credit customers registered in Samsun Microcredit Branch Directorate), P refers to the probability of using the microcredit, Q refers to probability of not using microcredit (1-P), Z refers to Z test value at level of % (1-α), α refers to significance and d refers to the margin of error (tolerance).

The minimum sample size to represent the population in the study is as follows;

n =[400*0.5*0.5*1.96*1.96] / [(400-1)*0.05*0.05*1.96*1.96] =100.30

The sample number determined based on the formula above is 100 people. However, 104 people participated in the survey with the help of Samsun Microcredit Branch officers during the survey process. Simple random sampling model was used in the population-sample selection in the study. "Simple random sampling models are defined as a research made to the whole of the universe or to a group to be taken from it in order to reach a general judgment about the universe" (Kılıç, 2013, p.45).

The questionnaire form consists three parts. In the first part, questions about the demographic characteristics of the participants, in the second part, questions about the economic characteristics of the participants, and in the third part questions about the microcredit usage process take place. The data obtained in the research were analyzed with the SPSS (Statistical Program for Social Sciences) program.

The study is important in terms of determining the situation of microcredit application in Samsun, the effect of microcredit on women's employment and women's empowerment, and revealing how effectively the application is carried out. The main questions/statements of the research can be listed as follows;

Q1: Microcredit is an effective tool to increase female labor force participation.
Q2: The use of microcredit is directly proportional to the increase in the income level of the household.
Q3: There has been a positive change in the social lives of women who have received microcredit.
  Q3a: The socialization opportunities of women using microcredit have improved.
  Q3b: Women using microcredit had greater gender equality.

Q3c: Women using microcredit are more courageous about entrepreneurship.
Q3d: Participation of women using microcredit in decision-making processes in the household has increased.
Q4: The self-confidence of women using microcredit has increased.
Q5: Women using microcredit provided employment opportunities to other women.
Q6: Microcredit was sufficient to meet the needs.
Q7: There is a semantic relationship between being successful in the business established with micro-credit and those who want to get microcredit again.
Q8: There is a semantic relationship between being successful in a microcredit business and having more gender equality after using micro-credit.
Q9: There is a semantic relationship between the status of being successful in the business established with microcredit and the educational status.

3.2 Research Gap

Samsun, one of Turkey's leading metropolitan cities, is a city where economic activities are quite intense. However, women, who make up almost half of the provincial population, cannot take part in these economic activities as much as they should and are struggling with the problem of poverty. Poverty and women's difficulties in inclusion in the labor market are important obstacles to the development of both the Province and the region. Micro-credit applications, which are seen as an important tool in reducing poverty and empowering women in the world, are also implemented in Samsun within the framework of Turkey Grameen Micro Credit Program. However, no study has been found in the literature examining the effects of related practices on women's empowerment and increasing employment in Samsun Province. This study will contribute to the development of the province and the region, as it will both fill the relevant gap in the literature and develop policies that will support the empowerment process of women, and thus, will reveal findings that may pave the way for increasing the welfare of the province and the region.

4. FINDINGS

In this section, the findings on the demographic and economic characteristics of the participants and the findings on the microcredit usage process are explained.

4.1 Findings Regarding the Demographic Characteristics of the Participants

The women who use microcredit utmost in the research area are between the ages of 42-49. The age group that uses microcredit the least is the age group of 18-25 (Table 2). When the distribution of the participants according to marital status was examined, it was determined that the women who were surveyed in the research area were mostly married. The rate of those who are married is 60.6%, who are single is 23.1% and who are divorced is 16.3%.

Table 2. Distribution of participants by age

		Frequency	Ratio (%)
Age	18-25	9	8.7
	26-33	20	19.2
	34-41	25	24.0
	42-49	36	34.6
	50 +	14	13.5
	Total	104	100

When the distribution of the participants according to their education level is analyzed, it was determined that the rate of primary school graduates is 39.4%, the rate of high school graduates is 45.2%, and the rate of associate/undergraduate graduates is 15.4%. The rate of microcredit utilization is very low among undergraduates with the highest level of education. Microcredit is mostly used by women with insufficient education level. In case of the distribution of the spouses of the participants according to their occupations, it was detected that the highest rate belonged to the women whose spouses were workers. This group is followed by those whose spouses are craftsmen (Table 3).

Table 3. Distribution of participants by the profession of spouse

		Frequency	Ratio (%)
Profession of spouse	Worker	26	41.9
	Craftsmen	14	22.6
	Farmer	5	8.1
	Retired	5	8.1
	Civil servant	3	4.8
	Other	9	14.5
	Total	62	100

4.2 Findings Regarding Participants' Economic Characteristics and Microcredit Use

In the research area, it has been determined that the monthly income of the families is mostly between 3500-4500 TL (Table 4). Those whose monthly income is between 2500-3500 TL are the second group that uses microcredit the most.

When the residence status of the participants in the house they live in is examined; it is revealed that the rate of those who live in their own house is 51% and the rate of those who live in rent is 45%. The rate of those living free of charge in a house belonging to their relatives is 3.8%.

Table 4. Distribution of participants by total monthly income before using micro credit

		Frequency	Ratio (%)
What is your family's total monthly income before using a microcredit?	0-1500 TL	1	1
	1500-2500 TL	13	12.5
	2500-3500 TL	30	28.8
	3500-4500 TL	35	33.7
	More than 4500 TL	25	24
	Total	104	100

In the research area, it was observed that 56.7% of the participants had social security and 43.3% did not before using micro credit. When the number of people living in the house where the participants live is searched, it has been determined that mainly 4 people live in the house. When the number of people working in the family of the women subjected to the research is examined, it has been determined that the rate of one person working in the family is 40.4%, the rate of two people working in the family is 49%, the rate of three people working in the family is 4.8%, and the rate of four or more people working in the family is 5.8%. Data presented in Table 5 show that, when the total monthly income distribution of the participants' families after using microcredit is examined, the group with the highest share is those with an income of more than 4500 TL. This group is followed by those with an income of 3500-4500 TL.

Table 5. Distribution of participants by total monthly income after using microcredit

		Frequency	Ratio (%)
What is your family's total monthly income after using microcredit?	1500-2500 TL	2	1.9
	2500 3500 TL	14	13.5
	3500-4500 TL	31	29.8
	More than 4500 TL	57	54.8
	Total	104	100

When Table 4 and 5 are examined together, it is found that the use of microcredit increases the monthly income of the participants. In the research area, the participants determined that 55% of them had employed before the micro-credit use and 45% did not. Handicrafts, preparing and selling home-cooking, craft activities, seasonal agricultural work, babysitting and daily domestic work were among the facilities performed by women before the use of microcredit. When the time period in which micro-credit was used for the first time was examined, it was revealed that micro-credit was overwhelmingly used in 2019 predominantly between the years 2009 and 2021. The significant decrease in this rate in 2021 compared to 2020 can be attributed to the negative economic impact of Covid-19 (Table 6).

Table 6. Distribution of participants according to their first microcredit usage year

		Frequency	Ratio (%)
When did you get the first micro credit? (Year)	2009	1	1
	2011	4	3.8
	2013	4	3.8
	2014	1	1
	2015	9	8.7
	2016	7	6.7
	2017	13	12.5
	2018	19	18.3
	2019	23	22.1
	2020	16	15.4
	2021	7	6.7
	Total	104	100

In the research area, concerning the microcredit usage frequency of the participants, it is determined that the rate of participants who use microcredit once is 17.3%, the rate of those who use it 2-3 times is 43.3%, the rate of those who take it 4-5 times is 17.3%, and the rate of those who take 6 times or more is 22.1%. It is observed that works that require manual labor such as needlework, knitting, sewing-embroidery, dowry products were placed on the top regarding the distribution of work done with the micro-credit (Table 7).

Table 7. Distribution of work done with microcredit

		Frequency	Ratio (%)
What type of work did you do with microcredit?	Production and sale of agricultural products such as jams, dairy products, local flavors	11	10.6
	Production and sale of products that require manual labor such as needlework, knitting, sewing-embroidery, dowry products	34	32.7
	Service-oriented jobs such as restaurant and cafe management	7	6.7
	Contributing to my spouse's existing business	8	7.7
	Catalog product sales, trade	34	32.7
	Other	10	9.6
	Total	104	100

When the distribution of success in the business established with microcredit is examined, it is determined that the rate of successful people is 96.2% and the rate of unsuccessful ones is 3.8%. The rate of self-employed is 70.2%, the rate of those who work with their spouses is 9.6%, the employment rate of the spouses is 2.9%, and the rate of those who employ workers is 17.3% in the businesses using microcredit. When the situation of creating additional employment other than the person using the micro credit is examined, it is determined that the users of microcredits provide employment to 1-2 people at most. When the distribution of the work to be done in the absence of microcredit support is examined, it is determined that the rate of those who will not work is 32.7%, which indicates an important result. In other words, it has come to light that one third of the women surveyed would not have the opportunity to work if microcredit was not used.

Table 8. Distribution of the participants according to the work they would have done if they had not received micro-credit

		n	%
What would you be doing now if you had not received the microcredit support?	I would not work	34	32.7
	I would try to develop my business with supports such as bank loans	8	7.7
	I would look for a job	16	15.4
	I would use various government grants	6	5.8
	I would continue at my (old) job	31	29.8
	Others	9	8.7
	Total	104	100

In the research area, 84% of the participants stated that their economic situation improved and 89% of the participants stated that their control over their spending increased after using microcredit. Moreover, 84% of the participants emphasized that they became more social, and 87% of them emphasized that their positive image around them increased after using microcredit. Furthermore, 95% of the participants emphasized that they tried to encourage the women in their environment about entrepreneurship after using microcredit. In the research area, 71% of the participants indicated that their positive expectations for the future increased and 90% of the participants remarked that their decision-making potential in both private and business life increased subsequent to the micro-credit use. On the other hand, 91% of the participants emphasized that they were disposed to use microcredit again and 77% of respondents mentioned that they gained gender equality after using micro-credit.

The findings of the study emphasize that microcredit practices greatly empower women, activate them in decision-making processes and socialize them. Previous research on the subject also supports the findings (Debnath et al., 2019; Shafique & Siddique, 2020; Aruna & Jyothirmayi, 2011; Swain & Wallentin, 2009; Niaz & Iqbal, 2019; Al-Shami et al., 2016).

5. CONCLUSION

Microcredit applications, which emerged under the leadership of Muhammed Yunus in Bangladesh in the world, are significant applications that pave the way empowering women and increasing women's participation in the workforce. With this study, it has been tried to determine the effectiveness of micro credit, which is one of the important tools in empowering women and increasing female labour force participation, specific to Samsun Province in Turkey. The method of the research is survey. Simple random sampling model was used in the population-sample selection and 104 women was surveyed. According to the findings obtained as a result of the survey, the Q1 question or statement was partially accepted. The rate of those who answered "I would not work" to the question "What would you be doing now if you had not received the microcredit support" was 32.7%, while the rate of those who answered "I was going to look for a job" is 15.4%. As it can be understood from this, the majority of the participants would not have been able to participate in the labor force if they had not taken microcredit. Question Q2 was as "Micro-credit usage and increase in household income level are directly proportional" and was accepted. Question S3 was "There has been a positive change in the social lives of women who have received micro-credit" and was accepted. Question Q4 is "Women using microcredit have increased their confidence in themselves and the future" and was partially accepted. During the survey women stated that their self-confidence increased after using microcredit, but they mentioned that they were not satisfied with the current economic situation and that they had concerns about the future. Question Q5 was "Women using microcredits provided employment opportunities to other women" and was partially accepted. When asked to those who create employment with microcredit, the question of "how many people have you employed" was answered by at most 1 person and then 2 people. Question Q6 is "Microcredit was sufficient to meet the needs". While 58 of the 104 participants answered "Yes" to this question, the number of those who answered "No" was 46. It is revealed that nearly half of the participants consider that microcredit is insufficient to meet their needs and they think that the amount of loans given should be increased more. Question Q7 is as follows: "There is a semantic relationship between being successful in the business established with microcredit and those who want to get microcredit again", and a semantic relationship could not be found as a result of the chi-square test. Both the successful and unsuccessful ones in the business they have established have stated that they want to get microcredit again. Question Q8 was as follows: "There is a semantic relationship between being successful in the business established with microcredit and having more gender equality after using microcredit" and was rejected. Although the number of unsuccessful ones is few, the participants think that they have more gender equality in the process they use microcredit. Question S9 was as follows: "There is a semantic relationship between being successful in the business established with micro-credit and educational status" and this question was also rejected. The reason why a semantic relationship could not be found in this test may be that the micro-credit application in Samsun is not fully known and that the loan amount is quite low, so it is insufficient for large-scale investments.

In Turkey, microcredit should be accepted as an active policy for the labour market and the support provided by the state for microcredit should be increased. Thus, it should be ensured that loans given to women in low amounts should be increased. In order to use microcredit more effectively, vocational and technical trainings for women should be expanded and women's education should be supported. It is very important for municipalities to play an active role in this area in increasing women's employment. Municipalities should support microcredits allocated to women, direct women using microcredits to the fields with high employment potential, and support women with various trainings. Social awareness should be created for the microcredit applications to reach more people. Practices such as giving sales/marketing guarantees to women using micro credit are important in ensuring the continuity of employment.

REFERENCES

Akbulut, Ö., & Yılız, N. (1999). *İstatistik analizlerde temel formüller ve tablolar*. Aktif Yayınevi.

Akkul, R. (2011). *Cinsiyetler arası gelir eşitsizliğini gidermede mikro kredi uygulamalarının etkinliği: Bilecik örneği* [Yüksek Lisans Tezi]. Bilecik Üniversitesi Sosyal Bilimler Enstitüsü.

Al-Shami, S. S. A., Razali, M. M., Majid, I., Rozelan, A., & Rashid, N. (2016). The effect of microfinance on women's empowerment: Evidence from Malaysia. *Asian Journal of Women's Studies, 22*(3), 318–337. doi:10.1080/12259276.2016.1205378

Alkan, I. (2018). Tarım sektöründe kadın emeği (Çarşamba Ovası Gündoğdu ve Damlataş köylerinde fındık, çeltik ve sebze üretimi özelinde bir irdeleme). Gazi Kitabevi.

Alptekin, D. (2014). Toplumsal cinsiyet eşitsizliği örüntüsünde kadının yoksulluğu ve yoksunlukları. In Yoksulluk ve Kadın içinde. Ayrıntı Yayınları.

Apaydın, S. (2015). *Yoksullukla mücadelede mikro kredi: Muş ili örneği [Yüksek Lisans Tezi]*. Dumlupınar Üniversitesi Sosyal Bilimler Enstitüsü.

Arıkan, R. (2018). Anket yöntemi üzerinde bir değerlendirme. *Haliç Üniversitesi Sosyal Bilimler Dergisi, 1*(1), 97-159.

Aruna, M., & Jyothirmayi, R. (2011). The role of microfinance in women empowerment: A study on the SHG Bank linkage program in Hyderabad (Andhra Pradesh). *Indian Journal of Commerce and Management Studies, 2*(4), 78–95.

Ata, N. (2006). Türkiye'de kadınların işgücüne katılma oranı hakkında bir not. *İşveren Dergisi, 44*(4), 19.

Ateş, G. & Öğütoğulları, E. (2012). Türkiye'de yoksullukla mücadelede mikrokredi uygulamaları. *Trakya Üniversitesi Sosyal Bilimler Dergisi, 14*(2), 33-53.

Aydın, B. (2012). *Yoksullukla mücadelede mikro kredinin Türkiye uygulamasının ekonomik açıdan değerlendirilmesi [Yüksek Lisans Tezi]*. Marmara Üniversitesi Sosyal Bilimler Enstitüsü.

Baltacı, N. (2011). *Kadınları güçlendirme mekanizması olarak mikrokredi [Uzmanlık Tezi]*. T.C Başbakanlık Kadının Statüsü Genel Müdürlüğü.

Çolakoğlu, C. (2016). *Yapabilirlikten yoksulluk bağlamında mikro kredi uygulaması: Grameen Bankası Sakarya ili örneği* [Yüksek Lisans Tezi]. Sakarya Üniversitesi Sosyal Bilimler Enstitüsü.

Debnath, D., Rahman, M. S., Acharjee, D. C., Latif, W. U., & Wang, L. (2019). Empowering women through microcredit in Bangladesh: An empirical study. *International Journal of Financial Studies, 7*(3), 37. doi:10.3390/ijfs7030037

Eyüboğlu, A., Özer, Ş., & Tanrıöver, T. (2000). Kentlerde kadınların iş yaşamına katılım sorunlarının sosyo-ekonomik ve kültürel boyutları. Başbakanlık K.S.S.G.M. Yayınları.

Fidan, F. & Yeşil, Y. (2014). Türkiye'de kadınların ekonomiye kazandırılması açısından mikro kredi: Bilecik örneği. *Girişimcilik ve Kalkınma Dergisi, 9*(2), 253-270.

Gökyay, Ç. (2008). *Türkiye'de mikro kredi uygulamaları ve istihdama yansımaları [Uzmanlık Tezi]*. Çalışma ve Sosyal Güvenlik Bakanlığı Türkiye İş Kurumu Genel Müdürlüğü.

Haspolat, E. (2010). *Neoliberalizmin kalkınma söylemi ve yoksullukla mücadele yöntemi olarak mikro kredi: Örnek ülke deneyimleri ve Türkiye [Yüksek Lisans Tezi].* Gazi Üniversitesi Sosyal Bilimler Enstitüsü.

Kabakçı, E. (2012). *Mikro kredinin kadın yoksulluğunu azaltmadaki rolü ve Eskişehir uygulaması [Yüksek Lisans Tezi].* Anadolu Üniversitesi Sosyal Bilimler Enstitüsü.

Karabıyık, İ. (2012). Türkiye'de çalışma hayatında kadın istihdamı. *Marmara Üniversitesi İİBF Dergisi, 32,* 231-260.

Kılıç, S. (2013). Örnekleme yöntemleri. *Journal of Mood Disorders, 3*(1), 44–60. doi:10.5455/jmood.20130325011730

KTB. (2022). *Samsun İl Kültür ve Turizm Müdürlüğü.* https://samsun.ktb.gov.tr/TR-59811/ekonomi---sanayi---ticaret.html

NiazM. U.IqbalM. (2019). *Effect of microfinance on women empowerment: A case study of Pakistan.* doi:10.2139/ssrn.3419834

Onaran, Ö. (2003). *Türkiye'de ihracat yönelimli büyüme politikalarının istihdam üzerindeki etkileri. In İktisadi kalkınma, kriz ve istikrar içinde.* İletişim Yayınları.

Özer, M. & Biçerli, K. (2003). Türkiye'de kadın işgücünün panel veri analizi. *Anadolu Üniversitesi Sosyal Bilimler Dergisi, 3*(1), 55-86.

Özmen, F. (2011). *Türkiye'de Kadın İşgücü İstihdamının Gelişiminde Mikro Kredi Uygulamaları [Doktora Tezi].* Celal Bayar Üniversitesi Sosyal Bilimler Enstitüsü.

Şahin, H. (2015). *Yoksullukla mücadelede mikrokredi yöntemi.* Available in: https://www.academia.edu/38149397/Yoksullukla_Mu_cadelede_Mikrokredi_Yo_ntemi

Şener, Ü. (2009). Kadın yoksulluğu. TEPAV (Türkiye Ekonomi Politikaları Araştırma Vakfı).

Serinikli, N. (2016). The importance of entrepreneurship in preventing the woman poverty: Woman cooperatives and micro-credit applications. *BJSS Balkan Journal of Social Sciences*, 598–609.

Seymen, S. (2011). *İl Özel İdaresi ve mikro kredi uygulamaları Kocaeli İl Özel İdaresi örneği* [Yüksek Lisans Tezi]. Kocaeli Üniversitesi Sosyal Bilimler Enstitüsü.

Shafique, O. & Siddique, N. (2020). The impact of microcredit financing on poverty alleviatıon and women empowerment: An empirical study on Akhuwat Islamıc microfinance. *PalArch's Journal of Archaeology of Egypt / Egyptology, 17*(8), 548-562.

Sürücü Bahar, H. (2015). *Yoksullukla mücadelede mikro kredi uygulamaları (Konya İli örneği) [Yüksek Lisans Tezi].* Selçuk Üniversitesi Sosyal Bilimler Enstitüsü.

Swain, R. B., & Wallentin, F. Y. (2009). Does microfinance empower women? Evidence from self-help groups in India. *International Review of Applied Economics, 23*(5), 541–556. doi:10.1080/02692170903007540

TGMP. (2022). *Türkiye Grameen mikrofinans programı.* Available in: https://prezi.com/view/ApSSyoPAShK6RXBMhDOG/

Toksöz, G. (2007). *Türkiye'de kadın istihdamının durumu.* Uluslararası Çalışma Örgütü.

TÜİK. (2022a). *Türkiye İstatistik Kurumu verileri*. https://data.tuik.gov.tr/Kategori/GetKategori?p=istihdam-issizlik-ve-ucret-108&dil=1

TÜİK. (2022b). *Türkiye İstatistik Kurumu verileri*. https://data.tuik.gov.tr/Kategori/GetKategori?p=Ulusal-Hesaplar-113

Ulutaş, Ç. Ü. (2009). Yoksulluğun Kadınlaşması ve Görünmeyen Emek. *Çalışma ve Toplum, 2,* 25-40.

UN. (2018). *Gender differences in poverty and household composition through the life cycle*. Available in: https://www.unwomen.org/sites/default/files/Headquarters/Attachments/Sections/Library/Publications/2018/SDG-report-Spotlight-01-Gender-differences-in-poverty-and-household-composition-en.pdf

UN. (2022). *UN Women*. Available in: https://data.unwomen.org/features/poverty-deepens-women-and-girls-according-latest-projections#:~:text=New%20projections%20of%20global%20poverty,372%20million%20men%20and%20boys)

Yunus, M. (1997). *Yoksulluğun bulunmadığı bir dünyaya doğru*. Doğan Kitapçılık.

ENDNOTES

1. This manuscript is the brief summary of M.S. Thesis of Bilgenur Şahbazoğlu (Microcredit Applications in Context of Empowering and Increasing The Labour Force Participation of Women: Case of Samsun Province) which has been accepted by Ondokuz Mayıs University Postgraduate Education Institute/Turkey as of September 2022.
2. Graduate student, Ondokuz Mayıs University, FEAS Economics Department, blgeshbz123@gmail.com, phone:0362-3121919-6017, ORCID:0000-0001-8778-4351.
3. Associate Professor (Corresponding Author), Ondokuz Mayıs University, FEAS Economics Department, isilalkan@omu.edu.tr, phone:0362-3121919-6017, ORCID: 0000-0002-1437-1967.

Chapter 7
Microfinance Schemes for Women Entrepreneurship in India:
A Case Study of Sikkim State

Sunil Kumar
https://orcid.org/0000-0002-2362-1972
Lovely Professional University, India

Soni Subedi
Lovely Professional University, India

ABSTRACT

In today's globalized world, women are recognizing in the field of entrepreneurship. This study is on five central government finance schemes—Deendayal Antyodaya Yojana-National Urban Livelihoods Mission (DAY-NULM), Pradhan Mantri Employment Generation Programme (PMEGP), Dairy Entrepreneurship Development Scheme (DEDS), North East Industrial and Investment Promotion Policy (NEIIPP), and Scheme of Fund for Regeneration of Traditional Industries (SFURTI)—applicable in the state of Sikkim. The aim of the chapter is to analyze the year wise growth of women beneficiaries. The data has been collected from government websites, journals, and through 'Right to Information Act 2005'. The study is descriptive in nature. Microsoft excel has been used for data visualization. The results of study showed a significant gender gap in the implementation of schemes, which need to be addressed through awareness and networking at ground level. The deeper penetration of financial schemes will result in more entrepreneurship ventures run and managed by females.

DOI: 10.4018/978-1-6684-8979-6.ch007

INTRODUCTION

Gender-focused entrepreneurship research started in the late 1970s. Recently, the scope has expanded to include female entrepreneurs in emerging economies and immigrant women in developed nations (De Vita *et al.*, 2014). Women entrepreneurship refers to any business or organization founded by a woman or a group of women. Women entrepreneurs represent those women who lead in initiating, organizing, and establishing a business. According to the Government of India, women entrepreneurs are defined as individuals who own and control an enterprise, with a minimum financial interest of 51 percent of the capital, and who ensure that at least 51 percent of the employment opportunities generated within the enterprise are offered to women (Rashmi, 2016). As observed by Paul Dana (2001), entrepreneurship holds substantial economic advantages. However, its teachability hinges on how one defines it. At the same time, certain aspects of entrepreneurship can be acquired through learning.

In a developing economy where financial growth is crucial, women entrepreneurs emerge as significant contributors. In a patriarchal society, surviving and succeeding in the competitive business landscape has always been a significant challenge for enterprising women. The deep-seated notion within society that only specific communities are entrepreneurial has been proven wrong. Today, one can observe women from all communities flourishing in various sectors, reaching top-level positions in their businesses. The current scenario and the perception of women have undergone a complete transformation.

Several factors influence women entrepreneurs, and one major influencer is the Government. Providing suitable support from society, family, and the Government to potential women entrepreneurs can significantly enhance the country's economic system (Geetha, 2019). Regularly updating the technological equipment used by women entrepreneurs can, in turn, lead to countless successes (Junare & Singh, 2016). In today's globalized world, women in entrepreneurship are gaining importance due to various government programs, schemes, benefits, policies, and training initiatives. The Central and State Governments offer numerous incentives and schemes designed to support potential and existing entrepreneurs. Recognizing the role of women in economic development can significantly increase through initiatives like startup and stand-up India (Manshani & Dubey, 2017). Government-sponsored development activities and skills training have empowered women entrepreneurs for their new ventures (Agarwal & Lenka, 2016).

Industrial development in Sikkim, particularly in Micro, Small, and Medium Enterprise development, has gained momentum since Sikkim became a tourist destination in the country. The Sikkim government is also dedicated to providing skills to its youth, enabling more individuals to become self-employed and create job opportunities.

GOVERNMENT SCHEMES/INSTITUTIONS IN VARIOUS COUNTRIES FOR WOMEN'S ENTREPRENEURSHIP

Tambunan (2009) discusses women's entrepreneurship in Asian developing countries, focusing on SMEs. While SMEs are crucial in the region, women entrepreneurs face obstacles like education and capital. Many become entrepreneurs out of necessity to improve family income. Increasing women's education and job opportunities may reduce their engagement in SME entrepreneurship. This paper explores the untapped potential of women's entrepreneurship in South Asia, where less than 10% of entrepreneurs are women. It reviews their profiles, challenges, and support initiatives by organizations, focusing on

SMEs. Notably, Wellalage and Locke (2017) found that in South Asia, female-owned SMEs are 3% less likely to face credit constraints than male-owned ones, revealing capital market imperfections in emerging economies. During the COVID-19 pandemic, women entrepreneurs in Asia and Europe focused on financial resources for economic sustainability (Sorensson & Ghannad, 2023).

Various institutions and Government-backed microfinance schemes for women entrepreneurship are launched worldwide. The purpose of all such institutions and schemes is to increase the financial inclusion and financial empowerment of women and their groups formally and systematically. Table 1 shows the details of these institutions/schemes.

Table 1. Government-backed microfinance schemes

Country	Institution/Scheme	Major Outcome(s)
Bangladesh	Grameen Bank	It offers microcredit to empower rural women entrepreneurs. It enables them to start businesses like farming, handicrafts, and trading.
	Bangladesh Rural Advancement Committee (BRAC)	BRAC provides microfinance to women entrepreneurs, focusing on skill development and capacity building. Their program offers training, credit access, and support for small business growth.
Philippines	ASA	ASA offers financial products like loans for income generation, housing, and education. Their strategy targets poverty reduction and empowerment through financial services.
	The Small Business Corporation (SBC)	SBC runs a low-interest loan initiative for microenterprises and small businesses.
Colombia	Fundación WWB Colombia	It provides microloans and financial education to aid women in business ventures. The focus is on social impact and empowering women economically.
Kenya	Jamii Bora Bank	It offers microfinance to women-owned small businesses with credit access, savings, and financial literacy training. The bank's initiatives foster economic growth and social development.
	Youth Enterprise Development Fund (YEDF)	The objective is to encourage entrepreneurship among youth, generate job prospects, and boost economic growth.
Malawi	MicroLoan Foundation	Operating in Africa, including Malawi, the foundation offers microfinance to women entrepreneurs, featuring small loans and training in finance, business skills, and agriculture.
Nigeria	The Small and Medium Enterprises Development Agency (SMEDAN)	The primary focus is to offer financial access, training, and capacity building to micro, small, and medium-sized enterprises (MSMEs) in diverse sectors.
Mauritius	The Self-Employment Programme (SEP)	It provides aid to unemployed individuals for launching micro and small businesses, aiming to lower unemployment and foster youth entrepreneurship.
Turkey	Women's Entrepreneurship Development Program (WEDP)	WEDP in Turkey aids women entrepreneurs with financial and non-financial incentives, providing grants, loans, and training to boost their involvement in economic activities.
Ghana	National Entrepreneurship and Innovation Plan (NEIP)	NEIP in Ghana is a government initiative providing financial aid, training, and capacity-building for young entrepreneurs to launch and expand businesses.
Pakistan	The Small and Medium Enterprises Development Agency (SMEDA)	SMEDA offers microfinance and support programs for small and medium-sized enterprises.

Source: Compiled by the author(s)

Across countries, microfinance institutions and government initiatives support women's entrepreneurship. Grameen Bank empowers rural women in Bangladesh, while SEWA Bank targets informal women workers. BRAC focuses on skill development, and ASA in the Philippines offers diverse financial products. Fundación WWB Colombia aids low-income women, and initiatives like NEIP in Ghana and WEDP in Turkey foster economic growth and gender equality.

WOMEN'S ENTREPRENEURSHIP IN INDIA: GOVERNMENT INITIATIVES AND IMPACT

In India, women entrepreneurship is much less prevalent in the formal sector. However, the Government of India have recognized the importance of encouraging women entrepreneurship, as a result of which multiple schemes have been launched across sectors to fulfil the dreams of aspiring women entrepreneurs and involve them in the workforce to support them with a stable income, thereby leading to the development of the economy of the country (Yadav & Unni, 2016). The Central and State Government has introduced several new schemes, programs and policies to empower women in both rural and urban areas (Rajalakshmi & Selvam, 2017). Barman and Saloi (2021) stated that it has become a major area of concern, and the Government needs to emphasize working towards alleviating urban poverty.

The Government of India (GOI) recognized that more enterprises offer better opportunities to the rural poor, especially the women, when there is a lack of availability of a conventional opportunity. The challenges faced by women in entrepreneurship are abundant. The majority of women cannot start their own venture due to a lack of access to both funds and skills (Jindal & Bhardwaj, 2016). Launching of various schemes by the Government has comforted the distressed women. Thakur et al. (2021) stated that DAY-NULM's programs helped in increasing the presence of women entrepreneurs on e-commerce websites, particularly in Amazon, where the "Amazon Saheli" program transformed the lives of a considerable number of women entrepreneurs by supporting them in their ventures.

Likewise, in the dairy sector, "Dairy Entrepreneurship Development Scheme (DEDS)" has been implemented by the "National Bank for Agriculture and Rural Development (NABARD)" of the GOI to generate self-employment opportunities for the rural people in the dairy sector, covering such activities as the improvement of milk "production, procurement, preservation, transportation, processing and marketing of milk" by offering subsidies (Tewari & Gakkhar, 2011). The scheme ensured that improved technologies reach rural women at the grassroots level to reduce the "drudgery" of agricultural women and help increase their work efficiency (Vaish & Tripathi, 2019).

The incorporation of new technologies will also help in alleviating the gender bias that exists in rural areas. Over the years, the GOI has undertaken commendable initiatives towards dairy development, particularly for women, by launching gender-specific schemes. As a result, there has been an overall improvement in women's socioeconomic status and livelihood. Well, a recent "credit-linked subsidy program" under the "Prime Minister's Employment Generation Programme (PMEGP)" has also been implemented to generate employment opportunities through the formation of fresh self-employment micro-enterprises in both rural and urban regions of the country. It is a Central scheme administered by the "Ministry of MSME" (Nagaiya & Begum, 2013).

The Government of India has emphasized popularizing women's entrepreneurship with the help of multiple training and support services. Since the development of entrepreneurship is closely linked with the development of MSMEs, the formation and development of these enterprises are of significant importance in countries like India, where they account for more than 95% of the total number of firms and are the largest source of employment especially for women (Singh & Manisha, 2013). According to the Ministry of MSME, more than Rs. 135 crore have been allocated for conducting multiple skill development programs nationwide through different government organizations (Chhabra et al., 2020). With the development of traditional industries, building innovative and traditional skills and creating long-term employment opportunities, the schemes empower women and increase their chances of becoming entrepreneurs (Bahl, 2012).

Microcredit through various financial services is instrumental in employment generation (Sahu et al., 2021). Although women play a secondary role in India, the issues related to the welfare of women have always been one of the main priorities among policymakers, as a result of which a remarkable shift has been observed in the approach to the issues and challenges faced by women (Singh & Singh, 2020). To promote women's Entrepreneurship, schemes must be implemented without any discrimination in society (Mahajan & Kamble, 2011). Women entrepreneurs can improve the country's general wealth and household income (Shah & Saurabh, 2015). But reaching out to the women regarding Government Schemes through various awareness programmes is a must. Implementation of schemes to help and support women entrepreneurs might not always be helpful unless the schemes are evaluated (Uma & Ramesh, 2018).

Case of Radhika Baburao Shinde: Empowering Women Through Entrepreneurship

Radhika Baburao Shinde's life is a testament to the remarkable power of entrepreneurship and unwavering determination in the face of daunting adversity. Hailing from a traditional family in the arid Satara district of India, Radhika's destiny took a profound turn when, at the tender age of 12, she married a man ten years her senior. Undeterred by the myriad challenges, Radhika aspired for a brighter future for herself and her three children. Her journey commenced in a region where a staggering 833 million people grappled with surviving on less than $3.20 per day. In this harsh environment, women like Radhika carried the weight of household duties and gruelling agricultural labour, casting a long shadow over her dream of breaking free from the relentless cycle of poverty. However, in 2014, a glimmer of hope appeared on Radhika's horizon when the Mann Deshi Foundation, a dedicated organization committed to empowering rural women through business acumen and financial assistance, entered her village. Offering vocational training at a nominal cost, Radhika determinedly seized this opportunity and successfully completed a rigorous 120-hour tailoring course. With her newly acquired skills, Radhika embarked on a dual journey, managing her tailoring business with her agricultural responsibilities. This entrepreneurial endeavour empowered her and ignited a beacon of hope for her children's future. Radhika defied the odds by earning an additional $5 per month, a significant sum in an area where the median monthly income barely reached $70. Nonetheless, her entrepreneurial spirit encountered resistance from her husband's family, who were apprehensive that her business pursuits might divert her attention from her farming duties. Despite numerous disputes, Radhika's determination remained unshaken (Mathew, 2019).

Radhika Baburao Shinde's remarkable narrative underscores the transformative potential of entrepreneurship, even amid the most daunting circumstances. Her journey from a young bride in a remote village to an empowered businesswoman is a profound inspiration for women confronting similar adversities. It also underscores the pivotal role of organizations like the Mann Deshi Foundation in dismantling barriers and empowering women in rural India, enabling them to forge a brighter future for themselves and their families. Radhika's indomitable spirit continues to guide and inspire countless others as they strive to break free from the cycle of poverty and inequality.

Methodology

This study is based on the secondary data. The data has been collected from various Government offices of the Government of Sikkim and through the Right to Information Act 2005. Data from published papers, websites and journals has been inferred while conducting this research. This study covers all the four districts of Sikkim. Below are the functioning Government financial schemes for women entrepreneurs in the State of Sikkim.

MICROFINANCE SCHEMES IMPLEMENTED IN SIKKIM

Deendayal Antyodaya Yojana-National Urban Livelihoods Mission (DAY-NULM): DAY-NULM is a Central scheme announced in 2011 but was implemented in the State of Sikkim from 2015-2016. The Ministry of Housing and Urban poverty alleviation is the implementing Central agency, whereas Sikkim Urban Development Agency, Government of Sikkim, is the nodal agency. Since urban poverty is increasing rapidly, Barman & Saloi (2021) stated that it has become a major area of concern, and the Government needs to emphasize working towards the alleviation of urban poverty. Therefore, the Government of India has introduced an innovative solution, the" DAY-NULM (Deendayal Antyodaya Yojana- National Urban Livelihoods Mission" program that aims at reducing poverty and vulnerability of the poverty-stricken urban households by facilitating their accessibility to "gainful self-employment opportunities," providing them with equipped shelters with all necessary amenities, addressing the concerns of their livelihood and offering institutional credit, social security and skills to meet new opportunities in the market.

Another underlying objective of DAY-NULM is to strengthen women's empowerment by providing entrepreneurship opportunities on a global platform to women across the country. It aims at providing accessibility of the products made by Self Help Groups (SHGs) to a large customer base, thereby strengthening the ability of women to create sustainable livelihoods in urban areas. This move by the GOI will be instrumental in unfolding urban women's entrepreneurship potential (Kuchibhotla, 2020). The mission has collaborated with Flipkart and Amazon for e-marketing SHG products across India (MHUA, 2020). Thakur et al. (2021) stated that DAY-NULM's programs helped in increasing the presence of women entrepreneurs on e-commerce websites, particularly in Amazon, where the "Amazon Saheli" program transformed the lives of a considerable number of women entrepreneurs by supporting them in their ventures.

It is shown in Figure 1 that in the year 2016-17, the total fund allocation under the scheme in the state was 111.57 Lakh (88.645 Lakhs Central Govt. share and 11.36 Lakhs State Govt. Share). Next year, 2017-18, the allocation under the scheme was increased to 90.94 Lakhs. In the year 2018-19, the allocation was 90.90 Lakhs.

Figure 1. Total fund allocation

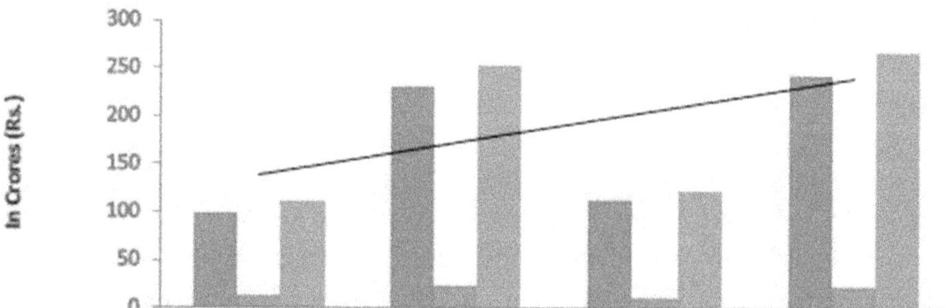

	2016-2017	2017-2018	2018-2019	2019-2020
Central share	98.9	231	112.23	243
State Share	12.67	23	11.23	24.3
Total	111.57	254	123.46	267.3

In 2018-19, the allocation was increased to 91.25 Lakhs. It is seen that 68 Lakh is still coming for various entrepreneurial opportunities. It is shown in Figure 2, that in the year 2015-16, the total number of trainings held was 32 where 125 women beneficiaries participated. Likewise, in 2016-17, the training increased to 71, where participation of women beneficiaries also increased. But in 2017-18, the training held decreased to 30, where women's participation also decreased to only 2%.

Figure 2. Total number of trainings

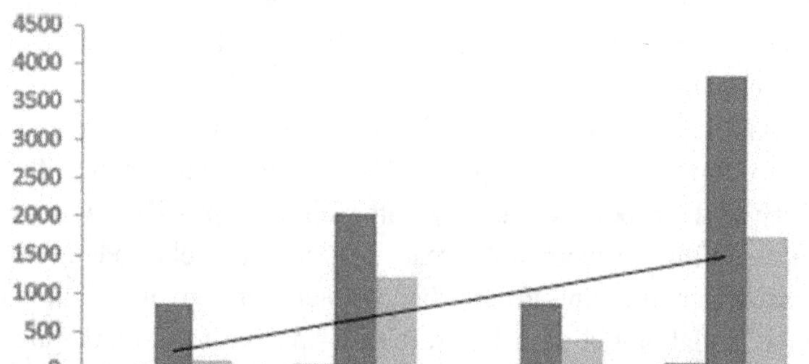

	2015-2016	2016-2017	2017-2018	Total
Total Number of Trainings	32	71	30	132
Total No of beneficiaries	869	2067	900	3863
Women Beneficiaries	125	1226	425	1776

Pradhan Mantri Employment Generation Programme (PMEGP): Pradhan Mantri Employment Generation Programme (PMEGP), a credit-linked subsidy programme) announced in 2008 by merging two schemes: Prime Minister's Rojgar Yojana (PMRY and the Rural Employment Generation Programme (REGP) *(Prime Minister's Employment Generation Programme)*. It is a Central scheme administered by the "Ministry of MSME" (Nagaiya & Begum, 2013). The scheme was implemented in the year 2008 in the State of Sikkim. The National Village Industries Commission (KVIC) functions as the Nodal Agency. At the state level, the scheme is implemented through State KVIC Directorates, State Khadi and Village Industries Boards (KVIBs), District Industries Centers (DICs) and banks. The targeted area of coverage is the East and North districts. The major beneficiaries of this program include the SCs, STs, OBCs and women who contribute approximately 5 percent of the project's total cost. Under the manufacturing sector, the maximum project cost is Rs.25 Lakhs; under the business sector, it is Rs. 10 Lakhs (Sharma, 2018).

The Self-Help Groups are a major beneficiary of the PMEGP program, availing subsidies under this scheme. Moreover, the scheme caters to the needs of more women than other respective categories, and the growth rate of women beneficiaries has been continuously increasing (Dangi, 2014). The Entrepreneurship Development Programme (EDP) under this scheme offers awareness to rural people regarding the managerial and operational aspects like "finance, production, marketing, enterprise management, banking formalities, and bookkeeping." In addition to this, training centres have also been established to provide training for self-employment. Furthermore, with the help of this scheme, subsidies, tax waivers and concessions are extended to women entrepreneurs at large in order to encourage them to take up entrepreneurship (Chavan & Murkute, 2016).

It is shown in Figure 3 that in the year 2008-09, the amount released was only 22.45 Lakhs. But in 2009-10, the amount was increased to 120.81 Lakhs. In 2010-11, there was a good increase in money to 154.24 Lakhs. In 2011-12, the amount was decreased to 113.37 Lakhs, followed by another decrease to 88.49 Lakhs in 2012-13.

Figure 3. 2008-09 amount

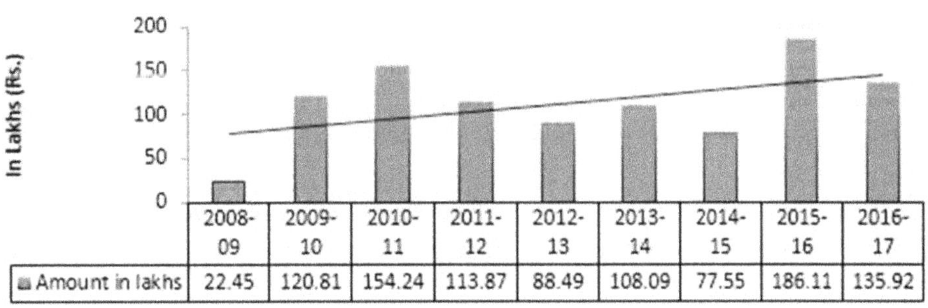

In 2013-14, there was a sharp increase to 108.09 Lakhs, which later decreased to 77.55 Lakhs in 2014-15. In 2015-16, there was a tremendous increase in the fund release to 186.11 Lakhs, but again, in 2016-17, the amount released decreased to 135.92.

In Figure 4, it is shown that in 2008-09, there were only three women beneficiaries, but in 2009-10 it was increased to 11. In 2010-11, there was a decline of women beneficiaries to 6, but it increased by 1, making it 7 in 2011-12. There was a decline in 2012-13 to 6, followed by a further decline in 2013-14 to 3.

Figure 4. Women beneficiaries in 2008-09

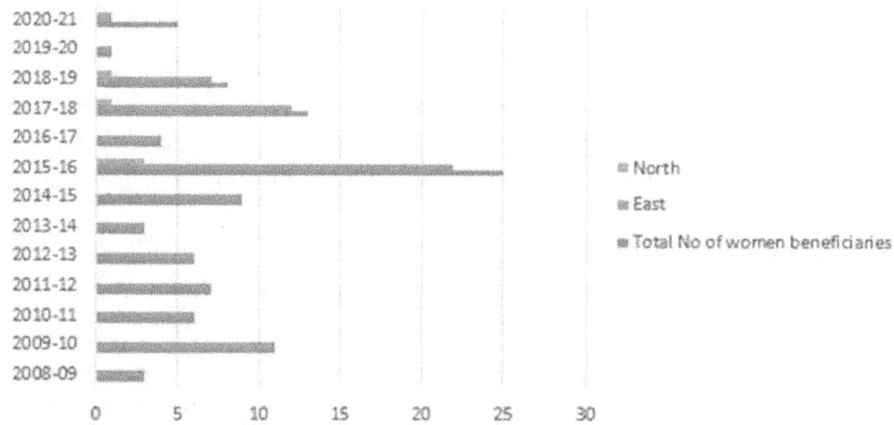

It was increased to 9 in the year 2014-15. In 2015-16, there was a tremendous increase of women beneficiaries to 25, followed by a decline in 2016-17 to only four women. Again, in 2017-18, a small increase was shown to 13 women beneficiaries, followed by a decline in 2018-19 to 8. In 2019-20, a frustrating decline was seen with only one woman. Again, a small increase is seen in 2020-21 to 5 women. So, only 0.7% participation of women beneficiaries is seen under this scheme.

Dairy Entrepreneurship Development Scheme (DEDS): The "Dairy Entrepreneurship Development Scheme (DEDS)" is a Central Scheme and has been implemented by the "National Bank for Agriculture and Rural Development (NABARD)" as a nodal agency to generate self-employment opportunities for the rural people in the dairy sector covering activities as the "improvement of milk production, procurement, preservation, transportation, processing and marketing of milk" by offering subsidies (Tewari & Gakkhar, 2011). Regional Rural and Urban Banks, Cooperative Banks, Commercial Banks, State Cooperative Agriculture and Rural Development Bank, and similar financial institutions eligible for the NABARD refinance facility are responsible for implementing the scheme (Dairy Entrepreneurship Development Programme).

The "Dairy Entrepreneurship Development Scheme (DEDS)" was implemented in 2008 in Sikkim. Activities like capacity building, cattle induction, fodder development, and entrepreneurship development for establishing dairy farms were the main thrust of the development. The dairy development in the state is in the three districts of Sikkim viz East, West and South. It has been implemented through the Sikkim Milk Union and North District through the North District Milk Union. The target area of coverage of the scheme is throughout the State of Sikkim. The scheme helps promote establishing modern-day dairy farms, introducing structural changes in the unorganized sectors and generating self-employment infrastructure primarily for the rural poor.

The major beneficiaries of this scheme are farmers, individual entrepreneurs, companies, and groups of unorganized sectors." Since rural women have been actively involved in "animal husbandry and dairy activities," the implementation of this scheme has been particularly helpful for them. The scheme ensured that improved technologies reach rural women at the grass root level so that they can reduce the "drudgery" of agricultural women and help increase their work efficiency (Vaish & Tripathi, 2019). The incorporation of new technologies will also help in alleviating the gender bias that exists the rural areas.

Over the years, the GOI has undertaken commendable initiatives towards dairy development, particularly for women, by launching gender-specific schemes. As a result, there has been an overall improvement in women's socioeconomic status and livelihood.

It is shown in Figure 5 that in the year 2016-17, the amount sanctioned was 9247818 Lakhs, where women beneficiaries are 32. Likewise, in the year 2017-18, the amount was reduced to 4340200, where women beneficiaries were 17. In 2018-19, the amount was further reduced to 2539400 Lakhs, reducing women beneficiaries to 7.

Figure 5. 2016-17 amount sanctioned

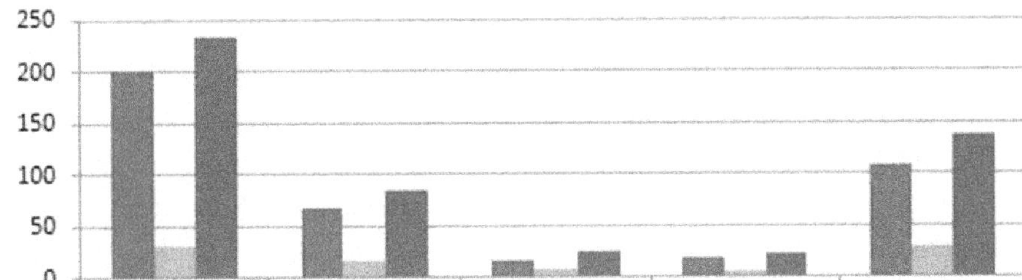

	2016-17	2017-18	2018-19	2019-20	2020-21
Male	201	68	17	18	108
Female	32	17	7	5	29
Total	233	85	24	23	137

Further, in 2019-20, there was an improvement to 3283800 Lakhs but a reduction in women beneficiaries to 5. But in 2020-21, there was a sharp increase of 10491600 Lakhs and the women beneficiaries to 29.

In Figure 6, it is shown that in the Farmers Awareness Programme, there are 1061 male participants, whereas female participants are only 510. Again, in capacity-building programmes, the male participants were 537, whereas 229 were female. 42% less as compared to male participants.

Figure 6. Farmers awareness programme

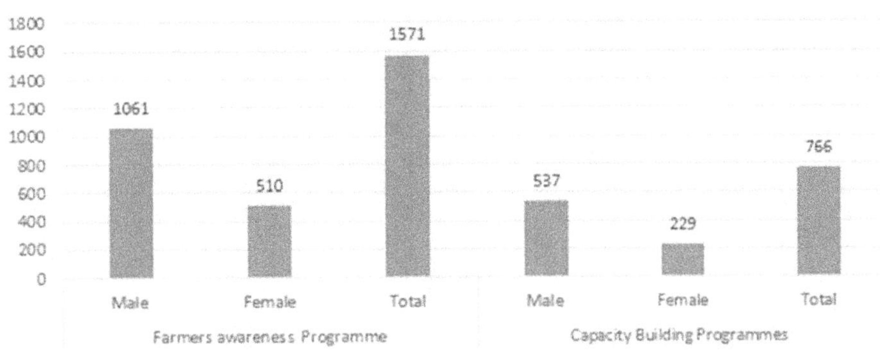

The Success Story of Ms. Pranita Pradhan Tiwari, a Dairy Farmer

Ms Pranita Pradhan Tiwari, a progressive farmer resident of Chota Singtam, East Sikkim, has been doing Dairy farming in Assam Lingzey, East Sikkim, for the last four years. She has done her Masters in Mass Communication. Currently, 23 cows, including calves, out of which 19 are under milking and selling 110 litres per day in the nearby market in Gangtok. She is using the latest automatic milking machine and producing subsidiary dairy products. She has employed three employees. Mrs. Pranita Pradhan Tiwari is a successful entrepreneur under DEDS. She benefitted from GOI (capital subsidy) under DEDS. She was awarded the Most Innovative Dairy Entrepreneur in 2018-19 on the occasion of "Gwala Diwas," celebrated on 1 July 2021.

The revised version of the erstwhile North East Industrial and Investment Promotion Policy (NEIIPP) is the *North East Industrial and Investment Promotion Policy (NEIIPP),* 2007. NEIIPP is a Central Scheme for the investors of North East India, implemented in 2007. Department of Industrial Policy and Promotion (DIPP) is the implementing agency of NEIIPP, 2007. North Eastern Development Finance Corporation Ltd, Guwahati is the nodal agency for disbursing subsidies under various schemes of NEIIPP, 2007. Each scheme component under the NEIIPP has its inbuilt provision of monitoring the scheme's implementation.

The main purpose of the scheme is to promote more MSMEs as they contribute to more employment generation. The State Government should also take more steps to establish Industrial Clusters, improve Government officials' training and conduct awareness generation activities among entrepreneurs. Figure 7 shows beneficiaries under the scheme.

It is shown in Figure 8 that the total amount released in the Central Capital Investment Subsidy Scheme from 2012-13 to 2020-21 is Rs. 30379995.11 crores. The industrial unit set up was 91, where males owned 81 units and females only 9.

Figure 7. Beneficiaries under the scheme

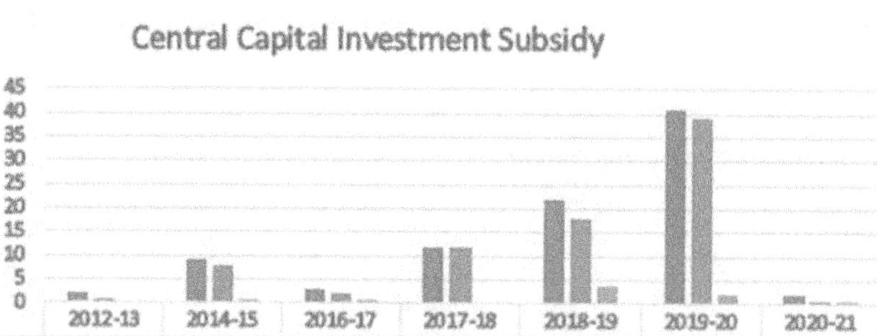

	2012-13	2014-15	2016-17	2017-18	2018-19	2019-20	2020-21
Number of Units	2	9	3	12	22	41	2
Male	1	8	2	12	18	39	1
Female	0	1	1	0	4	2	1

It is shown in Figure 8 that the total amount released in the Central Interest Subsidy Scheme from 2016-17 to 2019-20 was Rs. 99806568. The industrial unit set up was 32, where males owned 24 units and female only 7.

Figure 8. Total amount released in the central interest subsidy scheme from 2016-17 to 2019-20

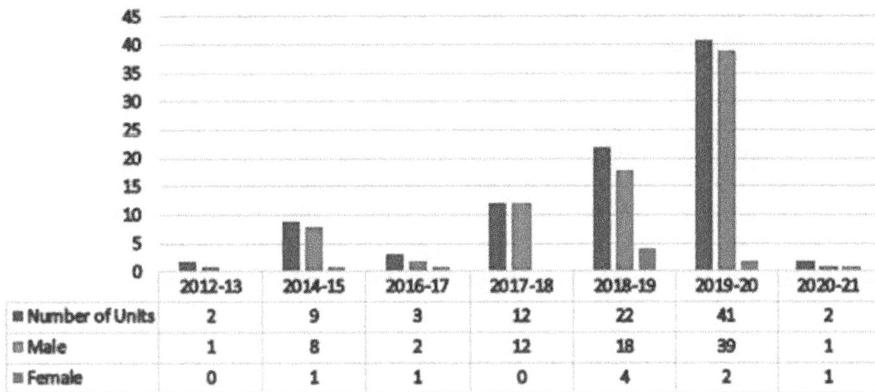

It is shown in Figure 9 that the total amount released by the Central Comprehensive Insurance Scheme from 2011-2021 was 69962015 crores. The industrial unit set up was 82, where males owned 72 units and females only 12.

Figure 9. Scheme of fund for regeneration of traditional industries (SFURTI)

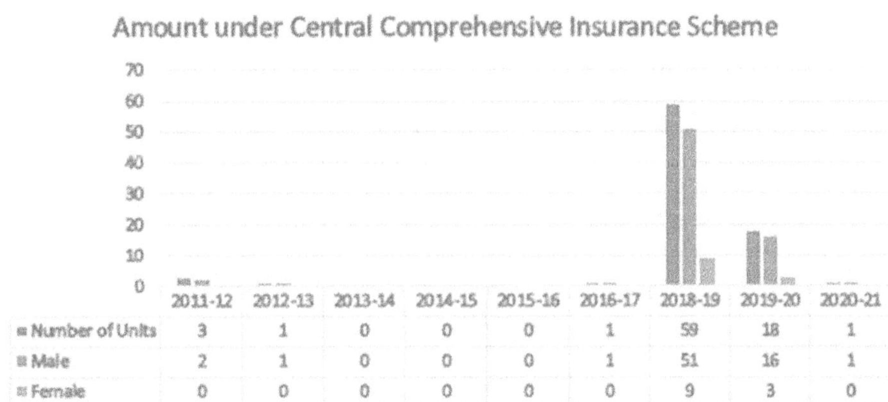

Scheme of Fund for Regeneration of Traditional Industries (SFURTI): According to Manikandan, the "Scheme of Fund for Regeneration of Traditional Industries (SFURTI)" has been implemented by the Ministry of Micro Small & Medium Enterprises with the primary objective to promote development in clusters such as the "khadi industries, village industries and coir industries." SFURTI scheme in the State of Sikkim was implemented in the year 2008, and KVIC is the implementing agency of this scheme. The scheme aims to arrange clusters of the "traditional industries and artisans" to increase their competitiveness and assist them in their long-term viability. In addition, providing sustained employment opportunities for "traditional industry artisans" and rural entrepreneurs is another objective.

The scheme developed 71 clusters nationwide with a total expenditure of Rs. 149.44 crores. The budget limit for the three clusters has been allotted between 1 crore and eight crore (Katoch, 2018). Eventually, it is proposed to develop 800 clusters with the Government of India and the Asian Development Bank's funding. The scheme facilitates the provisions of "skill training, capacity building, and design development." as well as hard interventions like "Common Facility Centres, Raw Material Banks (RMB), and training centres." The building and promotion of brand, e-commerce, and media marketing and developing connectivity among clusters are also a part of the interventions facilitated by the scheme. The scheme proposes to cover 4 lakh artisan beneficiaries, with a major part of these beneficiaries being women. Women's training is essentially done under this scheme to unfold their potential to perform traditional work even more efficiently without putting much effort into developing their skills. With the development of traditional industries, building innovative and traditional skills and creating long-term employment opportunities, this scheme empowers women and increases their chances of becoming entrepreneurs (Bahl, 2012).

Figure 10 shows that in 2012-13, the Government of India Assistance provided to the Sikkim Bee cluster was 72.50 Lakhs, where 118 were women artisans. In 2019-20, three Food processing clusters were opened where the GOI assistance was 234.71 Lakhs in each cluster. In West Sikkim Shitake Mushroom & Other Food Processing Cluster, the number of women artisans was 112. Likewise, in Norbuchoeling Shiitake Mushroom & Other Food Processing Cluster, there were 116 women artisans. In the Jorethang Sumbuk Shitake Mushroom & Other Food Processing Cluster, there were 98 women artisans. But in Moonew Tareybhir Enriched Composting/Vermi Composting Cluster, the GOI assistance was comparatively less with 196.89 Lakhs, where women artisans are 200. It is seen that 62 Lakhs amount is coming from the Government of India to encourage women artisans. More women participation is seen in this scheme.

Figure 10. Moonew Tareybhir enriched composting/Vermi composting cluster

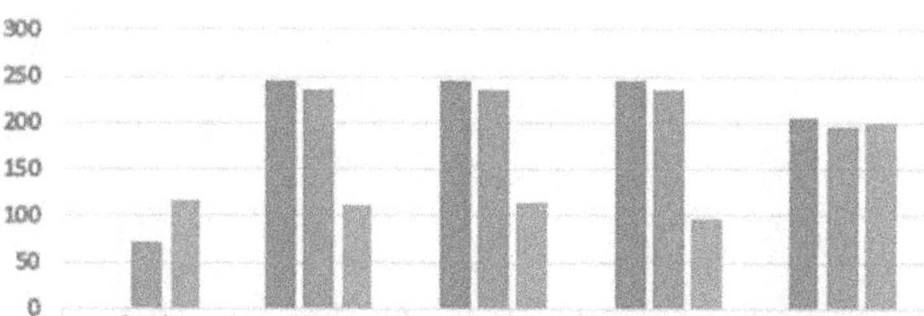

	South 2012-13	West 2019-20	South 2019-20	South 2019-20	South 2019-20
Total project cost		244.9	244.9	244.9	205.08
GOI Assistance In Lakhs	72.5	234.71	234.71	234.71	196.89
Women Artisians	118	112	116	98	200

DISCUSSIONS

Analysis shows that the Government is concerned about encouraging women to various entrepreneurial opportunities by allocating funds. A fluctuating trend is seen in women participation in Deendayal Antyodaya Yojana-National Urban Livelihoods Mission (DAY-NULM). The stress is on the grass-root level drive, educating women on training modules during livelihood generation. As the Pradhan Mantri Employment Generation Programme (PMEGP) is connected with various projects, it is evident that the funds are released according to the number of projects and the women beneficiaries. The year-wise increase in amount had led to increased participation of women beneficiaries. As the energizer and the Government's structured enhancement, networking has received the new initiative.

It is perceived that the amount sanctioned in the Dairy Entrepreneurship Development Scheme (DEDS) is directly coupled with women's entrepreneurial participation. The year the amount is decreased, automatically, it is seen that there is a decline in women's participation. Strains be on the part of the Government on robust proclamation, change in the policy/schemes and women opting for other suitable opportunities. The industrial units set up by women are inadequate, as the main idea of launching the North East Industrial and Investment Promotion Policy (NEIIPP) scheme is to encourage MSME and the creation of industrial units. Gender issues discouraging women in entrepreneurial activities still look prevalent. Lack of awareness generation activities among the entrepreneurs and rigid Government policies in setting up an industrial unit are imaged. It is discerned that the Scheme of Fund for Regeneration of Traditional Industries (SFURTI) have witnessed a satisfactory increase in women's participation. However, it is not linked to the amount of Government assistance. What attracted women is that they were the main target to participate in fair and reasonable Government policies and more awareness.

Sikkim, a small mountainous state, covers an area of 7096 sq. km (which accounts for 0.2% of the total area of India) with four districts. With a population of 6. 10 Lakhs, the sex ratio is 889 females per 1,000 males, with 323,057 males and 287,520 females. Sikkim is a mostly rural state; the capital, Gangtok, is the most significant urban area with around 98,000 inhabitants (Sikkim population 2011). Sikkim has achieved a literacy rate of 81.4%; the male literacy rate stands at 86.55 percent while the female is at 75.61 percent. Sikkim's Gross Domestic Product (GSDP) expanded at a high Compound Annual Growth Rate (CAGR) of 11.72 per cent between 2015-16 and 2018-19. Sector-wise contribution is shown at 11.62 percent in the primary sector, whereas the secondary sector at 61.56 per cent and the tertiary sector at 26.82 per cent in 2018-2019. The primary sector grew fastest growing between 2011-12 and 2018-19. There is a total 50 number of establishments in Sikkim under Women Entrepreneurs by nature of operation: 5071 in perennial, 211 in seasonal, and 22 in casual. The distribution of working enterprises in the state is 110 in micro, 12 in small, and 0 in medium. Likewise, by nature of manufacturing/ assembly/ processing activity, it is 105, 11 in services, and 6 in repairing and maintenance.

Sikkim was hardly recognized. The state took several years to transform itself from the rest of the fast-growing states. Sikkim was an agriculture-dependent state. It is only in the last 20-22 years that many developments in the manufacturing and service sectors came up. Over the decades, there has been a spurt in entrepreneurial investments due to Sikkim's natural bounties and pristine nature. Sikkim, a late entrant into the playground of skilled enterprise, is accelerating its growth. However, a more progressive mark can be celebrated if women eliminate the entrepreneurial challenges. MSME is a new feature in Sikkim's industrial arena; therefore, only scheme launching will not suffice. Understanding the need to reach out to a wider audience is essential. Based on the market demand, customized training programmes must be organized in various small centres, which will result in the rise of women.

CONCLUSION

Sikkim Government has been trying its best to set up industries to generate employment for potential entrepreneurs of Sikkim. Promotion of Khadi, small and village cottage industries have played a significant role in setting up the industries. It is evident from the study that the Central Government has been offering a vast range of investments. For a major boost, the share from the Central Government is much more than the state share. Very few initiatives are taken on the total outlay of the schemes. Observing the annual growth rate of the schemes, despite a decent number of subsidies and other benefits, none of the schemes have consistent growth. The number of entrepreneurs in the state of Sikkim is comparatively low. Women entrepreneurs are even less important for several reasons. Well, the Government is still committed to providing the ecosystem required for the entrepreneurs to flourish and grow in the state. Effectiveness, as well as the improvement of the schemes, will not be highlighted unless the schemes are evaluated. On a merit basis, placement opportunities are given on the training provided by concerned schemes to experience their skills. Ease of doing business can be likely only if the Government become flexible in terms of its policies. With a far-sighted objective to foster enterprise, intervention from countless factors must be minimized for sustainable development.

REFERENCES

Agarwal, S., & Lenka, U. (2016). An exploratory study on the development of women entrepreneurs: Indian cases. *Journal of Research in Marketing and Entrepreneurship*, *18*(2), 232–247. doi:10.1108/JRME-04-2015-0024

Bahl, J. (2012). Status of women entrepreneurship in rural India. *Asian Journal of Multidimensional Research*, *1*(2), 89–100.

Barman, D. K., & Saloi, T. (2021). Alleviation of Urban Poverty through DAY-NULM Scheme: A Study with Reference to Guwahati City. *International Journal of Management*, *11*(12), 2020.

Chavan, V. M., & Murkute, P. A. (2016). Role of women entrepreneurship in Indian economy. *International Journal of Science Technology and Management*, *5*(3), 604–612.

Chhabra, S., Raghunathan, R., & Rao, N. M. (2020). The antecedents of entrepreneurial intention among women entrepreneurs in India. *Asia Pacific Journal of Innovation and Entrepreneurship*, *14*(1), 76–92. doi:10.1108/APJIE-06-2019-0034

Dangi, N. (2014). Women entrepreneurship and growth and performance of MSMEs in India. *International Journal (Toronto, Ont.)*, *2*(4), 174–182.

De Vita, L., Mari, M., & Poggesi, S. (2014). Women entrepreneurs in and from developing countries: Evidences from the literature. *European Management Journal*, *32*(3), 451–460. doi:10.1016/j.emj.2013.07.009

Dey, A., Majumdar, K. K., Chakraborty, A. K., & Mandal, A. K. (2018). Women Empowerment in India–A Perspective. *Community Medicine*, *9*(8), 574–579.

Geetha, P. (2019). A Study on Women Entrepreneurs Awareness about Government Schemes-Special Reference to Kanniyakumari District. *Worldwide Diary of Business and Management Invention*, *8*(2), 1–7.

Jindal, M. K., & Bhardwaj, A. (2016). Entrepreneurship development in India: A new paradigm. *Proceedings of the world congress on engineering, 2*, 724-726.

Junare, S. O., & Singh, R. (2016). Technological Understanding and Usage vis-à-vis Knowledge of Government Schemes–A Study of Women Entrepreneurs of Selected Cities of Gujarat. *American Journal of Entrepreneurship*, *1*(1), 71–85.

Katoch, G. (2018). A Khadi and Village Industries Commission: Role, Challenges and Opportunity Ahead. *Pacific Business Review International*, *11*(2), 79–87.

Kuchibhotla, R. (2020). Self-Help Groups-Transforming Lives, Promoting & Sustain Women Empowerment. *The Management Accountant*, *55*(3), 28–31.

Mahajan, S. S., & Kamble, C. B. (2011). Government support to women entrepreneurship: A study of programmes implemented by MAVIM. *Indian Streams Research Journal*, *1*(11), 130–134.

Mandal, K. C. (2013, May). Concept and Types of Women Empowerment. In *International Forum of Teaching & Studies, 9*(2), 17-30.

Manshani, S., & Dubey, A. (2017). Startup Women in startup India: A study of women entrepreneurs in India. *International Journal of Business and Management*, *6*(4), 91–100.

Mathew, A. (2019). *Women struggle to break down barriers to starting a business.* International Monetary Fund.

Ministry of Housing & Urban Affairs. (2020). *Giving Impetus to the Women Entrepreneurs, Day -NULM Under Ministry of Housing and Urban Affairs Signs MoU with Amazon for E-Marketing of Products Made by Self Help Groups Across the Country*. PIB Delhi.

Nagaiya, D., & Begum, S. S. (2012). *Women entrepreneurship and small enterprises in India.* New Century Publications

Paul Dana, L. (2001). The education and training of entrepreneurs in Asia. *Education + Training*, *43*(8/9), 405–416. doi:10.1108/EUM0000000006486

Rajalakshmi, V., & Selvam, V. (2017). Impact of MGNREGA on women empowerment and their issues and challenges: A review of literature from 2005 to 2015. *Journal of Internet Banking and Commerce*, *22*(7), 1–13.

Rashmi, D. (2016). Women Entrepreneur in Micro, Small and Medium Enterprises in India-An overview. *International Journal of Managerial Studies and Research*, *4*(2), 60–64.

Sahu, T. N., Agarwala, V., & Maity, S. (2021). Effectiveness of microcredit in employment generation and livelihood transformation of tribal women entrepreneurs: Evidence from PMMY. *Journal of Small Business and Entrepreneurship*, 1–22. doi:10.1080/08276331.2021.1928847

Shah, H., & Saurabh, P. (2015). Women entrepreneurs in developing nations: Growth and replication strategies and their impact on poverty alleviation. *Technology Innovation Management Review*, *5*(8), 34–43. doi:10.22215/timreview/921

Sharma, S. (2018). Emerging dimensions of women entrepreneurship: Developments & obstructions. *Economic Affairs*, *63*(2), 337–346. doi:10.30954/0424-2513.2.2018.7

Singh, A., & Manisha, R. (2013). Women entrepreneurs in micro, small and medium enterprises. *International Journal of Management and Social Sciences Research*, *2*(8), 4–8.

Singh, S., & Singh, A. (2020). Women Empowerment in India: A Critical Analysis. *Tathapi*, *19*(44), 227–253.

Sinha, S. & UN.ESCAP. (2005). *Developing women entrepreneurs in South Asia: issues, initiatives and experiences*. Retrieved from: https://hdl.handle.net/20.500.12870/3557

Sörensson, A. & Ghannad, N. (2023). Entrepreneurial opportunities and difficulties under COVID-19 for women entrepreneurs in Asia and Europe. *Journal of Entrepreneurship in Emerging Economies*. doi:10.1108/JEEE-02-2023-0052

Tambunan, T. (2009). Women entrepreneurship in Asian developing countries: Their development and main constraints. *Journal of Development and Agricultural Economics*, *1*(2), 27–40.

Tewari, P., & Gakkhar, A. (2011). A study of opportunities extended to dairy women entrepreneurs under women's dairy development scheme. *Journal of Dairying, Foods & Home Sciences*, *30*(3), 178–181.

Thakur, H., Gupta, A., & Johnson, L. T. (2021). *Women engaging with markets from positions of strength: An exploratory understanding of Kudumbashree women's food service enterprises*. Academic Press.

Uma, S. N., & Ramesh, H. N. (2018). A study on government support for promoting women entrepreneurs in Karnataka state. *Int J Econ Manage Sci*, *7*, 521–525.

Vaish, S., & Tripathi, S. (2019). Empowering women dairy farmers through adoption of drudgery reducing technologies and availing government schemes. *Plant Archives*, *19*(1), 952–955.

Wellalage, N., & Locke, S. (2017). Access to credit by SMEs in South Asia: Do women entrepreneurs face discrimination. *Research in International Business and Finance*, *41*, 336–346. doi:10.1016/j.ribaf.2017.04.053

Yadav, V., & Unni, J. (2016). Women entrepreneurship: Research review and future directions. *Journal of Global Entrepreneurship Research*, *6*(1), 1–18. doi:10.118640497-016-0055-x

Chapter 8
Microfinancing for Women Economic Empowerment and Development:
Conceptual and Theoretical Considerations

Ndwakhulu Stephen Tshishonga
University of KwaZulu-Natal, South Africa

ABSTRACT

Microfinancing is pleaded as the strategic intervention for uprooting poverty and underdevelopment especially in the developing nations. Women in particular have been targeted as recipients for microfinancing and key actors in the microfinance industry. The growth of microfinance was juxtaposed against its failure to impact on women's empowerment and development; hence, women became over-indebted or turned to be the victim of predatory lenders. This chapter argues that microfinance, despite its financial inclusive agenda, is trapped in the neo-liberal development policies through the commercialisation of loans for profit making by commercial banks. Microfinance has emerged with specific focuses on microenterprises; hence, it lacks prospects for women investing in larger and productive businesses. This chapter therefore is anchored on conceptual and theoretical debates and complexities underpinning microfinance or microcredit in the Global South.

INTRODUCTION

Women, throughout the world' are defined by the scourge of "poverty, marginalisation and discrimination" (Agu, 2007, p. 32). For Bakoa & Syed (2018), marginalization of women is not only universal, bust also a long-time problem that has economic and social implications. Women from different spheres of life as Akor (2017) argues, are crowded with deprivation, neglect, exploitation and oppression. Inequalities and poverty are persistent factors that hinder effective participation of women towards realising their aspirations and their potential to build a safe and better world for all and contribute to the development

DOI: 10.4018/978-1-6684-8979-6.ch008

of their communities (Masuku & Jili, 2019). As a result of lack of financial means, women have more difficulty in establishing contacts and benefiting from the resources they need to become influential leaders (Holman, 2017). Similarly, the lack of access to formal and informal education and the lack of real training and capacity-building opportunities in most African societies, to the challenges faced by women their quest for economic, cultural, intellectual or personal self-emancipation is dire (Beerie et al., 2019). These challenges are further exacerbated by poverty and inequality which are acute among rural women especially in the African continent (Mutale & Mtapuri, 2023). Globally, women are subjected to low incomes due to labour force discrimination, and detrimental gender discrimination in resource allocation within their homes and societies (Stuart, 2018).

Thus, women compared to their male counterpart have became the product of patriarchy and neo-liberal systems that not only engender structural poverty, but also thrive on escalating inequality and underdevelopment (World Bank Group, 2018). Global economic systems have overtime created additional opportunities for men for self-determination at the expense of women (Holland, 2018). This has been signalled by the unrelenting masculinity in many economic processes seen in recent decades (Saqib, 2016). Women often receive attention as mothers and as a vulnerable fraction of the population (Kolovich, 2018). Programmes aimed at development were often aimed at tackling immediate poverty but not at empowering women (Karl, 2017). One way to unlock this potential is to seek women's economic empowerment through their participation in income-generating projects (Folayan, 2020). This has been explored in part in the emergence of gender and development, which evolved from women and development (Malhotra 2017). This chapter is more concerned about the use of microfinance as either the strategy for women economics empowerment or their disempowerment.

Empowerment in development is not without controversy, as there are often different perspectives on what constitutes empowerment (Frediani, Clark & Biggeri, 2019). There is also a risk that overly subjective measurements will provide inconclusive evidence. Economic empowerment provides incentives to change the traditional behavioural patterns to which a woman is bound as a dependent household member (Schneider, 2018). Empowerment often comes from within and individuals empower themselves, cultures, societies, institutions, and individuals can create conditions that facilitate or undermine the opportunities for empowerment (NZAID, 2007). Women's empowerment is essential for the eradication of poverty and hunger, and fully realizing human rights and achieving sustainable development (NZAID, 2007, p.24). Gender impartiality and empowered women are mechanisms for the dissemination of developmental attempts (Johnson, 2019). In this context, literature argues that investing in gender parity has a multiplier effect compared to other development investments (Willett, 2020). Nonetheless, it has been documented that woman economic empowerment, however compelling, cannot rely solely on microfinancing for poverty alleviation and economic development (Gendernet, 2011). In addition, African women face challenges in accessing finance due to their lack of collateral, legal and cultural barriers to for example, land and property ownership, discriminatory regulations, limited employment in the formal sector including lack of availability of financial products (Anyaegbunam & Alaga, 2015). These authors are critical of micro as they see nothing micro about women. Having said that, this chapter is conceptually and theoretically grounded on microfinance as the strategy for women empowerment or disempowerment.

BACKGROUND

Conceptualisation of Microfinance

Due to the prevalence of poverty, unemployment and underdevelopment globally more particularly in the developing nations, micro-finance or credit emerged to be the policy and programme interventions (Yadav & Mittal, 2016; and Mishra, 2021). Originally, the term was micro-credit which was later was subsumed into the broader notion of micro-finance and in this research micro-credit and micro-finance is used interchangeably. The two notions are differentiated as micro-credit on one hand is primarily concerned about the disbursement of financial resources and monitoring of repayments while micro-finance on the other hand, is more compressive as it involves insurance, loans and savings aimed at improving the well-being of the poor. Microfinance and credit are terms intrinsically linked and often used interchangeably (Imran et al., 2022). In essence, microfinance falls under the banking services provided to low-income individuals or groups who in most cases have no chance of accessing financial services from the commercial institutions (Kagan, 2023). Pragmatically, microfinance affords the poor loans which can be used for the establishment of small businesses yet within ethical lending practices. Most of smaller businesses and entrepreneurs are often disadvantaged as they are not eligible to secure credit services, hence microfinance came handy towards promoting entrepreneurship and inclusive growth.

Microfinance is broader than microcredit. Microfinance is inclusive of providing small loans for community collective projects together with other financial services in the form of small business advise (Ife, 2016). For Todaro & Smith (2020), microfinance is financial services given to people especially the poor who are unable to access such services from the commercial banks. While microcredit is more limited to the provision of small individual loans. These differences or interface led to the terminology trajectory from microcredit (1980s) through microfinance (1990s) to financial inclusion (2010s) (Gerard & Johnston, 2019, p. 878). Literature views microfinance to financial services in the form of small or micro amounts of money (see Gerard & Johnston, 2019). Bateman (2010, p. 1) conceives micro-finance as: ...the provision of tiny loans to poor individuals who establish or expand a simple income-generating activity, thereby supposedly facilitating their eventual escape from poverty. Furthermore, Das (2018) defines microfinance as a broad variety of services offered for the needy inclusive of microcredit, for entrepreneurs and small businesses lacking access to banking and other financial services. Microfinance refers to the provision of financial services, such as small loans, savings accounts, and insurance, to individuals and small businesses who do not have access to traditional banking services. Credit, on the other hand, refers to the borrowing of money with the promise to repay it later, often with interest (Adebola, 2021).

The benefits of microfinance extend beyond the direct effects of giving people a source for capital. Entrepreneurs who create successful businesses can then offer jobs and trade to help improve their community. Additionally, the International Finance Corp (IFC) has helped establish or improve credit reporting bureaus in 30 developing nations. It has also advocated for adding relevant laws that govern financial activities in developing countries (Kagan, 2023). The benefits of microfinance extend beyond the direct effects of giving people a source for capital. Entrepreneurs who create successful businesses, in turn, create jobs, trade, and overall economic improvement within a community. Empowering women in particular, as many microfinance organizations do, may lead to more stability and prosperity for families (Global Report, 2022).

According to Adebola (2022), microfinance provides access to financial services for people who would not have access to them otherwise. It can help to alleviate poverty by providing capital to people who want to start or expand small businesses. Microfinance can also help to promote financial inclusion and empower women, who often have limited access to financial services (Gerard & Johnston, 2019). Adebola (2022), states that access to credit can help small businesses to grow and create jobs, which can stimulate economic growth. Microfinance can help to reduce dependence on informal or exploitative lenders, who can be predatory and charge exorbitant interest rates. MFIs should help women to promote financial literacy and responsible borrowing.

As a financial strategy, microfinancing benefits low income earners especially women through granting them loans, savings, insurance and remittances. Sarumathi & Mohan (2011:1) ascertain that "microfinance, is banking the unbankables, bringing credit, savings and other essential financial services within the reach of millions of people who are too poor to be served by regular banks, in most cases because they are unable to offer sufficient collateral". Thus, within the neo-liberal framework, microfinance emerged to devolved responsibility for development to the individual as self-maximizer (McMichael, 2012). McMichael (2012, p. 220) went on to outline three functions associated with microfinance, namely: 1) providing credit to the poor as an entrepreneurial 'leg up', 2) deepening market relations and finally 3) enlarging financial opportunity in the form of legitimacy repair. Targeting women and granting them loans is considered as a substantial means of encouraging them and enhancing their financial status (Khursheed, 2022). Ali, Hatta, Azman & Islam (2017) concluded that "women have been intended for microfinance and microcredit because they tend to be mostly troubled by insufficiency than men, and the responsibility for the well-being of the household lies upon them". Thus, if women are actively involved and engaged in financial programmes and services, they do not only improve their household decision-making to become better, but they become positively impacted, as well as their economic empowerment (Ali & Hatta, 2012). Comparatively women are considered as better credit managers than men (Guillen, Mayo & Karelaia, 2018; and Le & Stefanczyk, 2018). Additionally, "access to credit is considered by development agencies as a crucial element of economic empowerment, as it can play a significant role in the process of emerging strategies of the livelihood of women 'given their responsibility in fulfilling both social and economic roles in society" (Ali & Hatta, 2012, p. 114). Contributing to the afore statement, Kato & Kratzer (2013) state that economic empowerment should also be directed to women because they are seen as passionate in development programmes and because they are responsibile for everyone within the household, particularly the children.

RESEARCH METHOD

This chapter employed qualitative research approach to conceptually understand microfinance and microcredit for women economic empowerment and poverty alleviation. Considering that chapter is non-empirical, documentary analysis and content analysis was used. In the context of this chapter, documentary data analysis was based on desktop and secondary data inclusive of books, book chapters, accredited articles, reports and governments policy documents. In line with the topic of this chapter, the dominant search of literature was on microfinancing and microcredit, inclusive of conceptual grounding of microfinancing, its historical emergence and its potential in empower women economically. Considering that this is the systematic literature review (Mengista, Soromessa & Legese, 2020), data was analysed and interpreted based on the thematic areas of microfinance and women economic development with the role and challenges as the underpinning areas of analsyis. A systematic literature review (SLR) is known for being systematic research method which is explicit, and reproducible in identifying, evaluating, and synthesizing the existing data (Del Amo, Erkoyuncu, Roy, Palmarini, & Onoufriou, (2018). As such, a systematic review is considered to be the key in the identification of all empirical evidence that fits the pre-specified inclusion criteria to answer a particular research question or hypothesis (Snyder, 2019). More than 60 sources were consulted towards writing this chapter. In this chapter, the systematic review allowed the authors to consult databases such as Scopus, Google Scholar, Science Direct were used in order to find relevant articles pertaining to microfinance and its role in poverty reduction and women economic empowerment. on the subject matter. Thus, this chapter used the framework of Search, Appraisal, Synthesis, and Analysis (SALSA) (Grant and Booth, 2009) as a methodology to determine the search protocols to be followed when using systematic literature review.

History of Microfinance

Microfinancing has a protracted history of existence and experimentation in both developed and developing worlds (Çetin & Keser, 2018). However, its origin is traceable to the work of Muhammed Yunus, a Professor of Economics at Chittagong University in the mid-1970s. The poverty and hunger experienced by many people in Bangladesh and the despair that they cause led Yunus to seek a different solution than the models predicted by economic theories. Yunus' ideas now form the basis of the Grameen financing model. The project, which began with a credit amounting to $27 US given to 42 needy persons, has become a giant financing model which is now being implemented in many countries all around the world (Yunus, 2003). Since its formation, the Grameen Bank provided the microlenders with low-interest loans aimed at fostering entrepreneurship among impoverished women (Bond, 2007; Mainsah, Heuer & Zhang, 2004).

Microcredits are an integral part of microfinancing. Çetin & Keser (2018) reinforce this relationship by highlighting that microcredit is part of the microfinance system and as such it has become one of the most successful economic development tools for aid agencies and non-governmental organizations all over the world. A microcredit is the credit given to a micro-entrepreneur by microfinance institutions for the purpose of establishing and improving small businesses. Microcredits are generally provided for needs like operating capital, the purchase of raw materials or equipment, or the purchase of manufacturing equipment (Ören et al, 2012; Özmen, 2012). The essence of the micro-credit project, which was first initiated by Grameen Bank in rural Bangladesh, involves lending small amounts of money to small-scale/micro entrepreneurs to help them start an enterprise or make an investment. While such small credits were more widely applicable in agriculture from the 1950s to the 1980s, since the 1980s, the main focus has shifted towards non-agricultural micro-entrepreneurs, especially women (Baltacı, 2011). In the Global South, microfinancing is spread to countries such as Bangladesh, Cambodia, India, Afghanistan, Democratic Republic of Congo, Indonesia, and Ecuador, inclusive of South Africa. The importance of microfinancing made Kagan (2023) to reveal that the global microfinance market was valued at an estimated $187 billion in 2022, and is expected to exceed $488 billion by 2030.

Women Economic Empowerment Through Microfinancing

Women's empowerment is a situation in which women are given the opportunity to participate fully in social, political and economic spheres of life (Tandon, 2018). Empowering women means creating an enabling environment for women to implement government programs and organizational policies that affect their lives (Chattopadhyay, 2017). Thus, women's empowerment implies moving from a state of oppression to a state where both the oppressor and the oppressed are equal socially, politically, and economically (Chattopadhyay, 2017). The concept of empowerment can be better understood when it is related to the social, educational, economic, political and psychological empowerment of women. In this regard, the women's social empowerment addresses issues of gender inequalities that exist between men and women in society (Srivstav, 2020). Women's empowerment is a major topic of discussion in development and economics. Economic empowerment enables women to control and benefit from resources, wealth, and income (Buvinic, 2016). It also increases the ability to manage risk and improve well-being. It relates to women's ability to make strategic life choices previously denied to them (Tandon, 2018). The world, nations, corporations, communities, and groups can benefit from women's empowerment (Fundie & Chisoro, 2015). It improves the quality and quantity of human resources available for development.

Women's economic empowerment is the ability of women to participate in, contribute to, and benefit from growth processes in a way that recognizes the value of their contributions, respects their dignity, and allows for a more equitable sharing of the benefits of the economy to negotiate growth (Periznieto, 2016). Economic empowerment improves women's access to economic resources and opportunities, including jobs, financial services, property and other productive assets, skills development and market intelligence (Buvinic, 2016). Women's economic participation and empowerment is fundamental in augumenting women's rights and empowering women to take control of their lives and exert influence in society (Sweden, 2017). It is about creating just and equal societies (Sweden, 2017). Women often face discrimination and persistent gender inequalities, with some women facing multiple discrimination and marginalization based on factors such as ethnicity or caste.

FINDINGS AND ANALYSIS

Women Advantages Through Micro-Finance

Although micro-finance has been recognized by the United Nations as a main tool to reduce poverty especially for developing countries, scholars of economics and community development differ in their view of micro-finance in alleviating poverty at the local level. On the positive side, Vletter (2006, p. 4) argues that micro-finance institutions accommodate low minimum deposits. This kind of support is easily extended to rural areas where the majority poor live and it is easy to adapt the use of micro-credit to the needs of local communities in promoting self-sustainable schemes. The African Development Bank (2006, pp. 7 & 9) shares this view and adds that micro-credit programs promote both sustainable levels of social and economic development at the community level. This considers the fact that about one billion people, the majority from developing countries who are poor and deprived from the basic living conditions have access to micro-credit programs, which have flexibility to be applied and adapted to the context of the communities. While micro-credits indeed promote Community Economic Development (CED) as initiated by NGOs, first because NGOs are familiarized with CED principles, which are people driven and second, because NGOs are localized and close to the people, it is crucial to consider the fact that the recipients of these schemes operate the related micro-enterprises in structural unbalanced environment (Thapa, 2018; and Schapper, 2017). Von Kotze (2009, p. 12) cautions the fact that the failure of such enterprise development through micro-credits is often attributed to the beneficiaries' incapacity without considering the structural unbalanced environment.

In order to meet the financial needs of the needy women in particular and further reduce women's dependency on informal financial sources, Tarig & Sangmi (2018) argue for the adoption of microfinance an its implementation. There is empirical evidence that point to potential of microfinance in empowering women beyond the inclavity of informal economies. Empowerment in the context of exclusion and marginalisation should touch on social, economic, political and psychological aspects of empowering women key asset in the Global South. The question is how the distribution of financial resources could be at the centre of addressing challenges facing women in a holistic matter? However, for microfinance to have impact on the persistence of socio-economic, political and psychological marginalisation, an integrated microfinance package based on education activism, awareness about laws and politics and training for capacity building is imperative (Li, Gan, & Hu, 2011 & Ali and Hatta, 2012).

There are, however, development scholars who are skeptical of micro-credit programmes. Morduch (1998, p. 28), for example argues that there is little evidence to show that micro-credit schemes focus on the real issues of consumption. The preoccupation of those who offer micro-credit loans is on institution building, particularly for the funding institutions. There is, Morduch argues, very little concern with the daily struggles of the poor. Thapa (2007, p.19) comes to a similar conclusion to Morduch having studied outreach and poverty reduction programmes that have been carried out by various MFIs. For Thapa, the priority of the majority of MFIs is to secure their institutional financial sustainability, and through this process the issue of poverty reduction by targeting the poorest of the poor has been compromised. MFIs are known to market themselves especially amongst the unbanked or underbanked individuals by the traditional banking services (Servon, 2017). In terms of gender disparity and low status of women in society, Debnath et al., (2019) note that women empowerment has been prioritised by development agencies and governments around the world especially the developing countries.

The Role of Microfinancial Institutions (MFIs)

Evidence from literature shows that MFIs are capable of reducing poverty, promote women's entrepreneurship, create employment opportunities and boost business growth by providing access to credit to underserved markets (Kumari, 2021). Thapa argues that the moderately poor have been legible for micro-credit schemes to the exclusion of the poor since the very poor are viewed as more likely to default on repayments. In this context, the exclusion of the poor who are in real need of the micro-credit schemes is related to securing institutional financial sustainability rather than outreaching the real intended beneficiaries.

Microfinance institutions promote the inclusion of unserved and underserved populations in the financial system with a special focus on female customers, SMEs, and the rural and urban poor (AFI, 2020). These institutions play an important role for example, during the COVID-19 pandemic some government support was channelled through financial institutions (CGAP 2020 and 2021). The social mission of microfinance involves reaching a large number of customers by offering small-scale financial services such as microcredit (Hudak, 2012). As such, the number of loan accounts at microfinance institutions can be larger than at commercial banks in some cases (e.g., Bangladesh, Bolivia, Cambodia, and Nepal) while the total outstanding loans at microfinance institutions tend to be significantly lower than those at commercial banks.

Bayai & Ikhide (2016) consider the issue of financial sustainability of MFIs from the perspective of their dependence on the donors. Since the MFIs are not themselves financially self-sustainable, their impact on providing micro-credit schemes in a sustainable way to beneficiaries is compromised. Due to their dependence on donors MFIs are likely to resort to two options: first to provide micro-credit schemes to the poor and charge the commonly established 20% interest rate or second, charge higher-than normal interest. Wang (2023) points out that with the first option MFIs may maximize their impact on promoting poverty alleviation, which is aligned with sustainable community development. However, this choice can lead to serious challenges regarding to operational costs. Operational costs are those costs that are directly linked to the running of the institution as to provide the services to the beneficiaries such as payment of water, electricity, taxes, fuel and so on. With the second option the MFIs may minimize their role as development agent, since their sustainability would be compromised by high beneficiary repayment default rates.

Women Disadvantages through Microfinance

Despite the positives attached to micro-finance model, the micro-finance is criticized as a 'poverty trap' which according to Bateman (2010, p. 1) is an antagonistic to sustainable economic and social development and so also to sustainable poverty reduction. In this regard, Willis (2005:20) argues that alternatives such as micro-credits are not neutral within a neo-liberal agenda while Thabethe, et al (2012, p. 2) are of the opinion that micro-credits rather inculcate a culture that compels communities to rely on their own devices without addressing structural inequalities. Affleck & Mellor (2006, p.13) assert that micro-credit strategy is premised on the fact that poor people in disadvantaged communities remain poor due to latent entrepreneurial opportunities that are often left untapped. Bateman (2010, p. 2) associates micro-finance as one of those 'feel good' public relations and marketing effort where human dignity and self-respect are lost as the poor in developing countries are increasingly forced to accept their permanent engagement with the most primitive, illegal, dangerous and demeaning business activities imaginable. For example, the success of microcredit was acknowledged in Nepal for aiding low-income women, however, McMichael (2012) demonstrated that microcredit contributed in reinforcing gender hierarchies and husbands being accused of helping themselves with business incomes. Through micro-credit institutions, microcredit earned a bad name as a 'death-trap' for the poor (Manzur, 2017, p. 33). In the context of Bangladesh, Hickel (2015) claimed that:

most microfinance loans are used to fund consumption to help people buy the basic necessities they need to survive. Therefore, borrowers do not generate income that can be used to repay existing loans. (Hickel, 2015 in Manzur, 2017, p. 33)

Mordeno (2010, p. 4) highlighted some of the limits attached to micro-credit programmes. The author went on to say that micro-credits or micro-finance have been the alternative for provision of credit, especially in the rural areas that have been neglected by the traditional commercial banks. Mordeno (2010) argues that although the majority of people, including the poor live in the rural areas, there have not been policy incentives for commercial banks to invest in the rural areas. In addition, rural communities lack collaterals to attract private credit. In order to balance this scenario, government and civil society through NGOs and other forms of funding from within the community have promoted micro-finance or micro-credit institutions as alternative funding for poor people's development initiatives.

Boateng, Boateng & Bampoe (2015) makes another critical point about the impact of micro-credit programs. He states that micro-finance schemes may improve the basic conditions at the household level. However, such impact is not, or is hardly ever transcended to community and national levels. The association of the positive impact of micro-credit programs/micro-finance schemes exclusively at the household level and not to community and national levels is both due to the provided minor loans to the beneficiaries and lack of adequate legislation for the operation of this category of business, which is linked to the informal sector. Minor loans do not enable the recipients to run fledged micro-enterprises and lack of adequate legislation hinders the state mainly at the local level to collect the taxes.

CONCLUDING REMARKS

While the strategy of micro-finance is in fact increasingly adopted, especially in developing countries as an alternative to mainstream financing, the environment of the implementation of the related micro-enterprises has not been concurrent with human right approach, which is core principle of social justice and community development. The chapter was dependent on conceptual and theoretical literature and debates on micro-finance with particular focus on women as recipients. It also profiled the challenges faced by women in accessing economic empowerment and development. However, due to high competitiveness in the area of micro-enterprises women in particular are excluded from accessing finances to develop their enterprises beyond micro-enterprises. The chapter is critical of micro-finance industry as a strategy for poverty reduction. Therefore, the chapter recommends financial inclusivity for women economic empowerment which embraces inclusive of training and support by governments, NGOs and CBOs operating in the development field. Capacity building for women economic empowerment should embrace Artificial Intelligence (AI) to activate innovative ideas for competitive enterprises. This should consider growing an integrated package geared towards growing macro-businesses for women. To deal with women dependency on micro-lenders, valuable lessons could be drawn from the traditional cooperatives and credit union schemes which are known in the global south for genuine economic empowerment.

REFERENCES

Adebola, S. (2022). *Embedded finance is the next big thing for sub-Saharan Africa*. https://www.linkedin.com>pulse

Affleck, A., & Mellor, M. (2006). Community development finance: A neo-market solution to social exclusion? *Journal of Social Policy*, *35*(2), 303–319. doi:10.1017/S0047279405009542

AFI. (2020). *AFI Annual Report 2020*. https://issu.com/afi7/docs_annual_report

Agu, S. (2007). 'Gender Equality Education and Women Empowerment' The Nigerian Challenge, Multi-Disciplinary. *Journal of Research and Development (Srinagar)*, *8*(2), 134–152.

Akor, F. O. (2017). Reflections on the Role of Women in the African Development Process: lessons from Nigeria. In A. Amtaika (Ed.), Socio-Economic Development in Africa: Challenges and Dynamics (pp. 325-345). Pan-African University Press.

Ali, I., Hatta, Z. A., Azman, A., & Islam, S. (2017). Microfinance as a development and poverty alleviation tool in rural Bangladesh: A critical assessment. *Asian Social Work and Policy Review, 11*(1), 14–15. doi:10.1111/aswp.12106

Anderson, R. M. (2017). Patient empowerment: Myths and misconceptions. *Patient Education and Counselling.*

Anyaegbunam, N., & Alaga, E. (2025). Think beyond microfinance when talking about businesswomen. *AfricanRenewal., 29*(2), 22–23.

Bako, M. J., & Syed, J. (2018). Women's marginalization in Nigeria and the way forward. *Human Resource Development International, 21*(5), 425–443. doi:10.1080/13678868.2018.1458567

Bayai, I., & Ikhide, S. (2016). Financing and financial sustainability of microfinance institutions (MFIs): A conceptual view. *Banks and Bank Systems, 11*(2), 21–32. doi:10.21511/bbs.11(2).2016.03

Beeri, I., Uster, A., & Vigoda-Gadot, E. (2019). Does performance management relate to good governance? A study of its relationship with citizens' satisfaction with and trust in Israeli local government. *Public Performance & Management Review, 42*(2), 241–279. doi:10.1080/15309576.2018.1436074

Boateng, G. O., Boateng, A. A., & Bampoe, H. S. (2015). Microfinance and poverty reduction in Ghana: Evidence from policy beneficiaries. *Review of Business & Finance Studies, 6*(1), 99–108.

Bond, P. (2007). Two economies, microcredit and the Accelerated and Shared Growth Initaitive for South Africa. *The Journal of Development Studies, 37*(2), 216–230.

Buvinic, M., & Furst-Nichols, R. (2016). Promoting Women's Economic Empowerment: What Works? *The World Bank Research Observer, 31*(1), 59–101.

Buvinic, M., & O'Donnell, M. (2016). *Revisiting what works: women, economic empowerment and smart design. Centre for Global Development Review.*

Bvuma, S., & Marnewick, C. (2020). Sustainable livelihoods of township small, medium and micro enterprises towards growth and development. *Sustainability (Basel), 12*(8), 31–49. doi:10.3390u12083149

Çetin, I., & Keser, H. Y. (2018). Women Entrepreneurship in MENA and Europe: Empowerment Through Microfinance. In R. C. Das (Ed.), *Microfinance and Its Impact on Entrepreneurial Development* (pp. 30–51). Sustainability, and Inclusive Growth.

CGAP. (2020/2021). *Social Assistance Payments in Response to Covid-19: The Role of Donors.* www.cgap.org

Chattopadhyay, A. (2017). Women's empowerment: What works? *Journal of International Development, 28*(3), 342–359.

Debnath, D., Rahman, S., Acharjee, D. C., Latif, W. U., & Wang, L. (2019). Empowering Women through Microcredit in Bangladesh: An Empirical Study. *International Journal of Financial Studies,·7*(37), 1-11. https://www.researchgate.net/publication/334159798

Del Amo, I. F., Erkoyuncu, J. A., Roy, R., Palmarini, R., & Onoufriou, D. (2018). A systematic review of Augmented Reality content-related techniques for knowledge transfer in maintenance applications. *Computers in Industry*, *103*, 47–71. doi:10.1016/j.compind.2018.08.007

Folayan, M. O.-B. (2020). *Women's economic empowerment, participation in decision-making and exposure to violence as risk indicators for early childhood caries*. Academic Press.

Frediani, A. A., Clark, D. A., & Biggeri, M. (2019). Human Development and the Capability Approach: The Role of Empowerment and Participation. In The Capability Approach, Empowerment and Participation: Concepts, Methods and Applications (pp. 3-36). London: Palgrave Macmillan.

Fundie, A. M. S., Chisoro, C., & Karodia, A. M. (2015). The Challenges Facing Informal Traders in the Hilbrow Area of Johannesburg. *Kuwait Chapter of the Arabian Journal of Business and Management Review*, *4*(6), 46–75. doi:10.12816/0018968

Grant, M. J., & Booth, A. (2009). A typology of review: An analysis of 14 review types and associated methodologies. *Health Information and Libraries Journal*, *26*(2), 91–108. doi:10.1111/j.1471-1842.2009.00848.x PMID:19490148

Guillen, L., Mayo, M., & Karelaia, N. (2018). Appearing self-confident and getting credit for it: Why it may be easier for men than women to gain influence at work. *Human Resource Management*, *57*(4), 839–854. doi:10.1002/hrm.21857

Holland, J. H. (2018). The global economy as an adaptive process. In *The economy as an evolving complex system* (pp. 117–124). CRC Press. doi:10.1201/9780429492846-7

Holman, M. R. (2017). Women in local government: What we know and where we go from here. *State & Local Government Review*, *49*(4), 285–296. doi:10.1177/0160323X17732608

Hudak, K. (2012). 'What next for micro-finance? How the broader financial context matters for effective micro0finance outreach'. *Journal of Developmental Entrepreneurship*, *17*(4), 1–19. doi:10.1142/S1084946712500239

Ife, J. (2016). *Community Development in an Uncertain World* (2nd ed.). Cambridge University Press. doi:10.1017/CBO9781316342855

Imran, M., Ul Haq, S., & Ozcatalbas, O. (2022). Role of Microcredit in Sustainable Rural Development. In *Sustainable Rural Development Perspective and Global Challenges* (pp. 1-22). London: IntechOpen.

Johnson, S. (2019). *Globalization and gender-dilemmas for microfinance organizations*. Small Enterprise Development.

Kagan, J. (2023). *Microfinance Definition: Benefits, History, and How It Works*. https://www.investopedia.com/terms/m/microfinance.asp#citation-20

Karl, E. N. (2017). Empowerment of youths in rural areas through agricultural development programmes: Implications for poverty reduction in South Africa. *Journal of Research in Agriculture and Forestry, 212*.

Khursheed, A. (2022). Exploring the role of microfinance in women's empowerment and entrepreneurial development: A qualitative study. *Future Business Journal*, *8*(1), 57. doi:10.118643093-022-00172-2

Kolovich, M. (2018). Fiscal policies and gender equality. In L. Kolovich (Ed.), *Fiscal Policies and Gender Equality* (pp. 1–8). International Monetary Fund.

Kumari, J. A. P. (2021). Instrument development of microfinance on poverty reduction: Pilot study in Sri Lankan microfinance sector. *Himalayan Journal of Economics and Business Management*, *2*(2), 8–16.

Kusi, A., Yussif, S., & Ismail, A. (2019). Access to micro credit by women entrepreneurs in Ghana: Sinapi aba Trust-Kumasi in retrospect. *International Journal of Academic Research in Business & Social Sciences*, *9*(9), 590–613. doi:10.6007/IJARBSS/v9-i9/6336

Li, X., Christopher, G., & Hu, B. (2011). The Credit Programme: A Case Study from Impact of Micro-credit on Women's Empower- Bangladesh: Evidence from China. *Journal of Chinese Economic and Business Studies*, *9*, 239–261. doi:10.1080/14765284.2011.592352

Mainsah, E, Heuer, S.R, Kalra, A & Zhang, Q. (2004). Grameen Bank: Taking capitalism to the poor. *Chazen Web Journal of International Business*.

Manzur, M. (2017). Impact of Non-Government Organisations and Microcredit Institutions on the Development of Bangladesh. *Political Science Undergraduate Review, 2*(2017), 30-35. https://journals.library.ualberta.ca/psur/index.php/psur/article/view/34/32

Masuku, M.M., & Jili, N.N. (2019). Public service delivery in South Africa: The political influence at local government level. *Journal of Public Affairs*, 1-7

McMichael, P. (2012). *Development and Social Change: A Global Perspective*. SAGE.

Mengista, W., Soromessa, T., & Legese, G. (2019). *Method for conducting systematic literature review and meta-analysis for environmental science research*. Elsevier B.V.

Mishra, P. (2021). Local Governance and Poverty Reduction in India: The Role of Micro-Finance. *Turkish Online Journal of Qualitative Inquiry, 12*(10).

Mordeno, K. (2010). *Micro-finance: The path to poverty alleviation*. http//stjliblog.wordpress.com/category/essay/content

Mphaka, P. L. (2017). *Strategies for Reducing Microfinance Loan Default in Low-Income Markets* [Doctoral dissertation]. Walden University.

Mutale, T. M., & Mtapuri, O. (2023). Rural Women's Perceptions of Poverty and Inequality in Mungwi District, Zambia. In O. Mtapuri (Ed.), *Poverty, Inequality, and Innovation in the Global South* (pp. 307–244). Palgrave Macmillan. doi:10.1007/978-3-031-21841-5_15

NZAID. (2007). *Achieving Gender Equality and Women Empowerment*. https://devpolicy.org>nzaid-achieving-gender-equality-and-women-empowerment

Opportunity International. (2022). *Global Report.* https://issuu.com/opportunity/docs/global-report-2022/2?ff&pageLayout=singlePage

Saqib, N. (2016). Women empowerment and economic growth: Empirical evidence from Saudi Arabia. *Advances in Management & Applied Economics.*

Schapper, A. (2017). Children's rights implementation as a multi-level governance process. *Human Rights Quarterly, 39*(1), 104–129.

Schneider, H. (2018). Empowerment in HCI-A survey and framework. In *Proceedings of the 2018 CHI Conference on Human Factors in Computing Systems* (pp. 1-14). 10.1145/3173574.3173818

Servon, L. (2017). *The unbanking of America: How the new middle class survives.* Houghton Mifflin Harcourt.

Snyder, H. (2019). Literature review as a research methodology: A review and guidelines. *Journal of Business Research, 104*, 333–339. doi:10.1016/j.jbusres.2019.07.039

Stuart, S. (2018). Advancing the economic empowerment and autonomy of women in the Caribbean through the 2030 Agenda for Sustainable Development. *ECLAC-Studies and Perspective – The Caribbean, 60.*

Tariq, S., & Sangmi, M.D. (2028). Microfinance and Women empowerment: A Brief Review of Literature. *Pacific Business Review International, 11*(3), 77–83.

Thabethe, N., Vhumani, M., & Nyuswa, M. (2012). Micro-credit as a community development strategy: a South African Case Study. *Community Development Journal, 47*(3), 423-435. https://www.jstor.org/stable/pdf/26

Thapa, N. B. (2018). *Empowering citizen and community through social mobilisation* [Doctoral dissertation].

Todaro, M. P., & Smith, S. C. (2020). *Economic Development.* Pearson.

Von Kotze, A. (2009). But what will we eat? Research questions and priorities for work and learning. In L. Cooper & S. Walters (Eds.), *Learning/Work: Turning Work and Lifelong Learning Inside Out* (pp. 16–29). HSRC Press.

Wang, F., Du, L., Tian, M., Liu, Y., & Zhang, Y. (2023). Sustainability of rural tourism in poverty reduction: Evidence from panel data of 15 underdeveloped counties in Anhui Province, China. *PLoS One, 18*(3), e0283048. doi:10.1371/journal.pone.0283048 PMID:36913402

World Bank Group. (2018). *An Incomplete Transition: Overcoming the Legacy of Exclusion in South Africa.* World Bank Group.

Yadav, S. B., & Mittal, R. (2016). Poverty Alleviation through Micro Finance in India: Empirical Evidences. *Research Journal of Humanities and Social Sciences, 7*(4), 259–267.

Chapter 9
Processes, Challenges, and Outcomes of the Self-Provision of Micro-Credit Schemes by Women's Groups in Chókwè Region, Mozambique

Ndwakhulu stephen Tshishonga
University of KwaZulu-Natal, South Africa

ABSTRACT

The majority of poor people in Mozambique have been excluded from getting loans, even from traditional financial institutions, since they do not have valuable assets or credit histories to enable them to be legible from those loans. This chapter focused on the self-provision of micro-credits by the community grouping from the 4th Neighbourhood in Chókwè district as the selected case study. This chapter examines and evaluates the effectiveness of micro-credit schemes in alleviating poverty and creating jobs for women. The chapter found that self-mobilization and solidarity were crucial in enhancing the self-provision of micro-credit schemes. The data for this chapter was obtained through the use of interviews with 20 women operating under self-credit schemes at 4th Neighbourhood in Chókwè region.

INTRODUCTION

Internationally, people are struggling because they are unable to access financial services, leaving them with limited income and job opportunities (Kato & Kratzer, 2013; Njiraini, 2015). According to the World Bank, 2 billion people, more than half of the world's adults, have no access to banking services (World Vision, 2019). When formalised microfinance is not available, families frequently have to rely on loans from traditional moneylenders who charge very high interest rates (Anyaegbunam & Alaga, 2025). Money obtained could be put to use for investment in their farms and feeding their families. Thus besides the high interest rates make it impossible for the poorest families to break even and move out of

DOI: 10.4018/978-1-6684-8979-6.ch009

this cycle of exploitation (Khursheed, 2022). Thus, the exclusion of the poor people especially women from the traditional financial institutions to access credit programmes in order to engage in livelihoods strategies to enhance their households' income and meet the basic needs, is a global concern especially in developing countries (Musau, 2015). This scenario has resulted in the emergence of global movement of both micro-finance institutions and community-based organizations with financial programmes tailored to the needs of poor people (World Vision, 2019). This chapter focuses on the self-provision of micro-credits by poor community-based groups in partnership with the World Vision. World vision is an international Christian NGO, which operates in Mozambique. The focus area of World Vision is to implement development programs to eradicate poverty in selected provinces in Mozambique. The majority of poor people in Mozambique do not have valuable assets or credit histories to enable them to benefit from loans, even from traditional financial institutions (Arnold, 2017).

For poverty to be addressed and jobs created, microfinancing is key. In essence, financial assistance in the form of micro-financial schemes, micro-enterprises should not only benefit the poor financially but should also empower them to manage and sustain their enterprises (Dias, 2007). Thus, loans are dispersed to facilitate localized development initiatives aimed at uprooting poverty and underdevelopment. As a result, a growing number of NGOs in Mozambique are engaged in micro-credit projects in partnership with poor community-based groups (CBGs), as a means of facilitating alternative financing. As a result of these micro-credit initiatives, local community groupings are able to initiate and run small businesses in partnership with NGOs. This thus allows poor communities to meet some of their basic needs such as housing, water, food security, education and health. Exclusion of the poor people from the traditional financial institutions to access credit programs in order to engage in livelihoods strategies to enhance their households' income and meet the basic needs, is a global concern especially in developing countries. This scenario has resulted in the emergence of global movement of both micro-finance institutions and community based organizations with financial programs tailored to the needs of poor people. Globally through micro-finance and community based organizations over ninety two million poor people have been reached out with more incidence to women, corresponding to 83%. The related benefits extended to 333 million family members (micro-credit summit campaign report, 2005; Reed, 2013). Nevertheless, globally it has been recognized that the financial programs tailored to meet the needs of the majority poor people may not be viewed in isolation. Therefore, the need to synchronize those tailored micro-credit programs with the perspective of the sustainable livelihood framework embedded with community development approach, which empower the poor people, especially women from the structural practices that are greatly linked to the exclusion of the poor communities from resources and opportunities (Bvuma & Marnewick, 2020).

This chapter is grounded on the self-provision of micro-credits by poor community-based groups in Chokwe District in Gaza Province in Mozambique. This type of micro-credit scheme is referred to as 'self-provision' since the funds are used to promote micro-credit lending is from the contributions made within the group members themselves and not from an external agency (Marceno, 2018). Therefore, the chapter examines and evaluates the effectiveness of micro-credit schemes in alleviating poverty. Objectives were to: 1) explore the roles, opportunities and advantages of micro-credit schemes operate in the Chókwè region, 2) examine the impact of self-provided micro-credit schemes on women socio-economic empowerment in Chokwe's Region and 3) is to determine the challenges faced by women micro-entrepreneurs within the Chokwe Region.

BACKGROUND

Chókwè District as the Site of the Study

The study upon which the data was obtained is located in Chókwè, a predominantly rural district in the Southern province of Gaza in Mozambique. Chókwè borders Guijá and Mabalane districts in the north; Xai-Xai and Bilene districts in the south; Chibuto district in the east and Magude and Massingir districts in the west. Massingir district in the northwest borders South Africa. (Public Administration Ministry: 2014) The Limpopo River is the main hydrographic resource of Southern Mozambique which runs through the length of the district. Its territory is comprised of 2.443 square kilometers with a population of 183 531. The majority of the population is female (102.946), which correspond to 56.1%. The male population is 80.585, which correspond to 43.9%. 72.000 people comprise the economically active population. There is an unemployment rate of 40%. The main economic activity is agriculture, which encompasses about 80% of active labour. 10% of active population is engaged in informal trading activity. Within this area, there are cycles of two types of climate features, namely droughts and floods (Statistics National Institute, 2016: 10).

According to the Poverty Annual Report (2014: 52) 60% of the population in Chókwè district is considered to be poor. The monthly average household income is $60 USD (United States Dollars). This is despite the fact that Chókwè district has high potential for agricultural development. About 40% of Mozambique's irrigated land is situated in this district. On average each household has access to about 1.5 hectare of land, corresponding to 10.000 hectares of land in total. This represents 5% of the total area of the district (Public Administration Ministry, 2014). The basic produced crops are maize, rice, variety of beans, cassava and sweet potatoes. Households also make use of the land to grow a wide range of vegetables, cashew-nuts, tobacco, sugar-cane and copra. There is also a number of farming companies in Chókwè district which produce cotton, rice, maize and tomato (Ismael, et al. 2021).

While there is great potential for food security and abundance in this district, this is constantly threatened by drought and floods. Floods are associated with loss of lives and the destruction of physical infrastructures (Njogu, 2021). Because of this, households in this district tend to store food such as cereal and cassava for future consumption. These foods can be stored for up to three months. However, natural disasters and the lack of resources for seed farming projects has meant that the harvest from the household farming is not been enough to satisfy the basic food needs of the people. These needs have to be met through non-farming income generation programmes such as making and selling of traditional beverages and remittances sent by the miners working in South Africa (Public Administration Ministry, 2014: 20).

A variety of NGOs and Community-Based organizations (CBOs) exist in Chókwè district whose aim is to alleviate the crisis associated with drought and floods, and poor resource management. Their activities range from community support for public health, micro-credit, and agriculture, small scale fishing etc. (Statistics National Institute, 2016, p.12). Chókwè district is also an ideal location for developmental intervention given the rich resources in this area and the entrepreneurial spirit of the people of the district. A number of commercial farming companies are also located in Chókwè hence it has great potential for creating (and sustaining) income generating activities. The regulated informal market activities by the local administrative body; the combination of both household farming to promote food security and commercial oriented crops production for trade with farming companies and potential for fishing are resources that can be mobilized in creating and sustaining income-generating activities by poor community-based groups (Public Administration Ministry, 2014: 20).

Figure 1. Administrative map of Mozambique with Gaza province and Chókwè district highlighted
Source: Public Administration Ministry (2014)

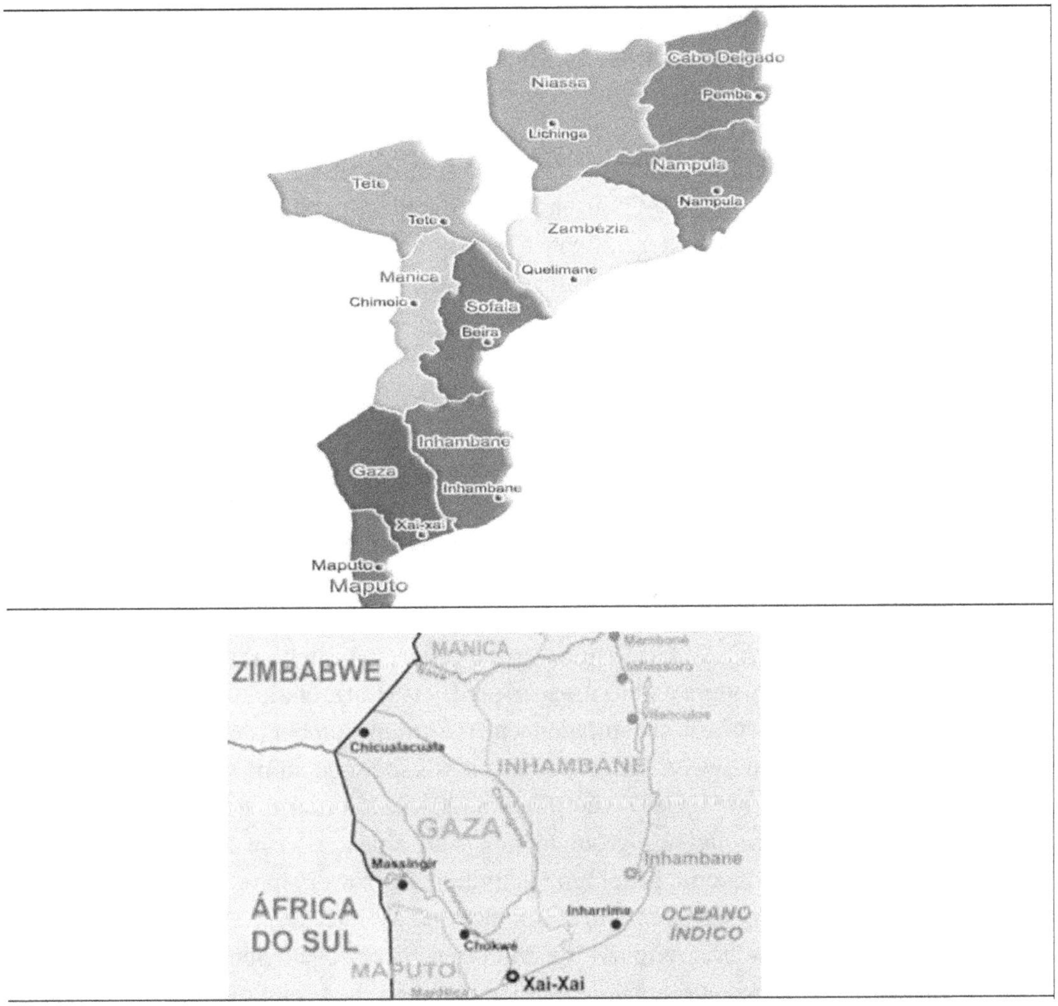

World Vision International has been operating in Mozambique since 1983. Initially it settled in Mozambique to respond to the needs of displaced people due to the civil war that escalated in the period 1986 to 1992. Currently it is implementing its programmes in the southern province of Gaza; central province of Tete; and norther provinces of Zambezia and Nampula. World Vision is a Christian organization and its mission is to alleviate poverty within the Christian principles (www.wvi.org/mozambique). The World Vision developmental programmes range from sponsorship for child education, health care, water and sanitation, small scale farming and natural disaster mitigation, especially for floods and droughts in the context of Mozambique. As a cross-cutting initiative for the communities that are beneficiaries from the World Vision programs, a model of ASCAS (Accumulative Savings and Credit Associations) for group self-provision of micro-credit scheme has been disseminated and especially the vulnerable people have been mobilized to participate in order to generate income and savings to meet their households' basic needs (Vletter, 2006). World Vision's savings groups have been partnering with VisionFund International to access additional loan capital (World Vision, 2020). For those groups or individuals who need more capital, VisionFund provides larger amounts than what the savings groups can provide, enabling members to increase their income and support the community's economic growth (World Vision, 2020). For the community groups that adhere to ASCAS model in addition to providing administrative support to establish the group organizational structure and conflict mediations, World Vision has also provided basic training for small business management. World Vision has also provided minor equipment and office supplies for the startup process (www.wvi.org/mozambique). The role of World Vision is to facilitate the promotion of ASCAS model through the self-provision of micro-credit schemes. This initiative is within the backdrop that the availability of household income in vulnerable communities is essential to access the basic needs and be able to better mitigate to emerging natural disasters. The ASCAS model is also viewed as a strategy to respond to the exclusion of the poor communities by the traditional financial institution (Swack and Manson, 1994; McMurtry, 1993).

In Chókwè district (and indeed throughout Mozambique), the World Vision has been promoting the creation of community groupings of poor households to mobilize funds for self-provision of micro-credit schemes for income generating activities and savings (Chaturvedi, 2016). These groupings and alternative funding are known as Accumulative Savings and Credit Associations (ASCAS). The aim of ASCAS program is to assist poor households in gaining access to credit, generating income and promoting savings in order to improve their basic living conditions, including food security. World Vision's role within this programme is to provide skills training, basic equipment (including a safe for each community-based group to keep the fund before it is deposited in the group's bank account), and office supplies (such as pens, calculators and writing pads). World Vision also assists each group to set up administrative structures to oversee administrative matters and to mediate conflicts (Lutz, et al. 2017).

The group administrative structure in consultation with the group members decides on which minimum contribution is acceptable. Depending on each group member's socio-economic status, each deposit may vary from 150 to 1000 MTs ($5 to 50 USD) (Chaturvedi, 2016). In order to promote the sustainability of the group fund, group members and non-group members are able to borrow amounts up to 50 000 Mt ($1600 USD) which is used for income generating activities. Borrowers have to reimburse the loan in four installments, which may vary between four to six months. An interest rate of about 10% is charged each time a client borrows from the group. At the end of each year cycle period, the generated profit from the accumulated group fund is proportionally shared among the group members.

LITERATURE ON MICROFINANCE AND CREDIT

Empowerment Through Microfinance

Due to the prevalence of poverty, unemployment and underdevelopment globally more particularly in the developing nations, micro-finance or credit emerged to be the policy and programme interventions (Yadav & Mittal, 2016; and Mishra, 2021). Access to financial services and credit is key in advancing development while lack of access to such services can constrain development (Imran, *Ul* Haq & Ozcatalbas, 2022). However, Imran et al., (2022) argue that low or no access to financial services especially for marginalised rural people whom are often ignored by conventional financial institutions such as banks and other microlending institutions. Thus, the need for development and the legacies of exclusion and marginalisation led the emergence of microfinance institutions and non-bank credit providers (World Bank Group, 2018). For micro-financing or credit, women are the primary target as women are characterised as the high-poverty group with low per capital incomes (Todaro & Smith, 2020). In addition, women are prone to experience poverty and other financial exclusion and hardships, women are often trusted to repay the loans on time and fundamental, microcredit has the potential to address gender disadvantages in society (Ife, 2016).

Microfinance and credit are terms intrinsically linked and often used interchangeably (Imran et al., 2022). Microfinance is broader than microcredit. Microfinance is inclusive of providing small loans for community collective projects together with other financial services in the form of small business advise (Ife, 2016). For Todaro & Smith (2020), microfinance is financial services given to people especially the poor who are unable to access such services from the commercial banks. While microcredit is more limited to the provision of small individual loans. These differences or interface led to the terminology trajectory from microcredit (1980s) through microfinance (1990s) to financial inclusion (2010s) (Gerard & Johnston, 2019: 878). Literature views microfinance to financial services in the form of small or micro amounts of money (see Gerard & Johnston, 2019). As a financial strategy, microfinancing benefits low income earners especially women through granting them loans, savings, insurance and remittances. Sarumathi and Mohan (2011:1) ascertain that "microfinance, is banking the unbankables, bringing credit, savings and other essential financial services within the reach of millions of people who are too poor to be served by regular banks, in most cases because they are unable to offer sufficient collateral". Thus, within the neo-liberal framework, microfinance emerged to devolved responsibility for development to the individual as self-maximizer (McMichael, 2012). McMichael (2012, p. 220) went on to outline three functions associated with microfinance, namely: 1) providing credit to the poor as an entrepreneurial 'leg up', 2) deepening market relations and finally 3) enlarging financial opportunity in the form of legitimacy repair. Targeting women and granting them loans is considered as a substantial means of encouraging them and enhancing their financial status (Khursheed, 2022). Ali, Hatta, Azman & Islam (2017) are of the view that, "women have been intended for microfinance and microcredit because they tend to be mostly troubled by insufficiency than men, and the responsibility for the well-being of the household lies upon them". Thus, if women are actively involved and engaged in financial programmes and services, they do not only improve their household decision-making to become better, but they become positively impacted, as well as their economic empowerment (Ali & Hatta, 2012). Additionally, "access to credit is considered by development agencies as a crucial element of economic empowerment, as it can play a significant role in the process of emerging strategies of the livelihood of women 'given their responsibility in fulfilling both social and economic roles in society" (Ali & Hatta, 2012: 114). Contributing to the afore statement, Kato and Kratzer (2013) state that economic empowerment also be directed to women because they are seen as passionate in development programmes and also that they take responsibility for everyone within the household, particularly the children.

Microfinance as a Challenge

Bayai & Ikhide (2016) raised the financial sustainability of MFIs from the perspective of their dependence on the donors. Since the MFIs are not themselves financially self-sustainable, their impact on providing micro-credit schemes in a sustainable way to beneficiaries is compromised. Linked with issue of MFIs dependence over donors, MFIs are likely to resort to two options: first to provide micro-credit schemes to the poor and charge the commonly established 20% interest rate or second, charge higher-than normal interest. Wang, Du, Tian, Liu & Zhang (2023) points out that with the first option MFIs may maximize their impact on promoting poverty alleviation, which is aligned with sustainable community development (Mishra,2021). However, this choice will lead to serious challenges regarding to operational costs. Operational costs are those costs that are directly linked to the running of the institution as to provide the services to the beneficiaries such as payment of water, electricity, taxes, fuel and so on. With the second option the MFIs may minimize their role as development agent, since their sustainability would be compromised by high beneficiary repayment default rates.

Microfinance "has been critiqued for adding to the duty-load of already burdened women, as they would now have to fulfil their customarily prescribed responsibilities of taking care of their children and household in addition to their economic programmes" (Ali & Hatta, 2012, p.115). It is clear that giving out loans and credits will not create any solution for women's empowerment but increases debt for women thus increasing their vulnerability in the globalised world (Al Mamun & Fazal, 2018). Services such as microfinance are directed towards women economic programmes with inefficient empowerment strategies and networks support, which can contribute to shifting all the burdens of household debt to these women (Debnath, Rahman, Acharjee, Latif & Wang 2019). Similarly, Ali and Hatta (2012:116) maintain that" the results of microfinance on incapacitated women cause debt, leading to challenges of withstanding women violence and in some cases subject women to violence from a spouse". Importantly, microfinance institutions do not have a long-term view of what happens to the programmes ran by their beneficiaries (Banerjee & Jackson, 2017; Kiunga, 2019). . Instead, they measure success in terms of the number of people enrolled and funds paid and recovered, not making a follow-up to find out if the program funded is still in existence, and to be aware of the surroundings in which these social transactions take place". Karim (2014) additionally ascertain that, women are often compelled by their partners to participate in microfinance activities meaning, they receive loans not for them, but for benefit of their husbands. Additionally, some women get grant on behalf of wealthy women in exchange for minimal amount of cash (Santoso, 2016). Therefore, the lack of fairness is likely to result in similar results which do not benefit women generally.

Although women are the most beneficiaries of micro-credit schemes, Noor, Isa & Nor (2021, p. 350) points out that the majority of women worldwide and particularly those from the developing countries, are not self-sufficient and lack autonomy and authority in regard to decision-making. Noor, Isa & Nor (2021, p. 351) argues that patriarchal practices and ideologies render women the poorest segment. Micro-credit has perpetuated gender division first because women have been equated with the term micro. Women, in accessing micro-credit, tend to access smaller loans than men, which has made it difficult for women to transcend from group-based recipient of micro-credit to individual recipient with flexibility to attain solid business (Kusi, Yussif & Ismail, 2019). In addition, Chinomona & Maziriri (2015) argues, women, while more reliable lenders, often lack business skills to effectively respond to markets environment namely opportunities and threats. The argument is that women's income generating activities have not been scrutinized in terms of the typology of activity, capital needed for the activity, duration of the activity and profitability of activity (Alam, Moir & Ibn-Boamah, 2021). Thus, the sustainability and viability of women's income generating activities are fundamental. However, progressive micro-credit program leaders have recognized this and have targeted women as recipients of micro-credit schemes (Le & Stefanczyk, J2018).. Micro-credit schemes through a variety of practices have been one of the main strategies devised to improve the socio-economic status of women, linked to income generating activities.

Case Study Context: 4th Neighbourhood at Chókwè

The 4th Neighbourhood is located in the greater Chókwè district. The majority of the members of the self-provision of micro-credit groupings live in the 4th Neighbourhood. The 4th Neighbourhood has common borders with other Neighbourhoods: the 1st Neighbourhood in the south; the 2nd Neighbourhood in the north; the 3rd Neighbourhood in the west and the 5th Neighbourhood in the east. There are 5 quarters and 25 blocks in this Neighbourhood. Each quarter is made up of 50 households and each block is made up of 10 households. The 4th Neighbourhood is divided into sections A and B. There are 12 blocks in section A and 13 blocks in section B (Public Administration Ministry, 2014). It is important to mention that there is the Neighbourhood secretary, who is responsible for the Neighbourhood affairs, the quarter chief who is responsible for the 50 households and the block chief who is responsible for the 10 households form part of the administrative structure. The affairs in the Neighbourhood at all the levels are liaised through summoned community meetings. The 4th Neighbourhood and the other Neighbourhoods in within Chókwè district are under the Chókwè municipality jurisdiction; that is, they are accountable to the Chókwè municipality (Public Administration Ministry, 2014).

Figure 2. Organogram of the 4th Neighbourhood local administrative structure

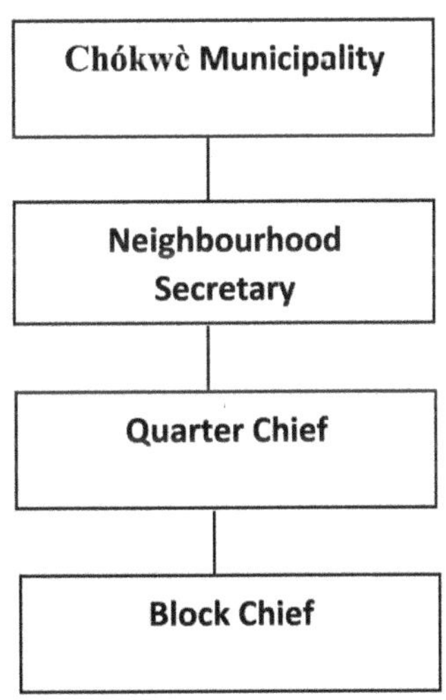

In the 4th Neighbourhood there is a primary school, the 4th Neighbourhood primary school, which is located in section A. The primary school has grades 1 to 5. The youth from this Neighbourhood go to the neighbouring 1st Neighbourhood to attend secondary level education, the 1st Neighbourhood secondary school. They may also choose to go to other primary and secondary schools in the 1st and 5th Neighbourhoods, which are the 1st and 5th Neighbourhoods' primary and secondary schools respectively. The other existing basic services, in the 4th Neighbourhood include health services from the 4th Neighbourhood local health facility, taped water and electricity. The 4th Neighbourhood local health facility is located in section B (Statistics National Institute, 2016).

Apart from the above-mentioned infrastructures related to basic services provision, the 4th Neighbourhood is characterized by untarred roads. Most of the households own houses made of reed with corrugated iron roofs. Some households own grass huts and few household own houses made by bricks (Statistics National Institute, 2016).

The main market is in the 4th Neighbourhood in section B, "o futuro melhor" market, which corresponds to better future market as translated in English. Some of the main service offered within the market include the sale of the basic food products such as rice, beans, potatoes, fresh and dried fish, maize flour, cooking oil and so on. Second hand clothes (used clothes) are also traded in the market. There is a local warehouse in the market that supplies the basic food products to the retailers. There are some workshops in the surrounding market, which offer services such as car repairing and welding (Poverty Annual Report, 2014). The social organization in the 4th Neighbourhood is mainly comprised by religious affiliation. While some community members attend Christian religion, the majority attend the African traditional religion, the "Zion" church. There are very few community members who attend the Muslim religion. It should be noted that the Muslim Religion is widely practiced in the Central and Northern regions of Mozambique and not in the Southern region as is the case of Chókwè district and the 4th Neighbourhood. In general some community members consult the traditional doctors in the 4th Neighbourhood (Statistics National Institute, 2016).

Figure 3. Community map: 4th Neighbourhood in Chókwè district

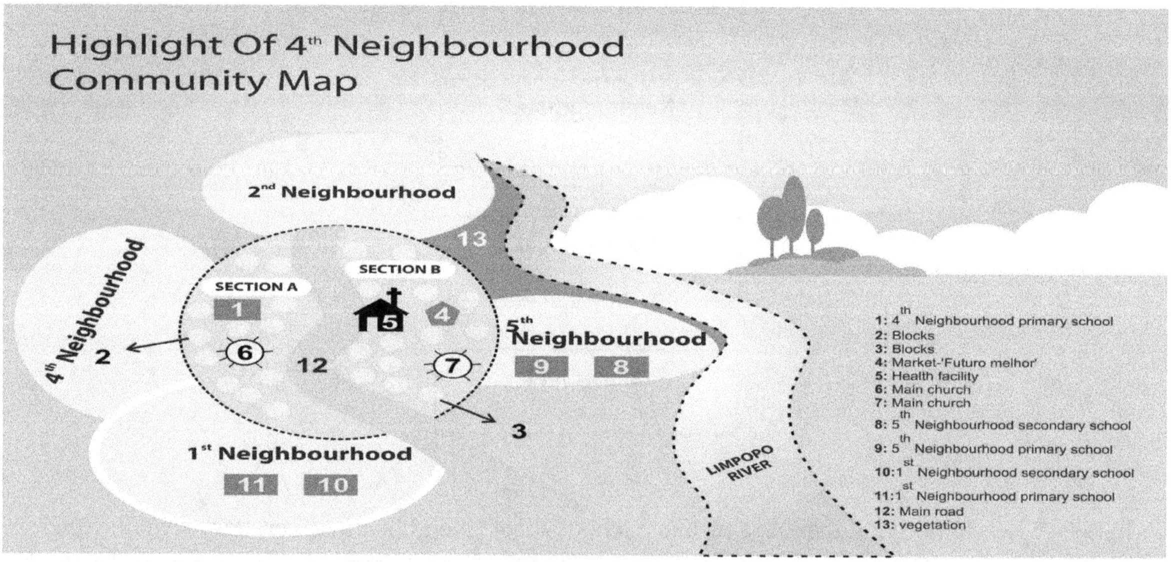

The main economic activity in the 4th Neighbourhood is agriculture, taking into account that its soil is fertile. In fact The Limpopo River, the main hydrographic resource of Southern Mozambique, which runs the length of the district also benefits the households in the 4th Neighbourhood. The basic produced crops by the household small scale farming are maize, rice, variety of beans, cassava and sweet potatoes. Households also produced typical commercial crops such as cashew-nuts, tobacco, sugar-cane and copra to supply to industrial farmers within the greater Chókwè region. Small scale fishing, raise cattle and informal trading also characterize the economic activity in the 4th Neighbourhood (Public Administration Ministry, 2014).

Although the 4th Neighbourhood and in fact the Chókwè region have fertile soil associated with the tropical weather, which is generally characteristic in Mozambique, there have been cyclical periods of floods. The most devastating sequels of the floods in the 4th Neighbourhood and Chókwè region have been the destruction of both household and government infrastructures. The destruction of infrastructure has forced the displacement of the communities to higher level land locations within Chókwè region or to other districts during the flooding periods (Ministry of Agriculture, 2009). The people from the 4th Neighbourhood often use firewood for cooking. They also buy charcoal brought in from the distant villages. Some of the villages that still produce charcoal from local bushes are Donga, Pelane, Newango and Chichongole. These villages are located in far distances, which range from 45 to 60 kilometers from the 4th Neighbourhood (Statistics National Institute, 2016).

METHODOLOGY

Considering that this study is qualitative in nature, both techniques such as individual interviews and systematic literature reviewer were used to collect data. Questions schedule was used to engage participants for this chapter. 20 participants were sampled from the members of the micro-credit schemes based in Chokwe District. The participants were sampled through the use of purposive and random selection techniques. Those selected to partake in the study had more than three years as members of the micro-credit schemes. and could share valuable information on role/benefits, impact and challenges of microfinance towards poverty reduction and job creation. Their ages varied from 22 to 66 years. Through the correlation between the age group and the number of the recipients of self-provided micro-credit schemes it was identified that 4 women were young and belonged to the age group of 22-23. 5 participants belonged to the age group of 34-37 and the majority adult 11 participants belonged to the age group of 45-66.

Table 1. Age variation of the recipients of the self-provided micro-credit schemes

Age Group	Recipients of Self-Provided Micro-Credit Schemes
22-23	4
34-37	5
45-66	11

Author's Analysis

Their level of education ranged from adult education, primary and secondary levels. Some of the participants did not attend school at all (none). The (2) young recipients of the self-provided micro-credit schemes attended the secondary level of education. And across the other age groups, the recipients of the self-provided micro-credit schemes attended primary (9), none (7) and adult education (2) levels. Therefore, there were recipients of the self-provided micro-credit schemes that according to their age groups (34-66 and 37-66) attended primary level of education or none of the level. In other words the age groups varied when correlated with the level of education of the participants of self-provided micro-credit schemes.

Table 2. Age group correlated to level of education

Age Group	Level of Education	Frequency
22-23	Secondary	2
34-66	Primary	9
37-66	None	7
45	Adult education	2

Author's Analysis

Participants were provided with three questions for them to answer. Questions asked to the participants were: 1) what role does the micro-credit scheme play in reducing poverty?, 2) What is the impact of micro-credit scheme on the reduction of poverty; 3) what are the challenges of micro-credit scheme in reducing poverty?

Second technique used for gathering data was the systematic literature review of literature on microfinance and credit in the context of women economic empowerment. Scopus, ScienceDirect and Google Scholars were mainly used as the databases for this chapter. Literature review was conducted based on peer-reviewed articles from local and international journals and publications pertaining to poverty reduction through microfinancing and credit. ScienceDirect is an online collection of published scientific research operated by the publisher (Gonçalves et al. 2018). While Scopus is an international database of peer-reviewed publications from all over the world (Ershov, Perevozchikova & Romanova, 2019). The third database used was Google scholar, which provides useful information on the conceptual and theoretical understanding of microfinance and credit. Apart from the articles obtained from the above-mentioned databases, the chapter also relied on peer-reviewed books and book chapters on advantages, opportunities and impact on microfinance for women empowerment.

FINDINGS AND ANALYSIS

Role/Opportunities and Advantages of Micro-Finance on Income-Generating Projects

The essence of micro-credit provision is that they accrued benefits linked with the generation of profit. The generated profit would enable the households not only to access valuable assets but also to improve their socio-economic status. The loans were determinant in promoting a shift on households' socio-economic status. Participants who owned relatively established fledging micro-businesses such as homemade bricks, maize, women's hair products, charcoal and tomatoes from their small-scale farming, mentioned to have experienced upwards shift on their socio-economic status. In fact those participants reported that the established micro-businesses, as part of self-employment promotion, have been a source of household income that enabled the attainment of the basic needs in a sustainable manner. A participant said that:

Definitely I am not rich, but somehow the type of the house, belongings, the degree of satisfaction of our basic needs in my family, and some of the services that we are able to pay for allowed us to improve our life in the community compared to other households. Although my house is not as big as others in the community it is a brick house, which is durable and offer more comfort. I used to sleep in a typical house in the community, which was made of reed and plastered with heavy sand.

The participants were proud of the durability of their properties. This is of extreme importance, when considering the fact that some of the basic needs may be accessed in periodical basis and depends on additional services for their sustainable use. A participant opinioned that:

Although I could have the water stored in my cemented water container, this water depended on the rain fall. Now the 1000 liter rubber container that I bought allows me to store water in it all the time. This is because it is removable, which enables it to be transported to the distant water source location to be filled with water in case we face some problems in the community in terms of drinking water. The generated profit also enables me to hire a small truck to carry the rubber container for the transportation purpose.

The income and profit generated from their small businesses afforded them an opportunity to improve their housing situation through the use of locally based and conventional resources. In addition, the generated profit enabled these households to have enough time to prepare their farms.

I still have my reed built house but it is comfortable now because its walls are now plastered with cement. Houses in the community are generally plastered with heavy sand. The floor of my house has also been upgraded with cement. This makes the house more comfortable. The other valuable thing that I managed to buy through the profit from my small business is the leather furniture that replaced the straw furniture. We used to take a lot of time ploughing the farm with oxen but now with the generated profit from the small business I hire a tractor. With the tractor the whole farm is ploughed in a single day, while it took several days when we used oxen. (Owner of maize business)

Owning the leather furniture, brick houses, rubber made water containers to store water, ability to hire a tractor to plough their household farms and bricks-built wall around the yard and other improvements in their households were indicators of upward mobility on their socio-economic status. The participants stressed that these belongings and the ability to access these services whether owned separately or partly still indicated an upward shift on household socio-economic status. Most of the study's participants mentioned owning a brick houses as the most valued aspect of their upward mobility.

The established fledging micro-enterprises promoted the generation of profit, the level of these micro-enterprises have enabled the participants to own a two roomed type of housing comprised of a bedroom and a sitting room. The houses tend to be 3 meters of high, and a length of 12 meters of which 9 meters are for the sitting room and 3 meters for the bedroom. The houses have two windows, one in the bedroom and the other in the sitting room. There is one door to the house. There is a curtain of the size of the door to close the entrance to the bedroom. The priority of the owners is to plaster the inside of the house, while gathering the funds to plaster the outside. The house is covered by corrugated iron. The inside walls are plastered with cement and the floor is also made of cement. Most of the houses and yards in the outskirts of Chókwè were built of reed and water containers were made of cement. Although the houses may have furniture, it is of low-quality materials. This is why brick houses, yards, rubber water containers and the leather furniture were mostly valued by the people. Most of the households used the rudimentary cattle system to plough their farms. However evidence from some of communities shows that ploughing land by tractor apart from being efficient is a quicker method (Statistics National Institute, 2016).

The self-provision of micro-credit schemes by the selected community groupings of Chókwè district provided an opportunity to the households to address their basic needs. Nevertheless, those participants who owned more established fledging micro-businesses attained relatively higher socio-economic status than others, and this enabled them to move to the horizontal level of social mobility. Guillen, et al. (2018) points out factors related to social mobility including education, discrimination and credit-limitation. Viewed in a holistic perspective the credit-limitation factor is crucial in that it has influence on both education and discrimination. Credit-limitation may particularly limit access to education, especially in relation to the majority poor people from developing countries in rural areas due to lack of enrolment fees, costs for school materials and long distances to access schools which is associated with transport costs.

In addition to some improved houses, brick-built walls to protect yards and rubber water containers that the researcher observed during an interaction with the participants, the oldest participant in the self-provision of micro-credit schemes characterized horizontal mobility based on the changes she had seen taking place particularly in the 4th Neighbourhood and in Chókwè district in general.

She added that:

Some of us have been implementing our small businesses before the self- provision of the schemes in the community, because of that the accumulated experiences have indeed enhanced the generation of profit in a sustainable manner. We are all from the same community, even long before the schemes we had this sense of community bondage that allows us to live as a group, share our problems and have solidarity. What I want to say is that the life of some households' recipients of the schemes have relatively improved when compared to other households recipients of the schemes. This does not mean that those households are now rich. But you can notice the difference in terms of their houses, yards, and some have bigger farms than before. The other important as a gain because of our business is the fact that almost all the children from that live in the households that benefit from the loans from our group at least go to school.

It is evidence from the deliberations above showed that women have benefited from the micro-credit schemes as beneficiaries. Through micro-credit schemes, women managed to generate money to secure assets and livelihoods, build their small businesses and further improve their socio-economic status.

Impact of Micro-Credit Schemes in Alleviating Poverty and Job Creation

The self-provision of micro-credit scheme project has been positive. All households have been unanimous over the positive impact of micro-credit schemes. The participants stressed that with the generated profit from their micro-businesses allowed them to buy monthly basic food stuff school materials and uniforms for those who have children attending school. The participants also mentioned that they were able to pay and access clean drinking water from the private water suppliers and pay for transport, especially for medical assistance in provincial capital:

Before starting my small business, it was difficult to have a decent meal for me and my children. For most of the days we had two meals namely, lunch and dinner. But for dinner we only had bread and tea. Sometimes we only ate once in a day. But now things have changed. Now with the profit from my business I am able to buy monthly basic food, which include 25 kilos of rice, 2 kilos of sugar, 2 liters of cooking oil and 5 kilos of maize flour. I buy beans from measured by a variety of cans from other informal traders. Once you have the basic food, mainly rice and maize flour to last for a month it becomes easy to get sauce. (Owner of vegetable business)

The government opened some public water taps but the water is not constant. But now with the profit I get from my small business I have clean water for our necessities, which I buy from the private water suppliers in the community. With the generated profit I am also able to buy at least a pair of uniform for my boy to wear when going to school. Putting on school uniform in mandatory, if it was not for my business maybe my child would not be attending school. (Owner of used clothes business)

The most concrete achievement that has been mentioned by the participants as a result of the generated profit from the small business is the improvement of their housing. There has been a significant replacement of the traditional reed built houses with more durable and comfortable bricks houses. The participants pointed out that before they joined the schemes, they were not able to make minimum savings. Thus they associate the savings to profits made in their micro-business.

The participants of the self-provision of micro-credit schemes are the heads of their households. Therefore, their households are women headed households. In this context they are the power holders at least at the household level since they are the decision makers. The participants mentioned that at the community level the income generated from their micro-business enabled them to exercise power and thus earn respect from the community members. This is because they were able to buy and take related presents and items to important events such as weddings and other ceremonies. In terms of acquiring a position of power in the community, one participant commented:

My business has helped me to buy chickens or other types of presents and take them to weddings. During the traditional ceremonies I also buy and take goats and thus my relatives are able to see that my household is also represented although it is headed by a woman. If you do not take presents especially to close relatives or neighbours, they also do not bring any present when you invite them to come to an event that you organize.

The discussed theories and the literature on micro-credit programs emphasized that although women are overwhelmingly the recipients of micro-credits worldwide and that in some cases there are positive impact at the household related to generated income through the corresponding micro-enterprise development, this does not necessarily empower women to partake in the decision-making process and gain self-esteem (Khursheed, 2022). Although women are the overwhelming recipients of micro-credit schemes, their schemes are associated with the survivalist type of micro-enterprise. In addition, women´s transition to robust business is viewed constrained due to the minimum loan size that they are allocated.

It was also pointed out that although the MFIs have channeled micro-credit schemes to the majority of women worldwide than men, the accrued positive impact has only enhanced welfare related basic needs such as health, food and water. Micro-credit programs failed to be associated with the empowerment principle for women to in fact recognize and challenge structural systems (Khursheed, 2022).

Therefore, although the MFIs targeted most of women as recipients of micro-credit schemes worldwide, and especially in developing countries, men still held power due to structural issues mainly related to gendered norms and patriarchal practices. In fact, the various perspectives of power discussed such as the individual, pluralist, structural and post structural perspectives of power had something in common, which pointed to exclusion of majority poor, especially women from resources and opportunities. The recipients of the self-provided micro-credit schemes from the community grouping of the 4th Neighbourhood in Chókwè district, in their capacity of the head of their households were empowered in terms of decision-making process at the household and community levels and through the corresponding micro-enterprises generated household income.

In relation to overall relatives and community expectation as indication of power status, the women recipients of the self-provided micro-credit schemes from the community grouping of 4th Neighbourhood in Chókwè district were enabled/empowered to comply with the role of meeting social expectations as ordinary men do, for example, provision of gifts in the wedding ceremonies. The fact that the women who headed their households not only were enabled by the implemented micro-enterprises to generate households' income and meet their basic needs and concurrently be able to fulfil social expectations as ordinary men do at the community level, was an indication of fostering gender equality.

The micro-enterprises that integrated the available local natural resources had relatively higher profits. Overall the advantage of use of local available natural resources was crucial (McKnight, 2017). This is along the utilizing of assets for the socio-economic development of the rural people as part of asset-based approach to community development (Kretzmann &McKnight (1993): Nel, 2022). As argued by Maclure (2022), ABCD could enable communities to a brighter future if they recognize their assets and strengths and use them positively. As such ABCD has been hailed to be capable of upskilling local people and empowering local associations by drawing on talents and existing strengths in order to effect change within communities (Warner & French, 2018). Nevertheless, all the schemes recipients were able to meet household basic needs through the generated income linked to their micro-enterprises.

Throughout various issues discussed in the literature review related to the positive impact of micro-credit, it was stressed that micro-credit recipients that borrow for minimum amounts generate less profits from their micro-enterprises compared to those who have borrowed larger amount. Comparatively women are considered as better credit managers than men (Guillen, Mayo & Karelaia, 2018; and Le & Stefanczyk, 2018). Indeed the study proved that the participants with minimum loans had their basic needs relatively met in a less sustainable way when compared to others. Some of the participant's had these to say:

I sell cool drinks outside the market. Many other people sell cool drinks in the same place with me. I have been able to sell, but the profit I generate is not that much. This is because the loans I have requested from the group schemes are not enough. This does not mean that the group schemes cannot give me the loan amount I need to implement my business properly. The problem is that I still want to practice and gain more experience. Although I still make a little profit I am not able to buy the necessary food to last for a whole month every month. My child still goes to school but I was not able to buy the school bag that he likes. (Owner of cool drinks business)

I sell cow and goat meat to my customers. Because of the sensitiveness of meat, I only buy the quantity of meat that can be distributed to my customers, and they pay me at the end of the month. While some customers are honest and they really pay me at the end of the month as soon as they receive their pay, others are not. The combination of the sensitiveness of meat and the strategy of my business, make me ask for less money from the scheme groups. Because of the dishonest customers, the profit base of my business is unstable and inadequate. So the provision of the basic needs, mainly food for my family depends on this situation in terms of the quantity and frequency that I buy that food. (Owner of the meat business)

In the same context, the beneficiaries who asked for larger loans or have accumulated loans have been able to attain durable basic needs such as improved housing compared to others. Moreover, Khursheed (2022) emphasized the need for women financial, social and economic environment Since all the micro-credit recipients in the selected community grouping in Chókwè district are women, it was not possible to determine whether they are better micro-credit managers than men as indicated in the literature review.

Challenges Faced by Micro-Finance Beneficiaries

The process of the running of micro-enterprises is complex in that, it does not take place in isolation. It involves relationships and sharing common resources by different stakeholders. Throughout the challenges related to the running of micro-businesses, the participants indicated the unfavourable environment created by the Chókwè Local Government and the unfair trading relations with trading partners from other provinces. Some of the challenges cited were that:

The Chókwè Local Government has provided us with minimum support. The municipality police confiscate our merchandises in spite of the daily rate we pay. Although the confiscated merchandise is supposed to be stored at the municipality, when we go there to claim them they are never returned to us. (Owner of maize business)

The inter provincial trading relations with trading partners from other provinces, mainly from Maputo province involve unfavorable negotiating power which is always against us. The trading partners from Maputo tend to fix the prices they want mainly due to our disorganization. On a trading day in the municipal market the farmers bring in from their farms lots of tomatoes, cabbages, green peppers, carrots and so on. Because the traders from other provinces know that some of these products quickly get rotten and that we cannot afford to take these products back home, we accept low prices. (Owner of vegetable businesses)

Disputes between small scale farmers and commercial farmers over the opened canals from the Limpopo River for irrigation purposes also remained unsolved. The participants highlighted that the frequency of disputes were notable during the drought period. During the drought period the Limpopo River levels recede and hinders households to access water from the canals to irrigate their small scale farms. The commercial farmers take the advantage of using pumping machines to pump the water from the canals to their farms. In terms of the water dispute from the canals for irrigation purposes one participant said:

During the drought period in Chókwè we face problems just to irrigate our farms and vegetable gardens. The main problem is not that the canals do not have some water. There is water but it does not reach our area because the commercial farmers pump it all with their pumping machines! The commercial farmers cannot even give us some time for the water to reach our area. They use their machines the whole day.

Maybe the commercial farmers would open their own canals because they have a lot of money. The Local Government is taking a lot of time to resolve this dispute, which is biased against us. I do not know whether the Local Government is not interested, or lacks the capacity to resolve this dispute.

The participants who owned fish micro-business pointed out the lack of freezers as challenging to them. This takes into account the fact that fish is a sensitive product:

Some days we do not manage to sell out all the fish, the remaining fish gets rotten because we do not have freezers to keep the fish. Although when there is much remaining fish sometimes we buy blocks of ice to keep it, this has not been often since the ice is expensive and we won't make daily profits. Lack of freezers hinders us to buy a lot of fish from the fisher men. Buying a lot of fish as retailers would really compensate the days of scarcity of fish, thus our business could not stop even a single day. We have to find a way to buy our own freezers.

The owners of the charcoal micro-business associated the challenges they faced with the transportation expenses and distances they have to travel to purchase the charcoal. One of the participants had this to say:

With the growing demand of the wood by the bakery's shops in order to produce the bread, the forest located in the surrounding areas have been cleared out. Therefore, we are forced to go to distant districts, such as Chicualacuala district, which is about 300 kilometers from Chókwè in order to buy the charcoal from the suppliers. The other challenge associated with buying charcoal in far districts such as Chicualacuala is the fact that we are forced to spend more than three days because a return journey depends on the availability of cars to hire to transport the merchandise back home. We also incur the cost of accommodation and food expenses when compared with buying charcoal in closer locations.

The use of human capital was fundamental in maximizing profit by women in their respective microenterprises. This perspective is concurrently reinforced by the principle of local economy embedded in community development approach (Al-Ami et al, 2015).

The first policy dimension was related to unfavourable environment that is at policy/legislative level between the Chókwè Municipality and the owners of micro-enterprises. This dimension is characterized by the informality of the trading process and minimum support by the Chókwè Municipality. The second dimension was related to the unbalanced relations between the micro-enterprises owners in farming related activities and the commercial farming sector in Chókwè district. The relation is favourable to the Chókwè commercial farming sector since they are financially powerful. The third dimension was related to the unbalanced relations between the micro-enterprises owners in the farming related activities and inter provincial trading partners. The trading relations between the micro-enterprises owners in the farming related activities and the trading partners from other provinces, mainly Maputo province as a typical urban province tend to be unbalanced on favour of the external trading partners from other provinces since they hold negotiation powers. The fourth dimension was more concerned about balancing relations between the micro-enterprises owners in the farming related activities and the trading partners from Gaza province (Chókwè district is within Gaza province). The trading relations tended to be balanced because of the same power level held by the trading partners.

FUTURE RESEARCH DIRECTIONS

The self-provision of micro-credit schemes by the community grouping and the related micro-enterprises in the 4th Neighbourhood in Chókwè district exposed other research areas in the field of micro-credit functioning. Further research in this area could provide a learning opportunity and best practice to be used throughout the country and other countries as well. Below, the researcher provides some topics that could be used for other research. There is a compelling need for research on the following: 1) Self-provision of micro-credit schemes by groupings of men; 2) A comparative study between the self-provision of micro-credit schemes by groupings of women and men, 3) A comparative study between the self-provision of micro-credit schemes and micro-credit schemes provided by an agency; 4) The impact of the self-provision of micro-credit schemes in the available local resources; 5) The impact of the self-provision of micro-credit schemes through partnership with the private sector; 6) The impact of the micro-credit schemes through establishment of co-ops; 7) The impact of the self-provision of micro-credit schemes in promoting employment; 8) The impact of micro-credit schemes for social mobility; 9) The impact of micro-credit schemes in promoting the satisfaction of basic needs at the household level; 11) The impact of trading relations in the initiated micro-enterprises through the self-provision of micro-credit schemes; 12) The sustainability of the promoted basic needs through the self-provision of micro-credit schemes and finally 13) The type of social mobility that is best promoted by self-provision of micro-credit schemes

CONCLUSION

The findings of this chapter have demonstrated how micro-credit schemes are operated in the Chókwè region, how the beneficiaries participate in the processes for the functioning of the schemes and how they have been enabled to properly manage their micro-enterprises. The findings have also demonstrated that equal power trading relations with the counterparts are crucial for a favourable environment in terms of running income generating activities by the beneficiaries. The findings show that the implemented micro enterprises had a positive impact in the satisfaction of the basic needs, while the micro-credit recipients who owned established fledging micro-enterprises were able to move to horizontal social mobility when compared to others. The survivalist-type of micro-enterprises, run by individuals was identified to have been common for all the beneficiaries. The integration of the available local resources maximized the generation of profits through micro-enterprises however the involvement of local government as partner in the process of micro-enterprises was minimum. The chapter findings also revealed that the beneficiaries would be able to sustain their micro-enterprises when the self-provision of the schemes ceased. Some of the micro-enterprises had a negative impact on the natural environment; therefore there is a need to integrate environmental awareness in the process of empowering beneficiaries.

REFERENCES

Al Mamun, A., & Fazal, S. A. (2018). *Effect of entrepreneurial orientation on competency and micro-enterprise performance*. Asia Pacific Journal of Innovation and Entrepreneurship. doi:10.1108/APJIE-05-2018-0033

Alam, J., Moir, R., & Ibn-Boamah, M. (2021). Gender and micro-credit: Who repays? Evidence from a Canadian individual-lending approach. *Journal of Small Business and Entrepreneurship, 33*(3), 249–267. doi:10.1080/08276331.2019.1606966

Ali, I., & Hatta, Z. A. (2012). Women's Empowerment or Disempowerment through Microfinance: Evidence from Bangladesh. *Asian Social Work and Policy Review, 6*(2), 111–121. doi:10.1111/j.1753-1411.2012.00066.x

Ali, I., Hatta, Z. A., Azman, A., & Islam, S. (2017). Microfinance as a development and poverty alleviation tool in rural Bangladesh: A critical assessment. *Asian Social Work and Policy Review, 11*(1), 14–15. doi:10.1111/aswp.12106

Anyaegbunam, N., & Alaga, E. (2015). Think beyond microfinance when talking about businesswomen. *Africa Renewal, 29*(2), 22–23. doi:10.18356/e422ba79-en

Arnold, G. (2017). *Africa: A Modern history: 1945-2015*. Atlantic Books.

Banerjee, S. B., & Jackson, L. (2017). Microfinance and the business of poverty reduction: Critical perspectives from rural Bangladesh. *Human Relations, 70*(1) 63–91. https://journals.sagepub.com/doi/pdf/10.1177/0018726716640865

Bvuma, S., & Marnewick, C. (2020). Sustainable livelihoods of township small, medium and micro enterprises towards growth and development. *Sustainability (Basel), 12*(8), 31–49. doi:10.3390u12083149

Chinomona, E., & Maziriri, E. T. (2015). Women in action: Challenges facing women entrepreneurs in the Gauteng Province of South Africa. *The International Business & Economics Research Journal, 14*(6), 835–850. doi:10.19030/iber.v14i6.9487

Ershov, B. A., Perevozchikova, L. S., & Romanova, E. V. (2019). Globalization and intensification of spiritual values in Russia in the philosophical aspect. *6th International Conference on Education and Social Sciences Abstracts & Proceedings*, 208-212.

Gerard, K., & Johnston, M. (2019). Explaining microfinance's resilience: The case of microfinance in Australia. *Globalizations, 16*(6), 876–893. doi:10.1080/14747731.2018.1560188

Gonçalves, E., Castro, J., Araújo, J., & Heineck, T. (2018). A systematic literature review of iStar extensions. *Journal of Systems and Software, 2018*(137), 1–33. doi:10.1016/j.jss.2017.11.023

Guillen, L., Mayo, M., & Karelaia, N. (2018). Appearing self-confident and getting credit for it: Why it may be easier for men than women to gain influence at work. *Human Resource Management, 57*(4), 839–854. doi:10.1002/hrm.21857

Ife, J. (2016). *Community Development in an Uncertain World* (2nd ed.). Cambridge University Press. doi:10.1017/CBO9781316342855

Imran, M., Ul Haq, S., & Ozcatalbas, O. (2022). Role of Microcredit in Sustainable Rural Development. In *Sustainable Rural Development Perspective and Global Challenges* (pp. 1-22). London: IntechOpen.

Karim, L. (2014). Analyzing Women's Empowerment. *Microfinance and Garment Labor in Bangladesh., 38*(2), 153–166.

Kato, M. P., & Kratzer, J. (2013). Empowering women through Microfinance: Evidence from Tanzania. *ACRN Journal of Entrepreneurship Perspectives.*, *2*(1), 31–59.

Khursheed, A. (2022). Exploring the role of microfinance in women's empowerment and entrepreneurial development: A qualitative study. *Future Business Journal, 8*(1), 1-13. https://www.ncbi.nlm.nih.gov/pmc/articles/PMC9735224/

Kiunga, C. (2019). *Effects of Micro-credit Programs on Women Economic Empowerment: a Case of Kajiado North Sub-County (2005-2018)* [Doctoral dissertation]. University of Nairobi.

Kretzmann, J. P., & McKnight, J. P. (1993). *Asset-based community development: Building communities from the inside out.* ACTA Publications.

Kusi, A., Yussif, S., & Ismail, A. (2019). Access to micro credit by women entrepreneurs in Ghana: Sinapi aba Trust-Kumasi in retrospect. *International Journal of Academic Research in Business & Social Sciences*, *9*(9), 590–613. doi:10.6007/IJARBSS/v9-i9/6336

Le, L. H., & Stefanczyk, J. K. (2018). Gender discrimination in access to credit: Are women-led SMEs rejected more than men-led? *Gender, Technology and Development*, *22*(2), 145–163. doi:10.1080/09718524.2018.1506973

Maclure, L. (2022). Augmentations to the Asset-Based Community Development Model to Target Power Systems. Taylor & Francis.

Marceno, S. (2018). Conditional Cash Transfers: Empowerment, Resilience and Good Behaviours in Development Policies. *Soft Power*, *5*(1), 119–144.

McKnight, J. (2017). *Asset-based community development: the essentials.* Asset-Based Community Development Institute.

McMichael, P. (2012). *Development and Social Change: A Global Perspective. Los Angela & London* SAGE.

Ministry of State Administration. (2014). *Profile of the districts.* http://www.govnet.gov.mz/

Musau, Z. (2015). Loans to Women=smart economics. *Africa Renewal*, *29*(2), 20–21. doi:10.18356/c828c83a-en

Nel, H. (2018). A comparison between the asset-oriented and needs-based community development approaches in terms of systems changes. *Practice*, *30*(1), 33–52. doi:10.1080/09503153.2017.1360474

Njiraini, J. (2015). Microfinance: Good for the poor? *Africa Renewal*, *29*(2), 24–25. doi:10.18356/97e702a4-en

Poverty Annual Report. (2014). http://www.iid.org.mz/G20-relatoriofinal

Psico, J. A. T., & Dias, J. F. (2007). *Social Performance Evaluation of Microfinance Institutions in Mozambique.* https://www.researchgate.net/publication/281098243_Social_Performance_Evaluation_of_Microfinance_Institutions_in_Mozambique

Santoso, D. B. (2016). *Credit Accessibility: The Impact of Microfinance on Rural Indonesian Households*. Lincoln University.

Statistics National Institute. (2016). *Demographics and Indicators*. INE. http//www.ine.gov.mz/estatisticas/estatisticas-demo

Todaro, M. P., & Smith, S. C. (2020). *Economic Development*. Pearson.

Vletter, F. (2006). *Micro-finance in Mozambique: Achievements, Prospects & Challenges*. Report of Mozambique Micro-Finance Facility. https://www.wvi.org/mozambique/about-us

Wang, F., Du, L., Tian, M., Liu, Y., & Zhang, Y. (2023). Sustainability of rural tourism in poverty reduction: Evidence from panel data of 15 underdeveloped counties in Anhui Province, China. *PLoS One*, *18*(3), e0283048. doi:10.1371/journal.pone.0283048 PMID:36913402

Warner, L. M., & French, D. P. (2018). Self-efficacy and its sources as determinants of physical activity among older people. In Palgrave handbook of ageing and physical activity promotion (pp. 231-250). Palgrave Macmillan. doi:10.1007/978-3-319-71291-8_12

World Bank Group. (2018). *An Incomplete Transition: Overcoming the Legacy of Exclusion in South Africa.* World Bank Group.

World Vision. (2019). *Fostering productivity and innovation.* https://www.wvi.org/sites/default/files/2019-12/Microfinance%202019.pdf

Chapter 10
The Role of Microfinance in Promoting Women's Empowerment:
A Socioeconomic Approach

Gertrude Amoakohene
Ghana Communication Technology University, Ghana

Joseph Nkyi
GTCU Business School, Ghana Communication Technology University, Ghana

Stephen Owusu Afriyie
https://orcid.org/0000-0002-8756-6378
GTCU Business School, Ghana Communication Technology University, Ghana

Mohammed Musah
GTCU Business School, Ghana Communication Technology University, Ghana

Peter Yao Lartey
Brock University, Canada

ABSTRACT

Women's economic empowerment is a technique meant to give them more authority over decisions, increase their income, and own assets. Since empowering women is essential to achieving the goals of development and reducing poverty, numerous attempts have been made to address this issue. Microfinance institutions (MFIs) have emerged as key tools over the past few decades to not only address poverty, but also to empower women in particular. It is believed that by employing microfinance, which has been shown to be one of the most effective approaches, women may gain some kind of personal empowerment. The primary objective of this research is to analyse how microfinance affects women's economic empowerment. Microfinance significantly boosts women's independent revenues, their levels of asset ownership, and their savings, which all contribute to their economic empowerment. The research also demonstrated that microfinance helps promote the growth of women's entrepreneurship and accessibility to business opportunities.

DOI: 10.4018/978-1-6684-8979-6.ch010

INTRODUCTION

Giving women control over their own lives, resources, and matters that have an impact on them is referred to as women empowerment. It essentially means conferring upon them the ability to self-decide. The process of empowerment is multidimensional, and it enables women to realize their full destiny and capabilities in all spheres of life. In fact, women's empowerment is central to the achievement of the triple goals of equality, development and social justice (Sinha et al., 2023). It makes women independent in decision making, identification, and utilization of resources. Empowering women gives them the power to take control of their lives and make decisions about their possessions. Empowerment of women include women's awareness of their rights, self-confidence, ability to regulate their life both indoors and beyond the house, and capacity to affect social change. The purpose includes fostering women's confidence in themselves, their freedom, and their right to influence societal change for themselves and others (Adam et al., 2022). Women empowerment is not a walk in the park. It demands concerted efforts because of ingrained societal constraints that sometimes, unfortunately, seek to keep women down below a certain level. Achieving this goal requires a multi-faceted approach, including education, healthcare, and economic enablement. That is where microfinance comes in - providing women with access to financial services like loans, savings, and insurance, even if they are excluded from traditional banking systems (Dhaoui, 2015). However, slowly but surely, things concerning women's microfinance-led developmental interventions are changing. The advent of microfinance as an economic strategy to lift underprivileged groups from poverty has been found to be quite helpful in advancing the long march towards women empowerment (Aruna & Jyothirmayi, 2011; Dhaoui, 2015; Rehman et al., 2014). By tackling poverty and supporting marginalized communities, microfinance has become a game-changer in the fight for women's empowerment and economic growth. The objective of this exploration aims to study the role of microfinance in promoting women's empowerment. In specific terms, the book chapter attempts to examine how microfinance has been used as a tool to enhance women's economic empowerment, decision-making power, overall well-being, considering operational challenges and societal constraints. Microfinance can be used as a tool to enhance women's economic empowerment, increase their agency and ultimately contribute to their general welfare and development. This is because microfinance creates employment opportunities for unemployed women thus increasing the level of their income and productive capacity (Alhassan et al., 2022).

LITERATURE REVIEW

Overview of Women Empowerment

The most vulnerable people in the world are women and children. However, if given more authority, women might become a formidable force. Women's empowerment was defined as improving their ability for decision-making at all levels. This includes giving them control over their lives, giving them an equitable chance to engage in society, and fostering their sense of value (Mohammed et al., 2022). Empowering women could be seen as a process. It takes time for the process develop. As such, it calls on women to advance and be given the same opportunities as males to engage in personal, social, and economic endeavours. Women must be included in all facets of society on an equal footing with men. Women would then have the freedom to make their own decisions and the authority to effect social change as a result. Improving the status of women would mean making them capable of controlling their lives in all spheres, including reproduction and all societal arenas. This makes it obvious that women empowerment is a pressing problem that requires a swift fix or an urgent solution.

Women Empowerment: A Multifaceted Perspective

Women's empowerment represents a complex and multi-dimensional concept that entails a transformative process where individuals previously deprived of their agency can gain and exercise this autonomy. This concept generally encompasses the following dimensions:

- **Political Empowerment**: Political empowerment of women entails their equal participation in decision-making processes, both within governmental institutions and in the broader political landscape. For instance, many countries have found success with quotas for women's representation in government bodies (Bauer & Burnet, 2013; McCann, 2013; Clayton, 2021).
- **Economic Empowerment**: In this respect, we're thinking about things like equal pay for equal work and other economic opportunities for women. Common methods of increasing women's economic independence include microcredit initiatives and vocational training (Ebrahimi et al., 2022; Sultana et al., 2023).
- **Social Empowerment**: This factor considers how women fare in society and how much sway they have over established beliefs and customs. Education is a key component in women's ability to achieve economic and political independence (Unterhalter et al., 2014).
- **Psychological Empowerment**: This factor considers how women feel about themselves, their abilities, and the change they can make. Self-worth is intrinsically linked to all other aspects, as earning material success or intellectual advancement can have a profound effect on one's sense of value (Yur'evna & Kristina, 2022).

Patriarchal societal structures, lack of economic and educational possibilities, violence and discrimination based on gender, and political and legal impediments are all factors that work against women's empowerment. However, these can be combated through a range of strategies, including government policies and programs, work by non-governmental organizations and civil society, education and awareness-raising, legal reforms and protection of women's rights, and economic and financial empowerment programs (UN Women, 2015).

RESEARCH METHODOLOGY

With this project, authors employed explanatory research to conduct investigations on the role of microfinance on women's economic empowerment. Using secondary sources which include books, journals, periodicals, and magazines, information was gathered to obtain insight into the relationship between microfinance and women empowerment. Additional information was acquired through conversations with some rural women entrepreneurs and MFIs. The current study is based on secondary data sources that were obtained from a number of publications and documents issued on microfinance and women empowerment to achieve the specified objective. The investigation searched for probable causal relationship between microfinance and the empowerment of women, and strategies to lessen poverty and provide these women more socioeconomic influence.

How Do Women Get Empowered?

According to European Institute for Gender Equality (2016), some of the tools needed to empower women include education, training, awareness raising, building self-confidence, expansion of choice, increasing access to and control over resources. Lyoussi & Kouchih (2023) also added that the actions to transform the structures and institutions that reinforce and perpetuate gender discrimination and inequality should be removed. In 1994, the United Nations Population Fund-UNFPA, an international development agency that works on population and development, sexual and reproductive health, and gender had a Conference on Population and Development in Cairo to propose some measures that could help empower women (UNFPA (1994). These are: (1) Setting policy and programme actions that will improve women's access to secure livelihood and economic resources. By so doing, it would be possible to enforce the elimination of legal barriers to women's involvement in public life. More efforts should be made by governments of nations to create social awareness through mass communication and effective training programmes. (2) To empower women, education is paramount as it would enable them acquire knowledge, skills and self-confidence necessary to participate fully in their developmental processes. More than one third of the world's adults, most of them women, have no access to printed knowledge, to new skills or to technologies that would improve the quality of their lives and help them shape and adapt to social and economic change. (3) There should not be any discrimination between men and women. Steps should be taken to ensure that this is achieved. (4) Countries should act to empower women and should take steps to eliminate inequalities between men and women as soon as possible by: (i) Establishing mechanisms for women's equal participation and equitable representation at all levels of the political process and public life in each community and society and enabling women to articulate their concerns and needs; (ii) Promoting the fulfilment of women's potential through education, skill development and employment, giving paramount importance to the elimination of poverty, illiteracy and ill health among women; (iii) Eliminating all practices that discriminate against women; assisting women to establish and realize their rights, including those that relate to reproductive and sexual health; (iv) Adopting appropriate measures to improve women's ability to earn income beyond traditional occupations, achieve economic self-reliance, and ensure women's equal access to the labour market and social security systems; (v) Eliminating violence against women; (vi) Eliminating discriminatory practices by employers against women, such as those based on proof of contraceptive use or pregnancy status; (vii) Making it possible, through laws, regulations and other appropriate measures, for women to combine the roles of child-bearing, breast-feeding and child-rearing with participation in the workforce. As concerns turn to inclusive economic systems, giving women chances to determine their own choices, and including decision-making can significantly contribute to the empowerment of women (Gupta & Roy, 2023). This strategy makes women take responsibility for their own lives, regain control, and develop the capacity for smart and sound decision-making. It bolsters the women's sense of self-esteem, self-determination, self-worth, and right to have an impact on societal change for both themselves as well as other people (Uruthirapathy, & Dyke, 2022).

Barriers to Women Empowerment

The COVID-19 pandemic threatened to reverse decades of progress gained in gender equality and women's rights, and the UN Secretary General asked states to put women and girls at the centre of the recovery process in 2020 (Ebrahim & Jones, 2021). This is a blatant sign that there are still significant obstacles to women's empowerment, and that momentous work is required to overcome them. Women's economic empowerment is not just a "women's issue" because it affects every person. There are four significant roadblocks that hinder women's economic growth: violence against women, discriminatory societal norms, unequal job opportunities, lack of access to financial resources. Rates of poverty reduction and economic growth deteriorate when women are excluded from economic and financial opportunities. According to the 2017 Report of Innovations for Poverty Action (IPA) on financial inclusion programme, many women are not economically solvent as they depend on their partners (Holloway et al., 2017), and this barrier of financial inclusion impact greatly on the economic empowerment of women. In developing countries, one in three married women still depend on their husbands for major family expenditures. More people must have access to and use high-quality financial products and services if inclusive economic growth and the eradication of poverty are to be achieved. Over the years, women's financial inclusion has not advanced much despite increasing global initiatives. The COVID-19 pandemic and other shocks continue to put women at a higher risk of financial vulnerability and exclusion than men, threatening to regress some of the gains achieved for the time being. The table below shows the various barriers that hinder women from been financially inclusive.

Table 1. Gender-based barriers to financial inclusions

Demand Side Barriers	Supply Side Barriers	Legal & Regulatory Barriers
Lack of bargaining power within the household	Inappropriate product offerings	Account opening requirements that disadvantage women
Concentration in lower-paying economic activities	Lack of gender-specific policies and practices for product design and marketing	Barriers to obtaining formal identification
Competing demands on women's time related to unpaid domestic work	Inappropriate distribution channels	Legal barriers to owning and inheriting property and other collateral
Lack of assets for collateral		Lack of gender-inclusive credit reporting systems
Lack of formal identification		
Reduced mobility due to time constraints or social norms		
Lower rates of cell phone ownership among women, needed to access many digital products		

Source: IPA (2017), Women's Economic Empowerment Through Financial Inclusion, p.3

The IPA report suggested that appropriately designed financial products could help overcome some of the barriers confronting women's empowerment. Financial inclusion improves a person's capacity to manage risk, start a business or invest in a business, and pay for significant expenses like educational pursuits or home enhancements.

Demand-Side Barriers

Women often lack the financial independence or societal standing to have equal say in financial decisions within households. According to Doepke et al. (2012), women are often overrepresented in fields with lower pay and fewer benefits, like domestic work or informal employment. Women are often expected to bear the brunt of unpaid domestic work, leaving less time for paid employment or entrepreneurial activities. Without formal identification, women cannot access formal financial systems or own property, a critical step in economic empowerment (Aker et al., 2016). Cultural norms may restrict women's mobility, limiting their ability to access markets or financial institutions. Lower rates of technology adoption among women can limit access to digital financial services and information (GSM Association, 2015). One of the main demand-side obstacles is financial illiteracy, which is lack of financial knowledge. This is because the majority of the poor women are illiterates, they are unaware of the goods and services available to them. Even the specifics of the programmes that are introduced for them are beyond their comprehension. They are reluctant to visit the bank. According to the research work of Solotaroff et al. (2019) and published by World Bank, financial literacy is crucial for first-time users because they are unable to meet all the documentation-related requirements and thus do not open bank accounts. Due to the fact that most rural women are unaware of the numerous banking products, services, and programmes that have been established for them, it tends to be a significant demand-side obstacle to financial inclusion (Hasan & Hoque, 2021). As a result, they are not enrolled in the specific programme that is introduced for them. Their ignorance is due to a number of factors, including little publicity for the programmes and illiteracy. Despite the fact that there may be programmes available to meet their specific needs, they are unaware of them. Also, low income earners who are largely unbanked, do not feel any pressure to open accounts because they have low incomes or are not financially capable (Huang et al., 2022). Sometime they spend all the earnings, and do not save any of it, since the they receive meagre income. Even if they decide to save, it will likely be a very small amount for which they will not require a bank account, but will instead store it at home.

Supply-side Barriers

Financial products are often designed with the needs of men in mind, ignoring the unique circumstances or needs of women (D'espallier et al., 2013). Most businesses do not consider gender-specific needs when designing or marketing products, thereby failing to tap into a market that could empower women economically. Traditional channels for financial service delivery may not be accessible for women due to cultural or logistical reasons, such as distance. Bank distance is a typical barrier for women in rural areas due to how far away bank branches are from residents' homes (Yan & Qi, 2021). Thus, it becomes quite challenging for them to visit the bank. The women find it quite difficult to visit the bank when it is apparent, they must leave their jobs in order to get a bank account. Consequently, they continue to be unbanked. Lack of trust develops as a result of the unsatisfactory bank encounter (Sharma et al., 2023). Sometimes, bank employees do not treat women from rural areas well. subsequently, such people stop believing in the banking system. Other unfavourable situations, such as having to wait in queue for a very long period before attended to. Sometimes, they are been told to return and gather all the paperwork they need. All these terrible experiences cause people to develop mistrust to utilise bank accounts and stop believing in traditional banking systems. Fadikpe et al. (2022) posits that high cost associated with banking services deprive poor women from patronising their offers. Although, it costs money for banks to provide financial services or products like credit cards, debit cards, passbooks, chequebooks, etc, but they are sometimes expensive for women who are low earners. Also, it is known that women with limited incomes are reluctant to open accounts due to requirements such as maintaining a minimum balance in the account, deduction of bank fees, fees for giving debit cards and ATM cards, etc.

Legal and Regulatory Barriers

According to the report by World Bank (2018) on women's financial inclusion and the law, discriminatory regulations can affect women's demand for financial services and impede their ability to save, borrow, pay, or insure themselves against risk. For example, limited access to and control over property constrain women's ability to provide collateral for loans. Similarly, gender differences in getting identification can make it more difficult for women to open bank accounts, especially where stringent identification requirements to do so exist. Laws might restrict women's legal ability that require consent or approval, typically from a husband, to engage in some daily operations. This may limit the financial inclusion of women. The report asserts that the husband is legally regarded as the head of household in 31 economies, which can have consequences ranging from government land allocation to who is eligible for government benefits inside a household. On a more fundamental level, the only nations where married women still require permission to open a bank account are Chad, Guinea-Bissau, and Niger. In Equatorial Guinea, a wife still requires her husband's consent before signing a legal document. Women's decision-making and mobility may be constrained by legal constraints. Women's decision-making and mobility may be constrained by legal constraints. In 31 economies, married women are not as free to select their residence as married men are. They are prohibited from working outside the home in 18 economies in the same way that a married man is. Additionally, in 17 countries (Afghanistan, Bahrain, Brunei Darussalam, the Arab Republic of Egypt, the Islamic Republic of Iran, Iraq, Jordan, Kuwait, Malaysia, Oman, Qatar, Saudi Arabia, Sudan, Syria, the United Arab Emirates, West Bank and Gaza, and the Republic of Yemen), married women are not permitted to travel outside the home in the same manner as married men. If this is the case, women can find it difficult to get to banks or other service providers and might not be able to reside somewhere that gives them the chance to work or access services or make a reliable income. Laws that limit women's ability to be financially independent also limit their access to and use of financial services. As corroborated by Mhlanga (2022), at least one law could limit women's economic opportunity and access to financial independence. For instance, women are less likely to have accounts, formal credit, or savings in countries where married women are not allowed to work. Women are more likely to utilise formal financial products in jurisdictions where they can be the head of the family or where they are not legally obligated to obey their husbands. Gender gaps in financial inclusion are greater for married women's access to bank accounts and their ability to borrow from a financial institution in areas where married women are not as free to select where to reside as men are (as seen in Figure 1).

Figure 1. Gender gaps in account ownership and capacity to borrow from a financial Institution are higher where women's mobility is constrained
Source:Women, Business and the Law (2018)

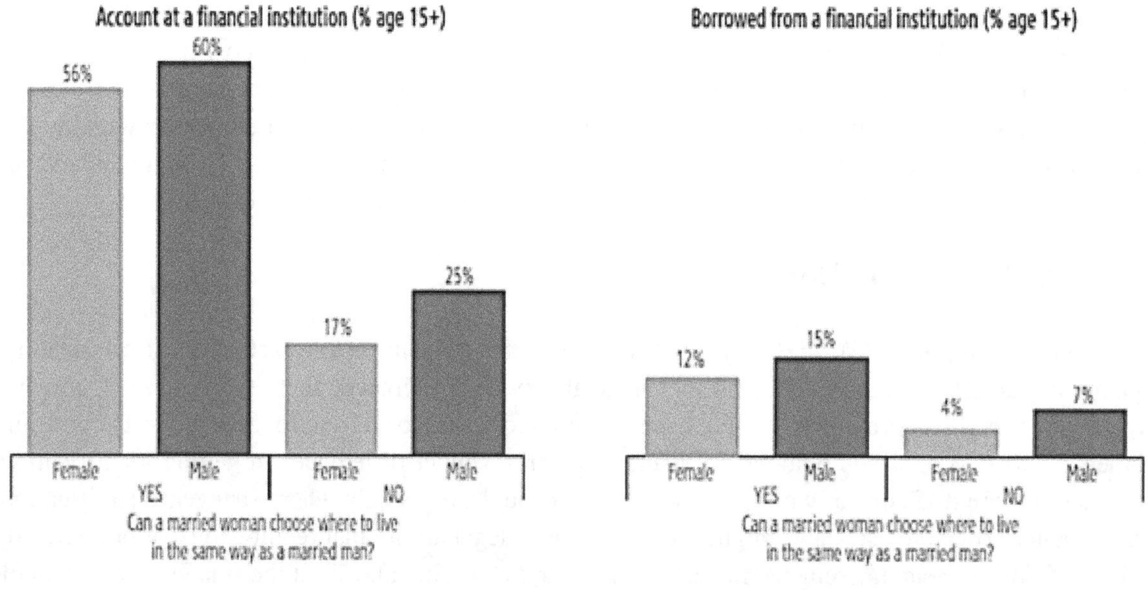

Microfinance Landscape: An Avenue for Women's Empowerment

Microfinance's emergence is profoundly tied to Dr. Muhammad Yunus's work and the establishment of the Grameen Bank in the 1970s (Yunus, 2003). Since then, MFIs have evolved and diversified, extending a broader range of services such as savings, insurance, and transfer services (Armendáriz & Morduch, 2010). The current global microfinance landscape reveals a plethora of institutions offering these services, with a particular emphasis on women's empowerment. Numerous MFIs target women due to their higher repayment rates and the significant impact of their economic activities on household welfare (Dotsey, 2022). Notable trends and innovations in microfinance for women's empowerment include the critical role of technology. Digital finance solutions have substantially broadened financial inclusion for women who face mobility constraints or discrimination (Duncombe & Boateng, 2009). Moreover, the creation of innovative financial products specifically tailored for women, such as group lending or flexible repayment schedules, has witnessed a significant increase in digital micro-lending (Shema, 2022). Despite these advancements, challenges persist in scaling up microfinance for women, including prevailing gender discrimination and social norms that restrict women's economic activity, lack of access to finance, regulatory barriers, and insufficient monitoring and evaluation mechanisms (Agier & Szafarz, 2013). However, opportunities and best practices for scaling up exist, such as leveraging partnerships and collaborations between various stakeholders, incorporating financial education, and advocating for a supportive regulatory environment (Luo & Cheng, 2022).

Role of Microfinance in Women Empowerment

Microfinance is a type of banking service provided to low income individuals and groups who otherwise would not have had access to formal financial services. Cull & Hartarska (2023) postulated that microfinance institutions (MFIs) have generated a considerable enthusiasm and hope for rapid poverty alleviation. Developing countries are typically where one may get these banking services. Many MFIs focus on helping women in particular. Many MFIs place a strong emphasis on assisting women. The MFIs organise various activities for small businesses and entrepreneurs to educate them on some principles of investment. Apart from providing entrepreneurial skills and knowledge on basic banking and saving account operation, the MFIs also offer startup capitals to the women. Microfinance has a considerable social and economic impact on both the person and the economy at large. By promoting self-employment, microfinance schemes benefit people, especially the disadvantaged in society to establish their own businesses. As asserted by Konadu & Biney-Assan (2007) because of the job opportunities microfinance provides, most individuals, especially the poor, have begun to limit their family sizes since it has become extremely difficult to work and care for multiple children at the same time. This stipulates that microfinance enables people, especially women, to have fewer children when they obtain employment. As women get work to do, through the microcredit from MFIs, they are able to take care of themselves and the family as well. Phan et al. (2023) explicate that microfinance has a correlation with household income and consumption patterns, which lowers poverty. This indicated that microfinance access increases people's incomes, which influences an uptick in their consumption patterns. As people become financially sound, it relieves the government of spending more in providing all fundamental necessities for its people, but rather put in more emphasis on sustainable development of the nation (Holmberg & Sandbrook, 2019). Microfinance initiatives mostly target women as their beneficiaries. Quagrainie et al. (2021) alluded that the loan amount does not only aid poor women in developing economically, but also improves gender equality, women's status within the family, their well-being, and their educational level. Additionally, microfinance programmes consider women to be a good credit risk due to their higher inclination to pay back the loans collected. As a result, MFIs target women since they have much lower default rates than males do. Men, on the other hand, are to a certain degree more interested in investing their money in risky business ventures, and are more likely to spend it on alcohol, tobacco, gambling or gaming (Gerard & Johnston, 2019). While a substantial portion of women's loans are sometimes directly invested in business ventures by their male folks, the responsibility for repayment rests on the women borrowers. For this reason, MFIs have introduced a number of cutting-edge programmes to financially support their female clientele. The MFIs play a vital role in advancing women's empowerment, since they increase women's resources, increase return on human capital by improving their affordability, and subsequently raise women's living standards. There is a profound linkage between microfinance and women's empowerment, with the former serving as a catalyst for transforming the lives of women, especially those from economically disadvantaged backgrounds. Microfinance, as posited by Akurugu et al. (2023), offers women the economic resources required to make strategic life decisions, thereby facilitating their empowerment. Alhassan et al. (2023) corroborated that microfinance is therefore intricately linked to poverty reduction in poor communities particularly in developing countries.

Impact of Microfinance on Poverty Reduction and Economic Development

Microfinance, as an essential financial service, provides an instrumental resource for individuals and small enterprises that are excluded from mainstream banking facilities (Ehigiamusoe, 2008). It was conceived in the 1970s by Dr. Muhammad Yunus in Bangladesh, and since its inception, it has significantly contributed to the economic growth of the country and facilitated substantial reduction in poverty (Yunus, 1999). Globally, the growth of Microfinance Institutions (MFIs) has been motivated by the core objective of delivering financial services like loans, savings, insurance, and money transfers to the marginalized population (Armendáriz & Morduch, 2010). Demonstrable proof of microfinance's positive impact on economic expansion and poverty mitigation can be found in the successful models of organizations such as Grameen Bank and BRAC in Bangladesh, SKS Microfinance in India, and BancoSol in Bolivia (Cull et al., 2007). Nevertheless, the efficacy of microfinance as a tool for poverty alleviation is a subject of debate. Critiques highlight its inability to penetrate the extremely impoverished strata of society, high-interest rates, and a propensity to cause over-indebtedness in certain cases (Bateman, 2010). However, when executed appropriately, microfinance can serve as a potent instrument for stimulating economic growth and reducing poverty levels (Banerjee, Karlan, & Zinman, 2015).

Social Empowerment of Women

Having a supportive environment through the use of various affirmative programmes and policies for the empowerment of women, as well as ensuring the availability of simple and equitable access to basic needs of life, is referred to as women's social empowerment (Ofori & Kashiwagi, 2022). Empowerment has become a buzzword in the field of human development, with a particular emphasis on reducing poverty, and involving underprivileged groups of women on political initiatives. For women, microfinance has demonstrated societal benefits. Christian et al., (2023) advocated that microfinance institutions have a considerable positive impact on women's social empowerment, because they significantly increase their ability to regulate their income, expenditure and domestic decision-making, which ultimately improves their welfare. According to Cooke & Amuakwa-Mensah (2022), women who participated in MFIs programme had greater financial independence, mobility, and control over household decisions. Moreover, Milazzo & Goldstein (2019) believe that women's involvement in MFIs improves family decision-making and discovered that family property ownership, media exposure, and institutional access are significant components in women's empowerment. In a similar vein, it has been demonstrated by Orkoh et al., (2022) that women are more significantly impacted by savings than males because savings increase their ability to make decisions about family planning, family spending, recreational activities, and behaviour. As a result, there is a need for an integrated microfinance programme that combines education with career development training to increase women's capacity building, and strengthen the correlation between microfinance and women's social empowerment.

Illustrations of Successful Microfinance Programs Targeting Women's Empowerment

Several examples of successful microfinance programs have significantly contributed to women's empowerment across different geographical and socio-economic contexts. Grameen Bank in Bangladesh is one of the most globally acclaimed and successful MFIs, particularly known for targeting women

(Yunus, 2007). Its model provides small loans to women without requiring collateral, enabling them to establish their businesses. It has positively influenced women's income, enhanced their decision-making capacity, and fostered a positive shift in societal perceptions about women's economic roles (Goetz & Sen Gupta, 1996). Another noteworthy example is the Self-Employed Women's Association (SEWA) Bank in India, a women-focused MFI providing financial services to poor, self-employed women. Recognizing that empowerment is a multifaceted process that goes beyond economic considerations, SEWA Bank provides not only credit but also financial literacy and business training (Chen, 1997). The Women's Microfinance Initiative (WMI) serves rural communities in East Africa. WMI's training and collateral-free loans to women have a high percentage of repayment. The initiative's effects on women's income and confidence have contributed to their overall empowerment (Ceesay, 2023). There are commonalities between these successful initiatives. They acknowledge the difficulties women have in obtaining conventional credit and aim their services squarely at this underserved demographic by providing collateral-free loans. Recognizing the multifaceted nature of empowerment, many also offer training in business skills, financial management, and leadership (Hennink et al., 2012). These initiatives have a far-reaching effect on women's empowerment and the economy as a whole. There is evidence that they improve family finances, education, and health, as well as alter society gender norms (Duvendack et al., 2011). However, it is commonly noted that additional study is needed in the areas of context-specific difficulties and the need for supplemental support services.

Challenges Faced by Women in Accessing Microloans

Microfinance can contribute significantly to the empowerment of women by enhancing their income levels, improving their financial management skills, and amplifying their decision-making capabilities within their households (Armendáriz & Morduch, 2010). Microloans allow women to start or grow enterprises, which increases their earnings potential. Microfinance, while highly beneficial, operates amidst a network of societal and cultural constructs that may present challenges to the empowerment of women. Additionally, loan repayment over time can bolster their financial management skills, and having control over economic resources can augment their decision-making power within households. Nonetheless, numerous obstacles impede women's access to financial services and their participation in the formal economy. Such hindrances may include societal gender biases, lack of collateral for securing loans, and deficient financial literacy (Johnson, 2004). Despite these benefits, microfinance presents limitations when it comes to empowering women. For instance, gender biases in loan disbursement and collection methods, the burden of unpaid care work, and patriarchal societal norms can hinder the empowerment potential of microfinance (Ebrahimi et al., 2022). Further, microfinance alone may not suffice to empower women; it needs to be complemented by other resources and services such as education, training, and social support networks (Cheston & Kuhn, 2002).

Strategies for Improving Microloan Recovery

The impact of microfinance on women's empowerment has been profound, yet it is not without its challenges and limitations. Concerns about the possible unaffordability of microloans and the subsequent accumulation of debilitating debt by borrowers have led some to argue that microfinance is counterproductive (Roodman & Morduch, 2014). Many people who rely on microfinance services, particularly women, also tend to lack basic financial literacy. Because of this, there is a possibility of squandering borrowed money and amassing uncontrollable debt (Hermes & Lensink, 2007). Using loans effectively is made more difficult when other resources, such business training, market access, and social support, are unavailable. Overemphasis on credit provision without proper accompanying mechanisms can limit microfinance's ability to realise its potential to empower women (Ebrahimi et al., 2022). However, there may be ways to lessen the impact of these problems. Improve women's ability to handle their money by combining microfinance services with financial education programmes (Agier & Szafarz, 2013). By combining microfinance with other forms of development like as education, healthcare, and business training, a more comprehensive approach to women's empowerment can be achieved (Morduch & Haley, 2002). Policy interventions can play a significant role in reducing high lending rates, ensuring regulation of microfinance institutions, and promoting their transparent and ethical operations. Many of the woes and frustrations of slow and distresses credits can be avoided by good loan supervision. Supervision helps to keep a good loan good. It may be visiting the borrowers' premises to investigate the general state of affairs. The credit monitoring process involves on-site visit, regular contacts as well as checking for compliance with loan agreements. Microfinance institutions should individually devise techniques and strategies to improve their monitoring systems. These approaches offer promising potential to enhance the effectiveness and sustainability of microfinance initiatives for women's empowerment. However, they necessitate a paradigm shift that perceives microfinance not merely as a financial instrument but as a critical component of broader social and economic development plans.

CONCLUSION

This research project accentuates that microfinance plays a significant role in increasing economic equality because of the connections involving poverty, women, and financial power. Women can enhance other aspects of their lives and improve the lives of their children when they have a greater amount of economic power. Microfinance is a useful tool that can support the growth of women's business and empowerment. In order to achieve stability, a developing nation must concentrate on the expansion and development of entrepreneurship. This is because individuals see microfinance as an opportunity for themselves to exhibit entrepreneurial dexterity, since it gives them a possibility to start their own businesses. Microfinance loan has demonstrated as a noteworthy and reliable source of income for women and significantly assisted them in raising their standards of living (Datta & Sahu (2022). However, the availability of microfinance for women makes them more empowered economically and socially.

REFERENCES

Adam, J. N., Adams, T., Gerber, J. D., & Amacker, M. (2022). The dilemma of women empowerment in informal artisanal and small-scale gold ore mining in Ghana. *Cogent Social Sciences*, *8*(1), 2108231. doi:10.1080/23311886.2022.2108231

Agier, I., & Szafarz, A. (2013). Microfinance and gender: Is there a glass ceiling in loan size? *World Development*, *42*, 165–181. doi:10.1016/j.worlddev.2012.06.016

Aker, J. C., Boumnijel, R., McClelland, A., & Tierney, N. (2016). Payment Mechanisms and Antipoverty Programs: Evidence from a Mobile Money Cash Transfer Experiment in Niger. *Economic Development and Cultural Change*, *65*(1), 1–37. doi:10.1086/687578

Akurugu, C. A., Nyuur, R. B., & Dery, I. (2023). Non-Governmental Organizations' approaches to women's empowerment amid the COVID-19 Pandemic: Towards decolonizing development praxis in northern Ghana. *World Development Sustainability*, 100079.

Alhassan, Y., Kuagbela, F., Nurokina, C. D., & Appiah, B. (2022). The Role of Microfinance in Africa: A Review of Outcomes from Ghana and Nigeria. *Microfinance and Sustainable Development in Africa*, 54-81. https://www.igi-global.com/chapter/the-role-of-microfinance-in-africa/293794

Alhassan, Y., Paul, G., Salia, S., & Nwagbara, U. (2023). Transforming Local Economies Through Microfinance in Rural Ghana: Evidence From a Review of Existing Literature. *Transforming Economies Through Microfinance in Developing Nations*, 1-19.

Armendáriz, B., & Morduch, J. (2010). *The Economics of Microfinance*. MIT Press.

Aruna, M., & Jyothirmayi, R. (2011). The Role of Microfinance in Women Empowerment: A Study on the SHG Bank Linkage Program in Hyderabad (Andhra Pradesh). *Indian Journal of Commerce and Management Studies*, *2*(4), 4.

Banerjee, A., Karlan, D., & Zinman, J. (2015). Six randomized evaluations of microcredit: Introduction and further steps. *American Economic Journal. Applied Economics*, *7*(1), 1–21. doi:10.1257/app.20140287

Bateman, M. (2010). *Why doesn't microfinance work? The destructive rise of local neoliberalism*. Zed Books Ltd. doi:10.5040/9781350223974

Bauer, G., & Burnet, J. E. (2013). Gender quotas, democracy, and women's representation in Africa: Some insights from democratic Botswana and autocratic Rwanda. *Women's Studies International Forum*, *41*, 103–112. doi:10.1016/j.wsif.2013.05.012

Ceesay, A. (2023). Women and Microfinance in The Gambia: A Path to Empowerment and Financial Inclusion. In K. A. Krawczyk & B. A. King (Eds.), *Women's Contributions to Development in West Africa: Ordinary Women, Extraordinary Lives* (pp. 99–118). Springer Nature. doi:10.1007/978-981-19-8190-6_5

Chen, M. A. (1997). *A Guide for Assessing the Impact of Microenterprise Services at the Individual Level*. SEEP Network.

Cheston, S., & Kuhn, L. (2002). Empowering women through microfinance. *Pathways out of poverty: Innovations in microfinance for the poorest families*, 167-228.

Christian, A. K., Atiglo, D. Y., Okyere, M. A., Obeng-Dwamena, A., Marquis, G. S., & Jones, A. D. (2023). Women's empowerment, children's nutritional status, and the mediating role of household headship structure: Evidence from sub-Saharan Africa. *Maternal and Child Nutrition*, *19*(3), 13520. doi:10.1111/mcn.13520 PMID:37092343

Clayton, A. (2021). How Do Electoral Gender Quotas Affect Policy? *Annual Review of Political Science*, *24*(1), 235–252. doi:10.1146/annurev-polisci-041719-102019

Cooke, E. F., & Amuakwa-Mensah, F. (2022). Microfinance loans, women's economic empowerment, and poverty: A case study of Baobab Microfinance Company. *Journal of Development Effectiveness*, *14*(1), 34–55. doi:10.1080/19439342.2021.1953568

Cull, R., Demirgüç-Kunt, A., & Morduch, J. (2007). Financial performance and outreach: A global analysis of leading microbanks. *Economic Journal (London)*, *117*(517), F107–F133. doi:10.1111/j.1468-0297.2007.02017.x

Cull, R., & Hartarska, V. (2023). Overview of microfinance, financial inclusion, and development. Handbook of microfinance, financial inclusion and development, 2-19.

D'espallier, B., Guérin, I., & Mersland, R. (2013). Focus on Women in Microfinance Institutions. *The Journal of Development Studies*, *49*(5), 589–608. doi:10.1080/00220388.2012.720364

Datta, S., & Sahu, T. N. (2022). How far is microfinance relevant for empowering rural women? An empirical investigation. *Journal of Economic Issues*, *56*(1), 97–112. doi:10.1080/00213624.2022.2019552

Dhaoui, I. (2015). *The role of Islamic Microfinance in Poverty Alleviation: Lessons from Bangladesh Experience*. https://mpra.ub.uni-muenchen.de/87358/

Doepke, M., Tertilt, M., & Voena, A. (2012). The Economics and Politics of Women's Rights. *Annual Review of Economics*, *4*(1), 339–372. doi:10.1146/annurev-economics-061109-080201

Dotsey, S. (2022). COVID-19 and Microcredit: Dissecting an NGO's Training, Financial Support, and Women Empowerment Programmes. *Social Sciences (Basel, Switzerland)*, *11*(9), 402. doi:10.3390ocsci11090402

Duncombe, R., & Boateng, R. (2009). Mobile phones and financial services in developing countries: A review of concepts, methods, issues, evidence and future research directions. *Third World Quarterly*, *30*(7), 1237–1258. doi:10.1080/01436590903134882

Duvendack, M., Palmer-Jones, R., Copestake, J. G., Hooper, L., Loke, Y., & Rao, N. (2011). *What is the evidence of the impact of microfinance on the well-being of poor people? The EPPI-Centre, Social Science Research Unit, Institute of Education*. University of London.

Ebrahim, C., Jack, A., & Jones, L. (2021). Women's economic empowerment and COVID-19: The case of vulnerable women with intersectional identities in Indonesia and Vietnam. *Enterprise Development & Microfinance*, *32*(1), 44–56. doi:10.3362/1755-1986.21-00007

Ebrahimi, R., Choobchian, S., Farhadian, H., Goli, I., Farmandeh, E., & Azadi, H. (2022). Investigating the effect of vocational education and training on rural women's empowerment. *Humanities & Social Sciences Communications*, *9*(1), 1. Advance online publication. doi:10.105741599-022-01187-4

Ehigiamusoe, G. (2008). The role of microfinance institutions in the economic development of Nigeria. *Publication of the Central Bank of Nigeria*, *32*(1), 17–25.

European Institute for Gender Equality (EIGE). (2016). *Gender equality training: Gender mainstreaming toolkit*. Author.

Fadikpe, A. A. A., Danquah, R., Aidoo, M., Chomen, D. A., Yankey, R., & Dongmei, X. (2022). Linkages between social and financial performance: Evidence from Sub-Saharan Africa microfinance institutions. *PLoS One*, *17*(3), e0261326. doi:10.1371/journal.pone.0261326 PMID:35231026

Gerard, K., & Johnston, M. (2019). Explaining microfinance's resilience: The case of microfinance in Australia. *Globalizations*, *16*(6), 876–893. doi:10.1080/14747731.2018.1560188

Goetz, A. M., & Gupta, R. S. (1996). Who takes the credit? Gender, power, and control over loan use in rural credit programs in Bangladesh. *World Development*, *24*(1), 45–63. doi:10.1016/0305-750X(95)00124-U

GSM Association. (2015). *Bridging the Gender Gap: Mobile Access and Usage in Low- and Middle-income Countries*. Academic Press.

Gupta, I., & Roy, A. (2023). What really empowers women? Taking another look at economic empowerment. *Journal of Social and Economic Development*, *25*(1), 17–31. doi:10.100740847-022-00215-y

Hasan, M., Le, T., & Hoque, A. (2021). How does financial literacy impact on inclusive finance? *Financial Innovation*, *7*(1), 1–23. doi:10.118640854-021-00259-9

Hennink, M., Kiiti, N., Pillinger, M., & Jayakaran, R. (2012). Defining empowerment: Perspectives from international development organisations. *Development in Practice*, *22*(2), 202–215. doi:10.1080/09614524.2012.640987

Hermes, N., & Lensink, R. (2007). The empirics of microfinance: What do we know? *Economic Journal (London)*, *117*(517), F1–F10. doi:10.1111/j.1468-0297.2007.02013.x

Holloway, K., Niazi, Z., & Rouse, R. (2017). Women's economic empowerment through financial inclusion: A review of existing evidence and remaining knowledge gaps. *Innovations for Poverty Action.*

Holmberg, J., & Sandbrook, R. (2019). Sustainable development: what is to be done? In *Policies for a small planet* (pp. 19–38). Routledge. doi:10.4324/9780429200465-1

Huang, J., Sherraden, M., Sherraden, M. S., & Johnson, L. (2022). Effective finance to increase financial well-being for low-income families: Empirical examination and policy implications. *The Journal of Consumer Affairs*, *56*(4), 1638–1657. doi:10.1111/joca.12484

Johnson, S. (2004). Gender norms in financial markets: Evidence from Kenya. *World Development*, *32*(8), 1355–1374. doi:10.1016/j.worlddev.2004.03.003

Konadu, A., & Biney-Assan, A. B. (2007). *The Role of Microfinance in the Empowerment of Women-An Example of Sinapi Aba Trust, Offinso Branch-Ghana* [Master's thesis]. Høgskolen i Agder.

Luo, W., & Cheng, J. (2022). Transition to sustainable business models for green economic recovery: Role of financial literacy, innovation and environmental sustainability. *Economic Change and Restructuring*, 1–24. doi:10.100710644-022-09408-1

Lyoussi, D., & Kouchih, A. (2023). Metaverse and Financial Inclusion Opportunities and Risks for the Banking Ecosystem. In *Influencer Marketing Applications Within the Metaverse* (pp. 205–224). IGI Global. doi:10.4018/978-1-6684-8898-0.ch013

McCann, J. (2013). *Electoral quotas for women: An international overview*. https://www.semanticscholar.org/paper/Electoral-quotas-for-women%3A-an-international-McCann/c4a06f4e4139807d8ee4239f7b05983816c7faff

Mhlanga, D. (2022). COVID-19 and digital financial inclusion: Policies and innovation that can accelerate financial inclusion in a post-COVID world through fintech. *African Journal of Development Studies, 2022*(si2), 79.

Milazzo, A., & Goldstein, M. (2019). Governance and women's economic and political participation: Power inequalities, formal constraints and norms. *The World Bank Research Observer, 34*(1), 34–64. doi:10.1093/wbro/lky006

Mohammed, F., Boateng, S. D., & Freeman, C. (2022). Effect of Access to Microfinance Support on Growth of Women Agro-Processing Enterprises in the Northern Region of Ghana. *International Journal of Business and Management, 10*(3).

Morduch, J., & Haley, B. (2002). *Analysis of the effects of microfinance on poverty reduction*. NYU Wagner Working Paper, 1014.

Ofori, E., & Kashiwagi, K. (2022). Impact of microfinance on the social performance of local households: Evidence from the Kassena Nankana East District of Ghana. *Sustainability (Basel), 14*(10), 6002. doi:10.3390u14106002

Orkoh, E., Claassen, C., & Blaauw, D. (2022). Poverty and Intrahousehold Gender Inequality in Time Use in Ghana. *Feminist Economics, 28*(4), 221–253. doi:10.1080/13545701.2022.2080854

Phan, C. T., Vo, T. T., & Vo, D. T. H. (2023). Can microcredit reduce vulnerability to poverty? Evidence from rural Vietnam. *Review of Development Economics, 27*(1), 608–629. doi:10.1111/rode.12951

Quagrainie, F. A., Adams, S., Kabalan, A. A. M., & Dankwa, A. D. (2021). Micro-entrepreneurship, sustainable development goal one and cultural expectations of Ghanaian women. *Journal of Entrepreneurship in Emerging Economies, 13*(1), 86–106. doi:10.1108/JEEE-11-2019-0174

Rehman, F. U., Nawaz, T., Ilyas, M., & Hyder, S. (2014). A Comparative Analysis of Mobile and Email Marketing Using AIDA Model. *Journal of Basic and Applied Scientific Research, 4*(6), 38–49.

Roodman, D., & Morduch, J. (2014). The impact of microcredit on the poor in Bangladesh: Revisiting the evidence. *The Journal of Development Studies, 50*(4), 583–604. doi:10.1080/00220388.2013.858122

Sharma, R., Mehta, K., Sidhu, N. K., & Vyas, V. (2023). Extending UTAUT2 Model With Sustainability and Psychological Factors in Adoption of Blockchain Technology for the Digital Transformation of Banks in India. In *Revolutionizing Financial Services and Markets Through FinTech and Blockchain* (pp. 27–43). IGI Global. doi:10.4018/978-1-6684-8624-5.ch003

Shema, A. (2022). Effects of increasing credit limit in digital microlending: A study of airtime lending in East Africa. *The Electronic Journal on Information Systems in Developing Countries, 88*(3), e12199. doi:10.1002/isd2.12199

Sinha, M., Mahapatra, S. S., Dutta, A., & Sengupta, P. P. (2023). Microfinance and women empowerment: An empirical analysis. In *Research Anthology on Microfinance Services and Roles in Social Progress* (pp. 1–13). IGI Global. https://www.igi-global.com/chapter/microfinance-and-women-empowerment-an-empirical-analysis/314741

Solotaroff, J. L., Kotikula, A., Lonnberg, T., Ali, S., & Jahan, F. (2019). *Voices to choices: Bangladesh's journey in women's economic empowerment*. World Bank Publications. doi:10.1596/978-1-4648-1374-0

Sultana, Y., Hazarika, P., Nu, F. R., V, A. F., & Javed, A. (2023). Women Empowerment Through Microfinance: Empirical Evidence from India (A Micro-Level Study). *Kepes, 21*(2), Article 2.

UNFPA, I. (1994). Program of Action. *Paragraph*, 8.

Unterhalter, E., North, A., Arnot, M., Lloyd, C., Moletsane, L., Murphy-Graham, E., Parkes, J., & Saito, M. (2014). *Interventions to enhance girls' education and gender equality. Education rigorous literature review*. Department of International Development.

Uruthirapathy, A., & Dyke, L. (2022). The influence of general causality orientations on self-esteem and perceived stress among undergraduate students in women-only colleges. *International Journal of Educational Management*, *36*(5), 766–783. doi:10.1108/IJEM-05-2021-0179

Vaessen, J. (2001). Accessibility of Rural Credit in Northern Nicaragua: The Importance of Networks of Information. *Journal of Microfinance/ESR Review*, *3*(2).

Women, U. N. (2015). *Progress of the World's Women 2015-2016: Transforming Economies, Realizing Rights*. UN Women. doi:10.18356/2d5f74e3-en

World Bank. (2018). *Women's Financial Inclusion and the Law*. World Bank.

Yan, Y., & Qi, S. (2021). Childhood matters: Family education and financial inclusion. *Pacific-Basin Finance Journal*, *65*, 101489. doi:10.1016/j.pacfin.2020.101489

Yunus, M. (1999). *Banker to the poor: The autobiography of Muhammad Yunus, founder of the Grameen Bank*. Oxford University Press.

Yunus, M. (2003). *Banker to the Poor: Micro-Lending and the Battle Against World Poverty*. Public Affairs.

Yur'evna, P. E., & Kristina, Y. (2022). Self-worth as a basis for the formation of self-esteem. *Modern Technologies and Scientific and Technological Progress*, *2022*(1), 361–362. doi:10.36629/2686-9896-2022-1-361-362

Chapter 11
The Role of Microfinance in Women Empowerment

Arohi Anand
Sarala Birla University, India

Animesh Karn
https://orcid.org/0000-0002-0359-8496
Amity University, Ranchi, India

ABSTRACT

Microfinance is often touted as a tool for women empowerment, as it provides financial services to individuals who are typically excluded from traditional banking systems. It is widely believed that access to microfinance can help women improve their financial situation, increase their agency and decision-making power, and ultimately lead to greater empowerment. In this context, the present study investigates the impact of microfinance on the lives of members of self-help groups operating in Ranchi, Jharkhand, India. The findings suggest that microfinance has the potential to empower women by providing them easier access to credit enabling them to achieve financial independence, learn income-generating skills, and increase say in household decision-making and participation in community activities.

I. INTRODUCTION

i. Definition of microfinance
ii. Importance of women empowerment
iii. Significance of studying the role of microfinance in women empowerment.

i. Definition of Microfinance

Microfinance refers to the provision of financial services to individuals with low incomes, specifically targeting those who lack access to conventional banking systems. It is a term used to describe the financial support offered to these underserved individuals, addressing their specific needs, and empowering

DOI: 10.4018/978-1-6684-8979-6.ch011

them economically. These financial services include small loans, savings accounts, insurance, and other financial products. The goal of microfinance is to provide these individuals with access to credit to help them start or expand small businesses, as well as to help them manage their finances more effectively.

The origins of microfinance can be traced back to several different countries and organizations. Founded by Muhammad Yunus in 1983, the Grameen Bank in Bangladesh stands as an early exemplar of microfinance. This innovative institution pioneered the practice of extending small loans to impoverished women residing in rural regions, enabling them to initiate small-scale enterprises and enhance their financial circumstances. Subsequently, microfinance has gained global recognition as a highly utilized approach for alleviating poverty and fostering economic progress.

There are several key features of microfinance that distinguish it from traditional banking services. First, microfinance institutions (MFIs) typically focus on providing financial services to the poor and marginalized, often in rural areas or urban slums. Second, MFIs emphasize the importance of building personal relationships with their clients, often through group lending models or other forms of social collateral. Finally, microfinance often involves smaller loan amounts and shorter repayment periods than traditional bank loans, as well as higher interest rates to compensate for the higher risk of lending to low-income borrowers.

One of the challenges of microfinance is ensuring that it has a positive impact on the lives of those it seeks to serve. While there is evidence that microfinance can help individuals improve their financial situation, some studies have raised concerns about the potential for microfinance to increase debt burdens or exacerbate poverty in certain cases. It is therefore important for microfinance institutions to carefully design their lending programs to ensure that they are not causing harm to clients.

In conclusion, microfinance is a tool that can help individuals who have been excluded from traditional banking services to access financial services and improve their economic situation. While there are challenges associated with implementing microfinance programs effectively, there is evidence that it can have a positive impact on poverty reduction and economic development.

ii. Importance of Women Empowerment

Women empowerment is closely linked to economic development. When women are empowered, they can actively contribute to the economy through increased labor force participation, entrepreneurship, and income generation. According to the World Bank, gender equality in the labor market could increase global GDP by $28 trillion by 2025 (World Bank, 2019). Empowered women invest a significant portion of their income in education, healthcare, and their families, leading to improved well-being and intergenerational progress. Empowering women is a key strategy in poverty alleviation efforts. Women are often disproportionately affected by poverty due to gender-based discrimination and limited access to resources. By providing women with education, skills training, and economic opportunities, they can break the cycle of poverty and become self-reliant. The United Nations Development Program (UNDP) notes that empowering women is essential for achieving sustainable development goals, including eradicating poverty (UNDP, 2020).

Women empowerment has a direct impact on health and education outcomes. When women are empowered, they have better access to healthcare services, leading to improved maternal and child health. Additionally, empowered women prioritize education, resulting in increased enrollment and improved educational outcomes for themselves and their children. The United Nations Educational, Scientific and Cultural Organization (UNESCO) highlights that investing in women's education leads to multiple societal benefits, including reduced child mortality, increased agricultural productivity, and enhanced resilience to climate change (UNESCO, 2020). Women empowerment is intrinsically linked to achieving gender equality and social justice. Empowered women challenge discriminatory social norms and practices, advocating for equal rights and opportunities. Promoting women's participation in decision-making processes, leadership roles, and political representation fosters a more inclusive and equitable society. The World Economic Forum's Global Gender Gap Report emphasizes that closing the gender gap and achieving gender equality can lead to more peaceful and just societies (World Economic Forum, 2020).

iii. Significance of Studying the Role of Microfinance in Women Empowerment

Women empowerment and microfinance are two interconnected concepts that have the potential to create positive social and economic change in the lives of women, particularly in developing countries. Let us explore these concepts in more detail.

1. Women Empowerment: The concept of women empowerment entails empowering women to have autonomy in their lives, exercise decision-making power, and engage actively in social, economic, and political domains. It involves addressing gender-based inequalities, discrimination, and barriers that restrict women's opportunities.

Empowered women can contribute to their families, communities, and societies in several ways. They are more likely to pursue education, access healthcare, engage in economic activities, and participate in decision-making processes. Attaining sustainable development goals relies not only on upholding fundamental human rights but also on fostering gender equality and empowering women.

2. Microfinance: Microfinance is a financial service strategy that caters to the needs of underserved individuals, particularly those with limited incomes and inadequate access to traditional banking facilities. It encompasses the provision of small loans, savings opportunities, insurance, and various other financial products, with a specific focus on women who face barriers in accessing formal financial systems. Microfinance institutions (MFIs) aim to alleviate poverty, promote entrepreneurship, and support economic development in underserved communities.

Microfinance can play a crucial role in empowering women by offering them access to financial resources and tools. Historically, women have faced challenges in accessing formal financial services due to cultural, social, and economic barriers. Microfinance fills this gap by providing financial services tailored to the needs of women, enabling them to start or expand businesses, generate income, and enhance their economic independence.

Linking Women Empowerment and Microfinance

Microfinance programs that specifically target women have been successful in promoting women's empowerment. Here are some keyways in which microfinance contributes to women's empowerment:

a. Economic Empowerment: Microfinance provides women with capital to start or expand businesses, leading to increased income and economic independence. This empowerment enhances their decision-making power within the household and broader community.
b. Skill Development: Microfinance institutions often offer training and capacity-building programs to borrowers, including financial literacy, entrepreneurship, and vocational skills. These programs enhance women's knowledge and abilities, boosting their confidence and self-esteem.
c. Social Empowerment: Access to financial services can challenge gender norms and empower women to challenge traditional roles. Women's participation in economic activities and their increased income can lead to greater social recognition and influence within their families and communities.
d. Education and Health: Increased income from microfinance can enable women to invest in education and healthcare for themselves and their families. Educated and healthy women are better equipped to make informed decisions and contribute to their communities.
e. Community Development: When women are economically empowered, they often invest in the welfare of their families and communities. They become agents of change, promoting social development, and influencing positive transformations in their societies.

Overall, by providing financial services and support, microfinance can be a powerful tool in advancing women's empowerment. However, it is important to note that microfinance alone cannot address all the complexities related to gender inequality. It should be complemented by broader efforts, such as policy reforms, gender-responsive programs, and addressing social norms and cultural barriers, to create sustainable and long-term change.

Case #1: Grameen Bank in Bangladesh

The Grameen Bank, founded by Nobel laureate Muhammad Yunus in Bangladesh, is one of the most renowned microfinance institutions globally. It has played a significant role in empowering women and alleviating poverty in rural communities. The Grameen Bank's approach focuses on providing small loans to predominantly women borrowers, known as "Grameen borrowers."

Impact on Economic Empowerment: One notable impact of Grameen Bank's microfinance program is the economic empowerment of women. By providing small loans without collateral requirements, the bank enables women to start income-generating activities. Borrowers receive financial training and support to develop business plans and manage their enterprises effectively.

For example, Fatima Begum, a Grameen borrower, used a microloan to start a small tailoring business. With her increased income, she was able to improve her family's living conditions, provide education for her children, and expand her business. She became an influential figure in her community and a role model for other women entrepreneurs.

Impact on Social Empowerment: Microfinance through Grameen Bank has also had a profound impact on social empowerment. Women borrowers become active participants in decision-making processes at both the household and community levels. As they gain economic independence, their opinions and voices are recognized and valued.

Shahnaz, another Grameen borrower, used her microloan to purchase a cow and started a dairy business. As her business thrived, she gained respect in her village and became a member of the local community council. Shahnaz actively advocated for the needs and rights of women in her community, challenging traditional gender roles and promoting women's empowerment.

Impact on Education and Health: Access to microfinance has enabled women to invest in education and healthcare, leading to improved outcomes for themselves and their families. With increased income, women can afford to send their children, especially daughters, to school. This breaks the cycle of intergenerational poverty and empowers future generations.

Moreover, Grameen Bank introduced the concept of microfinance-based health insurance, allowing borrowers to access affordable healthcare services. Women like Nazma, a Grameen borrower, were able to receive necessary medical treatments for themselves and their family members, thus improving their overall well-being.

Community Development: The impact of Grameen Bank's microfinance program extends beyond individual borrowers. As empowered women invest in their families and communities, there is a ripple effect on community development. They actively engage in social initiatives, such as sanitation campaigns, education programs, and women's rights advocacy. For instance, Amina, a Grameen borrower, used her microloan to set up a small grocery store. With her increased income, she supported the education of disadvantaged children in her village and initiated awareness campaigns on women's health and hygiene.

This example exemplifies the positive impact of microfinance on women's empowerment. By providing financial services and support to women, the bank has enabled them to overcome socio-economic barriers, gain economic independence, and become influential members of their communities. The case demonstrates the transformative power of microfinance in fostering women's empowerment and contributing to sustainable development.

Case #2: SEWA Bank in India

SEWA (Self Employed Women's Association) Bank is a pioneering microfinance institution in India that focuses on empowering women in the informal sector. Established in 1974, SEWA Bank has played a vital role in promoting financial inclusion, entrepreneurship, and social empowerment among marginalized women.

Impact on Economic Empowerment: SEWA Bank provides financial services, including loans, savings, and insurance, to its members, who are predominantly women working in the informal sector. By accessing microloans, women can start or expand their businesses, ranging from small-scale trading to artisanal work.

For example, Raji, a member of SEWA Bank, received a microloan to purchase a sewing machine and materials. With her newfound business, she was able to generate a stable income, provide for her family's needs, and even employ other women from her community. Through the support of SEWA Bank, Raji gained economic independence and became a successful entrepreneur.

Impact on Social Empowerment: SEWA Bank's microfinance program has had a significant impact on the social empowerment of women. It provides a platform for women to come together, share experiences, and collectively address issues they face. The bank also offers training programs on financial literacy, business management, and leadership, equipping women with essential skills and knowledge.

For instance, Geeta, a member of SEWA Bank, participated in leadership training and capacity-building workshops organized by the bank. She developed strong leadership skills and became a prominent advocate for the rights of women in the informal sector. Geeta's involvement in SEWA Bank's activities empowered her to challenge societal norms and fight for better working conditions and social protections for women.

Impact on Education and Health: Access to microfinance has enabled women to invest in education and healthcare for themselves and their families. SEWA Bank encourages members to save regularly, promoting a culture of financial discipline and resilience.

For instance, Meena, a member of SEWA Bank, used her savings and a microloan to pay for her daughter's higher education. As a result, her daughter was able to pursue a college degree, breaking the cycle of limited opportunities in their family. Meena's investment in education not only empowered her daughter but also inspired other women in her community to prioritize education for their children.

Community Development: SEWA Bank's microfinance program has contributed to community development by empowering women to be agents of change. As women gain economic independence and social empowerment, they actively participate in community initiatives and decision-making processes. For example, Sita, a member of SEWA Bank, established a successful tailoring business with the help of microfinance. She used her influence and business acumen to organize skill development programs for women in her community. Through these programs, she not only provided employment opportunities but also fostered a sense of unity and collective progress among women.

SEWA Bank's microfinance program has played a pivotal role in empowering women in the informal sector in India. By providing financial services, training, and a platform for collective action, SEWA Bank has enabled women to break free from the cycle of poverty, gain economic independence, and become influential change agents in their communities.

Case Study #3: Bandhan Microfinance in India

Bandhan Microfinance is one of the leading microfinance institutions in India. Stemming from the Bandhan Financial Services Limited, a not-for-profit society founded in 2001, Bandhan Microfinance has matured into a commercial bank–Bandhan Bank–with over 1000 branches and over 5000 banking outlets across the country. Set up initially as a microcredit institution, it provided small loans to the tune of Rs.1000–3000 to women from the economically weaker sections of suburban Kolkata. In less than a decade, it emerged as the largest microfinancing institution in India.

In 2015, it acquired the universal banking license from the Reserve Bank of India and transferred its microlending business and existing customers to the newly created banking entity, the Bandhan Bank. As of June 2023, the Bank has mobilized Rs.1,08,479 crores as deposits from over three crore customers. Over 84% of the bank's advances are in retail and micro-entrepreneur segment.

Becoming a bank has helped Bandhan Microfinance unshackle itself from the rules that bound microfinancing institutions while retaining the microcredit nature of its lending. For example, it has enabled Bandhan Bank to offer a higher upper limit of Rs.1,50,000 as borrowings to individual borrowers and also offer credit to ones who already have such loans from two other microfinancing institutions (which is not possible in the case of a purely MFI institution).

Over half of its customer base has been with Bandhan for more than 19 years with an average borrowing of Rs.39,000. This longstanding relationship with its customers has helped Bandhan build a system of financial trust as it knows the entire lifecycle of its customers. This enables it to offer the lowest microlending rate in the industry.

The rapid rise of Bandhan Bank is built upon its success as a microfinancing enterprise focusing on financial inclusion and women empowerment. Even after transforming itself into a banking institution, it continues to nurture its core value of financial inclusion and caters largely to its decades-old clientele of micro-borrowers.

Case Study #4: NABARD – Composting for Success

NABARD in association with a local NGO, Ankur Abhian, imparted training for income generation through vermicompost and vegetable cultivation using micro-irrigation to SHG families of Lohardaga district in Jharkhand. The SHG members were struggling to increase their income levels despite forming the group several months ago. Training was imparted to 162 members.

Members took a loan of Rs. 40,000 from their own groups to purchase vermicompost units and invest in micro-irrigation infrastructure. As a result of the training and subsequent micro-financing, participating member were able to increase their incomes from Rs.1,500 to Rs.3,000 per month. The groups as a whole were able to do a business of Rs.8,00,000 by selling vermicompost to the local NGOs and to the nodal agency implementing plantation drive under the MGNRES (Mahatma Gandhi National Rural Employment Guarantee Scheme).

II: LITERATURE REVIEW

i. Theoretical Frameworks for Understanding Microfinance and Women Empowerment

Women empowerment can be understood from several theoretical frameworks drawn from diverse disciplines. Elements derived from these frameworks can be used to trace connections between microfinance and women empowerment.

Economic Empowerment Framework focuses on the economic aspects of women's empowerment through microfinance. It emphasizes that providing access to financial services, such as microcredit and savings, can enhance women's economic capabilities and improve their overall well-being. It argues that access to capital allows women to start and expand businesses, generate income, and gain greater control over financial resources, which in turn leads to increased decision-making power and autonomy.

The Capability Approach, developed by economist Amartya Sen and philosopher Martha Nussbaum, views empowerment as the expansion of individuals' capabilities or freedoms to lead lives they value. In the context of microfinance and women, this framework emphasizes that empowerment goes beyond economic factors and should also encompass social, political, and educational dimensions. It focuses on enabling women to develop their own capabilities, make choices, and participate fully in society, with microfinance acting as a means to facilitate this broader empowerment.

Social Capital Framework highlights the importance of social networks, relationships, and community support in empowering women through microfinance. It suggests that access to financial services can enhance social capital by strengthening women's social connections, building trust, and fostering collective action. Through participation in microfinance groups or networks, women can gain valuable social resources, knowledge, and support, which contribute to their empowerment beyond the economic sphere.

Feminist Empowerment Framework examines the gendered power dynamics and structural inequalities that shape women's lives. It recognizes that women's empowerment is not solely an individual endeavor but requires addressing broader socio-cultural norms and systemic barriers. In the context of microfinance, this framework analyzes how microfinance programs can challenge or reinforce existing gender inequalities. It emphasizes the need for gender-responsive approaches that promote women's agency, challenge gender norms, and address structural barriers to empower women effectively.

The EMERGE (Evidence-based Measures of Empowerment for Research on Gender Equality) initiative views women empowerment as both a process and an outcome and provides a framework to quantify its constructs. It postulates that the empowerment process begins with (i) the consciousness of possible choices that exist beyond socially imposed marginalization; next, (ii) one must be convinced of their right to make such choices to result in any (iii) agency to exercise them. These choices are then evaluated against achievement of self-determined goals (see Figure–1).

Figure 1. The empowerment process model
Source: Report of the EMERGE Team, April 2021.

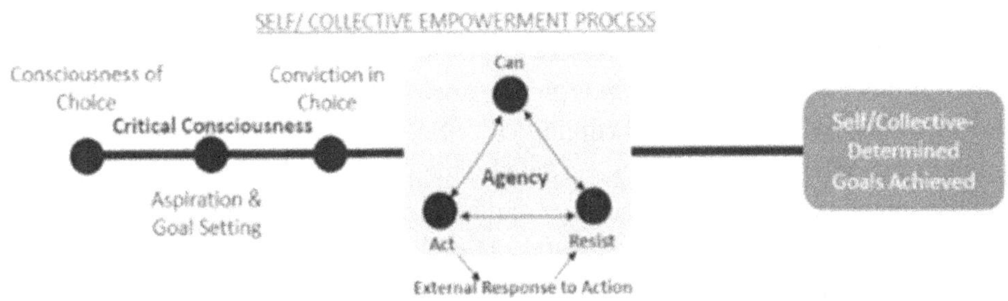

According to this model, women first must become conscious of their marginalization in order to aspire to be liberated from it. Once this consciousness sets in, women must aspire and set goal(s); conviction towards the goals set makes it easier to overcome obstacles and challenges in achieving them. Any exercise of choice (agency) may be met with retaliation by the oppressor (individuals or social power structure) and has to be resisted in order to realize the goals set. Results of the agency are then evaluated against the aspired goals for future action. Viewed from this perspective, microfinance becomes a mean or strategy to achieve empowerment that financial independence brings along.

These theoretical frameworks offer different lenses to understand the complex relationship between microfinance and women's empowerment. It is important to note that the effectiveness of microfinance programs in empowering women can vary based on contextual factors, program design, and implementation strategies.

ii. Review of Studies on Microfinance and Women Empowerment

According to Shaw (2004), the most impoverished households have limited access to formal education, which severely hampers their overall productivity. In addition, inadequate healthcare and malnutrition significantly contribute to limiting the capabilities of these households. Illiteracy and a general lack of education impact impoverished individuals negatively and impede their comprehension of credit acquisition processes.

Malhotra, Schuler and Boender (2002) highlight the fact that while the recognition of empowerment as a crucial driver of development has taken place, institutions like the World Bank and other development agencies have yet to establish a reliable approach to assess and analyze the diverse dimensions of empowerment. Empowerment is a multifaceted and dynamic process that poses challenges when it comes to measuring it. This complexity arises from the interplay between factors– socio-economic, and political–that influence empowerment.

The term 'empowerment' has been employed to encompass a broad spectrum of ideas and to depict a multitude of outcomes. The term has been used more often to advocate for certain types of policies and intervention strategies than to analyze them, as demonstrated by a number of documents from the United Nations (UNDAW 2001; UNICEF 1999), the Association for Women in Development (Everett 1991), Feminist activist writings often promote empowerment of individuals and organizations of women (Sen and Grown 1987; Jahan 1995; Kumar 1993) but vary in the extent to which they conceptualize or discuss how to identify it. An alternative perspective in the field of development advocates for social inclusion within institutions as the primary avenue for empowering individuals. However, this approach has occasionally blurred the distinction between empowerment and participation.

Capitalism, top-down approaches to development, and/or poverty itself are seen as sources of dis-empowerment that must be challenged by bringing "lowers"—the poor and disenfranchised (Chambers 1997)—into the management of community and development processes. The growth of civil society and participatory development methods at both macro-and meso-levels of society are usually proposed as the mechanisms by which empowerment takes place (Friedmann 1992; Chambers 1997). For example, Narayan et al. (2000a) focus on state and civil society institutions at both national and local levels, including informal institutions such as kinship and neighborhood networks. In the context of social exclusion, micro level institutions, such as marriage and the household, are typically not regarded as components of civil society or even the state. However, within the household, the interpersonal dynamics of gender are recognized as integral to the issue of social exclusion and require targeted efforts for transformation.

Morduch and Armendariz (2005) report that, in general, women accounted for 71% of the total borrowers in Microfinance Institutions (MFIs) and, in particular, 95% of the borrowers affiliated with Grameen Bank were females, and this percentage continued to rise until 2011. Previous researchers have also highlighted that MFIs specifically target women due to their significantly lower default rates compared to men (Al- Mamun, Wahab, Mazumder, & Su, 2014; Kevane & Wydick, 2001). As a result, MFIs have introduced various innovative schemes to provide financial support to their female clients. The role of MFIs in empowering women is crucial as it enhances their resources, improves their affordability, thereby increasing returns on their human capital, and ultimately elevating their living standards.

Katherine Esty (2017) identified several key factors that contributed to the groundbreaking success of Grameen Bank in Bangladesh: visionary leadership, challenging established norms, building a dedicated team, effective communication, adaptability, and the perseverance to overcome challenges.

Microfinance and Women Empowerment in India

Participation of women in microfinance-backed self-help groups not only improves the monetary position of the participating members but also generates employment opportunities for other women. This, Mathur and Agrawal (2017) say, results in improved standard of living among women.

Sharma (2019) in his study of a successful and a failing SHG in Manipur, put forth the following reasons for the success of Ningol Sintha SHG which mainly engaged in embroidery and wool knitting: i) members were sensitized about the objectives and given training before they undertook the activity, ii) more than 80% women were educated above high school, iii) a good rapport with the supporting agency (NCUI–Women Cooperative Education Project), iv) 50% members were young, unmarried and energetic, v) working together gave a good working environment, vi) machinery were new and suitable, vii) established marketing of the finished goods, viii) the group procured raw materials in bulk and thus enjoyed economies of scale, ix) their group leader (45 years old) was calm, cool, and wise. The unsuccessful SHG, Laima SHG, which primarily operated in the Bori (nuggets) making business, encountered several significant challenges. The members of the SHG lacked proper training, which hindered their ability to effectively carry out their business activities. The SHG members were unaware that certain raw materials, such as black lentils and urad dal, were not locally produced. This lack of knowledge affected their ability to source the necessary materials for their business. The SHG also faced challenges in marketing its products and competing with established markets. They also struggled with the absence of a well-organized distribution channel. The SHG did not receive sufficient support from relevant line departments, which limited their ability to address and overcome the challenges they faced. The SHG lacked access to timely credit as the financial institution providing support to the SHG exhibited a non-cooperative attitude, which impeded their business operations and growth. Stronger members within the SHG exploited their position, causing problems and inequality within the group. As a result, the SHG struggled with weak financial management practices, including the diversion of funds towards personal consumption, marriages, and house construction, instead of business development.

Studying the impact of microlending by Bandhan Microfinance in Tinsukia district of Assam, Baruah, Bora, and Deka (2022) found that while availing microcredit enabled women to enhance the economic dimension of their empowerment, it left the other dimensions namely, sociocultural, and political, unimpacted.

Khan, Bhat and Sangmi (2022) found similar results in their study of microfinance-backed women entrepreneurs in Kashmir, India. They conclude that while female entrepreneurs are more empowered than female non-entrepreneurs in all dimensions of empowerment, the impact of microfinancing on political and social empowerment of women remained less effective.

But Kumar *et al* (2021) contend and assert that not only entrepreneurship empowers women but also that the improvement in economic and social status of women is more significant particularly when microfinance is accessed through participation in SHGs.

Microfinancing Structure in India

Micro Finance Institutions (MFIs) currently operate in 29 States, 4 Union Territories and 563 districts in India. The reported 168 MFIs with a branch network of 10,233 and 89,785 employees have reached out to more than 3 crore clients with an outstanding loan portfolio of Rs. 46,842 crores. The average loan outstanding per borrower stood at Rs. 12,751 and 85% of loans were used for income generation purposes. In India, microcredit operates through two main channels: self-help groups and microfinancing institutions.

Self-Help Groups (SHGs)

Self-Help Groups (SHGs) are unofficial, homogenous organizations with 10 to 20 members that operate democratically and with participatory administration. SHGs are predominately made up of women. Table–1 shows state wise total number of SHG's:

Table 1. State-wise number of SHGs and membership

State/Union Territory Name	Number of SHGs	Minority Category-Wise Members				
		SC	ST	Minority	Others	PWD
Andhra Pradesh	853067	1866671	589882	2	6472282	274423
Assam	339644	370536	678048	1163673	1578674	3333
Bihar	1054957	2999779	224747	1385476	7591174	5781
Chhattisgarh	259538	317079	1165648	17258	1282511	121367
Gujarat	271002	287545	831413	78119	1485246	34015
Jharkhand	273058	508776	1047175	192353	1454313	23506
Karnataka	258074	563025	255079	154966	2065715	118419
Kerala	253988	408697	71356	641528	2395988	101015
Madhya Pradesh	442531	979649	1898050	81324	2269089	76747
Maharashtra	598199	792861	886902	211786	4062826	110576
Odisha	529875	1011903	1317321	85003	3037040	87720
Rajasthan	260018	706501	907475	91052	1155702	62582
Tamil Nadu	320283	1048399	62873	149169	2375261	360182
Telangana	439701	1005872	627454	146106	2907905	17031
Uttar Pradesh	720009	2554842	71857	462768	4390238	277788
West Bengal	1068316	3610085	765049	2849584	3748747	94155
Haryana	57590	279639	337	41675	267767	2593
Himachal Pradesh	42474	103200	16619	3104	216400	1945
Jammu And Kashmir	81665	82444	47528	3122	515170	4210
Punjab	41292	283527	57	14370	114895	4923
Uttarakhand	55724	105860	23314	22509	262597	11465
Arunachal Pradesh	8289	249	61106	957	2888	1347
Manipur	7791	1762	22025	7607	49057	388
Meghalaya	44208	4115	404000	15915	4292	5881
Mizoram	9772	104	76557	0	25	1313
Nagaland	14129	118	120438	5	292	1967
Sikkim	5631	3120	19798	5719	23230	752
Tripura	46866	97158	145718	32868	144809	2901
Andaman And Nicobar	1182	8	294	1852	9440	110
Goa	3652	1100	8732	3774	33403	117
Ladakh	551	1	4070	13	135	26
Lakshadweep	328	1	3718	22	0	104
Puducherry	4354	13740	231	1916	38675	857
Dadra & Nagar Haveli and Daman & Diu	925	302	7874	18	1404	81

Source: National Rural Livelihoods Mission Report, Ministry of Rural Development.

The SHG's members accumulate savings among themselves before becoming qualified to apply for credit. This program is known as the Self-Help Group-Bank Linkage Program (SHG-BLP) since the procedure of acquiring loans connects them to established banking institutions.

With a reach of 14.20 crore families, the SHG-BLP model is one of the most popular and successful microfinance programs in the world. Table–2 shows the overall development of the program's SHG linkage with the banking sector between 2019–2020 and 2021–2022.

Table 2. Progress under SHG–bank linkage program

	2019-20	2020-21	2021-22
Number of SHGs having Saving Bank Accounts (in lakhs)	97.96 (5.6%)	103.29 (5.4%)	108.87 (5.4%)
Savings of SHGs with Banks (in Rs. Crore)	25,055 (14.7%)	28,709 (14.6%)	32,908 (14.6%)
Number of SHGs provided with Bank Loan during the year (in lakhs)	24.15 (-0.8%)	25.42 (5.3%)	26.79 (5.4%)
Bank Loan disbursed to SHGs during the year (in Rs. Crore)	82,928 (-0.9%)	87,375 (5.4%)	92,147 (5.5%)
Number of SHGs having outstanding Bank Loan at the end of the year (in lakhs)	54.75 (-0.2%)	57.64 (5.3%)	60.74 (5.4%)
Bank Loan outstanding against SHGs at the end of the year (in Rs. Crore)	2,16,892 (-0.1%)	2,28,434 (5.3%)	2,40,936 (5.5%)
Number of SHGs covered under Credit Guarantee Fund Scheme for SHGs during the year (in lakhs)	1.95 (-11%)	2.18 (11.8%)	2.44 (11.9%)
Amount of Bank Loan covered under Credit Guarantee Fund Scheme for SHGs during the year (in Rs. Crore)	6,132 (-10%)	6,833 (11.4%)	7,642 (11.8%)

Figures in parentheses indicate decrease/increase over previous year.
Source: Status of Microfinance in India (2021-22), NABARD

Micro Finance Institutions

In India, MFIs not only offer micro-credit but also provide other financial services like savings, insurance, remittance and non- financial services like counselling, training and support to start a small business activity.

Under the MFI model, loans are given through the mechanism of Joint Lending Groups (JLGs). JLGs are informal groups of 4-10 members engaged in similar economic activity and are willing to jointly repay the loan taken by the members of the JLG from the MFIs. Loans given to JLG could be individual loan or a group loan.

Microfinance in Jharkhand

Jharkhand has a total of 61 microfinancing institutions (as on 2021) with active loans to the tune of Rs. 10.58 crore (see Table–3). The average ticket size of the loans is Rs.32,752 per SHG member.

Table 3. Savings, disbursement, and outstanding loans to SHGs in Jharkhand

Savings With SHGs (in Lakh Rupees)		**Loans Disbursed to SHGs (in Lakh Rupees)**		**Loans Outstanding (in Lakh Rupees)**	
Number of SHGs	Savings Amount	Number of SHGs	Disbursed Amount	Number of SHGs	Outstanding Amount
2,82,181	38,577.12	63,231	57,846.37	1,38,502	1,05,898.66

What is interesting is that while public sector commercial banks have classified loans to the tune of over Rs.3000 lakh as non-performing assets, they form only 5.21% of their total outstanding loans to the SHGs. But in case of private sector commercial banks, the NPAs of Rs.297.31 constitute over 60% of their outstanding loans to the SHGs.

Jharkhand has more than two lakhs registered SHGs with more than 26 lakh members. Table–4 presents district-wise distribution of SHG's in Jharkhand:

Table 4. District-wise number of SHGs and members in Jharkhand

Sl. No.	**District**	**SHG Count**	**Member Count**
1	Ranchi	18,702	2,39,435
2	Lohardaga	5,004	66,221
3	Gumla	8,357	1,08,400
4	Simdega	6,618	86,080
5	Palamu	17,658	2,21,030
6	Latehar	7,847	95,575
7	Garhwa	10,484	1,24,048
8	West Singhbhum	11,151	1,48,528
9	East Singhbhum	13,478	1,69,055
10	Dumka	13,394	1,65,880
11	Sahebganj	9,197	1,23,496
12	Pakur	6,594	84,663
13	Godda	10,655	1,35,118
14	Hazaribagh	14,827	1,89,221
15	Chatra	11,092	1,36,366
16	Giridih	16,920	2,30,608
17	Bokaro	13,768	1,76,926
18	Ramgarh	7,198	89,434
19	Khunti	5,969	77,765
Total		2,08,913	26,67,849

Of these, savings of more than 1.72 lakh SHGs have been linked with banks amounting to Rs.32,830.85 lakhs from more than 21 lakh members. The number of exclusively women SHGs is 1,52,417 with 19,03,147 members.

III. OBJECTIVES OF THE STUDY

The present study examines the extent to which microfinance interventions contribute to women's economic empowerment by analysing their literacy level, improvements in income level, decrease in indebtedness and sense of economic empowerment.

Hypothesis

Microfinance interventions positively impact women's economic empowerment by increasing their literacy level, access to healthcare, income level, level of debt-freeness and degree of economic empowerment.

Methodology

The study profiles the SHGs in the city of Ranchi, capital of a district of the same name as well as of the Jharkhand state. Jharkhand is an eastern state of India and one of the states having substantial population of tribals. It has historically been part of the state of Bihar which, in turn, is part of a group of most economically backward states in India. Jharkhand has 2,71,132 SHGs of which 740 have fewer than 5 members and none had more than 20 members each (Ministry of Rural Development, 2023).

Sample Size 10 SHGs with 20 members each. That comes to 200 people.	**Data Collection** Personal interviews of the members of the SHGs through a structured questionnaire.	**Data Analysis** Descriptive statistics.

The microfinancing institutions studied employ a large number of (mostly) young men as field staff who live in the vicinity of the areas where the programs are to run. When a new operation commences, these field staff visit nearby economically weaker communities and backward localities and explain in community gatherings and organized meetings that the program will provide credit to poor and assetless women in order to help them start income earning activities.

To become eligible for participation and receiving credit, women are asked to form small groups. Each women member is required to have a bank account; the field staff helps unbanked women open a 'Jan Dhan' (zero-cost) account. After assessing the dynamics of the groups, weekly meetings are organized where savings are deposited and loans are advanced. While loans are advanced to individual members, there is no collateral and the group members collectively are responsible for ensuring repayments by individual borrowers. The participating members are free to decide which income generating activity will they employ their loans for, but members are required to undergo mandatory training programs that help them assess the economic viability of an activity and organize the selected one.

IV. RESULTS ANALYSIS AND DISCUSSION

Demographically (see Table–5), close to 70 percent of the SHG members were of the age group 25–55 years. Married women constituted 93 percent of the sample. Female literacy rate was found to be 51.36, which is quite close to the female literacy rate of 52.04 at the national level (Registrar General and Census Commissioner of India, 2013). Most (175) of the women interviewed, either joined a literacy program or learnt new skills related to income generation activities of their respective SHGs.

Table 5. Demographic profile of the SHG members

Age Distribution		Marital Status		Monthly Earning	
Age in Years	**Percent**	**Marital Status**	**Percent**	**Amount (in Rs.)**	**Percent**
15–25	08.07	Married	93.0	Up to 2000	01.91
26–35	13.10	Unmarried	03.4	2000–4000	19.09
36–45	45.45	Widowed	03.2	4000–6000	63.35
46–55	22.35	Divorced	00.3	6000 and above	15.65
56 and above	11.03				

Most of the women (63.35%) earned between Rs.4000–6000 per month with 175 of them affirming increase in their income levels after becoming members of SHGs. Few members (33) had debt and other financial liabilities; their main source of borrowing being NGOs, relatives, and friends—none had borrowed from banks. Though borrowing from NGOs had helped them a lot, they also suffered huge losses as the intermediaries assigned by the credit organizations absconded with huge sums of money. Nevertheless, most of them (29 out of 33) were able to repay the monies owned due to increased income from the SHGs.

Only half of the members who had taken loans, were aware of the rate of interest charged at the time of borrowing. These loans were taken mainly for investment (starting home-based businesses such as saree painting, basket making, etc.) and productive purposes (working capital finance– mainly for buying cattle and selling vegetables). There were no cases of taking loans for consumption purposes.

The respondents were unanimous in asserting that joining SHGs had positively impacted their lives. The four main advantages cited by them were (i) improved social status, (ii) acquisition of new assets, (iii) better housing, and (iv) an increase in spending on food; repayment of prior debts, easier access to credit facilities, better education, involvement in community activities, increased involvement in household decision-making, and a lighter workload the acquisition of new skills came next (see Table–6).

Most of the women asserted that attending training programs had the largest impact on their ability to repay the loans. One interviewee said, "[attending] the training made me realize the mistakes I made in may earlier attempts at earning money. I learnt the value of incremental savings." Learning a new skill helped members start their own microenterprise: "I learnt the art of making wicker baskets that are in great demand by the vegetable vendors and 'kirana' general store keepers. This helped me become suppliers to 20 such clients." (interviewee #5).

Table 6. Benefits of joining SHGs

Serial No.	List of Benefits	Responded Yes
1	Increased income level	175
2	Learnt a new skill	175
3	Easier access to credit facilities	175
4	Repaid old loans	029
5	Better education	050
6	Bought new assets	065
7	Better housing	095
8	Better social status	170
9	More empowered in household decision	050
10	Increased participation in social activities	076

Being able to build 'pucca' houses or repair a dilapidated accommodation unit were the immediate impact of money earned through self-enterprise. Being able to support the education of their children was the most meaningful expense that they could engage in. "I was over-the-moon by being able to repair the leaky roof over my children's bedroom…they couldn't do their homework when it rained. Now they study for extra hours." (interviewee #37).

But the largest impact of the entire experience–becoming a member of the SHG, availing loan for self-enterprise, and repaying the borrowings on time–was the respect that they earned within their communities, especially their peer group. "I was considered good-for-nothing, not valued at all. Family did not take well my decision to join the SHG. But now that I bring in almost the same amount of money as my husband does, everybody thinks that I am really smart…they value me now and even ask for my advice." (interviewee #56)

V. CONCLUSION

Joining SHGs has an unequivocal positive impact on the lives of its members, especially women. Cutting across the religion, caste, income, and age boundaries, women are the most marginalized section of the India society. SHGs give them an opportunity for financial independence and, hence, of having a greater say in household decision-making. Success outside the house tends to enhance the self-esteem as well as social worth of the women.

The biggest issue facing women, especially in the tribal belt, is their lack of access to both a proper (non-exploitative and stable) credit channel and a skill set that can help generate income in for a long-term. SHGs, as per the present study, help alleviate both problems. Thus, microfinancing through SHGs has the potential to enhance the regular economic lives of women by providing them with a ready credit channel, a consistent market and a strong skill set.

REFERENCES

Al-Mamun, A., Wahab, S. A., Mazumder, M. N., & Su, Z. (2014). Empirical Investigation on the Impact of Microcredit on Women Empowerment in Urban Peninsular Malaysia. *Journal of Developing Areas*, 287–306.

Baruah, I., Bora, M., & Deka, M. B. (2022). Impact of Bandhan Microfinance on Empowerment of Rural Women in Tinsukia District of Assam. *Asian Journal of Agricultural Extension. Economia e Sociologia*.

Bateman, M. (2010). *Why doesn't microfinance work? The destructive rise of local neo-liberalism*. Zed Books. doi:10.5040/9781350223974

Bradley, S. W., McMullen, J. S., Artz, K., & Simiyu, E. M. (2012). Capital is not enough: Innovation in developing economies. *Journal of Management Studies*, *49*(4), 684–717. doi:10.1111/j.1467-6486.2012.01043.x

Chemin, M. (2008). The benefits and costs of microfinance: Evidence from Bangladesh. *The Journal of Development Studies*, *44*(4), 463–484. doi:10.1080/00220380701846735

De Soto. (2000). *The Mystery of Capital: Why Capitalism Triumphs in the West and Fails Everywhere Else*. Academic Press.

Diochon, M., & Ghore, Y. (2016). Contextualizing a social enterprise opportunity process in an emerging market. *Social Enterprise Journal*, *12*(2), 107–130. doi:10.1108/SEJ-11-2015-0032

Hagen, E. E. (1963). *How economic growth begins: a theory of social change. University of Illinois at Urbana-Champaign's Academy for Entrepreneurial Leadership Historical Research Reference in Entrepreneurship*. Free Press.

Kabeer, N. (1999). Resources, agency, achievements: Reflections on the measurement of women's empowerment. *Development and Change*, *30*(3), 435–464. doi:10.1111/1467-7660.00125

Katherine, E. (2017). Lessons from Muhammad Yunus and the Grameen Bank: Leading Long-Term Organizational Change Successfully. In S. A. Tirmizi & J. D. Vogelsang (Eds.), *Leading and Managing in the Social Sector: Strategies for Advancing Human Dignity and Social Justice* (pp. 31–39). Springer.

Kevane, M., & Wydick, B. (2001). Microenterprise Lending to Female Entrepreneurs: Sacrificing Economic Growth for Poverty Alleviation? *World Development*, *29*(7), 1225–1236. doi:10.1016/S0305-750X(01)00032-8

Kevane, M., & Wydick, B. (2001). Microenterprise lending to female entrepreneurs: Sacrificing economic growth for poverty alleviation? *World Development*, *29*(7), 1225–1236. doi:10.1016/S0305-750X(01)00032-8

Khan, S. T., Bhat, M. A., & Sangmi, M.-U.-D. (2022). Can microfinance-backed entrepreneurship be a holistic empowerment tool for women? Empirical evidence from Kashmir Valley, India. *Journal of Business and Socio-Economic Development*, 117-136.

Kumar, N., Raghunathan, K., Arrieta, A., Amir, J., & Pandey, S. (2021). The power of the collective empowers women: Evidence from self-help groups in India. *World Development, 146*, 105579. doi:10.1016/j.worlddev.2021.105579 PMID:34602708

Malhotra, A., Schuler, S. R., & Boender, C. (2002). Measuring Women's Empowerment as a Variable in International Development. *Workshop on Poverty and Gender: New Perspectives, 28.* 10.1037/e597202012-004

Mathur, P., & Agrawal, P. (2017). Self-help groups: a seed for intrinsic empowerment of Indian rural women. *Equality, Diversity and Inclusion: An International Journal.*

Ministry of Rural Development. (2023, June 28). *SHGs Profile Entry Status.* Retrieved from Aajeevika: https://nrlm.gov.in/shgReport.do?methodName=showIntensiveStateWiseReport

Morduch, J. (1999). The Microfinance Schism. *World Development, 28*(4), 617–629. doi:10.1016/S0305-750X(99)00151-5

Morduch, J., & Armendariz, B. (2005). *The Economics of Microfinance.* MIT Press.

Otero, M. (1999). Bringing development back into microfinance. *Small Enterprise Development, 10*(1), 9–20.

Registrar General and Census Commissioner of India. (2013). *The Census of India 2011.* Ministry of Home Affairs, Government of India.

Schuler, S. R., Islam, F., & Rottach, E. (2010). Women's empowerment revisited: A case study from Bangladesh. *Development in Practice, 20*(7), 840–854. doi:10.1080/09614524.2010.508108 PMID:20856695

Sharma, A. D. (2019). Empowering Women through SHGs – Evidence from a Case Study of SHGs in Imphal East District, Manipur. *Economic Affairs, 64*(1). Advance online publication. doi:10.30954/0424-2513.1.2019.3

Shaw, J. (2004). Microenterprise Occupation and Poverty Reduction in Microfinance Programs: Evidence from Sri Lanka. *World Development, 32*(7), 1247–1264. doi:10.1016/j.worlddev.2004.01.009

United Nations Development Program (UNDP). (2020). *Gender Equality and Women's Empowerment.* Retrieved from https://www.undp.org/sustainable-development-goals/gender-equality

United Nations Educational, Scientific and Cultural Organization (UNESCO). (2020). *Why is Gender Equality Important for Sustainable Development?* Retrieved from https://en.unesco.org/gem-report/gender-and-education/why-gender-equality-important-sustainable-development

World Bank. (2019). *Toward Gender Equality in East Asia and the Pacific: A Companion to the World Development Report.* Retrieved from https://openknowledge.worldbank.org/handle/10986/31337

World Economic Forum. (2020). *The Global Gender Gap Report 2020.* Retrieved from https://www.weforum.org/reports/gender-gap-2020-report-100-years-pay-equality

APPENDIX: INTERVIEW SCHEDULE

Name:
Age:
Name and Address of the SHG:

1. Marital Status:
   Married
   Unmarried
   Widow
   Divorce

2. Number of children:
   Sons
   Daughters
   None

3. Nature of family:
   Joint Family
   Nuclear Family

4. Number of members in your family:
   Male
   Female

5. Educational Status:
   Literate
   Illiterate

6. If literate up to:
   Up to primary
   Less than middle
   Middle and above

7. Do you attend any literacy/educational program / training program conducted in this village by government or NGOs?
   Yes
   No

8. Have you learned any new skills after joining SHG?
   Yes
   No

9. Age group of SHG members:
   15-25 yrs.
   26-35 yrs.
   36- 45 yrs.
   46-55 yrs.
   56 and above

10. Income before joining the SHG:
    Up to 1000 Rs
    1000-2000 Rs
    2000-5000 Rs
    5000 and above

11. Income after joining the SHG:
    Up to 2000 Rs
    2000-3000 Rs
    4000-5000 Rs
    6000 and above

12. What assets did you buy after joining SHG?
    1. ___________
    2. ___________
    3. ___________

13. What kind of house did you live in before joining SHG?
    Pucca house
    Katcha house
    Semi pucca house
    Semi Katcha house

14. After joining SHG, were there any changes in the house?
    Yes: ______________________
    No: ______________________

15. Was there any loan on you before joining SHG?
    Yes
    No

16. Were you able to repay your loan after joining SHG?
    Yes
    No

17. What has been the source of borrowing?
    Cooperative Society
    Banks
    Block office
    NGOs
    Landlords
    Friends and relatives
    Sahukars

18. Are you aware of the rate of interest paid by you or your spouse?
    Yes
    No

19. For what purpose did you take the loans?
    Consumption
    Investment
    Productive
    Unproductive

20. Are you aware of the health programs running in your village?
    Yes
    No

21. Have you used these health benefit schemes?
    Yes
    No

22. After joining SHG, do you see a marked improvement in yourself or among your family members?
    Yes
    No

23. Did you have the right to make household decisions before joining SHG?
(Household Expenses, childbirth, medical expenses, your income, voting and entertainment)
    Yes
    No

24. Do you have the right to make major household decisions after joining SHG?
(Household Expenses, childbirth, medical expenses, your income, voting and entertainment)
    Yes
    No

Chapter 12
Women Entrepreneurs in Turkey:
The Empirical Analysis of Microcredit Applications and Economic Growth Relations

Serdar Yener
Sinop University, Turkey

Aykut Arslan
Piri Reis University, Turkey

Ayşegül Eda Kop
Sinop University, Turkey

ABSTRACT

Women entrepreneurship is explained by the women-owned business that create economic value. Since there are potential differences between men and women entrepreneurships, this study aims to provide a detailed analysis of how micro-credits help women entrepreneurship in development and economic growth. The data used for this research is obtained from Grameen Microfinance and Statistical Institute. The obtained data is analysed to examine the relationship between women entrepreneurships and economic development. Firstly, a model is developed to test the influence of unit of used microcredit in Turkey and unit change in the number of women who work in their own business. The impact of micro-credit in Turkey on women's employment is analysed with regression analysis. Secondly, the ARDL bounds testing approach model is employed to investigate the influence of number of women entrepreneurships and economic growth. This relation elicits the contribution of micro-credits to Turkey's economy.

DOI: 10.4018/978-1-6684-8979-6.ch012

1. INTRODUCTION

The majority of women in the world and Turkey did not have chance to obtain equal opportunities in education and social life because of social and cultural limitations. This influenced their existence in the business world as compared to men's position. When women's ratio in the entire world population and their contribution to the world economy are compared, women's contribution to gross domestic product (GDP) is found less than it is expected (Hammawa and Hashim, 2016). According to Soysal (2010), an individual's societal behaviour patterns, quality and level of education, general economic conditions have significantly affected entrepreneurship. A great number of developing or developed countries have supported women entrepreneurship since the 2000s with various programmes that aim to get benefit from the idle women labor force. Micro-credit practices aim to support self-employment of (primarily) women and other disadvantaged groups (such as immigrants and minorities) to benefit from this idle labour, consequently to avoid poverty. The micro-credit practices have been started in the 2000s in Turkey while in 1970s in the world. They have been becoming more and more important and speeding up in recent years. In the literature, the relationship between micro-credit and women entrepreneurship has been analysed by using qualitative research, mainly conducting case studies (e.g. Maîtrot and Nino-2017; Seenivasan, 2015; Hulme, and Maitrot, 2014). Some of these studies have not supported the expected results of micro-finance, and are not influenced enough to trigger development. Although these studies in the literature provide valuable insights, they are limited to small sampling. Despite providing precious contribution, the existing literature is limited with narrow samples that only consist of local results. Therefore, micro-credits for women entrepreneurship and consequently its economical results were not correlated with macro data. The objective of this study is to analyse the impact of triggering factors of micro-credits on women entrepreneurship, hence, its influence on economic development by benefitting quantitative methods. On the contrary to the majority of studies (e.g. Hulme and Maitrot, 2014; Copestake et al., 2015), micro-credit is not a way to aim to alleviate the absolute poverty, however, micro-credits are discussed as determinant for women entrepreneurships who find opportunities. The findings of this study show that micro-credit has a significant impact on triggering women entrepreneurship on development and economic growth. These findings contradict to the arguments in the previous studies (e.g. Robinson and Watson, 2001; Kevane ve Wydick, 2001; Karnani, 2007).

2. LITERATURE

2.1. Women Entrepreneurships

The studies that examined the correlation between entrepreneurship and economic growth generally reveal a positive correlation. Therefore, entrepreneurships are seen as 'locomotive of country development' (Karlsson et al., 2009). Entrepreneurship is essential for continuity of communal process according to demand approach to economic development and defined as the person who discovers opportunities in any environment and gathers all the factors together to derive profit as seen in entrepreneurship literature (Kuratko, 2009). From a broader perspective, entrepreneurship is a process that starts a business, owns a business, improves and grows business (Bridge, 1998, p.35). Although entrepreneurship has been started to research as a business phenomenon in 1960s in USA, studies on women entrepreneurship have been neglected until 1990s in the literature (Loza, 2017). The reasons behind the lack of previous studies on women entrepreneurship are (1) not having a big women group in terms of quantity, (2) not appearing on popular media frequently, and (3) not considering the potential differences between men and women (Jennings and Brusch, 2013). Müftüoğlu and Durukan (2004, p. 35) define women entrepreneurship as 'Women who take the calculated risks in the market economy, focusing on market directly, producing and selling goods and services that can be converted into cash, running a business, registering for tax, registering for chambers of commerce and industry such as The Union of Chamber of Merchants and Craftsmen[1], The Confederation of Turkish Tradesmen and Craftsmen (TESK) or The Union of Chambers and Commodity Exchanges of Turkey (TOBB), working under one of the social security institutions or employing other people.' In this study, women entrepreneurship is used for women who create economic value by owning a business. According to Hisrich and Peters (1998), there are significant differences between women and men entrepreneur such as the source of motivation, age to start the enterprise, the people from whom they get support for enterprise, the industries to enterprise, education background, usage of resources, their expereince area and etc. Brush and Hisrich (1999) state that the differences between women and men entrepreneurs are the results of the combination of personal, social and cultural characteristics. Gundry et al. (2002) highlight that the influence of industry, family, culture and goal orientation on women enterprise should be examined. They continue with emphasizing the requirements to increase the studies on women entrepreneurship especially in developing countries. According to Hanson (2009), the potentials of women entrepreneurship are repressed because of various systematic difficulties. As Goyal and Yadav (2014) stated, women have problems to find financial support and they face socio-cultural bias. Aidis et al. (2007) compared women and men entrepreneurship in Litvania and Ukraine that are under transition economy, and examined differences with institutionalization theory. While the traditional role of women in society is incompatible with the idea of women entrepreneurship, thus cultural traditions and societal customs, a member state of EU, Litvaina, however overly developed formal institutions influence men and women entrepreneurship positively. Nowadays, although women are still exposed to glass ceiling in entrepreneurship, many countries realise the potential contribution of women to economic growth. According to GEM (Global Entrepreneurship Monitoring) Women Entrepreneurship Report of 2016-2017, 163 million of women were starting new businesses in 74 countries throughout the world. Plus, another 111 million were running established businesess. Consequently, entrepreneur women contribute to their families in terms of income and contribute to their society in terms of employment and contribute to the world in terms of value-added products and services (GEM, 2017). Worldbank report (2017) indicates that women mostly prefer to establish sole proprietorship rather than limited liability corporations (LLC), on average only one-third of new LLCs are initiated by women (Meunier et al., 2017). Buttner and Moore (1997) state the prominent factors that push women entrepreneurship are (1) balancing family-work life, (2) survival pressures, (3) not being satisfied with the previous job, (4) economic collapse and (5) unemployment. According to the results of a study that examined 129 women managers and professionals who quitted from their jobs and started up their own business, women define success as self-fulfillment' and 'goal achievement' rather than high profit and turnover. Buttner and Moore (1997) argue that enterprises have benefits on liberating women, achieving more professional satisfaction, and use their entrepreneurship as a tool for career growth. According to the study that examines the reasons of women to start up a business based on various cities in Turkey, it is found that factors such as getting a profit, providing an extra income to the family, working independently, having a social life, prove themselves, being productive, passion for success become prominent (Soysal, 2010). Therefore, the factors that support women entrepreneurship are both push factors such as getting profit and pull factors such as obtaining social status. Thus, entrepreneurship may mean for women more than bringing extra income to home. However, there are differences between women's entrepreneurship motivations and success criteria based on the information that women entrepreneurs have variety levels of human and social capital. Çetindamar et al. (2012) examined the influence of various capital (financial, human and family) on women and men entrepreneurs. They found that all 3 capitals increase the ratio of being entrepreneur regardless of gender. Surprisingly, the impact of human capital on women entrepreneurs is found as more than men entrepreneurs. According to the findings of Ufuk and Özgen (2001) who examined 220 married women entrepreneurs in Ankara, entrepreneurship influences women's social, economic, and personal lives positively, while it influences the roles of family life negatively. In the factor driven economies and efficiency driven economies, the tendency of women entrepreneurship is higher because of needing income and not having a better alternative job (Meena, 1992). According to Carrington (2006), women prefer to run mainly traditional businesses. Because of requiring less capital and equipment, food, clothing, hygiene and similar industries are preferred by women in Turkey (Nayır, 2008; Çelik ve Özdevecioğlu, 2001). The reason for women tend towards entrepreneurship in underdeveloped and developing countries is explained with need. Moreover, the actions of opportunity-driven entrepreneurship are seen as play a part as the main foundation of entrepreneurship approaches in innovation-driven economies (GEM, 2017). While the ratio of women entrepreneurship's necessity-driven entrepreneurship activities among total entrepreneurial activity (TEA) is 13% in the USA -as an innovation-driven economy-, this ratio increases to 36% in Sub-saharan Africa. This ratio is approximately 24% in Turkey as a country that is in a transition period from an efficiency-driven economy to an innovation-driven economy. When the total ratio of human resources' effective use -which is considered as an indicator of economic efficiency- is checked, the efficiency of economies can be presented by comparing the population of women and their contribution to GNP (Hisrich et al., 2008).

2.2. Micro-Credit

The reason behind the increase of the given importance of micro-credit and finance practices is losing the influence of development programmes that applied in less developed and developing countries before 1980s with globalization (Gökyay, 2008). Women became more active in politics and economy with the transition of women's movement to women empowerment activities in Turkey after 1980s (Gökakın, 2000). However, the continuation of the patriarchal mentality rarefies the spreading of women movement (Soysal, 2010). Microfinance policies that gain importance in Turkey, as well as in the world provide entrepreneurship opportunities for women and other groups (such as immigrants and minorities) who stayed out of the economy because of various social reasons at least in order to ease standing on their own feet.

The most important financial target of microfinance systems is to eliminate income differences between regions and genders and to fight poverty (Aygar, 2013). The concept of microfinance includes micro-credit not only to provide microcredits to poor people but also to provide services such as savings, retirement, consumer loans, insurance and money transfer (Aygar, 2013). According to Development Bank reports 2007, micro financing is defined as ''financial services that are provided to poor or low income level people, family and micro entrepreneurship (that has employees less than 9 (1-9)]. In this concept, micro-credit is defined in this paper as 'the credit that is given to micro-entrepreneurship to develop business by a micro financial organization'. Micro financial organisations cover a variety of financial organisations that include micro-finance enterprises, non-governmental organizations, commercial banks and credit unions. These credits are based on trust, and given without guarantor or guarantee, and are aimed to give to people in need to improve their business and to create opportunity not to eat fish or teach fishing, but to help them find the equipment for fishing (Dündar, 2007). Therefore, an entrepreneur needs to realize the job opportunities and have a business idea. According to GEM 2017 report, opportunity perceptions of Turkish women increased by 32% from 2014 to 2016 and the proportion to female to male opportunity perception increased to 7% for the same year interval. The increase in perception of opportunity can be indicator of more women to found their own business if required financial support provided.

Micro-credit practices have been started in Bangladesh to help poor people found the business or develop their business since 1976. After 1990s, it has been started to be detected as an important factor to fight against poverty by national and international organisations. In 1997, micro credit summit gathered and United Nations announced year 2005 as "Micro-credit year". In this summit, it is aimed to reach the poorest 100 million families in the world and especially women members of the families between the years 1997-2005 (Gökyay, 2008). According to results, approximately 80 million families who mostly live in Asia, benefit from microcredit practices. In 2006, microcredit summit that gathered in Halifax Canada aimed to reach the world's poorest 175 million families and increase their daily income by more than $1 by 2015. Furthermore, besides qualitative targets; quantitative targets such as strengthening women, self-sustaining, building stable financial structure have been added to the targets (Öz and Colakoğlu, 2014). According to Microcredit Summit Campaign 2012 reports, 137.5 million poor, who 82.3% of them are women, were reached by microcredit by end of 2010.

In the Member States and regions of the European Union, micro-credit is used as a means to encourage self-employment and development of micro-enterprises (especially for women and minorities), and it can be argued that micro-credit can play an important role in growth and 'flexi-curity' (the combination of flexibility and social security) . In EU, micro-credit refers loans less than € 25000; and micro-enterprise refers business that has less than 10 employees and 2 million euros of yearly revenue (COM, 2007; COM, 2006). Microcredit programmes in European Union showed different results based on regions. For instance, the expected results had not been found in France. The most important reason for this in France is the salary deduction of people who benefit from micro credits and not getting support from their social environment because of individual culture while paying back the credits (Gökyay, 2008). Moreover, exactly opposite results were found in the north region of Norway. In this region, men's being busy with fishing, women's not having any businesses caused by depopulation. Thus, protection of the population by offering/providing a field of occupation is aimed and has been successful. Therefore, micro credits show important results to find solutions not always for financially, but also for social problems (Gökyay, 2008).

Foundation for the support of women's work (*Kadın Emeğini Değerlendirme Vakfı*-KEDV) started to apply this first time in 2002 in the Marmara region of Turkey (Gökyay, 2008). In 2002, KEDV found MAYA that is Turkey's first microcredit organization, and aims to give required credits to women in order them to accomplish small size enterprises or grow their business (Öz ve Çolakoğlu, 2014). MAYA gave first credits in August 2002 in Kocaeli, in June 2003 in Istanbul, in August 2004 in Duzce, in November 2005 in Sakarya (www.kedv.org.tr as cited in Öz ve Çolakoğlu, 2014).

Another enterprise about microcredits in Turkey is Turkey waste prevention foundation (*Türkiye İsrafı Önleme Vakfı - TİSVA*) that started Turkey Grameen Microfinance (*Türkiye Grameen Mikrofinans*) programme (Öz ve Çolakoğlu, 2014). First attempts started in 1996, but the positive results could not be obtained. Then, a pilot project in Diyarbakir was applied to 12 people by giving ₺ 500 cheques in 2003. Later on, Grameen Microfinance Programme widened to 68 cities. In 2013, approximately 120000 women were reached, and the total amount of given credit reached up to 270 million Turkish Liras (TİSVA, 2013). Turkey Grameen Microfinance Programme (TGMP) sets their target group as women who live in villages or cities and below the poverty line and suggest loan condition as offering 5 women who live in the same village or town to group together (Aydın, 2012). Öz and Çolakoğlu's (2014) research on women who get benefitted from micro-credits in Sakarya, found that these women are extremely satisfied with micro-credits and micro-credits practices contributed significantly to the women's economic and social lives. According to Karapınar's (2010) study on women who benefitted micro-credit in Bursa, 53% of women grow their business with micro-credits, 47% of women use micro-credits to found a new business. Approximately half of women graduated only from primary school and none of them have a graduate degree. Their businesses are found as labor-intensive work such as handcrafted lace, clothing, and home textiles. Although 32% of women stated that their family income increased significantly, 66% of women's family income increased slightly. Karapınar (2010) highlighted that the families' income has not decreased. The results of this study also invalidated the critiques that weekly repayments of microcredits bring additional burden to poor people for the sample in this study.

Micro and small enterprises are a productive part of Turkish economy; however, supply of microfinance services is limited in terms of people served and the range of services offered (Karatas and Helvacioglu, 2008). In Turkey, the number of organisations that are working on only microfinance is less than number of traditional financial organisations. Institutions and organisations such as commercial banks, non-bank financial intermediaries, associations, cooperatives, cooperative unions, foundations provide microfinance services as possible as their regulations permit (Aygar, 2013). Legal regulations are needed in Turkey in order microfinance practices to run in a systematic, comprehensive and effective way by experienced institutions (Aygar, 2013). According to Gökyay (2008), needs to be supported by education and social responsibility projects for micro financial policies not to be inadequate on its own. Moreover, many micro-enterprises that are operating in a similar area should build cooperatives to maintain their sustainability. Furthermore, required funding is transferred to the customers by the microfinance institutions with low cost (Aygar, 2013). Financial institutions' mistrust of the women to their repayments of entrepreneur women who applied for credit pose an obstacle for women (Soysal, 2010).

With the authorities' promoting enterpreneurship behaviour in the markets and suporting structural transformation, supporting to the enterpreurship behaviours of individuals who can see the opportunities in the market by micro finance practices contribute to the market equilibrium (Gries and Naude, 2010). Microfinance practices are important not only contribution to increase family income, but also women empowerment (McCarter, 2006). However, empowerment is not always seen in the studies conducted in Turkey (Adaman and Bulut, 2007; Örenet al. 2007; Baltacı, 2011).

According to GEM's 2017 report, in developing countries or countries with transition economies, microcredits are thought to increase women's enterpreneurship because of the need for enterpreneurship motivation and low expectations of women entrepreneurship (Kyaruzi and Markovic, 2009). Considering behaviours of individuals are in need for a driving force, the satisfaction level of these needs and efficiency depend on social institutions (laws, norms, etc.) and practices (Braunerhjelm, 2010).

2.3. Theoretical Background

In the literature, there is not enough source of theoretical background about the impact of micro-finance. Theoretical approach such as push-pull and ripple effect is preferred. In this study, the fact that microcredits increase women's entrepreneurship will be explained by the nudge theory. Thaler and Sunstein

(2008) defined nudge as 'is any aspect of the choice architecture that alters people's behaviour in a predictable way, without forbidding any options or significantly changing their economic incentives'. According to Sunstein (2014), both private sector and public institutions started to focus on policies in nudge form in the last years because of low cost and its potencial contribution to the economic targets. Sunstein (2014) stated that the aim of nudge practices is making life simpler, safer and navigate people easier. Nudges provide freedom of making decisions and freedom of choice (such as GPS systems show the shortest road, but do not force people to use this route) (Sunstein, 2014). During David Cameron's coalition government period in 2010, the department that found as 'Behaviorial Insights Team' (BIT) called 'nudge unit' (Mols et al., 2015). Although the number of such kind of practices increases, many researchers argue that nudge techniques can not help for everything. Although Mols et al. (2015) predominantly agreed with this view, they stated that nudge can be enough and appropriate in some situations. According to Mols et al. (2015), nudge tactic must not be adopted in every condition because of its low cost, the other tactics to change the behaviour must be applied when it is not enough. Therefore, the effectiveness of nudge tactics may vary according to the situation. For instance, while more coercive policies are more suitable for pay taxes, nudge can produce very productive results for the policies to increase the entrepreneurship. It is because intention and will are ready, the only requirement is the driivng force. In this context, it can be said that microcredit practices have a mitigating effect on financial difficulties for business start-ups and act as a poke for people to bring their intention to life. According to the results of a study that analysed women entrepreneurs in Bangladesh, microcredits help to solve financial problems, however, women's entrepreneur roles have a larger share in growing the business (Munny and Weiyu, 2011). These studies show that microcredit is not enough alone for enterprises for sustainability and growth, however, it has a driving role during the process of women's starting up their own businesses. According to Carter and Cannon (1992), considering individuals who have entrepreneur characteristics can show entrepreneurial behavior if possibilities and conditions are met, and if these environmental conditions are provided -as nudge theory suggests- the entrepreneurship level can be increased. The individuals can be adversely affected by the factors that cause market imbalance in the developing and transition economy countries. They can discover the opportunities that emerged from imbalance. These individuals' support via microfinance under nudge theory can indirectly increase the development.

2.4. Objectives of the Study and Research Gap

Research Gap

Although there have been some previous studies conducted on entrepreneurship (Bridge, 1998, Kuratko, 2009), studies on women entrepreneurship lack in the literature (especially until the 1990s) for various reasons such as not having many women entrepreneurship, lack of media interest, and not considering the gender difference in entrepreneurship (Loza, 2017, Jennings and Brusch, 2013). This study addresses this gap by focusing on measures of how the use of micro-credits by women entrepreneurships affects the number of women entrepreneurships and economic growth namely real GDP and real income. Additionally, in the prior studies, the relationship between micro-credit and women entrepreneurship has been examined by exploring case studies. Not all of these studies found supporting results of triggering development. Since these studies based on qualitative research that means limited number of case studies, their valuable insights cannot go beyond displaying local results. Therefore, it is possible to say that micro-credits for women entrepreneurship and their influence on the economy were not examined by using macro data. In order to fill this research gap, this research aims to explain their relationship with quantitative methods. Based on these research gaps, the following key research questions are identified:

- How does the number of used microcredits by women entrepreneurships in Turkey affect the number of women who work in their own business?
- How does microcredit use in Turkey influence economic growth (real GDP and real income)? After identifying these research questions, the following hypothesis is determined:
- H_{1a}: There is a positive relationship between the unit of used microcredit in Turkey and the number of women who work in their own business.
- H_{1b}: There is a positive relationship between microcredit use in Turkey and economic growth.

Objectives of the Study

Based on these research gaps and identified hypothesis, two main objectives are determined for this study. It is firstly aimed to analyse the impact of micro-credits used in Turkey on women entrepreneurship and secondly to examine the contribution of micro-credits on Turkey's economy based on the same data source.

2.5. Women Entrepreneurs in Turkey: The Empirical Analysis of Microcredit Applications and Economic Growth Relations

In this study, the panel data was extracted from Turkey Grameen Microfinance, and Turkish Statistical Institute. Accordingly, the econometric analysis has been done in 2 steps. Firstly, regression analysis is used to analyse the impact of micro credit in Turkey on women's employment between 1999-2020. In the second analysis, ARDL bounds testing approach is used to analyse the contribution of micro-credits on Turkey's economy in the same years.

3. ANALYSIS

3.1. Development of Women Employment in Turkey: Microcredit Application Relationship Analysis

3 variables (as can be seen in Table 1) are used in the first econometric analysis model. These variables are the number of women who own business, amount of provided credits in Turkey, and the number of microcredit users. The data that is analysed is monthly data.

Dummy variables are used in the regression models in order to include qualitative variables. The dummy variables that are added to the model as dependent and independent variables are shown in the econometric model. In other words, dummy variables are used in the econometric model however they cannot be measured numerically. For instance, in the econometric model which is related to product harvest; if the size of the cultivated area and the fertility of the soil are measurable variables, the variable that is regarding the month of harvest is dummy variable. The used equation is shown in the model (1).

Table 1. Variables, symbols, and data sources

Variables	Symbol	Source of Data
The number of women who own business (*Kendilerine ait işlerde çalışan kadınların Miktari*)	KİÇKS	Turkey Grameen Microfinance
Amount of Provided Credits in Turkey (*Türkiye'de Kullandırımı Sağlanan Kredi Tutarı*)	TKMKT	Turkey Grameen Microfinance
The Number of Microcredit Users (*Mikro Kredi Kullananları Sayısı*)	MKKS	Turkish Statistical Institute

$$Y_t = \beta_0 + \beta_1 X_t + \beta_2 Dummy + \varepsilon_t \quad (1)$$

X: the amount of used microcredit
ε_t: Error term

According to equation (1), the reason to add dummy variable is the contraction of credit use because of the influence of the global crisis just 1 year before the start year of 2009. Especially during the crisis, regardless of the increase in demand for credit use, the unwillingness of the banks to give credits what is called as credit rationing is discussed.

The variables used in economic modelling are expected to be stable in order to give correct results. The concept of stability is not defined as a continuous increase or decrease of variables in a determined time. However, it is defined as its scattering along the horizontal axis in a determined time. Before the econometric analysis, KPSS unit root test is applied to variables for identifying their stability. The hypothesis of KPSS unit root test is seen in H_0 and H_1. H0 hypothesis stated that the series is stable which means does not contain any unit root, unlike ADF and PP unit root tests. H1 hypothesis stated that the series is not being stable and contain unit root (Kwiatkowski, Phillips, Schmidt and Shin, 1992, p.165).

Hypothesis are set up as follows:

$H_0 = \sigma_0^2 = 0$ does not contain unit root. Variable is stable.
$H_1 = \sigma_0^2 \neq 0$ does contain unit root. Variable is not stable.

The condition to test the related hypothesis in KPSS test is shown in equation (1)

$$y_t = \varepsilon_t + r_t + \varepsilon_t \quad (2)$$

In equation (2), the indicative coefficient that points trends, expresses random and disturbance term. The relationship indicated by the lagged value of the random term is shown in equation (2).

$$r_t = r_{(c-1)} + u_t \quad (3)$$

In equation (3), u term refers to the error term between itself and a lagged value of the random term. KPSS unit root test is applied on variables, results are shown in Table 2.

Table 2. KPSS unit root test results (at level)

		Schwarz Information Criteria Level of Significance		
Variable	**LM Statistics**	**1%**	**5%**	**10%**
KİÇKS	0.1788**	0.216	0.146	0.119
TKMKT	0.7981*	0.216	0.147	0.119
MKKS	0.7111*	0.216	0.147	0.119

According to KPSSS results in Table 2, H0 which states that the series is stable for all series was rejected. In other words, series are not stable.

Table 3. KPSS unit root test results (first difference)

		Schwarz Information Criteria Level of Significance		
Variable	**Statistic**	**1%**	**5%**	**10%**
KİÇKS	0.0671	0.216	0.146	0.119
TKMKT	0.0121	0.216	0.147	0.119
MKKS	0.1300	0.216	0.148	0.119

In Table 3, the variables, that the first differences are calculated, have become stable. In other words, the degree of integration of variables is one. If series are stable at the same level, the long-term relationship between them is required to be tested. In this study, after ensuring the stability of variables, regression analysis is done.

Table 4. Regression results

Variable	Coefficient	Standard (Std.) Error	T Statistic	Sig.
TKMKT	0.04523	0.00099	6.21	0
Dummy	-13954	20112	-5.44	0
C	881123	112421	53.111	0
R Square	0.96		Akaike Information Criteria	24.132
Adjusted R Square	0.90		Schwarz Information Criteria	24.767
Sig.	-254		Hannan Quinn Information Criteria	24.612
F Statistic	65567		Durbin Watson Statistics	1.34
Sig (F Statistic)	0.00			

As seen in F-Test in Table (4), F value (65567) is above the table value when p value is lower than 0.05. Therefore, this model is significant. T statistics value (5.21) is above table value. This shows that model is significant. According to Regression results in Table (4), every 1 unit of used microcredit in Turkey causes 0.045 unit change in the number of women who work in their own business. Thus, H1a is supported. R square is the coefficient that the regression analysis's correlation coefficient and the direction and size of the relationship between independent variables. Statistically, R square value is expected to be between -1 and +1, The R square value of this study is calculated as 0.96 which is statistically significant and as expected.

3.2. The Analysis of Microcredit Applications Economic Growth Relationship in Turkey

In this analysis, the relationship between Microcredit and Economic Growth is tested by using ARDL bounds testing approach. Monthly data are added to the variables in the analysis. The used variables, symbols, and data source are shown in Table 5.

Table 5. Variables, symbols, and data sources

Variable	Symbol	Data Source
Real GDP (Reel GSYİH)	Y	TÜİK
The Amount of Used Microcredit	MFC	Turkey Grameen Microfinance

Model to use is seen:

$$Y = \beta_0 + \beta_1 MFC_t + \mu_t \tag{4}$$

In equation (4) Y refers to real GDP (reel SYH), $\beta 0$ refers to inclination or constant parameter, $MFCt$ refers to credit given in t time, $\beta 1$ refers to vector coefficient of micro finance credits and μt refers to stochastic term.

Before estimations of the econometric relationship between growth and microcredit, unit root test is applied to the variables that are included in analysis (See table 6 and 7).

Table 6. KPSS unit root test results (at level)

		Schwarz Information Criteria Level of Significance		
Variable	LM Statistics	1%	5%	10%
Y	0.1618**	0.216	0.146	0.119
MFC	0.7131*	0.216	0.147	0.119

Table 7. KPSS unit root test results (at level)

		Schwarz Information Criteria Level of Significance		
Variable	**LM Statistics**	**1%**	**5%**	**10%**
Y	0.0341	0.216	0.146	0.119
MFC	0.0141	0.216	0.147	0.119

After the stability tests of variables included in the analysis, ARDL bounds testing approach is used for the cointegration relationship between two variables. The main advantages of ARDL model that was developed by Pesaran and Shin (1996) if variables are either I(1) or I(0), it is possible to do integration testing and possible to find significant results.

The used ARDL model is shown in equation (5) and (6).

$$\Delta_{ln}Y_t = \delta_0 + \delta_1 Y_{t-1} + \delta_2 MFC_{t-1} + \sum_{i=1}^{n} \delta_3 \Delta l_n Y_{t-1} + \sum_{i=0}^{n} \delta_4 \Delta l_n MFC_{t-1} + \mu_{1t} \quad (5)$$

$$\Delta_{ln}MFC_t = \hat{I}_0 + \hat{I}_1 MFC_{t-1} + \hat{I}_2 Y_{t-1} + \sum_{i=1}^{n} \hat{I}_3 \Delta l_n MFC_{t-1} + \sum_{i=0}^{n} \hat{I}_4 \Delta l_n Y + \mu_{2t} \quad (6)$$

Y_t in equation (5) and (6) refers to the real gross domestic production t time, MFC_t refers to given microcredit in t time, l values refer to logarithmic values of variables, ώ and δ refer to the constant term and Δ refers to difference values.

Table 8. F statistics for boundary testing

Dependent Variable	Function	F Statistics
LY	LY (REEL Y / MFC)	0.6512
LMFC	LMFC (MFC/ REEL Y)	6.132
	Critical Values	
	5%	10%
Lower Bound	3.66	3.01
Upper Bound	4.8	4.24

According to the table that was created by Pesaran et al. (2001), lower and upper bound threshold values under 5% and 10% significance levels are displayed in Table 8. If F statistic calculated at any significant level is above an upper threshold value, null hypothesis that argues not being long-term is rejected. If F statistic is lower than lower threshold value, the null hypothesis is accepted. If calculated F statistic is between lower and upper threshold values, a definite interpretation cannot be made and alternative cointegration tests are used. According to the results, when MFC is a dependent variable, there is a cointegration relationship (F statistic is above the critic values).

In the analysis, with the consideration of Likelihood (LR) Final Prediction Error (FPE), Akaike Information Criterion (AIC), Shwarz Information Criterion (SC), and Hannan-Quinn Information Criterion (HQ) criteria on variables, the most suitable lag length has been determined.

Table 9. Determining the suitable lag length

Lag Length	LR	FPE	AIC	SC	HQ
0	121.412	5.11	71.77	69.743	62.910
1	101.612	2.71	54.12	66.311	61.2213
2	41.161	1.64	65.60	66.387	62.412
3	12.323*	8.09*	64.111*	66.141*	64.112*
4	5.444	1.31	66.413	66.398	64.312
5	4.301	1.04	64.208	66.765	65.387

As seen in Table 8, the best lag length is identified as 3. According to the situation of MFC is a dependent variable, calculated long term ARDL estimations are displayed in Table 9.

Table 10. Long-term ARDL estimation

Variable	Coefficient	Standard Error	T Value	P Value
LY (Dependent Variable)				
LMFC	0.0512*	0.00145	2.7121	0.0051
R^2= 0.165		*DW*: 2.103		

In Table 9, according to the long-term estimation results, the long-term elasticity of real income is estimated as positive (0.00612) as expected. This result shows that there is a positive relationship between microcredit use in Turkey and economic growth. Thus, H1b is accepted. This is statistically significant at 1 percent level. According to this result, 1% increase in microcredits in Turkey causes 0.05% increase in real GDP. After long-term coefficient estimations, short-term coefficients are estimated by using the error correction model and displayed in Table 10.

Table 11. ARDL short-term coefficients (error corrections)

	Coefficient	Standard Error	t Statistic
LMFC	0.0410	0.011	-3.000**
ECM_{t-1}	-0.1779	0.361	-3.320***

*, ** and *** represents10%, 5% and 1% significance level respectively

According to results in Table (10), when MFC increases %1, real income as a dependent variable increases 0.04%. Furthermore, short-term deviations during the terms that were analysed converge towards the equilibrium point in the long run.

The coefficient of EC (-1) is estimated as -0.178. The result shows that in case of any external or internal shock that deviates from balance, about 18% of it can be corrected after one period. In other words, short term deviations reach long term balance in approximately 5.5 years.

4. DISCUSSION/CONTRIBUTION OF THE STUDY

This study proposes and empirically tests a model of how micro-credit affect women entrepreneurship in the context of development and economic growth. It is proposed that there is a positive relationship between microcredit use in Turkey and the number of women who work in their own business as well as economic growth (real GDP and real income). The research findings are explained in detail in the analysis section. Following that, primary research findings will be explained briefly, with a discussion of the theoretical and practical contribution, as well as managerial implications.

4.1. Theoretical Contribution

This study makes two important contributions to the literature on women entrepreneurship and micro-credits. To do so, the influence of micro-credit on women's employment as an important factor in terms of contribution of women entrepreneurships to the economy is identified. Unique to our study, we suggest that the use of micro-credit across Turkey (according to the data based on years between 1999-2020) has a positive influence not only on (1) the number of women who work/operate in their own business but (2) economic growth (real GDP and real income). Although these findings contradict the arguments in the earlier research (e.g. Robinson and Watson, 2001; Kevane and Wydick, 2001; Karnani, 2007; Karlan and Zinman, 2011), there are studies (see De Vita et al., 2014) that back up the findings of this study as well.

First, regression analysis is used to examine the impact of microcredit on women's employment in Turkey (in the years between 1999-2020). The existing literature is extended by testing key assumptions about the number of women who own businesses, the number of credits supplied in Turkey, and the number of microcredit users. This study adds new knowledge to the literature in which argues that women are struggling to find financial support for their businesses (Goyal and Yadav, 2014). For instance, the regression analysis of this study displays that micro-credit used in Turkey increases the number of women who work in their own business. This finding supports the literature which argues the micro-credits as a determinant for women entrepreneurships to find opportunities (Dündar, 2007, GEM 2017). This study highlights that providing opportunities to women with micro-credits increases the support to women who found their business. This finding supports the previous studies that show micro-credits can support women in various ways economically and socially (McCarter, 2006, Gökyay, 2008, Öz and Çolakoğlu, 2014) for instance growing their business and founding new business (Karapınar, 2010). This finding supports the GEM 2017 report which argues that micro-credits have a positive influence on the number of women entrepreneurships in developing countries or countries with transition economies (Kyaruzi and Markovic, 2009).

Secondly, after regression analysis, the contribution of micro-credits on Turkey's economy (years between 1999-2020) in terms of Real GDP (Reel GSYİH) is analyzed with the ARDL bounds testing approach. In this analysis, the relationship between Microcredit and Economic Growth is tested with the addition of monthly data into the variables in the analysis. This analysis displays a positive relationship between microcredit use in Turkey and economic growth. Microcredit increases real GDP by around 0.4-0.5 unit per each unit increase. Additionally, according to our findings, if there is any external or internal shock that deviates from a balance of about 18%, this short-term deviation can reach long term balance in approximately 5,5 years.

Finally, the primary contribution of our study is that if women are given more chances and financial support through micro-credits, their contribution to the gross domestic product (GDP) will increase. Whereas some scholars suggest that women's contribution to gross domestic product (GDP) is less than it is expected compared to the women's ratio in the entire world population and their contribution to the world economy (Hammawa and Hashim, 2016). However, in this study, our finding is consistent with the prior studies that argue entrepreneurships have a positive influence on economic growth (Karlsson et al., 2009), but also our study extends the current understanding of entrepreneurship concept by providing empirical support about women entrepreneurships that has both theoretical and practical importance.

4.2. Practical Contribution and Managerial Implications

Finally, this study also contributes to practice by providing important implications for academics and practitioners studying micro-credits given to women entrepreneurships on Turkey's economy. The information from the existing literature is combined within the model, by adding new relationships to the existing knowledge. Based on the results of this study, researchers suggest that micro-credit used in Turkey creates a positive value in the number of women who work in their own business as supported by Karapınar (2010) and McCarter (2006). This kind of support behaves as a stimulator and encourages women to involve in the workforce. In this case, the finding reveals that micro-credits given to women entrepreneurs would be beneficial for both women's employment and economic growth.

The contribution of micro-credits on economy is shown as positively related to the number of given micro-credits. This result demonstrates that providing micro-credits to women entrepreneurships help to allocate these limited resources of micro-credits appropriately to increase the number of women who work in their own business and as a result having a positive influence on economic growth (real GDP and real income) if women entrepreneurship is supported. This contribution has important implications for the use of micro-credits by women entrepreneurships who have only limited resources and may need more financial support. Hence, the model can serve as guidance for given micro-credits to women entrepreneurships. Secondly, financial and economic opportunities and support will be transformed into positive outcomes, and the economic growth of real income and real GDP will be higher. Even these results may have short term deviations, this can reach balance in long term in approximately 5.5 years.

Summary of Findings

In sum, as the results of this study demonstrate and it is supported in the literature, micro-credits given to women support them financially in various ways, including growing their business, founding new business, raising family income, and making major contributions to their economic lives (McCarter, 2006, Karapınar 2010, Öz and Çolakoğlu, 2014). Thus, research findings have shown that the capability of women entrepreneurship is promising in the long term. Given micro-credits to women entrepreneurships can positively influence both women in business, and economy in overall, and economic growth which is promising results in long term.

5. LIMITATIONS AND FUTURE RESEARCH

5.1. Limitations

As this study is based on secondary data, we acknowledge some limitations. Firstly, this research is based on women entrepreneurship in Turkey. Due to limitations, the data for the study was collected by using a sample from a single location-Turkey. Such kind of geographical boundaries of this study limits the generalizability of research findings. Therefore, further research would extend the generality of the results. Secondly, limiting the research area and data range between 1999 and 2020 is a limitation of this research. Thirdly, the global economic crisis that occurred in 2008 had a negative influence on micro-credits because banks were not willing to give credits although demand for credit use increased. Lastly, industry difference is not considered in this research which may provide different results, especially in the women-intense industries.

5.2. Future Research

This study focuses on women entrepreneurship and micro-credits effect on women entrepreneurship. Future research should examine the effects of different variables and corresponding relationships with women entrepreneurship. We encourage future studies to (1) examine the influence of enterprise and its sustainability in the long term, (2) understand how much of micro credit practices used for need or growing and innovative entrepreneurship, (3) examine the flexibility of giving individual microcredit and increasing the amount of microcredit, (4) analyse the data by widening the research area, and data range extended before 1999 and after 2020, (5) analyse the results after extending geographical boundaries of this study, (6) examine industry differences, if obtained data provide data from different industries, (7) to test this model in other economic settings, both transitional and developed, and to cross validate it for greater generalization.

6. CONCLUSION

The results of this study indicate that micro-credits trigger women entrepreneurship in development and economic growth and make a meaningful effect. The concept of this study is women who started entrepreneurship; therefore, new studies are needed to understand how enterprise was or will be sustainable in the long term. Moreover, the actual desired result is women to proceed with innovative or growth-oriented entrepreneurship more than need entrepreneurship. Regardless of whether economic growth and development or social equality and justice are viewed, the main target is to set sail for a growing and innovative entrepreneurship that makes a difference. In this concept, understanding how much of micro credit practices supports for need entrepreneurship, how much of it supports for growing and innovative entrepreneurship need further research. Transition to more flexible policies such as giving individual microcredit and increasing the amount of microcredit are needed to be evaluated.

REFERENCES

Adaman, F., & Bulut, T. (2007). *500 Milyonluk Umut Hikayeleri*. İletişim.

Aidis, R., Welter, F., Smallbone, D., & Isakova, N. (2007). Female entrepreneurship in transition economies: The case of Lithuania and Ukraine. *Feminist Economics, 13*(2), 157–183. doi:10.1080/13545700601184831

Aydın, B. (2012). *Yoksullukla Mücadelede Mikro Kredinin Türkiye Uygulamasının Ekonomik Açıdan Değerlendirilmesi* [Marmara Üniversitesi Sosyal Bilimler Enstitüsü Yayınlanmamış Yüksek Lisans Tezi]. Marmara Üniversitesi.

Aygar, K. (2013). *Mikro Finans ve Türkiye için Öneriler*. Sermaye Piyasaları Kurulu. Ortaklıklar Finansmanı Dairesi.

Baltacı, Ö. (2011). *Kadınları Güçlendirme Mekanizması Olarak Mikrokredi* [Uzmanlık Tezi]. T.C Başbakanlık Kadın Statüsü Genel Müdürlüğü.

Braunerhjelm, P. (2010). *Entrepreneurship, innovation and economic growth*. Swedish Entrepreneurship Forum and the Royal Institute of Technology Working Paper 2010/2.

Bridge, S., O'Neill, K., & Cromie, S. (1998). *Understanding Enterprise, Entrepreneurship and Small Business*. Macmillan. doi:10.1007/978-1-349-26171-0

Brush, C., & Hisrich, R. D. (1999). Women-owned businesses: why do they matter? In *Are small firms important? Their role and impact* (pp. 111–127). Springer. doi:10.1007/978-1-4615-5173-7_7

Carrington, C. (2006). Women entrepreneurs. *Journal of Small Business and Entrepreneurship, 19*(2), 83–94. doi:10.1080/08276331.2006.10593360

Carter, S., & Cannon, T. (1992). *Women as entrepreneurs: A study of female business owners, their motivations, experiences and strategies for success*. Academic Press.

Çelik, C., & Özdevecioğlu, M. (2001). *Kadın Girişimcilerin Demografik Özellikleri ve Karşılaştıkları sorunlara İlişkin Nevşehir İlinde Bir Araştırma*. Orta Anadolu Kongresi (Nevşehir).

Çetindamar, D., Gupta, V. K., Karadeniz, E. E., & Egrican, N. (2012). What the numbers tell: The impact of human, family and financial capital on women and men's entry into entrepreneurship in Turkey. *Entrepreneurship and Regional Development, 24*(1-2), 29–51. doi:10.1080/08985626.2012.637348

Commission of The European Communities (COM) (2006). *Implementing the Community Lisbon Programme: Financing SME Growth – Adding European Value*. Author.

Commission of The European Communities (COM) (2007). *A European initiative for the development of micro-credit in support of growth and employment*. Author.

Copestake. (2015). *Towards a plural history of microfinance*. Bath Papers in International Development and Wellbeing Working Paper No.40. http://www.bath.ac.uk/cds/

De Vita, L., Mari, M., & Poggesi, S. (2014). Women entrepreneurs in and from developing countries: Evidences from the literature. *European Management Journal*, *32*(3), 451–460. doi:10.1016/j.emj.2013.07.009

Dündar, O. (2007). *Mikro Finansman. Türkiye Kalkınma Bankası Ekonomik ve Sosyal Araştırmalar Müdürlüğü*. http://www.kalkinma.com.tr/data/file/raporlar/ESA/ga/2007-GA/GA-07-05-28_Mikro_Finansman.pdf

GEM (Global Entrepreneurship Monitoring). (2017). *Women's Entrepreneurship 2016/2017 Report*. GEM.

Gökakın, Z. Ö. (2000). *Doksanlı Yılların Yeni Kahramanları: Türkiye'de Girişimci Kadın Profili* (Vol. 8). Yönetim ve Organizasyon Kongresi Bildiriler Kitabı.

Gökyay, Ç. (2008). *Türkiye'de Mikro Kredi Uygulamaları ve İsdihdama Yansımaları*. T.C. Çalışma ve Sosyal Güvenlik Bakanlığı, Türkiye İş Kurumu Genel Müdürlüğü.

Goyal, P., & Yadav, V. (2014). To be or not to be a woman entrepreneur in a developing country? *Psychosociological Issues in Human Resource Management*, *2*(2), 68–78.

Gries, T., & Naudé, W. A. (2010). Entrepreneurship and Structural Economic Transformation. *Small Business Economics*, *34*(1), 13–29. doi:10.100711187-009-9192-8

Gundry, L. K., Ben-Yoseph, M., & Posig, M. (2002). Contemporary perspectives on women's entrepreneurship: A review and strategic recommendations. *Journal of Enterprising Culture*, *10*(1), 67–86. doi:10.1142/S0218495802000141

Hammawa, Y., & Hashim, N. (2016). Women-micro entrepreneurs and sustainable economic development in Nigeria. *IOSR Journal of Business and Management*, *18*(1), 27–36.

Hanson, S., & Blake, M. (2009). Gender and entrepreneurial networks. *Regional Studies*, *43*(1), 135–149. doi:10.1080/00343400802251452

Hisrich, R. D., & Peters, M. P. (1998). Enterpreneurship (4th ed.). Academic Press.

Hisrich, R. D., Peters, M. P., & Shepherd, D. A. (2008). *Entrepreneurship* (7th ed.). McGraw-Hill Co. Inc.

Hulme, D., & Maitrot, M. (2014). Has Microfinance Lost Its Moral Compass? *Economic and Political Weekly*, *49*(48), 77–85.

Jennings, J. E., & Brush, C. G. (2013). Research on women entrepreneurs: Challenges to (and from) the broader entrepreneurship literature? *The Academy of Management Annals*, *7*(1), 663–715. doi:10.5465/19416520.2013.782190

Karapınar, K. (2010). *Türkiye'de yerel kalkınma modeli olarak mikrofinans sistemi: Bursa örneği* [Master's thesis]. Çanakkale Onsekiz Mart Üniversitesi Sosyal Bilimler Enstitüsü.

Karatas, A., & Helvacioglu, A. D. (2008, October). The microcredit strategies for SMEs in Turkey in the EU Harmonization Process. In *8th Global Conference on Business and Economics* (pp. 18-19). Academic Press.

Karlan, D., & Zinman, J. (2011). Microcredit in Theory and Practice: Using Randomized Credit Scoring for Impact Evaluation. *Science*, *332*(6035), 1278–1284. doi:10.1126cience.1200138 PMID:21659596

Karlsson, C., Johansson, B., & Stough, R. (2009). *Entrepreneurship and Development – Local Processes and Global Patterns. Cesis WP 160*. The Royal Institute of Technology.

Karnani, A. (2007). Do Women Benefit from Microcredit. *The Perspective of Women's Entrepreneurship in the Age of Globalization*, 129.

Kevane, M., & Wydick, B. (2001). Microenterprise lending to female entrepreneurs: Sacrificing economic growth for poverty alleviation? *World Development*, *29*(7), 1225–1236. doi:10.1016/S0305-750X(01)00032-8

Kuratko, D. F. (2009). The entrepreneurial imperative of the 21st century. *Business Horizons*, *52*(5), 421–428. doi:10.1016/j.bushor.2009.04.006

Kwiatkowski, D., Phillips, P. C., Schmidt, P., & Shin, Y. (1992). Testing the null hypothesis of stationarity against the alternative of a unit root: How sure are we that economic time series have a unit root? *Journal of Econometrics*, *54*(1-3), 159–178. doi:10.1016/0304-4076(92)90104-Y

Kyaruzi, I. S., & Markovic, M. R. (2009). *Female Entrepreneursip and Local Economic Growth*. Outskirt Press.

Loza, E. (2017). Female entrepreneurship theory: A multidisciplinary review of resources. *JWEE*, (1-2), 26–64.

Maîtrot, M., & Niño-Zarazúa, M. (2017). *Poverty and wellbeing impacts of microfinance: What do we know?* (WIDER Working Paper 2017/190). United Nations University. https://www.wider.unu.edu/sites/default/files/Publications/Working-paper/PDF/wp2017-190.pdf

McCarter, E. (2006). Women and microfinance: Why we should do more. *U. Md. LJ Race, Religion. Race, Gender & Class (Towson, Md.)*, *6*, 353.

Meena, R. (1992). Gender Research/Studies in Southern Africa: An Overview. In R. Meena (Ed.), Gender in Southern Africa: Conceptual and Theoretical Issues (pp. 15–87). Academic Press.

Meunier, F., Krylova, Y., & Ramalho, R. (2017). *Women's Entrepreneurship: How to Measure the Gap between New Female and Male Entrepreneurs?* World Bank Group, Policy Research Working Paper 8242. https://documents.worldbank.org/curated/en/704231510669093889/pdf/WPS8242.pdf

Microcredit Summit Campaign. (2012). *State of the Microcredit Summit Campaign Report 2012*. A Project of Results of Educational Fund.

Mols, F., Haslam, S. A., Jetten, J., & Steffens, N. K. (2015). Why a nudge is not enough: A social identity critique of governance by stealth. *European Journal of Political Research*, *54*(1), 81–98. doi:10.1111/1475-6765.12073

Moore, D. P., Buttner, E. H., Wong-MingJi, D. J., & Sullivan, S. E. (2017). *Women Entrepreneurs: Moving Beyond the Glass Ceiling*. Academic Press.

Müftüoğlu, T., & Durukan, T. (2004). *Girişimcilik ve KOBİ'ler*. Gazi Kitabevi.

Munny, K. N., & Weiyu, Z. (2011). *The Role of Micro-credit for women entrepreneurs: The Case of Banglades* [Master Thesis]. University of Gavle. http://www.diva-portal.org/smash/get/diva2:543989/FULLTEXT01.pdf

Nayır, D. Z. (2008). İşi ve Ailesi Arasındaki Kadın: Tekstil ve Bilgi İşlem Girişimcilerinin Rol Çatışmasına Getirdikleri Çözüm Stratejileri. *Ege Academic Review*, *8*(2), 631–650. doi:10.21121/eab.2015221924

Ören(2007)

Öz, C. S., & Çolakoğlu, C. (2014). Türkiye'de Mikro Kredi Uygulamasının Sakarya İli Özelinde İncelenmesi. *Calisma Ve Toplum*, *43*(4).

Pesaran, M. H., Shin, Y., & Smith, R. (2001). Bound testing approaches to the analysis of level relationships. *Journal of Applied Econometrics*, *16*(3), 289–326. doi:10.1002/jae.616

Pesaran, M. H., Shin, Y., & Smith, R. J. (1996). Testing for the'Existence of a Long-run Relationship' (No. 9622). Faculty of Economics, University of Cambridge.

Robinson, S., & Watson, J. (2001). Female entrepreneur underperformance: A puzzle for the information age. *Journal of International Information Management*, *10*(1), 4.

Seenivasan, R. (2015). High Interest Rates Are an Amorality in Microfinance. *Economic and Political Weekly*, *50*(3), 75–77.

Soysal, A. (2010). Türkiye'de Kadın Girişimciler: Engeller ve Fırsatlar Bağlamında Bir Değerlendirme. *Ankara Üniversitesi SBF Dergisi*, *65*(1), 83-114.

Sunstein, C. R. (2014). Nudging: A very short guide. *Journal of Consumer Policy*, *37*(4), 583–588. doi:10.100710603-014-9273-1

Thaler, R., & Sunstein, C. (2008). *Nudge: The Gentle Power of Choice Architecture*. Yale University Press.

TİSVA. (2013). *Girişimciliği Sağlayarak, Yoksulluğun Bir Başkasına İhtiyaç Olmadan Azaltılması Modeli: Türkiye Grameen Mikro Finans Programı, Sakarya Grameen Bankası Mikrofinans Şubesi'nden temin edilen broşür*. TISVA.

Ufuk, H., & Özgen, Ö. (2001). Interaction between the business and family lives of women entrepreneurs in Turkey. *Journal of Business Ethics*, *31*(2), 95–106. doi:10.1023/A:1010712023858

ENDNOTE

[1] *Esnaf ve Sanatkarlar Birlikleri ve Odaları- original in Turkish*

Chapter 13
Women's Financial Inclusion

Peterson K. Ozili
https://orcid.org/0000-0001-6292-1161
Central Bank of Nigeria, Nigeria

ABSTRACT

The purpose of this study is to examine women financial inclusion. Some barriers to women financial inclusion were highlighted. Some strategies to increase women financial inclusion were also identified such as providing greater financial education for women, greater access to formal credit for women-owned businesses, microfinance designed for women, government loan schemes for women, adequate legal identification for women, affordable mobile phones for women, and laws that criminalize gender discrimination against women.

1. INTRODUCTION

This paper explores financial inclusion for women.

Women financial inclusion refers to access and use of affordable financial services for women (Bhatia and Singh, 2019). It also refers to bringing women into formal financial system so that they can use existing formal financial services to improve their welfare and the welfare of their households. Some progress has been made to increase financial inclusion for women such as proving women with cheap mobile phones and using fintech to deliver financial services to women (Mushtaq et al, 2023). Despite these efforts, women still lag behind in financial inclusion according to the 2021 Global Findex Report.

In some parts of the world, women continue to face greater financial exclusion than men for different reasons, such as societal culture and a rigid patriarchal system, among others (Ghosh and Vinod, 2017; Kulkarni and Ghosh, 2021). Women financial exclusion is further worsened by unforeseen shocks, like the COVID-19 pandemic, wars, discriminatory laws, and ethnic conflicts, all of which have reversed some of the gains made so far in extending useful and affordable financial services to women (Demirgüç-Kunt et al, 2013; Setiawan et al 2023). And, even when women own a formal account, there are still problems of low account usage, account inactivity, large number of dormant accounts, digital illiteracy, and a reluctance to use formal accounts for day-to-day transactions among women (Ghosh and Vinod, 2017; Saluja et al, 2023). In other societies, divorce, separation, and widowhood affect women more

DOI: 10.4018/978-1-6684-8979-6.ch013

negatively than men, and it affects women's ability to access and use a wide range of financial services (Demirgüç-Kunt et al, 2013). As a result, divorced women are more likely to be poorer than divorced men after separation (Demirgüç-Kunt et al, 2013). Also, some commercial banks design financial products and services that are more attractive to men than women, thereby neglecting women's needs and preferences (Chavan, 2008).

There is a need to increase financial inclusion for women to improve women's access and use of financial services which would enable them to be financially independent and economically empowered in society. Targeted financial inclusion for women will enable women to generate income, access essential services, and protect their basic standards of living, which are essential to live a meaningful life and to foster gender equality in society (Hendriks, 2019). This paper explores women financial inclusion. It highlights some barriers to women financial inclusion and several avenues for increasing financial inclusion for women.

The discussion in this paper contributes to the literature that examine financial inclusion for vulnerable groups. Such studies include (Mavrinac and Chin, 2004; Kyrgidou and Petridou, 2013; Jarecke et al, 2014; Zins and Weill, 2016; Tran et al, 2018; Ozili, 2020a; Ozili, 2021). This study extends the literature by focusing on financial inclusion for women who are a vulnerable group. The discussion in this paper also contributes to the literature that examine the possible solutions for expanding financial inclusion. Such studies include Sapovadia (2018), Atkinson and Messy (2013), Ozili (2023), and Ozili (2022b).

The rest of the paper is organized in the following way. Section 2 presents some barriers for increasing women financial inclusion. Section 3 presents some strategies for increasing financial inclusion for women. Section 4 highlights some real-world programs for increasing women financial inclusion. Section 5 presents the conclusion of the study.

2. BARRIERS TO WOMEN FINANCIAL INCLUSION

Below are some barriers that hinder women financial inclusion. Some of these barriers are also faced by men but women are disproportionately affected by them because of their gender. They include:

Economic Barriers

- Low-income for women compared to men.
- Lack of credit histories for women
- Time and mobility constraints
- Unequal access to technology
- The presence of a well-functioning and trusted informal financial system in rural areas
- Lack of tangible assets to use as collateral for loans.
- Lack of financial services designed to meet the needs and preferences of women.
- Financial digitization risks that affect women disproportionally than men

Cultural Barriers

- Unequal inheritance rights
- Inter-role conflicts in the home
- Barriers to women's access and control over property
- Socio-cultural constraints
- Small number of female-headed households

Institutional, Political, and Social Barriers

- The widening gender gap
- Lack of decision-making power
- Political instability
- Coup and war
- Limited women leadership in the formal financial sector
- Legal constraints
- Unwillingness of government to design public policies that are targeted at women.

Technological Barriers

- Digital illiteracy
- Lack of access to broadband internet
- Lack of access to affordable mobile phones
- Financial illiteracy

3. STRATEGIES FOR EXPANDING WOMEN FINANCIAL INCLUSION

Below are some strategies or ideas that could help to increase financial inclusion for women in society.

3.1. Greater Financial Education for Women

Financial education will increase financial knowledge especially for women (Mavrinac and Chin, 2004; Jarecke et al, 2014). Increasing women's financial knowledge is beneficial for women who struggle to find a convenient way to pay taxes and healthcare bills. Greater financial education for women will make women aware of financial services that are available to them which they can use to meet their needs (Mavrinac and Chin, 2004). Financial education will also enable women to learn the skills and knowledge they need to conveniently access and use the appropriate formal financial services that meet their personal, family, and economic needs (Kyrgidou and Petridou, 2013); thereby giving women a chance to be socially and economically empowered. Greater financial education for women financial inclusion will also teach women about the financial products and services they need for accumulating assets, generating income, managing financial risks, and fully participating in the economy.

3.2. Greater Formal Credit for Women-Owned Businesses

Women's businesses are important assets for social and economic growth (Ellis, 2007; Tran et al, 2018). However, it is nearly impossible for women entrepreneurs to sustain their business without access to formal credit or loans since financial assistance from family and friends is mostly insufficient and cannot be relied on. Many women entrepreneurs are unable to receive formal loans on adequate terms to meet their needs. This results in many women-owned businesses that are financially excluded. Women entrepreneurs desire affordable and convenient funding to boost their small and medium scale businesses. But their inability to access cheap formal credit affects the survival of their business which is their source of livelihood. Convenient access to loans for women entrepreneurs will increase financial inclusion for women-owned SMEs, and will also lead to job and wealth creation, poverty reduction, empowerment, and overall socio-economic development. Formal loans should be extended to women-owned small businesses through their bank account as this will increase financial inclusion for women-owned businesses. The business case for extending more loans to women-owned small businesses is that women tend to be more loyal customers, they run profitable businesses, and they pay back on time.

3.3. Microfinance Designed for Women

Microfinance is the provision of financial services in a sustainable manner to help low-income and poor individuals and families take advantage of income-generating activities and better cope with risk (Beck, 2015). Microfinance products and services for women could be loans that are small loan amounts and collateral-free. Microfinance institutions can also use group-social capital as collateral in the absence of credit history. Increasing women's access to micro financial services would lead to greater gender equality and nondiscrimination. Women's ability to access micro loans and saving products is a significant factor contributing to the sustainable livelihoods of women and communities (Wellalage and Locke, 2017). Women would benefit greatly if many microfinance institutions (MFIs) target female clients because it leads to women's empowerment by positively influencing women's decision-making power and enhancing their overall socio-economic status. Microfinance targeted at women also has the potential to make a significant contribution to gender equality and promote sustainable livelihoods and better working conditions for women.

3.4. Existing Government Loan Schemes for Women

Government loans for women are a way to increase financial inclusion for women. In many developing societies, there are no government interventions to increase access to formal credit for women. The lack of intervention widens the inequality between men and women in access to formal credit and is a setback for women financial inclusion. However, in societies where there are extensive government interventions in improving citizen's welfare, the government may provide loan schemes for women. Such loan schemes may take the form of low-interest loans, and such loans can be paid directly into the formal account of women beneficiaries, thereby increasing women financial inclusion.

3.5. Humanitarian Cash Transfer Programs for Women

Humanitarian cash transfer programs are programs launched by governments, international aid agencies and national civil society organizations to provide financial assistance directly to victims of humanitarian crises and where the victims, who are the beneficiaries of the program, can decide to purchase what they need most from local markets (Bailey and Harvey, 2015). The cash transfer is paid into the bank account of the victims, and they can spend it where, how, and when the recipient chooses. Women tend to be more adversely affected during humanitarian crises than men, and women are usually the most conspicuous victims of humanitarian crises. Therefore, direct cash transfer payments should be paid into the account of female victims of humanitarian crises to assist them in meeting their essential food and non-food needs, and to assist them in situations where opportunities for employment, income, livelihood, or economic production are extremely limited or have ceased to exist because of humanitarian crisis.

3.6. Introducing Digital Financial Capability Programs From Women

Financial capability programs are designed to assist people in acquiring knowledge, skills, and tools necessary to engage constructively with the formal financial system (Atkinson et al, 2007; Robb and Woodyard, 2011). Women need financial capability programs because many of them may not be very confident in their ability to set and reach a financial goal. Some women have never been taught how to manage their money using a digital bank app (Lusardi and de Bassa Scheresberg, 2017). Also, some women approaching retirement age may not have a financial retirement plan, and older women may feel uncomfortable in learning to use online financial technology compared to younger women. There is a need to establish digital financial capability programs for women both old and young. Such programs, if well-designed, will teach women how to use digital tools to develop individualized financial goals and foster good financial management practices. A digital financial capability program can teach women how to use digital bank apps and other digital tools to control spending, develop a sustainable budget, establish, or improve credit score, design, and manage a financial plan, build financial confidence, and to carryout secure banking transactions.

3.7. Adequate Legal Identification for Women

Lack of legal identity is crucial for wellbeing in society. People who lack legal identification will find it difficult to access basic services such as health care, education, banking services, insurance, and social welfare payments (Dermish et al, 2011; Ozili, 2022a). People need to be legally identified in society so that it is easy to identify who is using the services provided by the government and the private sector. Women also need to be legally identified to enable them access and use the services provided by the government and the private sector. Ensuring that every woman has a legal identity is crucial for achieving women financial inclusion because, without it, women cannot own a formal account. Therefore, policy-makers should ensure that all women have a legal identity, and all barriers to women's access to legal ID should be removed. Also, stringent identity documentation requirements should not be imposed on women as it is one of the commonly cited reasons why unbanked women say they do not have a formal account. Legislation could be introduced to ensure that every girl child and female adult has a legal ID which will give them easy access to a formal account.

3.8. Easy Access to Affordable Mobile Phones for Women

Lack of easy access to mobile phones can hinder financial inclusion because digital financial inclusion is difficult to achieve without extensive mobile phone ownership (Tchouassi, 2012; Ozili, 2020b). Mobile phones can be used to access financial services remotely (Ozili, 2018). Mobile phones are an effective channel to expand digital financial inclusion for women since many women who are financially excluded have a mobile phone (Buteau et al, 2021). Digital financial services through mobile phones can be used to expand financial inclusion for rural women by giving women digital access to a financial institution account or a mobile money service which they can use to perform day to day transactions, and to engage more effectively in the formal economy. Public policies can be issued to subsidize the cost of mobile phone ownership for women. There is also a need to subsidize the cost of internet connectivity for women to enable them carry out mobile banking services with low-cost internet broadband (Ozili, 2018). There should also be free SIM cards and free SIM card registrations for women so that obtaining a fully operational mobile phone will become easier and cheaper.

3.9. Support the Payment of Women's Social Welfare Benefits Into Their Account

Social welfare programs can be designed to protect women from economic risks, social risks, and insecurities of life. When social welfare programs are targeted at women, the benefits accruing to women can be paid into their account (Gabor and Brooks, 2017). This will foster financial inclusion among women. Government should support the payment of women's social welfare (financial) benefits directly into the digital account of women. This will ensure that all female beneficiaries will own an account, and the account will be under women's control which will allow them to perform a range of digital financial transactions including payments, without any undue control from their husbands or the male head in the family. Paying women's social welfare benefits directly into their digital account will also offer women greater privacy and control over their money and contribute to their financial security.

3.10. Enact Laws That Criminalize Gender Discrimination Against Women

Gender discrimination against women exist in many forms. It prevents women from competing fairly with men for the same opportunities. Gender discrimination against women also affects women's access to formal financial services (Demirgüç-Kunt et al, 2013). This is because financial institutions intentionally or unintentionally make certain financial services more accessible to men than women, especially investment and saving products, and they charge a higher interest rate on loans issued to single women while charging lower interest rate on loans issued to single men. This type of gender discrimination discourages women from joining the formal financial sector and can increase the level of financial exclusion for women. Existing discriminatory laws can also affect women's demand for financial services and impede their ability to save, borrow or insure themselves against risk. Introducing laws that criminalize gender discrimination against women can help to give women equal access to available financial products and services. When such laws are in place, women will not be discriminated based on their gender, and they will be motivated to own a formal account and freely access the same formal financial services that are available to men.

4. REAL-WORLD PROGRAMS TO INCREASE WOMEN FINANCIAL INCLUSION

Some existing real-world programs aimed at increasing women financial inclusion, as shown in table 1, include the Denarau Action Plan (DAP), the Affirmative Finance Action for Women in Africa program (AFAWA), the African Union's Women and Youth Financial and Economic Inclusion Initiative, the World Bank's Women Entrepreneurs Finance Initiative, etc.

Table 1. Real-world programs to increase women financial inclusion

Country	Program	Purpose
Nigeria	Framework for Advancing Women's Financial Inclusion In Nigeria	This framework provides the blueprint for driving sustainable access to and usage of financial services by women in Nigeria
Alliance for Financial Inclusion (AFI) member-countries	Denarau Action Plan (DAP)	The Denarau Action Plan identifies measures that AFI members can take to increase the number of women with access to quality and affordable financial services globally and close the financial inclusion gender gap, noting that the goals of financial access, usage and quality should be pursued in parallel and in a responsible and sustainable manner.
African countries	Affirmative Finance Action for Women in Africa (AFAWA) program	AFAWA is a partnership set to increase financial inclusion for women-led enterprises across the African continent. It is a program developed by the African Development Bank
Costa Rica	Implementation of actions to close the financial gaps between women and men in Costa Rica and its pilot program	This program aims to help the country to develop financial products that meet the specific needs of women and thereby help close gender gaps.
Solomon Islands	The National Women's Financial Inclusion Policy: 2022-2026	The policy aims to initiate digital financial services (DFS) and facilitate the provision of fast, safe, and affordable financial services – especially to women and rural families.
Ghana	National Financial Inclusion and Development Strategy (NFIDS) 2018–2023	It aims to support the government of Ghana's vision of increasing the availability of a broad range of affordable and quality financial services that meet the needs of all Ghanaians and are provided by sound, responsible, and innovative financial institutions.
Philippines	National strategy for financial inclusion 2022 to 2028	It aims to achieve the vision of driving financial inclusion toward broad-based growth and financial resilience for everyone including women
Zimbabwe	Zimbabwe National Financial Inclusion Strategy	It aims to increase the level of ¬financial inclusion in the country through interventions targeted at minimizing the barriers to financial inclusion for identified priority segments that include women, MSMEs, youth, and rural and smallholder farmers.
African union countries	African Union's Women and Youth Financial and Economic Inclusion Initiative	It aims to enable financing opportunities and parity in employment for at least 1 million African women and youth by 2030.
World Bank	Women Entrepreneurs Finance Initiative	It aims to unlock the potential of women entrepreneurs. The new Women Entrepreneurs Finance Initiative (We-Fi) will enable more than $1 billion in financing to improve access to capital, provide technical assistance, and invest in projects and programs that support women and women-led SMEs in World Bank Group client countries.
Pakistan	National Financial Inclusion Strategy	A strategy for building a dynamic and inclusive financial sector to support Pakistan's growth in the 21st century.

5. CONCLUSION

The purpose of this study is to discuss women financial inclusion. Some barriers to women financial inclusion were highlighted. Some strategies to increase women financial inclusion were also identified such as providing greater financial education for women, greater access to formal credit for women-owned businesses, microfinance designed for women, government loan schemes for women, adequate legal identification for women, affordable mobile phones for women, and laws that criminalize gender discrimination against women.

The implication is that countries should take bold actions to increase financial inclusion for women by removing many obstacles that keep women financially excluded. Policymakers should leverage on existing technological innovations that can advance financial inclusion for women. There is also a need to create a favourable regulatory environment that allow innovations to thrive especially innovations that increase women financial inclusion. It is equally important to ensure that existing laws support women financial inclusion. This may require legal reforms to advance women's financial inclusion.

Future research can examine the effect of women financial inclusion on economic growth. Such studies should document evidence of how women financial inclusion affects economic growth. Future research can also identify other causes of financial exclusion for women.

REFERENCES

Atkinson, A., McKay, S., Collard, S., & Kempson, E. (2007). Levels of financial capability in the UK. *Public Money & Management*, *27*(1), 29–36. doi:10.1111/j.1467-9302.2007.00552.x

Atkinson, A., & Messy, F. A. (2013). *Promoting financial inclusion through financial education: OECD/INFE evidence, policies, and practice*. Academic Press.

Bailey, S., & Harvey, P. (2015). *State of evidence on humanitarian cash transfers*. Overseas Development Institute Background Note.

Beck, T. (2015). *Microfinance*. Independent Evaluation Group.

Bhatia, S., & Singh, S. (2019). Empowering women through financial inclusion: A study of urban slum. *Vikalpa*, *44*(4), 182–197. doi:10.1177/0256090919897809

Buteau, S., Rao, P., & Valenti, F. (2021). Emerging insights from digital solutions in financial inclusion. *CSI Transactions on ICT*, *9*(2), 105–114. doi:10.100740012-021-00330-x

Chavan, P. (2008). Gender inequality in banking services. *Economic and Political Weekly*, 18–21.

Demirgüç-Kunt, A., Klapper, L. F., & Singer, D. (2013). Financial inclusion and legal discrimination against women: evidence from developing countries. *World Bank Policy Research Working Paper*, (6416).

Dermish, A., Kneiding, C., Leishman, P., & Mas, I. (2011). Branchless and mobile banking solutions for the poor: A Survey. *Innovations, 6*(4).

Ellis, A. (2007). *Gender and economic growth in Tanzania: Creating opportunities for women.* World Bank Publications.

Gabor, D., & Brooks, S. (2017). The digital revolution in financial inclusion: International development in the fintech era. *New Political Economy*, *22*(4), 423–436. doi:10.1080/13563467.2017.1259298

Ghosh, S., & Vinod, D. (2017). What constrains financial inclusion for women? Evidence from Indian micro data. *World Development*, *92*, 60–81. doi:10.1016/j.worlddev.2016.11.011

Hendriks, S. (2019). The role of financial inclusion in driving women's economic empowerment. *Development in Practice*, *29*(8), 1029–1038. doi:10.1080/09614524.2019.1660308

Jarecke, J., Taylor, E. W., & Hira, T. K. (2014). Financial literacy education for women. *New Directions for Adult and Continuing Education*, *2014*(141), 37–46. doi:10.1002/ace.20083

Kulkarni, L., & Ghosh, A. (2021). Gender disparity in the digitalization of financial services: Challenges and promises for women's financial inclusion in India. *Gender, Technology and Development*, *25*(2), 233–250. doi:10.1080/09718524.2021.1911022

Kyrgidou, L. P., & Petridou, E. (2013). Developing women entrepreneurs' knowledge, skills, and attitudes through e-mentoring support. *Journal of Small Business and Enterprise Development*, *20*(3), 548–566. doi:10.1108/JSBED-04-2013-0061

Lusardi, A., & de Bassa Scheresberg, C. (2017). *Financial capability and financial literacy among working women: New insights*. Academic Press.

MavrinacS. C.ChinW. P. (2004). *Financial education for women in Asia Pacific*. doi:10.2139/ssrn.695042

Mushtaq, R., Dastane, O., Rafiq, M., & Başar, B. D. (2023). Women financial inclusion research: A bibliometric and network analysis. *International Journal of Social Economics*, *50*(8), 1169–1185. doi:10.1108/IJSE-06-2022-0438

Ozili, P. K. (2018). Impact of digital finance on financial inclusion and stability. *Borsa Istanbul Review*, *18*(4), 329–340. doi:10.1016/j.bir.2017.12.003

Ozili, P. K. (2020). Contesting digital finance for the poor. *Digital Policy, Regulation & Governance*, *22*(2), 135–151. doi:10.1108/DPRG-12-2019-0104

Ozili, P. K. (2020). Theories of financial inclusion. In *Uncertainty and challenges in contemporary economic behaviour* (pp. 89–115). Emerald Publishing Limited. doi:10.1108/978-1-80043-095-220201008

Ozili, P. K. (2021). Financial inclusion research around the world: A review. *The Forum for Social Economics*, *50*(4), 457–479. doi:10.1080/07360932.2020.1715238

Ozili, P. K. (2022a). Can central bank digital currency increase financial inclusion? Arguments for and against. In *Big Data Analytics in the Insurance Market* (pp. 241–249). Emerald Publishing Limited. doi:10.1108/978-1-80262-637-720221013

Ozili, P. K. (2022b). Digital financial inclusion. In *Big Data: A game changer for insurance industry* (pp. 229–238). Emerald Publishing Limited. doi:10.1108/978-1-80262-605-620221015

Ozili, P. K. (2023). CBDC, Fintech and cryptocurrency for financial inclusion and financial stability. Digital Policy, Regulation and Governance, 25(1), 40-57.

Robb, C. A., & Woodyard, A. (2011). Financial knowledge and best practice behavior. *Financial Counseling and Planning*, *22*(1).

Saluja, O. B., Singh, P., & Kumar, H. (2023). Barriers and interventions on the way to empower women through financial inclusion: A 2 decades systematic review (2000–2020). *Humanities & Social Sciences Communications*, *10*(1), 1–14. doi:10.105741599-023-01640-y

Sapovadia, V. (2018). Financial inclusion, digital currency, and mobile technology. In Handbook of Blockchain, Digital Finance, and Inclusion, Volume 2 (pp. 361-385). Academic Press. doi:10.1016/B978-0-12-812282-2.00014-0

Setiawan, B., Phan, T. D., Medina, J., Wieriks, M., Nathan, R. J., & Fekete-Farkas, M. (2023). Quest for financial inclusion via digital financial services (Fintech) during COVID-19 pandemic: Case study of women in Indonesia. *Journal of Financial Services Marketing*, 1–15. doi:10.105741264-023-00217-9

Tchouassi, G. (2012). Can mobile phones really work to extend banking services to the unbanked? Empirical lessons from selected Sub-Saharan Africa countries. *International Journal of Developmental Science*, *1*(2), 70–81.

Tran, T. K. V., Elahi, E., Zhang, L., Abid, M., Pham, Q. T., & Tran, T. D. (2018). Gender differences in formal credit approaches: Rural households in Vietnam. *Asian-Pacific Economic Literature*, *32*(1), 131–138. doi:10.1111/apel.12220

Wellalage, N., & Locke, S. (2017). Access to credit by SMEs in South Asia: Do women entrepreneurs face discrimination. *Research in International Business and Finance*, *41*, 336–346. doi:10.1016/j.ribaf.2017.04.053

Zins, A., & Weill, L. (2016). The determinants of financial inclusion in Africa. *Review of Development Finance, 6*(1), 46-57.

Compilation of References

Adaman, F., & Bulut, T. (2007). *500 Milyonluk Umut Hikayeleri*. İletişim.

Adam, J. N., Adams, T., Gerber, J. D., & Amacker, M. (2022). The dilemma of women empowerment in informal artisanal and small-scale gold ore mining in Ghana. *Cogent Social Sciences*, *8*(1), 2108231. doi:10.1080/23311886.2022.2108231

Adebola, S. (2022). *Embedded finance is the next big thing for sub-Saharan Africa*. https://www.linkedin.com>pulse

Affleck, A., & Mellor, M. (2006). Community development finance: A neo-market solution to social exclusion? *Journal of Social Policy*, *35*(2), 303–319. doi:10.1017/S0047279405009542

AFI. (2020). *AFI Annual Report 2020*. https://issu.com/afi7/docs_annual_report

Agarwal, S., & Lenka, U. (2016). An exploratory study on the development of women entrepreneurs: Indian cases. *Journal of Research in Marketing and Entrepreneurship*, *18*(2), 232–247. doi:10.1108/JRME-04-2015-0024

Agier, I., & Szafarz, A. (2013). Microfinance and gender: Is there a glass ceiling in loan size? *World Development*, *42*, 165–181. doi:10.1016/j.worlddev.2012.06.016

Agu, S. (2007). 'Gender Equality Education and Women Empowerment' The Nigerian Challenge, Multi-Disciplinary. *Journal of Research and Development (Srinagar)*, *8*(2), 134–152.

Aidis, R., Welter, F., Smallbone, D., & Isakova, N. (2007). Female entrepreneurship in transition economies: The case of Lithuania and Ukraine. *Feminist Economics*, *13*(2), 157–183. doi:10.1080/13545700601184831

Akbulut, Ö., & Yılız, N. (1999). *İstatistik analizlerde temel formüller ve tablolar*. Aktif Yayınevi.

Aker, J. C., Boumnijel, R., McClelland, A., & Tierney, N. (2016). Payment Mechanisms and Antipoverty Programs: Evidence from a Mobile Money Cash Transfer Experiment in Niger. *Economic Development and Cultural Change*, *65*(1), 1–37. doi:10.1086/687578

Akgeyik, T. (2017). Türkiye'de kadınların işgücü piyasasına katılımını etkileyen faktörler: TÜİK verileri üzerine bir analiz. *Journal of Social Policy Conferences*, (70), 31-53.

Akkul, R. (2011). *Cinsiyetler arası gelir eşitsizliğini gidermede mikro kredi uygulamalarının etkinliği: Bilecik örneği* [Yüksek Lisans Tezi]. Bilecik Üniversitesi Sosyal Bilimler Enstitüsü.

Akor, F. O. (2017). Reflections on the Role of Women in the African Development Process: lessons from Nigeria. In A. Amtaika (Ed.), Socio-Economic Development in Africa: Challenges and Dynamics (pp. 325-345). Pan-African University Press.

Aksoy, N., Felek, Ş., Yayla, N., & Çeviş, İ. (2019). Türkiye'de Kadın İstihdamı ve Etkileyen Faktörler. *Journal of Management and Economics Research*, *17*(3), 146–163.

Akudugu, M. A. (2014). *Farm Credit and Agricultural Productivity in Ghana* [PhD Thesis]. School of Agriculture, Policy and Development, University of Reading, Reading, UK.

Akudugu, M. A. (2010). Assessment of access to financial capital by rural people in Ghana: The case of the Upper East Region. *Savings and Development*, *34*(2), 169–189.

Akudugu, M. A. (2012). Estimation of Determinants of Credit Demand by Rural Banks in Ghana's Upper East Region. *Asian Journal of Agriculture and Rural Development*, *2*(2), 189–200.

Akudugu, M. A. (2012). Estimation of the determinants of credit demand by farmers and supply by Rural Banks in Ghana's Upper East Region. *Asian Journal of Agriculture and Rural Development*, *2*(2), 179–190.

Akudugu, M. A., & Alhassan, A.-R. (2012). The climate change menace, food security, livelihoods and social safety in northern Ghana. *International Journal of Sustainable Development and World Policy*, *1*(3), 80–95.

Akudugu, M. A., Dittoh, S., & Mahama, E. S. (2012). The Implications of Climate Change on Food Security and Rural Livelihoods: Experiences from Northern Ghana. *Journal of Environment and Earth Science*, *2*(3), 21–29.

Akudugu, M. A., Egyir, I. S., & Akwasi, M.-B. (2009). Access to credit from rural banks in Ghana: The case of women farmers in the Upper East Region. *Ghana Journal of Development Studies*, *6*(2), 142–167.

Akudugu, M. A., Egyir, I. S., & Akwasi, M.-B. (2009). Women farmers' access to credit from rural banks in Ghana. *Agricultural Finance Review*, *69*(3), 284–299. doi:10.1108/00021460911002671

Akudugu, M. A., Garforth, C. J., & Dorward, P. (2013). Improvement in Crop Production in Ghana: Is it due to Area Expansion or Increased Productivity? *Developing Country Studies*, *3*(1), 176–186.

Akurugu, C. A., Nyuur, R. B., & Dery, I. (2023). Non-Governmental Organizations' approaches to women's empowerment amid the COVID-19 Pandemic: Towards decolonizing development praxis in northern Ghana. *World Development Sustainability*, 100079.

Al Mamun, A., & Fazal, S. A. (2018). *Effect of entrepreneurial orientation on competency and micro-enterprise performance*. Asia Pacific Journal of Innovation and Entrepreneurship. doi:10.1108/APJIE-05-2018-0033

Alam, J., Moir, R., & Ibn-Boamah, M. (2021). Gender and micro-credit: Who repays? Evidence from a Canadian individual-lending approach. *Journal of Small Business and Entrepreneurship*, *33*(3), 249–267. doi:10.1080/08276331.2019.1606966

Alene, A., & Manyong, V. M. (2007). The Effect of Education on Agricultural Productivity under Traditional and Improved Technology in Northern Nigeria: An Endogenous Switching Regression Analysis. *Empirical Economics*, *32*(1), 141–159. doi:10.100700181-006-0076-3

Alhassan, Y., Kuagbela, F., Nurokina, C. D., & Appiah, B. (2022). The Role of Microfinance in Africa: A Review of Outcomes from Ghana and Nigeria. *Microfinance and Sustainable Development in Africa*, 54-81. https://www.igi-global.com/chapter/the-role-of-microfinance-in-africa/293794

Alhassan, Y., Paul, G., Salia, S., & Nwagbara, U. (2023). Transforming Local Economies Through Microfinance in Rural Ghana: Evidence From a Review of Existing Literature. *Transforming Economies Through Microfinance in Developing Nations*, 1-19.

Alhassan, A.-R., Akudugu, M. A., & Akuriba, M. A. (2023). The Double Bottom Line in Microfinance: Implications for the Performance Measurement Practices of Microfinance Institutions. In Y. Alhassan & U. Nwangbara (Eds.), *Transforming Economies Through Microfinance in Developing Nations*. IGI Global. doi:10.4018/978-1-6684-5647-7.ch002

Al-hassan, S., & Sagre, B. (2006). Microcredit and poverty alleviation: An analysis of the performance of women in microcredit activities in the Kassena/Nankana District of Ghana. *Ghana Journal of Development Studies*, *3*(2), 41–56.

Ali, I., & Hatta, Z. A. (2012). Women's Empowerment or Disempowerment through Microfinance: Evidence from Bangladesh. *Asian Social Work and Policy Review*, *6*(2), 111–121. doi:10.1111/j.1753-1411.2012.00066.x

Ali, I., Hatta, Z. A., Azman, A., & Islam, S. (2017). Microfinance as a development and poverty alleviation tool in rural Bangladesh: A critical assessment. *Asian Social Work and Policy Review*, *11*(1), 14–15. doi:10.1111/aswp.12106

Alkan, I. (2018). Tarım sektöründe kadın emeği (Çarşamba Ovası Gündoğdu ve Damlataş köylerinde fındık, çeltik ve sebze üretimi özelinde bir irdeleme). Gazi Kitabevi.

Al-Mamun, A., Wahab, S. A., Mazumder, M. N., & Su, Z. (2014). Empirical Investigation on the Impact of Microcredit on Women Empowerment in Urban Peninsular Malaysia. *Journal of Developing Areas*, 287–306.

Alptekin, D. (2014). Toplumsal cinsiyet eşitsizliği örüntüsünde kadının yoksulluğu ve yoksunlukları. In Yoksulluk ve Kadın içinde. Ayrıntı Yayınları.

Al-Shami, S. S. A., Razali, M. M., Majid, I., Rozelan, A., & Rashid, N. (2016). The effect of microfinance on women's empowerment: Evidence from Malaysia. *Asian Journal of Women's Studies*, *22*(3), 318–337. doi:10.1080/12259276.2016.1205378

Alvarez, A. D. (1998, July) *Transformational development program.* Kabalikat Para sa Maunlad na Buhay (KMBI - A Microfinance NGO). Unpublished Manuscript.

Alvarez, A. D. (1999, October). *Microfinance: An alternative tool in the fight against poverty. An Introduction to Microfinance.* Unpublished Paper.

Alvarez, A. D. (2001, June 8) *Katuwang Resource Center, Inc.* (2nd ed.). Concept Paper.

Anang, B. T., & Amikuzuno, J. (2015). Factors Influencing Pesticide Use in Smallholder Rice Production in Northern Ghana. *Agriculture, Forestry and Fisheries*, *4*(2), 77–82. doi:10.11648/j.aff.20150402.19

Anderson, R. M. (2017). Patient empowerment: Myths and misconceptions. *Patient Education and Counselling.*

Anyaegbunam, N., & Alaga, E. (2025). Think beyond microfinance when talking about businesswomen. *AfricanRenewal.*, *29*(2), 22–23.

Anyaegbunam, N., & Alaga, E. (2015). Think beyond microfinance when talking about businesswomen. *Africa Renewal*, *29*(2), 22–23. doi:10.18356/e422ba79-en

Apaydın, S. (2015). *Yoksullukla mücadelede mikro kredi: Muş ili örneği [Yüksek Lisans Tezi].* Dumlupınar Üniversitesi Sosyal Bilimler Enstitüsü.

Arıkan, R. (2018). Anket yöntemi üzerinde bir değerlendirme. *Haliç Üniversitesi Sosyal Bilimler Dergisi, 1*(1), 97-159.

Armendariz, B. A., & Morduch, J. (2005). *The Economics of Microfinance.* MIT Press.

Armendáriz, B., & Morduch, J. (2010). *The Economics of Microfinance*. MIT Press.

Arnold, G. (2017). *Africa: A Modern history: 1945-2015.* Atlantic Books.

Arshad, A. (2023). Nexus between financial inclusion and women empowerment: Evidence from developing countries. *Gender in Management*, *38*(4), 561–580. doi:10.1108/GM-04-2022-0125

Arslan, M. (2020). *Türkiye'de kadın istihdamı ve ekonomik büyüme arasındaki ilişki* (Publication Number 643103) [Master's thesis]. İstanbul Gelişim University, İstanbul. tez.yok.gov.tr

Aruna, M., & Jyothirmayi, R. (2011). The Role of Microfinance in Women Empowerment: A Study on the SHG Bank Linkage Program in Hyderabad (Andhra Pradesh). *Indian Journal of Commerce and Management Studies*, *2*(4), 4.

Aruna, M., & Jyothirmayi, R. (2011). The role of microfinance in women empowerment: A study on the SHG Bank linkage program in Hyderabad (Andhra Pradesh). *Indian Journal of Commerce and Management Studies*, *2*(4), 78–95.

Asfaw, S. (2010). *Estimating Welfare Effect of Modern Agricultural Technologies: A Micro-Perspective from Tanzania and Ethiopia International Crops Research Institute for the Semi-Arid Tropics*. ICRISAT.

Ata, N. (2006). Türkiye'de kadınların işgücüne katılma oranı hakkında bir not. *İşveren Dergisi*, *44*(4), 19.

Ateş, G. & Öğütoğulları, E. (2012). Türkiye'de yoksullukla mücadelede mikrokredi uygulamaları. *Trakya Üniversitesi Sosyal Bilimler Dergisi*, *14*(2), 33-53.

Atieno, R. (2001). *Formal and informal institutions' lending policies and access to credit by small-scale enterprises in Kenya: An empirical assessment*. African Economic Research Consortium Research Paper 111.

Atkinson, A., & Messy, F. A. (2013). *Promoting financial inclusion through financial education: OECD/INFE evidence, policies, and practice*. Academic Press.

Atkinson, A., McKay, S., Collard, S., & Kempson, E. (2007). Levels of financial capability in the UK. *Public Money & Management*, *27*(1), 29–36. doi:10.1111/j.1467-9302.2007.00552.x

Awunyo-Vitor, D., & Abankwah, V. (2012). Substitutes or complements: Formal and informal credit demand by maize farmers in Ashanti and Brong Ahafo Regions of Ghana. *Journal of Agricultural Science*, *7*(1), 1–13.

Ayamga, M., Sarpong, D. B., & Asuming-Brempong, S. (2006). Factors influencing the decision to participate in micro-credit programmes: An illustration for Northern Ghana. *Ghana Journal of Development Studies*, *3*(2), 57–65.

Aydın, B. (2012). *Yoksullukla Mücadelede Mikro Kredinin Türkiye Uygulamasının Ekonomik Açıdan Değerlendirilmesi* [Marmara Üniversitesi Sosyal Bilimler Enstitüsü Yayınlanmamış Yüksek Lisans Tezi]. Marmara Üniversitesi.

Aydın, B. (2012). *Yoksullukla mücadelede mikro kredinin Türkiye uygulamasının ekonomik açıdan değerlendirilmesi [Yüksek Lisans Tezi]*. Marmara Üniversitesi Sosyal Bilimler Enstitüsü.

Aygar, K. (2013). *Mikro Finans ve Türkiye için Öneriler*. Sermaye Piyasaları Kurulu. Ortaklıklar Finansmanı Dairesi.

Baffour-Kyei, V., Mensah, A., Owusu, V., & Horlu, G. S. A. K. (2021). Artisanal Small-Scale Mining and Livelihood Assets in Rural Southern Ghana. *Resources Policy*, *71*, 101988. doi:10.1016/j.resourpol.2021.101988

Bahl, J. (2012). Status of women entrepreneurship in rural India. *Asian Journal of Multidimensional Research*, *1*(2), 89–100.

Bailey, S., & Harvey, P. (2015). *State of evidence on humanitarian cash transfers*. Overseas Development Institute Background Note.

Bako, M. J., & Syed, J. (2018). Women's marginalization in Nigeria and the way forward. *Human Resource Development International*, *21*(5), 425–443. doi:10.1080/13678868.2018.1458567

Baltacı, N. (2011). *Kadınları güçlendirme mekanizması olarak mikrokredi [Uzmanlık Tezi]*. T.C Başbakanlık Kadının Statüsü Genel Müdürlüğü.

Baltacı, Ö. (2011). *Kadınları Güçlendirme Mekanizması Olarak Mikrokredi* [Uzmanlık Tezi]. T.C Başbakanlık Kadın Statüsü Genel Müdürlüğü.

Bammeke, T. O. A. (2003). *Accessibility and Utilization of Agricultural Information in the Economic Empowerment of Women Farmers in South Western Nigeria*. University of Ibadan.

Banchirigah, S. M. (2006). How have reforms fuelled the expansion of artisanal mining? Evidence from Sub-Saharan Africa. *Resources Policy*, *31*(3), 165–171. doi:10.1016/j.resourpol.2006.12.001

Banchirigah, S. M. (2008). Challenges with eradicating illegal mining in Ghana: A perspective from the grassroots. *Resources Policy*, *33*(1), 29–38. doi:10.1016/j.resourpol.2007.11.001

Banchirigah, S. M., & Hilson, G. (2010). De-agrarianization, re-agrarianization and local economic development: Re-orienting livelihoods in African artisanal mining communities. *Policy Sciences*, *43*(2), 157–180. doi:10.100711077-009-9091-5

Banerjee, S. B., & Jackson, L. (2017). Microfinance and the business of poverty reduction: Critical perspectives from rural Bangladesh. *Human Relations, 70*(1) 63–91. https://journals.sagepub.com/doi/pdf/10.1177/0018726716640865

Banerjee, A., Karlan, D., & Zinman, J. (2015). Six randomized evaluations of microcredit: Introduction and further steps. *American Economic Journal. Applied Economics*, *7*(1), 1–21. doi:10.1257/app.20140287

Barman, D. K., & Saloi, T. (2021). Alleviation of Urban Poverty through DAY-NULM Scheme: A Study with Reference to Guwahati City. *International Journal of Management*, *11*(12), 2020.

Barretta, C. B., Reardon, T., & Webb, P. (2001). Nonfarm income diversification and household livelihood strategies in rural Africa: Concepts, dynamics, and policy implications. *Food Policy*, *26*(4), 315–331. doi:10.1016/S0306-9192(01)00014-8

Baruah, I., Bora, M., & Deka, M. B. (2022). Impact of Bandhan Microfinance on Empowerment of Rural Women in Tinsukia District of Assam. *Asian Journal of Agricultural Extension. Economia e Sociologia*.

Bateman, M. (2010). *Why doesn't microfinance work? The destructive rise of local neoliberalism*. Zed Books Ltd. doi:10.5040/9781350223974

Bauer, G., & Burnet, J. E. (2013). Gender quotas, democracy, and women's representation in Africa: Some insights from democratic Botswana and autocratic Rwanda. *Women's Studies International Forum*, *41*, 103–112. doi:10.1016/j.wsif.2013.05.012

Bayai, I., & Ikhide, S. (2016). Financing and financial sustainability of microfinance institutions (MFIs): A conceptual view. *Banks and Bank Systems*, *11*(2), 21–32. doi:10.21511/bbs.11(2).2016.03

Beck, T. (2015). *Microfinance*. Independent Evaluation Group.

Bedük, A. (2005). Türkiye'de çalışan kadın ve kadın girişimciliği. *Elektronik Sosyal Bilimler Dergisi*, *3*(12), 106–117.

Beeri, I., Uster, A., & Vigoda-Gadot, E. (2019). Does performance management relate to good governance? A study of its relationship with citizens' satisfaction with and trust in Israeli local government. *Public Performance & Management Review*, *42*(2), 241–279. doi:10.1080/15309576.2018.1436074

Beken, N. (2020). Covid-19 pandemi sürecinde kadın istihdamı: Türkiye örneği. *Iğdır Üniversitesi Sosyal Bilimler Dergisi*, 47-74.

Belderbos, R., Carree, M., Diederen, B., Lokshin, B., & Veugelers, R. (2004). Heterogeneity in R&D Cooperation Strategies. *International Journal of Industrial Organization*, *22*(8-9), 1237–1263. doi:10.1016/j.ijindorg.2004.08.001

Bhatia, S., & Singh, S. (2019). Empowering women through financial inclusion: A study of urban slum. *Vikalpa*, *44*(4), 182–197. doi:10.1177/0256090919897809

Blattner, C. E. (2020). Just Transition for Agriculture? A Critical Step in Tackling Climate Change. *Journal of Agriculture, Food Systems, and Community Development*, *9*(3), 53–58. doi:10.5304/jafscd.2020.093.006

Boateng, G. O., Boateng, A. A., & Bampoe, H. S. (2015). Microfinance and poverty reduction in Ghana: Evidence from policy beneficiaries. *Review of Business & Finance Studies*, *6*(1), 99–108.

Bond, P. (2007). Two economies, microcredit and the Accelerated and Shared Growth Initaitive for South Africa. *The Journal of Development Studies*, *37*(2), 216–230.

Bouasria, M., Ashta, A., & Ratsimalahelo, Z. (2020). Bottlenecks to Financial Development, Financial Inclusion, and Microfinance: A Case Study of Mauritania. *Journal of Risk and Financial Management, 13*(10), 239. . doi:10.3390/jrfm13100239

Bradley, S. W., McMullen, J. S., Artz, K., & Simiyu, E. M. (2012). Capital is not enough: Innovation in developing economies. *Journal of Management Studies*, *49*(4), 684–717. doi:10.1111/j.1467-6486.2012.01043.x

Braunerhjelm, P. (2010). *Entrepreneurship, innovation and economic growth.* Swedish Entrepreneurship Forum and the Royal Institute of Technology Working Paper 2010/2.

Bridge, S., O'Neill, K., & Cromie, S. (1998). *Understanding Enterprise, Entrepreneurship and Small Business*. Macmillan. doi:10.1007/978-1-349-26171-0

Brush, C., & Hisrich, R. D. (1999). Women-owned businesses: why do they matter? In *Are small firms important? Their role and impact* (pp. 111–127). Springer. doi:10.1007/978-1-4615-5173-7_7

Bryceson, D. F. (1999). *Sub-Saharan Africa betwixt and between: Rural livelihood practices and policies.* Afrika-Studiecentrum (Leiden University) Working Paper 43.

Bryceson, D. F. (2002). The Scramble in Africa: Reorienting Rural Livelihoods. *World Development*, *30*(5), 725–739. doi:10.1016/S0305-750X(02)00006-2

Bryceson, D. F., & Jonsson, J. B. (2010). Gold digging careers in rural Africa: Small-scale miners' livelihood choices. *World Development*, *38*(3), 379–392. doi:10.1016/j.worlddev.2009.09.003

Buteau, S., Rao, P., & Valenti, F. (2021). Emerging insights from digital solutions in financial inclusion. *CSI Transactions on ICT*, *9*(2), 105–114. doi:10.100740012-021-00330-x

Buvinic, M., & Furst-Nichols, R. (2016). Promoting Women's Economic Empowerment: What Works? *The World Bank Research Observer*, *31*(1), 59–101.

Buvinic, M., & O'Donnell, M. (2016). *Revisiting what works: women, economic empowerment and smart design. Centre for Global Development Review.*

Bvuma, S., & Marnewick, C. (2020). Sustainable livelihoods of township small, medium and micro enterprises towards growth and development. *Sustainability (Basel)*, *12*(8), 31–49. doi:10.3390u12083149

Carrington, C. (2006). Women entrepreneurs. *Journal of Small Business and Entrepreneurship*, *19*(2), 83–94. doi:10.1080/08276331.2006.10593360

Carter, S., & Cannon, T. (1992). *Women as entrepreneurs: A study of female business owners, their motivations, experiences and strategies for success.* Academic Press.

Cavlak, H., & Akpınar, İ. E. (2019). Türkiye-Avrupa Birliği katılım müzakereleri sürecinde sosyal politika ve istihdam projelerinde kadının yeri. *International Journal of Economics Administrative and Social Sciences*, *2*(1), 40–58.

Ceesay, A. (2023). Women and Microfinance in The Gambia: A Path to Empowerment and Financial Inclusion. In K. A. Krawczyk & B. A. King (Eds.), *Women's Contributions to Development in West Africa: Ordinary Women, Extraordinary Lives* (pp. 99–118). Springer Nature. doi:10.1007/978-981-19-8190-6_5

Çelik, C., & Özdevecioğlu, M. (2001). *Kadın Girişimcilerin Demografik Özellikleri ve Karşılaştıkları sorunlara İlişkin Nevşehir İlinde Bir Araştırma*. Orta Anadolu Kongresi (Nevşehir).

Çetindamar, D., Gupta, V. K., Karadeniz, E. E., & Egrican, N. (2012). What the numbers tell: The impact of human, family and financial capital on women and men's entry into entrepreneurship in Turkey. *Entrepreneurship and Regional Development*, *24*(1-2), 29–51. doi:10.1080/08985626.2012.637348

Çetin, I., & Keser, H. Y. (2018). Women Entrepreneurship in MENA and Europe: Empowerment Through Microfinance. In R. C. Das (Ed.), *Microfinance and Its Impact on Entrepreneurial Development* (pp. 30–51). Sustainability, and Inclusive Growth.

CGAP. (2020/2021). *Social Assistance Payments in Response to Covid-19: The Role of Donors*. www.cgap.org

Chandan Kumar Goyal. (2008). *Financial Inclusion in the North-eastern Region of India with Special Reference to Assam*. The ICFAI University Press.

Chandra, B. S. (2011). Growth through Financial inclusion in India. *Journal of International Business Ethics*, *4*(1), 2011.

Chattopadhyay, A. (2017). Women's empowerment: What works? *Journal of International Development*, *28*(3), 342–359.

Chaudhary & Kumari. (2022). Impact of Financial Inclusion on Women Empowerment: A Case Study of Ranchi District. *International Journal for Research in Applied Science & Engineering Technology*, *10*(8), 1388-1398. doi:10.22214/ijraset.2022.46423

Chavan, P. (2008). Gender inequality in banking services. *Economic and Political Weekly*, 18–21.

Chavan, V. M., & Murkute, P. A. (2016). Role of women entrepreneurship in Indian economy. *International Journal of Science Technology and Management*, *5*(3), 604–612.

Chavas, J.-P., & Falco, S. D. (2012). On the role of risk versus economies of scope in farm diversification with an application to Ethiopian farms. *Journal of Agricultural Economics*, *63*(1), 25–55. doi:10.1111/j.1477-9552.2011.00319.x

Chemin, M. (2008). The benefits and costs of microfinance: Evidence from Bangladesh. *The Journal of Development Studies*, *44*(4), 463–484. doi:10.1080/00220380701846735

Chen, M. A. (1997). *A Guide for Assessing the Impact of Microenterprise Services at the Individual Level*. SEEP Network.

Cheston, S., & Kuhn, L. (2002). Empowering women through microfinance. *Pathways out of poverty: Innovations in microfinance for the poorest families*, 167-228.

Chhabra, S., Raghunathan, R., & Rao, N. M. (2020). The antecedents of entrepreneurial intention among women entrepreneurs in India. *Asia Pacific Journal of Innovation and Entrepreneurship*, *14*(1), 76–92. doi:10.1108/APJIE-06-2019-0034

Chinomona, E., & Maziriri, E. T. (2015). Women in action: Challenges facing women entrepreneurs in the Gauteng Province of South Africa. *The International Business & Economics Research Journal*, *14*(6), 835–850. doi:10.19030/iber.v14i6.9487

Christian, A. K., Atiglo, D. Y., Okyere, M. A., Obeng-Dwamena, A., Marquis, G. S., & Jones, A. D. (2023). Women's empowerment, children's nutritional status, and the mediating role of household headship structure: Evidence from sub-Saharan Africa. *Maternal and Child Nutrition*, *19*(3), 13520. doi:10.1111/mcn.13520 PMID:37092343

Clayton, A. (2021). How Do Electoral Gender Quotas Affect Policy? *Annual Review of Political Science*, *24*(1), 235–252. doi:10.1146/annurev-polisci-041719-102019

Cochran, W. G. (1977). The Estimation of Sample Size. *Sampling Techniques*, *3*, 72–90.

Cohen, J. (1992). Statistical Power Analysis. *Current Directions in Psychological Science*, *1*(3), 98–101. doi:10.1111/1467-8721.ep10768783

Çolakoğlu, C. (2016). *Yapabilirlikten yoksulluk bağlamında mikro kredi uygulaması: Grameen Bankası Sakarya ili örneği* [Yüksek Lisans Tezi]. Sakarya Üniversitesi Sosyal Bilimler Enstitüsü.

Commission of The European Communities (COM) (2006). *Implementing the Community Lisbon Programme: Financing SME Growth – Adding European Value*. Author.

Commission of The European Communities (COM) (2007). *A European initiative for the development of micro-credit in support of growth and employment.* Author.

Conning, J., & Udry, C. (2005). *Rural Financial Markets in Developing Countries, Economic Growth Centre.* Yale University, and Centre Discussion Paper No. 914.

Cooke, E. F., & Amuakwa-Mensah, F. (2022). Microfinance loans, women's economic empowerment, and poverty: A case study of Baobab Microfinance Company. *Journal of Development Effectiveness*, *14*(1), 34–55. doi:10.1080/19439342.2021.1953568

Copestake. (2015). *Towards a plural history of microfinance*. Bath Papers in International Development and Wellbeing Working Paper No.40. http://www.bath.ac.uk/cds/

Cornejo, J., & McBride, W. (2002). *Adoption of Bioengineered Crops*. Agricultural Economics Report No. 810. Academic Press.

Cull, R., & Hartarska, V. (2023). Overview of microfinance, financial inclusion, and development. Handbook of microfinance, financial inclusion and development, 2-19.

Cull, R., Demirgüç-Kunt, A., & Morduch, J. (2007). Financial performance and outreach: A global analysis of leading microbanks. *Economic Journal (London)*, *117*(517), F107–F133. doi:10.1111/j.1468-0297.2007.02017.x

D'espallier, B., Guérin, I., & Mersland, R. (2013). Focus on Women in Microfinance Institutions. *The Journal of Development Studies*, *49*(5), 589–608. doi:10.1080/00220388.2012.720364

Dai, X., Qian, S., & Zhang, J. (2022). *Sustainable financial inclusion as a source of green environment? Evidence from selected regional comprehensive economic partnership countries.* Economic Research-Ekonomska Istraživanja., doi:10.1080/1331677X.2022.2035244

Dangi, N. (2014). Women entrepreneurship and growth and performance of MSMEs in India. *International Journal (Toronto, Ont.)*, *2*(4), 174–182.

Danso-Abbeam, G., Ansah, I. G. K., & Ehiakpor, D. S. (2014). Microfinance and Micro-Small-Medium Scale Enterprises (MSME's) in Kasoa Municipality, Ghana. *British Journal of Economics, Management and Trade*, *4*(12), 1939–1956.

Datta, S., & Sahu, T. N. (2022). How far is microfinance relevant for empowering rural women? An empirical investigation. *Journal of Economic Issues*, *56*(1), 97–112. doi:10.1080/00213624.2022.2019552

Dawuni, P., Mabe, F. N., & Tahidu, O. D. (2021). Effects of Village Savings and Loan Association on Agricultural Value Productivity in Northern Region of Ghana. *Agricultural Finance Review*, *81*(5), 657–674. doi:10.1108/AFR-02-2020-0024

De Soto. (2000). *The Mystery of Capital: Why Capitalism Triumphs in the West and Fails Everywhere Else*. Academic Press.

De Vita, L., Mari, M., & Poggesi, S. (2014). Women entrepreneurs in and from developing countries: Evidences from the literature. *European Management Journal*, *32*(3), 451–460. doi:10.1016/j.emj.2013.07.009

Debnath, D., Rahman, S., Acharjee, D. C., Latif, W. U., & Wang, L. (2019). Empowering Women through Microcredit in Bangladesh: An Empirical Study. *International Journal of Financial Studies,·7*(37), 1-11. https://www.researchgate.net/publication/334159798

Debnath, D., Rahman, M. S., Acharjee, D. C., Latif, W. U., & Wang, L. (2019). Empowering women through microcredit in Bangladesh: An empirical study. *International Journal of Financial Studies*, *7*(3), 37. doi:10.3390/ijfs7030037

Del Amo, I. F., Erkoyuncu, J. A., Roy, R., Palmarini, R., & Onoufriou, D. (2018). A systematic review of Augmented Reality content-related techniques for knowledge transfer in maintenance applications. *Computers in Industry*, *103*, 47–71. doi:10.1016/j.compind.2018.08.007

Demirgüç-Kunt, A., & Klapper, L. (2012). *Financial inclusion in Africa: An Overview*. World Bank Policy Research Working Paper WPS No. 6088.

Demirgüç-Kunt, A., Klapper, L. F., & Singer, D. (2013). Financial inclusion and legal discrimination against women: evidence from developing countries. *World Bank Policy Research Working Paper*, (6416).

Demurger, S., Fournier, M., & Yang, W. (2010). Rural households' decisions towards income diversification: Evidence from a township in northern China. *China Economic Review*, *21*, 32–44. doi:10.1016/j.chieco.2010.05.007

Deogharia, P. C. (2018). Diversification of Agriculture: A Review. *Journal of Economic and Social Development*, *14*(1), 46–59.

Department of Agrarian Reform (DAR). (2016). https://www.dar.gov.ph/

Department of Trade and Industry. (2019) *2019 MSME Statistics*. https://www.dti.gov.ph/resources/msme-statistics/

Dermish, A., Kneiding, C., Leishman, P., & Mas, I. (2011). Branchless and mobile banking solutions for the poor: A Survey. *Innovations*, *6*(4).

Dey, A., Majumdar, K. K., Chakraborty, A. K., & Mandal, A. K. (2018). Women Empowerment in India–A Perspective. *Community Medicine*, *9*(8), 574–579.

Dhaoui, I. (2015). *The role of Islamic Microfinance in Poverty Alleviation: Lessons from Bangladesh Experience*. https://mpra.ub.uni-muenchen.de/87358/

Di Falco, S., Veronesi, M., & Yesuf, M. (2011). Does Adaptation to Climate Change Provide Food Security? A Micro-Perspective from Ethiopia. *American Journal of Agricultural Economics*, *93*(3), 829–846. doi:10.1093/ajae/aar006

Diochon, M., & Ghore, Y. (2016). Contextualizing a social enterprise opportunity process in an emerging market. *Social Enterprise Journal*, *12*(2), 107–130. doi:10.1108/SEJ-11-2015-0032

Doepke, M., Tertilt, M., & Voena, A. (2012). The Economics and Politics of Women's Rights. *Annual Review of Economics*, *4*(1), 339–372. doi:10.1146/annurev-economics-061109-080201

Dorward, A. (2009). Integrating contested aspirations, processes and policy: Development as hanging in, stepping up and stepping out. *Development Policy Review*, *27*(2), 131–146. doi:10.1111/j.1467-7679.2009.00439.x

Dotsey, S. (2022). COVID-19 and Microcredit: Dissecting an NGO's Training, Financial Support, and Women Empowerment Programmes. *Social Sciences (Basel, Switzerland)*, *11*(9), 402. doi:10.3390ocsci11090402

Dücan, E., & Polat, M. A. (2017). Kadın istihdamının ekonomik büyümeye etkisi: OECD ülkeleri için panel veri analizi. *Çukurova Üniversitesi Sosyal Bilimler Enstitüsü Dergisi, 26*(1), 155-170.

Duncombe, R., & Boateng, R. (2009). Mobile phones and financial services in developing countries: A review of concepts, methods, issues, evidence and future research directions. *Third World Quarterly, 30*(7), 1237–1258. doi:10.1080/01436590903134882

Dündar, O. (2007). *Mikro Finansman. Türkiye Kalkınma Bankası Ekonomik ve Sosyal Araştırmalar Müdürlüğü.* http://www.kalkinma.com.tr/data/file/raporlar/ESA/ga/2007-GA/GA-07-05-28_Mikro_Finansman.pdf

Durukan, L. (2021). Türkiye'de kadın girişimcilerin desteklenmesinde KOSGEB'in rolü. *Gazi İktisat ve İşletme Dergisi, 7*(1), 17–37.

Duvendack, M., Palmer-Jones, R., Copestake, J. G., Hooper, L., Loke, Y., & Rao, N. (2011). *What is the evidence of the impact of microfinance on the well-being of poor people? The EPPI-Centre, Social Science Research Unit, Institute of Education.* University of London.

Ebrahim, C., Jack, A., & Jones, L. (2021). Women's economic empowerment and COVID-19: The case of vulnerable women with intersectional identities in Indonesia and Vietnam. *Enterprise Development & Microfinance, 32*(1), 44–56. doi:10.3362/1755-1986.21-00007

Ebrahimi, R., Choobchian, S., Farhadian, H., Goli, I., Farmandeh, E., & Azadi, H. (2022). Investigating the effect of vocational education and training on rural women's empowerment. *Humanities & Social Sciences Communications, 9*(1), 1. Advance online publication. doi:10.105741599-022-01187-4

Ehigiamusoe, G. (2008). The role of microfinance institutions in the economic development of Nigeria. *Publication of the Central Bank of Nigeria, 32*(1), 17–25.

Ellis, A. (2007). *Gender and economic growth in Tanzania: Creating opportunities for women.* World Bank Publications.

Ellis, F. (1998). Household strategies and rural livelihood diversification'. *The Journal of Development Studies, 35*(1), 1–38. doi:10.1080/00220389808422553

Ellis, F. (2000). *Rural Livelihoods and Diversity in Developing Countries.* Oxford University Press.

Ellis, F. (2000). The determinants of rural livelihood diversification in developing countries. *Journal of Agricultural Economics, 51*(2), 289–302. doi:10.1111/j.1477-9552.2000.tb01229.x

Ellis, F. (2006). Agrarian change and rising vulnerability in rural sub-Saharan Africa. *New Political Economy, 11*(3), 387–397. doi:10.1080/13563460600841025

Erdoğan, S., & Yaşar, S. (2018). Türkiye'de kadın istihdamının gelişimi: Konya-Karaman örneği. *Karamanoğlu Mehmetbey Üniversitesi Sosyal ve Ekonomik Araştırmalar Dergisi, 20*(34), 18–28.

Ershov, B. A., Perevozchikova, L. S., & Romanova, E. V. (2019). Globalization and intensification of spiritual values in Russia in the philosophical aspect. *6th International Conference on Education and Social Sciences Abstracts & Proceedings*, 208-212.

Eswaran, M., & Kotwal, A. (1990). Implications of Credit Constraints for Risk Behavior. Oxford Economic Papers. *New Series, 42*(2), 473–482.

European Institute for Gender Equality (EIGE). (2016). *Gender equality training: Gender mainstreaming toolkit.* Author.

Eurostat. (2020). *Women's Employment in the EU.* https://ec.europa.eu/eurostat/en/web/products-eurostat-news/-/edn-20200306-1

Eurostat. (2022). *More Women Than Men Outside the Labour Fource*. https://ec.europa.eu/eurostat/en/web/products-eurostat-news/-/ddn-20220622-1

Eyüboğlu, A., Özer, Ş., & Tanrıöver, T. (2000). Kentlerde kadınların iş yaşamına katılım sorunlarının sosyo-ekonomik ve kültürel boyutları. Başbakanlık K.S.S.G.M. Yayınları.

Fadikpe, A. A. A., Danquah, R., Aidoo, M., Chomen, D. A., Yankey, R., & Dongmei, X. (2022). Linkages between social and financial performance: Evidence from Sub-Saharan Africa microfinance institutions. *PLoS One*, *17*(3), e0261326. doi:10.1371/journal.pone.0261326 PMID:35231026

Fallah, B., Bergolo, M., Saadeh, I., Abu Hashhash, A., & Hattawy, M. (2021). The Effect of Labour-Demand Shocks on Women's Participation in the Labor Force: Evidence from Palestine. *The Journal of Development Studies*, *57*(3), 400–416. doi:10.1080/00220388.2020.1806246

Family Code of the Philippines. (1987). *Property relations between husband and wife*. Executive Order No. 209.

Feder, G., Lau, L. J., Lin, J. Y., & Luo, X. (1990). The Relationship Between Credit and Productivity in Chinese Agriculture: A Microeconomic Model of Disequilibrium. *American Journal of Agricultural Economics*, *72*(5), 1151–1157. doi:10.2307/1242524

Feder, G., & Umali, D. L. (1993). The Adoption of Agricultural Innovations: A Review. *Technological Forecasting and Social Change*, *43*(3-4), 215–239. doi:10.1016/0040-1625(93)90053-A

Fernandez, M. R. (2003, October). *Dynamics of communication of women involved in microfinance projects: A model for women empowerment* [Unpublished Dissertation]. College of Mass Communication, University of the Philippines, Diliman.

Fernandez, M. R. (2002). Dynamics of communication of women involved in microfinance projects. *Danyag. Journal of the Humanities and Social Sciences, 7*(2), 161–172.

Fidan, F. & Yeşil, Y. (2014). Türkiye'de kadınların ekonomiye kazandırılması açısından mikro kredi: Bilecik örneği. *Girişimcilik ve Kalkınma Dergisi, 9*(2), 253-270.

Folayan, M. O. B. (2020). *Women's economic empowerment, participation in decision making and exposure to violence as risk indicators for early childhood caries*. Academic Press.

Frediani, A. A., Clark, D. A., & Biggeri, M. (2019). Human Development and the Capability Approach: The Role of Empowerment and Participation. In The Capability Approach, Empowerment and Participation: Concepts, Methods and Applications (pp. 3-36). London: Palgrave Macmillan.

Freeman, H. A., Simeon, K. E., & Jabar, M. A. (1998). Credit Constraints and Smallholder Dairy Production in the East African highlands: Application of a Switching Regression Model. *Agricultural Economics*, *19*(1-2), 33–44. doi:10.1111/j.1574-0862.1998.tb00512.x

Fundie, A. M. S., Chisoro, C., & Karodia, A. M. (2015). The Challenges Facing Informal Traders in the Hilbrow Area of Johannesburg. *Kuwait Chapter of the Arabian Journal of Business and Management Review*, *4*(6), 46–75. doi:10.12816/0018968

Gabor, D., & Brooks, S. (2017). The digital revolution in financial inclusion: International development in the fintech era. *New Political Economy*, *22*(4), 423–436. doi:10.1080/13563467.2017.1259298

Gálvez-Sánchez, F.J., Lara-Rubio, J., Verdú-Jóver, A.J., & Meseguer-Sánchez, V. (2013) Research Advances on Financial Inclusion: A Bibliometric Analysis. *Sustainability, 13*, 3156. doi:10.3390/su13063156

Gardiner, K., & Miller, J. (2006). How Low-Paid Employees Avoid Poverty: An Analysis by Family Type and Household Structure. *Journal of Social Policy*, *35*(3), 351–369. doi:10.1017/S0047279406009822

Geetha, P. (2019). A Study on Women Entrepreneurs Awareness about Government Schemes-Special Reference to Kanniyakumari District. *Worldwide Diary of Business and Management Invention*, *8*(2), 1–7.

GEM (Global Entrepreneurship Monitoring). (2017). *Women's Entrepreneurship 2016/2017 Report*. GEM.

Gerard, K., & Johnston, M. (2019). Explaining microfinance's resilience: The case of microfinance in Australia. *Globalizations*, *16*(6), 876–893. doi:10.1080/14747731.2018.1560188

Ghana Statistical Service (2021). *2021 Population and Housing Census - Regional Analytical Report-Northern Region Census Report*. Author.

Ghana Statistical Service. (2008). *Ghana Living Standards Survey.* Report Number 5. Government of Ghana.

Ghosh, S., & Vinod, D. (2017). What constrains financial inclusion for women? Evidence from Indian micro data. *World Development*, *92*, 60–81. doi:10.1016/j.worlddev.2016.11.011

Göcen, S. (2020). Ekonomik Gelişme ve Kadın İş Gücü İstihdamı: Türkiye İçin Nedensellik İlişkisi İncelemesi. *Uluslararası İktisadi ve İdari İncelemeler Dergisi*, (29), 45–60.

Godquin, M. (2006). Finance rurale au Bangladesh et aux Philippines [Rural finance in Bangladesh and the Philippines]. In *Economies et finances.* Université Panthéon-Sorbonne - Paris I.

Goetz, A. M., & Gupta, R. S. (1996). Who takes the credit? Gender, power, and control over loan use in rural credit programs in Bangladesh. *World Development*, *24*(1), 45–63. doi:10.1016/0305-750X(95)00124-U

Gökakın, Z. Ö. (2000). *Doksanlı Yılların Yeni Kahramanları: Türkiye'de Girişimci Kadın Profili* (Vol. 8). Yönetim ve Organizasyon Kongresi Bildiriler Kitabı.

Gökyay, Ç. (2008). *Türkiye'de Mikro Kredi Uygulamaları ve İsdihdama Yansımaları*. T.C. Çalışma ve Sosyal Güvenlik Bakanlığı, Türkiye İş Kurumu Genel Müdürlüğü.

Gökyay, Ç. (2008). *Türkiye'de mikro kredi uygulamaları ve istihdama yansımaları [Uzmanlık Tezi]*. Çalışma ve Sosyal Güvenlik Bakanlığı Türkiye İş Kurumu Genel Müdürlüğü.

Gonçalves, E., Castro, J., Araújo, J., & Heineck, T. (2018). A systematic literature review of iStar extensions. *Journal of Systems and Software*, *2018*(137), 1–33. doi:10.1016/j.jss.2017.11.023

Goyal, P., & Yadav, V. (2014). To be or not to be a woman entrepreneur in a developing country? *Psychosociological Issues in Human Resource Management*, *2*(2), 68–78.

Grameen Bank. (1986). *Grameen bank: A bank for the poor.* Dhaka: Grameen Bank Grameen Foundation. https://grameenfoundation.org/

Grant, M. J., & Booth, A. (2009). A typology of review: An analysis of 14 review types and associated methodologies. *Health Information and Libraries Journal*, *26*(2), 91–108. doi:10.1111/j.1471-1842.2009.00848.x PMID:19490148

Greene, W. H. (2003). *Econometric analysis*. Pearson Education India.

Greene, W. H. (2008). *Econometric Analysis* (6th ed.). Pearson.

Gries, T., & Naudé, W. A. (2010). Entrepreneurship and Structural Economic Transformation. *Small Business Economics*, *34*(1), 13–29. doi:10.100711187-009-9192-8

GSM Association. (2015). *Bridging the Gender Gap: Mobile Access and Usage in Low- and Middle-income Countries.* Academic Press.

Guillen, L., Mayo, M., & Karelaia, N. (2018). Appearing self-confident and getting credit for it: Why it may be easier for men than women to gain influence at work. *Human Resource Management, 57*(4), 839–854. doi:10.1002/hrm.21857

Gujarati, D. M. (2006). *Essentials of Econometrics* (3rd ed.). McGraw Hill International.

Gülcan, C. (2021). Nitel Bir Veri Toplama Araci: Odak (Focus) Grup Tekniğinin Uygulanişi Ve Geçerliliği Üzerine Bir Çalişma. *Mersin Üniversitesi Sosyal Bilimler Enstitüsü Dergisi, 4*(2), 94–109.

Gundry, L. K., Ben-Yoseph, M., & Posig, M. (2002). Contemporary perspectives on women's entrepreneurship: A review and strategic recommendations. *Journal of Enterprising Culture, 10*(1), 67–86. doi:10.1142/S0218495802000141

Gupta, I., & Roy, A. (2023). What really empowers women? Taking another look at economic empowerment. *Journal of Social and Economic Development, 25*(1), 17–31. doi:10.100740847-022-00215-y

Hagen, E. E. (1963). *How economic growth begins: a theory of social change. University of Illinois at Urbana-Champaign's Academy for Entrepreneurial Leadership Historical Research Reference in Entrepreneurship.* Free Press.

Haggblade, S., Hazell, P., & Reardon, T. (2010). The rural non-farm economy: Prospects for growth and poverty reduction. *World Development, 38*(10), 1429–1441. doi:10.1016/j.worlddev.2009.06.008

Hammawa, Y., & Hashim, N. (2016). Women-micro entrepreneurs and sustainable economic development in Nigeria. *IOSR Journal of Business and Management, 18*(1), 27 36.

Hanson, S., & Blake, M. (2009). Gender and entrepreneurial networks. *Regional Studies, 43*(1), 135–149. doi:10.1080/00343400802251452

Haritha, M., & Prasad Reddy, A. (2023). *Microfinance, Financial Inclusion & Women Empowerment.* https://ssrn.com/abstract=4399783

Hasan, M., Le, T., & Hoque, A. (2021). How does financial literacy impact on inclusive finance? *Financial Innovation, 7*(1), 1–23. doi:10.118640854-021-00259-9

Haspolat, E. (2010). *Neoliberalizmin kalkınma söylemi ve yoksullukla mücadele yöntemi olarak mikro kredi: Örnek ülke deneyimleri ve Türkiye [Yüksek Lisans Tezi].* Gazi Üniversitesi Sosyal Bilimler Enstitüsü.

Hausman, J. A. (1983). Specification and Estimation of Simultaneous Equation Models. In Z. Griliches & M. Intriligator (Eds.), *Handbook of econometrics*. North Holland Press. doi:10.1016/S1573-4412(83)01011-9

Hendriks, S. (2019). The role of financial inclusion in driving women's economic empowerment. *Development in Practice, 29*(8), 1029–1038. doi:10.1080/09614524.2019.1660308

Hennink, M., Kiiti, N., Pillinger, M., & Jayakaran, R. (2012). Defining empowerment: Perspectives from international development organisations. *Development in Practice, 22*(2), 202–215. doi:10.1080/09614524.2012.640987

Hermes, N., & Lensink, R. (2007). The empirics of microfinance: What do we know? *Economic Journal (London), 117*(517), F1–F10. doi:10.1111/j.1468-0297.2007.02013.x

Hilson, G., & Garforth, C. (2012). 'Agricultural poverty' and the expansion of artisal mining in Sub-Saharan Africa: Experiences from Southwest Mali and Southeast Ghana. *Population Research and Policy Review, 31*(2).

Hilson, G. (2002). The environmental impact of small-scale gold mining in Ghana: Identifying problems and possible solution. *The Geographical Journal, 168*(1), 57–72. doi:10.1111/1475-4959.00038

Hilson, G. (2009). Small-scale mining, poverty and economic development in sub-Saharan Africa: An overview. *Resources Policy*, *34*(1-2), 1–5. doi:10.1016/j.resourpol.2008.12.001

Hilson, G. (2010). Once a miner, always a miner: Poverty and livelihood diversification in Akwatia, Ghana. *Journal of Rural Studies*, *26*(3), 296–307. doi:10.1016/j.jrurstud.2010.01.002

Hilson, G. (2020). Formalization Bubbles: A Blueprint for Sustainable Artisanal and Small-Scale Mining (ASM) in Sub-Saharan Africa. *The Extractive Industries and Society*, *7*(4), 1624–1638. doi:10.1016/j.exis.2020.11.001

Hirano, K., & Imbens, G. W. (2004). The Propensity score with Continuous Treatments. Applied Bayesian Modeling and Causal Inference from incomplete-data. *Perspectives*, *226164*, 73–84.

Hisrich, R. D., & Peters, M. P. (1998). Enterpreneurship (4th ed.). Academic Press.

Hisrich, R. D., Peters, M. P., & Shepherd, D. A. (2008). *Entrepreneurship* (7th ed.). McGraw-Hill Co. Inc.

Holland, J. H. (2018). The global economy as an adaptive process. In *The economy as an evolving complex system* (pp. 117–124). CRC Press. doi:10.1201/9780429492846-7

Holloway, K., Niazi, Z., & Rouse, R. (2017). Women's economic empowerment through financial inclusion: A review of existing evidence and remaining knowledge gaps. *Innovations for Poverty Action.*

Holman, M. R. (2017). Women in local government: What we know and where we go from here. *State & Local Government Review*, *49*(4), 285–296. doi:10.1177/0160323X17732608

Holmberg, J., & Sandbrook, R. (2019). Sustainable development: what is to be done? In *Policies for a small planet* (pp. 19–38). Routledge. doi:10.4324/9780429200465-1

Huang, J., Sherraden, M., Sherraden, M. S., & Johnson, L. (2022). Effective finance to increase financial well-being for low-income families: Empirical examination and policy implications. *The Journal of Consumer Affairs*, *56*(4), 1638–1657. doi:10.1111/joca.12484

Hudak, K. (2012). 'What next for micro-finance? How the broader financial context matters for effective micro0finance outreach'. *Journal of Developmental Entrepreneurship*, *17*(4), 1–19. doi:10.1142/S1084946712500239

Hulme, D., & Maitrot, M. (2014). Has Microfinance Lost Its Moral Compass? *Economic and Political Weekly*, *49*(48), 77–85.

Hussain, A., & Thapa, G. B. (2015). Fungibility of Smallholder Agricultural Credit: Empirical Evidence from Pakistan. *European Journal of Development Research.*

IFAD. (2003). *Ghana: Women's access to formal financial services.* Retrieved from https://www.ifad.org/gender/learning/sector/finance/42.htm

Ife, J. (2016). *Community Development in an Uncertain World* (2nd ed.). Cambridge University Press. doi:10.1017/CBO9781316342855

Iiyama, M. (2006). *Livelihoods diversification patterns among households and their implications on poverty and resource use: A case study from a Kerio River Basin Community.* LUCID Working Paper Series 51.

Imran, M., Ul Haq, S., & Ozcatalbas, O. (2022). Role of Microcredit in Sustainable Rural Development. In *Sustainable Rural Development Perspective and Global Challenges* (pp. 1-22). London: IntechOpen.

Iyanda, J. O., Afolami, C. A., Obayelu, A. E., & Ladebo, O. J. (2014). Social Capital and Access to Credit among Cassava Farming Households in Ogun State, Nigeria. *Journal of Agriculture and Environmental Sciences*, *3*(2), 175–196.

Janmejaya, S., & Neeraj, A. (2011). *Financial Inclusion: From Obligation to Opportunity*. Boston Consulting Group Publications.

Jarecke, J., Taylor, E. W., & Hira, T. K. (2014). Financial literacy education for women. *New Directions for Adult and Continuing Education*, *2014*(141), 37–46. doi:10.1002/ace.20083

Jennings, J. E., & Brush, C. G. (2013). Research on women entrepreneurs: Challenges to (and from) the broader entrepreneurship literature? *The Academy of Management Annals*, *7*(1), 663–715. doi:10.5465/19416520.2013.782190

Jindal, M. K., & Bhardwaj, A. (2016). Entrepreneurship development in India: A new paradigm. *Proceedings of the world congress on engineering*, *2*, 724-726.

Jocano, F. L. (1997). *Filipino value system: A cultural definition*. PUNLAD Research House, Inc.

Johnson, S. (2004). Gender norms in financial markets: Evidence from Kenya. *World Development*, *32*(8), 1355–1374. doi:10.1016/j.worlddev.2004.03.003

Johnson, S. (2019). *Globalization and gender-dilemmas for microfinance organizations*. Small Enterprise Development.

Junare, S. O., & Singh, R. (2016). Technological Understanding and Usage vis-à-vis Knowledge of Government Schemes–A Study of Women Entrepreneurs of Selected Cities of Gujarat. *American Journal of Entrepreneurship*, *1*(1), 71–85.

Kabakçı, E. (2012). *Mikro kredinin kadın yoksulluğunu azaltmadaki rolü ve Eskişehir uygulaması [Yüksek Lisans Tezi]*. Anadolu Üniversitesi Sosyal Bilimler Enstitüsü.

Kabeer, N. (1999). Resources, agency, achievements: Reflections on the measurement of women's empowerment. *Development and Change*, *30*(3), 435–464. doi:10.1111/1467-7660.00125

Kabunga, N. S., Dubois, T., & Qaim, M. (2012). Yield effects of tissue culture Bananas in Kenya: Accounting for selection bias and the role of complementary inputs. *Journal of Agricultural Economics*, *62*(2), 444–464. doi:10.1111/j.1477-9552.2012.00337.x

Kagan, J. (2023). *Microfinance Definition: Benefits, History, and How It Works*. https://www.investopedia.com/terms/m/microfinance.asp#citation-20

Kagider. (2023). *KAGİDER Hakkında*. https://kagider.org/tr/kurumsal/hakkimizda

Karabıyık, İ. (2012). Türkiye'de çalışma hayatında kadın istihdamı. *Marmara Üniversitesi İİBF Dergisi, 32,* 231-260.

Karapınar, K. (2010). *Türkiye'de yerel kalkınma modeli olarak mikrofinans sistemi: Bursa örneği* [Master's thesis]. Çanakkale Onsekiz Mart Üniversitesi Sosyal Bilimler Enstitüsü.

Karatas, A., & Helvacioglu, A. D. (2008, October). The microcredit strategies for SMEs in Turkey in the EU Harmonization Process. In *8th Global Conference on Business and Economics* (pp. 18-19). Academic Press.

Karim, L. (2014). Analyzing Women's Empowerment. *Microfinance and Garment Labor in Bangladesh.*, *38*(2), 153–166.

Karl, E. N. (2017). Empowerment of youths in rural areas through agricultural development programmes: Implications for poverty reduction in South Africa. *Journal of Research in Agriculture and Forestry, 212.*

Karlan, D., & Zinman, J. (2011). Microcredit in Theory and Practice: Using Randomized Credit Scoring for Impact Evaluation. *Science*, *332*(6035), 1278–1284. doi:10.1126cience.1200138 PMID:21659596

Karlsson, C., Johansson, B., & Stough, R. (2009). *Entrepreneurship and Development – Local Processes and Global Patterns. Cesis WP 160*. The Royal Institute of Technology.

Karnani, A. (2007). Do Women Benefit from Microcredit. *The Perspective of Women's Entrepreneurship in the Age of Globalization*, 129.

Kassie, M., Pender, J., Yesuf, M., Kohlin, G., Bluffstone, R., & Mulugeta, E. (2008). Estimating Returns to Soil Conservation Adoption in the Northern Ethiopian Highlands. *Agricultural Economics*, *38*(2), 213–232. doi:10.1111/j.1574-0862.2008.00295.x

Katherine, E. (2017). Lessons from Muhammad Yunus and the Grameen Bank: Leading Long-Term Organizational Change Successfully. In S. A. Tirmizi & J. D. Vogelsang (Eds.), *Leading and Managing in the Social Sector: Strategies for Advancing Human Dignity and Social Justice* (pp. 31–39). Springer.

Katoch, G. (2018). A Khadi and Village Industries Commission: Role, Challenges and Opportunity Ahead. *Pacific Business Review International*, *11*(2), 79–87.

Kato, M. P., & Kratzer, J. (2013). Empowering women through Microfinance: Evidence from Tanzania. *ACRN Journal of Entrepreneurship Perspectives.*, *2*(1), 31–59.

Katuwang Resource Center, Inc. (KRCI). (n.d.). *Microfinance*. https://www.katuwang.com/services/microfinance

Kavak, Y. (1997). Eğitim, İstihdam ve İşsizlik İlişkileri. *Hacettepe Üniversitesi Eğitim Fakültesi Dergisi*, *13*(13), 21–26.

Kazi, S., Raza, B., & Al-Jalaly, S. Z. (2015). Rural Women's Access to Credit and Extension: A Strategy for Change. *Pakistan Development Review*, *34*(4), 753–765.

Kedv. (2023). *KEDV Hakkında*. https://www.kedv.org.tr/kedv-hakkinda

Kevane, M., & Wydick, B. (2001). Microenterprise Lending to Female Entrepreneurs: Sacrificing Economic Growth for Poverty Alleviation? *World Development*, *29*(7), 1225–1236. doi:10.1016/S0305-750X(01)00032-8

Khan, S. T., Bhat, M. A., & Sangmi, M.-U.-D. (2022). Can microfinance-backed entrepreneurship be a holistic empowerment tool for women? Empirical evidence from Kashmir Valley, India. *Journal of Business and Socio-Economic Development*, 117-136.

Khursheed, A. (2022). Exploring the role of microfinance in women's empowerment and entrepreneurial development: A qualitative study. *Future Business Journal*, *8*(1), 1-13. https://www.ncbi.nlm.nih.gov/pmc/articles/PMC9735224/

Khursheed, A. (2022). Exploring the role of microfinance in women's empowerment and entrepreneurial development: A qualitative study. *Future Business Journal*, *8*(1), 57. doi:10.118643093-022-00172-2

Kibaara, B. (2006). *Rural Financial Services in Kenya: What is Working and Why*. Tegemeo Working paper (25).

Kılıç, S. (2013). Örnekleme yöntemleri. *Journal of Mood Disorders*, *3*(1), 44–60. doi:10.5455/jmood.20130325011730

Kiunga, C. (2019). *Effects of Micro-credit Programs on Women Economic Empowerment: a Case of Kajiado North Sub-County (2005-2018)* [Doctoral dissertation]. University of Nairobi.

Kocabaş, İ. Ü., & Küçükbay, F. (2023). Türkiye'de Kadınların İşgücüne Katılım Oranını Etkileyen Faktörlerin Ekonometrik Analizi. *Hak İş Uluslararası Emek ve Toplum Dergisi*, *12*(32), 29–51. doi:10.31199/hakisderg.1202393

Kocher, A. (1997). An Empirical Investigation of Rationing Constraints in Rural Credit Markets in Indian. *Journal of Development Economics*, *53*(2), 339–371. doi:10.1016/S0304-3878(97)00020-5

Kolovich, M. (2018). Fiscal policies and gender equality. In L. Kolovich (Ed.), *Fiscal Policies and Gender Equality* (pp. 1–8). International Monetary Fund.

Konadu, A., & Biney-Assan, A. B. (2007). *The Role of Microfinance in the Empowerment of Women-An Example of Sinapi Aba Trust, Offinso Branch-Ghana* [Master's thesis]. Høgskolen i Agder.

Korkmaz, A. N., & Budak, S. (2022). Ekonomik (İktisadi) Kalkınma ve Kadın: Türkiye Örneği. *Mehmet Akif Ersoy Üniversitesi Uygulamalı Bilimler Dergisi, 6*(1), 197–223. doi:10.31200/makuubd.1084496

Kretzmann, J. P., & McKnight, J. P. (1993). *Asset-based community development: Building communities from the inside out.* ACTA Publications.

Ksgm. (2023). *Projelerimiz.* https://www.aile.gov.tr/Ksgm/Faaliyetler/Projelerimiz/

KTB. (2022). *Samsun İl Kültür ve Turizm Müdürlüğü.* https://samsun.ktb.gov.tr/TR-59811/ekonomi---sanayi---ticaret.html

Kuchibhotla, R. (2020). Self-Help Groups-Transforming Lives, Promoting & Sustain Women Empowerment. *The Management Accountant, 55*(3), 28–31.

Kulkarni, L., & Ghosh, A. (2021). Gender disparity in the digitalization of financial services: Challenges and promises for women's financial inclusion in India. *Gender, Technology and Development, 25*(2), 233–250. doi:10.1080/09718524.2021.1911022

Kumari, J. A. P. (2021). Instrument development of microfinance on poverty reduction: Pilot study in Sri Lankan microfinance sector. *Himalayan Journal of Economics and Business Management, 2*(2), 8–16.

Kumar, N., Raghunathan, K., Arrieta, A., Amir, J., & Pandey, S. (2021). The power of the collective empowers women: Evidence from self-help groups in India. *World Development, 146*, 105579. doi:10.1016/j.worlddev.2021.105579 PMID:34602708

Kumar, S. (2022). *Financial Inclusion of Women: Current Evidence from India. ORF Issue Brief No. 600.* Observer Research Foundation.

Kuratko, D. F. (2009). The entrepreneurial imperative of the 21st century. *Business Horizons, 52*(5), 421–428. doi:10.1016/j.bushor.2009.04.006

Kusi, A., Yussif, S., & Ismail, A. (2019). Access to micro credit by women entrepreneurs in Ghana: Sinapi aba Trust-Kumasi in retrospect. *International Journal of Academic Research in Business & Social Sciences, 9*(9), 590–613. doi:10.6007/IJARBSS/v9-i9/6336

Kwiatkowski, D., Phillips, P. C., Schmidt, P., & Shin, Y. (1992). Testing the null hypothesis of stationarity against the alternative of a unit root: How sure are we that economic time series have a unit root? *Journal of Econometrics, 54*(1-3), 159–178. doi:10.1016/0304-4076(92)90104-Y

Kyaruzi, I. S., & Markovic, M. R. (2009). *Female Entrepreneursip and Local Economic Growth.* Outskirt Press.

Kyrgidou, L. P., & Petridou, E. (2013). Developing women entrepreneurs' knowledge, skills, and attitudes through e-mentoring support. *Journal of Small Business and Enterprise Development, 20*(3), 548–566. doi:10.1108/JSBED-04-2013-0061

Lee, L. (1978). Unionism and Wage Rates: A simultaneous Equation Model with Qualitative and Limited Dependent Variables. *International Economic Review, 19*(2), 415–433. doi:10.2307/2526310

Le, L. H., & Stefanczyk, J. K. (2018). Gender discrimination in access to credit: Are women-led SMEs rejected more than men-led? *Gender, Technology and Development, 22*(2), 145–163. doi:10.1080/09718524.2018.1506973

Li, X., Christopher, G., & Hu, B. (2011). The Credit Programme: A Case Study from Impact of Microcredit on Women's Empower- Bangladesh: Evidence from China. *Journal of Chinese Economic and Business Studies, 9*, 239–261. doi:10.1080/14765284.2011.592352

Lokshin, M., & Sajaia, Z. (2004). Maximum Likelihood Estimation of Endogenous Switching Regression Models. *The Stata Journal*, *4*(3), 282–289. doi:10.1177/1536867X0400400306

Loza, E. (2017). Female entrepreneurship theory: A multidisciplinary review of resources. *JWEE*, (1-2), 26–64.

Luo, W., & Cheng, J. (2022). Transition to sustainable business models for green economic recovery: Role of financial literacy, innovation and environmental sustainability. *Economic Change and Restructuring*, 1–24. doi:10.100710644-022-09408-1

Lusardi, A., & de Bassa Scheresberg, C. (2017). *Financial capability and financial literacy among working women: New insights*. Academic Press.

Lyoussi, D., & Kouchih, A. (2023). Metaverse and Financial Inclusion Opportunities and Risks for the Banking Ecosystem. In *Influencer Marketing Applications Within the Metaverse* (pp. 205–224). IGI Global. doi:10.4018/978-1-6684-8898-0.ch013

Mabrouk, F., Bousrih, J., Elhaj, M., Binsuwadan, J., & Alofaysan, H. (2023). Empowering Women through Digital Financial Inclusion: Comparative Study before and after COVID-19. *Sustainability (Basel)*, *15*(12), 9154. doi:10.3390u15129154

Maclure, L. (2022). Augmentations to the Asset-Based Community Development Model to Target Power Systems. Taylor & Francis.

Maddala, G. (1983). *Limited Dependent and Qualitative Variables in Econometrics*. Cambridge University Press. doi:10.1017/CBO9780511810176

Madhavi, A. L. (2011). Financial Inclusion: Options for Micro, Small and Medium Enterprises. Synergy, 9(2).

Mahajan, S. S., & Kamble, C. B. (2011). Government support to women entrepreneurship: A study of programmes implemented by MAVIM. *Indian Streams Research Journal*, *1*(11), 130–134.

Mainsah, E, Heuer, S.R, Kalra, A & Zhang, Q. (2004). Grameen Bank: Taking capitalism to the poor. *Chazen Web Journal of International Business*.

Maîtrot, M., & Niño-Zarazúa, M. (2017). *Poverty and wellbeing impacts of microfinance: What do we know?* (WIDER Working Paper 2017/190). United Nations University. https://www.wider.unu.edu/sites/default/files/Publications/Working-paper/PDF/wp2017-190.pdf

Maity, S. (2023). Financial inclusion also leads to social inclusion—Myth or reality? Evidences from self-help groups led microfinance of Assam. *Journal of Innovation and Entrepreneurship*, *12*(1), 42. doi:10.118613731-023-00307-x

Malhotra, A., Schuler, S. R., & Boender, C. (2002). Measuring Women's Empowerment as a Variable in International Development. *Workshop on Poverty and Gender: New Perspectives, 28.* 10.1037/e597202012-004

Manda, J., Alene, A. D., Gardebroek, C., Kassie, M., & Tembo, G. (2016). Adoption and impacts of sustainable agricultural practices on maize yields and incomes: Evidence from Rural Zambia. *Journal of Agricultural Economics*, *67*(1), 130–153. doi:10.1111/1477-9552.12127

Mandal, K. C. (2013, May). Concept and Types of Women Empowerment. In *International Forum of Teaching & Studies, 9*(2), 17-30.

Manshani, S., & Dubey, A. (2017). Startup Women in startup India: A study of women entrepreneurs in India. *International Journal of Business and Management*, *6*(4), 91–100.

Manzur, M. (2017). Impact of Non-Government Organisations and Microcredit Institutions on the Development of Bangladesh. *Political Science Undergraduate Review, 2*(2017), 30-35. https://journals.library.ualberta.ca/psur/index.php/psur/article/view/34/32

Marceno, S. (2018). Conditional Cash Transfers: Empowerment, Resilience and Good Behaviours in Development Policies. *Soft Power, 5*(1), 119–144.

Masuku, M.M., & Jili, N.N. (2019). Public service delivery in South Africa: The political influence at local government level. *Journal of Public Affairs*, 1-7

Mathew, A. (2019). *Women struggle to break down barriers to starting a business.* International Monetary Fund.

Mathur, P., & Agrawal, P. (2017). Self-help groups: a seed for intrinsic empowerment of Indian rural women. *Equality, Diversity and Inclusion: An International Journal.*

MavrinacS. C.ChinW. P. (2004). *Financial education for women in Asia Pacific.* doi:10.2139/ssrn.695042

McCann, J. (2013). *Electoral quotas for women: An international overview.* https://www.semanticscholar.org/paper/Electoral-quotas-for-women%3A-an-international-McCann/c4a06f4e4139807d8ee4239f7b05983816c7faff

McCarter, E. (2006). Women and microfinance: Why we should do more. *U. Md. LJ Race, Religion. Race, Gender & Class (Towson, Md.), 6*, 353.

McKinsey Global Institute Report. (2023). https://www.mckinsey.com/featured-insights/sustainable-inclusive-growth/future-of-america/financial-inclusion-and-sustainable-inclusive-growth-in-action

McKnight, J. (2017). *Asset-based community development: the essentials.* Asset-Based Community Development Institute.

McMichael, P. (2012). *Development and Social Change: A Global Perspective. Los Angela & London.* SAGE.

McMichael, P. (2012). *Development and Social Change: A Global Perspective.* SAGE.

MCPI Regular Members. (2002-2023). *Microfinance Council of the Philippines.* https://microfinancecouncil.org/regular-members/

McQuail, D., & Widahl, S. (1993). Communication models for the study of mass communications (2nd ed.). Longman Singapore Publishers (Pto.) Ltd.

Meena, R. (1992). Gender Research/Studies in Southern Africa: An Overview. In R. Meena (Ed.), Gender in Southern Africa: Conceptual and Theoretical Issues (pp. 15–87). Academic Press.

Mengista, W., Soromessa, T., & Legese, G. (2019). *Method for conducting systematic literature review and meta-analysis for environmental science research.* Elsevier B.V.

Meunier, F., Krylova, Y., & Ramalho, R. (2017). *Women's Entrepreneurship: How to Measure the Gap between New Female and Male Entrepreneurs?* World Bank Group, Policy Research Working Paper 8242. https://documents.worldbank.org/curated/en/704231510669093889/pdf/WPS8242.pdf

Mhlanga, D. (2022). COVID-19 and digital financial inclusion: Policies and innovation that can accelerate financial inclusion in a post-COVID world through fintech. *African Journal of Development Studies, 2022*(si2), 79.

Microcredit Summit Campaign. (2012). *State of the Microcredit Summit Campaign Report 2012.* A Project of Results of Educational Fund.

Milazzo, A., & Goldstein, M. (2019). Governance and women's economic and political participation: Power inequalities, formal constraints and norms. *The World Bank Research Observer, 34*(1), 34–64. doi:10.1093/wbro/lky006

Ministry of Housing & Urban Affairs. (2020). *Giving Impetus to the Women Entrepreneurs, Day -NULM Under Ministry of Housing and Urban Affairs Signs MoU with Amazon for E-Marketing of Products Made by Self Help Groups Across the Country*. PIB Delhi.

Ministry of Rural Development. (2023, June 28). *SHGs Profile Entry Status.* Retrieved from Aajeevika: https://nrlm.gov.in/shgReport.do?methodName=showIntensiveStateWiseReport

Ministry of State Administration. (2014). *Profile of the districts.* http://www.govnet.gov.mz/

Mishra, P. (2021). Local Governance and Poverty Reduction in India: The Role of Micro-Finance. *Turkish Online Journal of Qualitative Inquiry, 12*(10).

Mohammed, F., Boateng, S. D., & Freeman, C. (2022). Effect of Access to Microfinance Support on Growth of Women Agro-Processing Enterprises in the Northern Region of Ghana. *International Journal of Business and Management, 10*(3).

Mols, F., Haslam, S. A., Jetten, J., & Steffens, N. K. (2015). Why a nudge is not enough: A social identity critique of governance by stealth. *European Journal of Political Research, 54*(1), 81–98. doi:10.1111/1475-6765.12073

Moore, D. P., Buttner, E. H., Wong-MingJi, D. J., & Sullivan, S. E. (2017). *Women Entrepreneurs: Moving Beyond the Glass Ceiling*. Academic Press.

Mordeno, K. (2010). *Micro-finance: The path to poverty alleviation.* http//stjliblog.wordpress.com/category/essay/content

Morduch, J., & Haley, B. (2002). *Analysis of the effects of microfinance on poverty reduction.* NYU Wagner Working Paper, 1014.

Morduch, J. (1999). The Microfinance Schism. *World Development, 28*(4), 617–629. doi:10.1016/S0305-750X(99)00151-5

Motsholapheko, M. R., Kgathi, D. L., & Vanderpost, C. (2011). Rural livelihoods and household adaptation to extreme flooding in the Okavango Delta, Botswana. *Physics and Chemistry of the Earth, 36*, 984–995. doi:10.1016/j.pce.2011.08.004

Mphaka, P. L. (2017). *Strategies for Reducing Microfinance Loan Default in Low-Income Markets* [Doctoral dissertation]. Walden University.

Mpuga, P. (2010). Constraints in Access to and Demand for Rural Credit: Evidence from Uganda. *African Development Review, 22*(1), 115–148. doi:10.1111/j.1467-8268.2009.00230.x

Müftüoğlu, T., & Durukan, T. (2004). *Girişimcilik ve KOBİ'ler*. Gazi Kitabevi.

Muhongayirea, W., Hitayezub, P., Mbatiac, O. L., & Mukoya-Wangiad, S. M. (2013). Determinants of Farmers' Participation in Formal Credit Market in Rural Rwanda. *Journal of Agricultural Science, 4*(2), 87–94.

Munny, K. N., & Weiyu, Z. (2011). *The Role of Micro-credit for women entrepreneurs: The Case of Banglades* [Master Thesis]. University of Gavle. http://www.diva-portal.org/smash/get/diva2:543989/FULLTEXT01.pdf

Muriithi, P., Horner, D., Pemberton, L., & Wao, H. (2018). Factors influencing Research Collaborations in Kenyan Universities. *Research Policy, 47*(1), 88–97. doi:10.1016/j.respol.2017.10.002

Musau, Z. (2015). Loans to Women=smart economics. *Africa Renewal, 29*(2), 20–21. doi:10.18356/c828c83a-en

Mushtaq, R., Dastane, O., Rafiq, M., & Başar, B. D. (2023). Women financial inclusion research: A bibliometric and network analysis. *International Journal of Social Economics, 50*(8), 1169–1185. doi:10.1108/IJSE-06-2022-0438

Mutale, T. M., & Mtapuri, O. (2023). Rural Women's Perceptions of Poverty and Inequality in Mungwi District, Zambia. In O. Mtapuri (Ed.), *Poverty, Inequality, and Innovation in the Global South* (pp. 307–244). Palgrave Macmillan. doi:10.1007/978-3-031-21841-5_15

Mwangi, I. W., & Sichei, M. M. (2011). Determinants of access to credit by individuals in Kenya: A comparative analysis of the Kenya National FinAccess Surveys of 2006 and 2009. *European Journal of Business and Management, 3*(3), 206–226.

Nagaiya, D., & Begum, S. S. (2012). *Women entrepreneurship and small enterprises in India*. New Century Publications.

Nageswara Rao, N. D. S. V. (2010). Financial Inclusion –Banker's Perspective. Bank Quest, 81(4).

Nayır, D. Z. (2008). İşi ve Ailesi Arasındaki Kadın: Tekstil ve Bilgi İşlem Girişimcilerinin Rol Çatışmasına Getirdikleri Çözüm Stratejileri. *Ege Academic Review, 8*(2), 631–650. doi:10.21121/eab.2015221924

Nel, H. (2018). A comparison between the asset-oriented and needs-based community development approaches in terms of systems changes. *Practice, 30*(1), 33–52. doi:10.1080/09503153.2017.1360474

NiazM. U.IqbalM. (2019). *Effect of microfinance on women empowerment: A case study of Pakistan*. doi:10.2139/ssrn.3419834

Niehof, A. (2004). The significance of diversification for rural livelihood systems. *Food Policy, 29*(4), 321–338. doi:10.1016/j.foodpol.2004.07.009

Njiraini, J. (2015). Microfinance: Good for the poor? *Africa Renewal, 29*(2), 24–25. doi:10.18356/97e702a4-en

NobelPrize.org. (2023). Muhammad Yunus - Biographical. *The Nobel Peace Prize 2006.* Nobel Prize Outreach AB 2023. https://www.nobelprize.org/prizes/peace/2006/yunus/biographical/

Ntifo-Siaw & Bosompem. (2008). *Microfinance as Poverty Alleviation Tool: Case Study of Social Investment Fund Interventions in the Central Region – Ghana.* Governance and Sustainable Development. Marcel Hughes Publicity Group.

Nweke, F. L., Spencer, D. S. C., & Lynam, J. K. (2002). *The Cassava Transformation.* Michigan State University Press.

Nyangena, W., & Köhlin, G. (2008). *Estimating Returns to Soil and Water Conservation Investments: An Application to Crop Yield in Kenya.* Environment for Development Discussion Paper Series, EfD DP 08-32.

NZAID. (2007). *Achieving Gender Equality and Women Empowerment.* https://devpolicy.org>nzaid-achieving-gender-equality and women empowerment

Obisesan, A. A., & Akinlade, R. J. (2013). Credit constraints and Poverty among Nigerian farming Households. *Agricultural Journal, 8*(2), 94–100.

Ofori, E., & Kashiwagi, K. (2022). Impact of microfinance on the social performance of local households: Evidence from the Kassena Nankana East District of Ghana. *Sustainability (Basel), 14*(10), 6002. doi:10.3390u14106002

Ojone, J. E. (2023). Religious importance of microfinance bank: A Christian perspective. *International Journal of Scientific and Management Research, 6*(7), 50-70. doi:10.37502/IJSMR.2023.6704

Omar, M. A., & Inaba, K. (2020). Does financial inclusion reduce poverty and income inequality in developing countries? A panel data analysis. *Journal of Economic Structures, 9*(1), 37. doi:10.118640008-020-00214-4

Onaran, Ö. (2003). *Türkiye'de ihracat yönelimli büyüme politikalarının istihdam üzerindeki etkileri. In İktisadi kalkınma, kriz ve istikrar içinde.* İletişim Yayınları.

Opportunity International. (2022). *Global Report.* https://issuu.com/opportunity/docs/global-report-2022/2?ff&pageLayout=singlePage

Ören(2007)

Orkoh, E., Claassen, C., & Blaauw, D. (2022). Poverty and Intrahousehold Gender Inequality in Time Use in Ghana. *Feminist Economics, 28*(4), 221–253. doi:10.1080/13545701.2022.2080854

Osarfo, D., Senadza, B., & Nketiah-Amponsah, E. (2016). *The Impact of Nonfarm Activities on Rural Farm Household Income and Food Security in the Upper East and Upper West Regions of Ghana*. Academic Press.

Osumanu, I. K. (2020). Small-Scale Mining and Livelihood Dynamics in North-Eastern Ghana: Sustaining Rural Livelihoods in a Changing Environment. *Progress in Development Studies, 20*(3), 208–222. doi:10.1177/1464993420934223

Otero, M. (1999). Bringing development back into microfinance. *Small Enterprise Development, 10*(1), 9–20.

Owusu-Antwi, G., & Antwi, J. (2010). The Analysis of the Rural Credit Market in Ghana. *The International Business & Economics Research Journal, 9*(8). doi:10.19030/iber.v9i8.611

Öz, C. S., & Çolakoğlu, C. (2014). Türkiye'de Mikro Kredi Uygulamasının Sakarya İli Özelinde İncelenmesi. *Calisma Ve Toplum, 43*(4).

Özer, M. & Biçerli, K. (2003). Türkiye'de kadın işgücünün panel veri analizi. *Anadolu Üniversitesi Sosyal Bilimler Dergisi, 3*(1), 55-86.

Ozili, P. K. (2018). Impact of digital finance on financial inclusion and stability. *Borsa Istanbul Review, 18*(4), 329–340. doi:10.1016/j.bir.2017.12.003

Ozili, P. K. (2020). Contesting digital finance for the poor. *Digital Policy, Regulation & Governance, 22*(2), 135–151. doi:10.1108/DPRG-12-2019-0104

Ozili, P. K. (2020). Financial Inclusion Research around the World: A Review. Advance online publication. doi:10.2139srn.3515515

Ozili, P. K. (2020). Theories of financial inclusion. In *Uncertainty and challenges in contemporary economic behaviour* (pp. 89–115). Emerald Publishing Limited. doi:10.1108/978-1-80043-095-220201008

Ozili, P. K. (2021). Financial inclusion research around the world: A review. *The Forum for Social Economics, 50*(4), 457–479. doi:10.1080/07360932.2020.1715238

Ozili, P. K. (2022a). Can central bank digital currency increase financial inclusion? Arguments for and against. In *Big Data Analytics in the Insurance Market* (pp. 241–249). Emerald Publishing Limited. doi:10.1108/978-1-80262-637-720221013

Ozili, P. K. (2022b). Digital financial inclusion. In *Big Data: A game changer for insurance industry* (pp. 229–238). Emerald Publishing Limited. doi:10.1108/978-1-80262-605-620221015

Ozili, P. K. (2023). CBDC, Fintech and cryptocurrency for financial inclusion and financial stability. Digital Policy, Regulation and Governance, 25(1), 40-57.

Özmen, F. (2011). *Türkiye'de Kadın İşgücü İstihdamının Gelişiminde Mikro Kredi Uygulamaları* (Publication Number 286661) [Doctoral dissertation]. Celal Bayar University, Manisa. tez.yok.gov.tr

Özmen, F. (2011). *Türkiye'de Kadın İşgücü İstihdamının Gelişiminde Mikro Kredi Uygulamaları [Doktora Tezi]*. Celal Bayar Üniversitesi Sosyal Bilimler Enstitüsü.

Öztürk, S., & Karataş, M. (2020). Türkiye'de Kadınların İstihdam Edilmelerini Zorlaştıran Faktörler. *Hak İş Uluslararası Emek ve Toplum Dergisi, 9*(24), 180–204. doi:10.31199/hakisderg.747129

Özyılmaz, A. M. (2016). *Türkiye'de kadın girişimciliği ve girişimci kadınların karşılaştıkları sorunlar üzerine bir araştırma* (Publication Number 436702) [Master's thesis]. Hacı Bektaş Veli University, Nevşehir. tez.yok.gov.tr

Pal, M., Gupta, H., & Joshi, Y. C. (2022). Social and economic empowerment of women through financial inclusion: Empirical evidence from India. *Equality, Diversity and Inclusion*, *41*(2), 294–305. doi:10.1108/EDI-04-2021-0113

Patton, M. Q. (1990). *Qualitative evaluation methods*. SAGE Publications.

Paul Dana, L. (2001). The education and training of entrepreneurs in Asia. *Education + Training*, *43*(8/9), 405–416. doi:10.1108/EUM0000000006486

Pekel, E. (2019). Eğitim ve İstihdam İlişkisinin Değerlendirilmesi. In *Cataloging-In-Publication Data* (p. 268). Internatinonal Balkan and Near Eastern Social Sciences Congress Series.

Pesaran, M. H., Shin, Y., & Smith, R. J. (1996). Testing for the'Existence of a Long-run Relationship' (No. 9622). Faculty of Economics, University of Cambridge.

Pesaran, M. H., Shin, Y., & Smith, R. (2001). Bound testing approaches to the analysis of level relationships. *Journal of Applied Econometrics*, *16*(3), 289–326. doi:10.1002/jae.616

Petrick, M. (2004). Farm investment, credit rationing, and governmentally promoted credit access in Poland: A cross-sectional analysis. *Food Policy*, *29*(3), 275–294. doi:10.1016/j.foodpol.2004.05.002

Phan, C. T., Vo, T. T., & Vo, D. T. H. (2023). Can microcredit reduce vulnerability to poverty? Evidence from rural Vietnam. *Review of Development Economics*, *27*(1), 608–629. doi:10.1111/rode.12951

Philippine Commission on Women. (n.d.-a). *Agriculture, fisheries and forestry*. https://pcw.gov.ph/agriculture-fisheries-and-forestry/

Philippine Commission on Women. (n.d.-b). *Micro, small and medium enterprises (MSMEs) development*. https://pcw.gov.ph/micro-small-and-medium-enterprises-development/

Philippine Commission on Women. (n.d.-c). *Mission and Vision*. https://pcw.gov.ph/mission-and-vision/

Philippine Deposit Insurance Corporation (PDIC). (2008). *Bulletin No. 2008-02*. Philippine Deposit Corporation Official Website. pdic.gov.ph

Philippine News Agency (PNA). (2008, February 1). *PDIC takes over four branches of CRBA Banks*. Iloilo City, Philippines. pdic.gov.ph

Philippine Statistics Authority. (2016). psa.gov.ph

Philippine Statistics Authority. (2023, March 24). *Press Release 2023-119. HomePoverty Statistics*. psa.gov.ph

Pokhriyal, A. K., & Ghildiyal, V. (2011). Progress of Microfinance and Financial Inclusion: A Critical Analysis of SHG-Bank Linkage Program in India. *International Journal of Economics and Finance*, *3*(2). doi:10.5539/ijef.v3n2p255

Poverty Annual Report. (2014). http://www.iid.org.mz/G20-relatoriofinal

Press Kit. (2003, April 25-27). *1st Community Press Summit*. Kalibo, Aklan and Boracay.

Psico, J. A. T., & Dias, J. F. (2007). *Social Performance Evaluation of Microfinance Institutions in Mozambique*. https://www.researchgate.net/publication/281098243_Social_Performance_Evaluation_of_Microfinance_Institutions_in_Mozambique

Quagrainie, F. A., Adams, S., Kabalan, A. A. M., & Dankwa, A. D. (2021). Micro-entrepreneurship, sustainable development goal one and cultural expectations of Ghanaian women. *Journal of Entrepreneurship in Emerging Economies*, *13*(1), 86–106. doi:10.1108/JEEE-11-2019-0174

Quaye, W. (2008). Food Security Situation in Northern Ghana, Coping Strategies and Related Constraints. *African Journal of Agricultural Research*, *3*(5), 334–342.

Rahji, M. A. Y., & Fakayode, S. B. (2009). A multinomial logit analysis of agricultural credit rationing by commercial banks in Nigeria. *International Research Journal of Finance and Economics*, (24), 90–100.

Rajalakshmi, V., & Selvam, V. (2017). Impact of MGNREGA on women empowerment and their issues and challenges: A review of literature from 2005 to 2015. *Journal of Internet Banking and Commerce*, *22*(7), 1–13.

Rashmi, D. (2016). Women Entrepreneur in Micro, Small and Medium Enterprises in India-An overview. *International Journal of Managerial Studies and Research*, *4*(2), 60–64.

Registrar General and Census Commissioner of India. (2013). *The Census of India 2011*. Ministry of Home Affairs, Government of India.

Rehman, F. U., Nawaz, T., Ilyas, M., & Hyder, S. (2014). A Comparative Analysis of Mobile and Email Marketing Using AIDA Model. *Journal of Basic and Applied Scientific Research*, *4*(6), 38–49.

Report of Expert Committee on Harnessing the India Post Network for Financial Inclusion. (2010, June 16). Department of Financial Services, Department of Economic Affairs, Department of Post and Invest India Economic Foundation (IIEF).

Robb, C. A., & Woodyard, A. (2011). Financial knowledge and best practice behavior. *Financial Counseling and Planning*, *22*(1).

Robinson, S., & Watson, J. (2001). Female entrepreneur underperformance: A puzzle for the information age. *Journal of International Information Management*, *10*(1), 4.

Roodman, D. (2011). Fitting Fully Observed Recursive Mixed-Process Models with CMP. *The Stata Journal*, *11*(2), 159–206. doi:10.1177/1536867X1101100202

Roodman, D., & Morduch, J. (2014). The impact of microcredit on the poor in Bangladesh: Revisiting the evidence. *The Journal of Development Studies*, *50*(4), 583–604. doi:10.1080/00220388.2013.858122

Sachin, J. (2011). Financial Inclusion: Involving the Uninvolved through Product, Channel and Marketing Innovations. Bank Quest, 82(2).

Şahin, H. (2015). *Yoksullukla mücadelede mikrokredi yöntemi*. Available in: https://www.academia.edu/38149397/Yoksullukla_Mu_cadelede_Mikrokredi_Yo_ntemi

Şahin, D. K. (2022). Kadın İstihdamının Ekonomik Büyümeye Etkisi: Ampirik Bir Analiz. *Uluslararası Ekonomi ve Yenilik Dergisi*, *8*(2), 277–288. doi:10.20979/ueyd.1135131

Şahinoğlu, T., & Ağırkaya, M. B. (2021). Kadın İstihdamını Etkileyen Unsurlar ve Bu Unsurların Demografik Özelliklerle İlişkisi: Erzurum İli Örneği. *İktisadi İdari ve Siyasal Araştırmalar Dergisi, 6*(16), 398-421.

Sahu, T. N., Agarwala, V., & Maity, S. (2021). Effectiveness of microcredit in employment generation and livelihood transformation of tribal women entrepreneurs: Evidence from PMMY. *Journal of Small Business and Entrepreneurship*, 1–22. doi:10.1080/08276331.2021.1928847

Sakyi, S., Abu, B. M., & Nkegbe, P. K. (2020). Effects of farm credit access on agricultural commercialization in Ghana: Empirical evidence from the northern Savannah ecological zone. *African Development Review*, *32*(2), 150–162. doi:10.1111/1467-8268.12424

Salayo, N. D., Perez, M. L., Garces, L. R., & Pido, M. D. (2012). Mariculture development and livelihood diversification in the Philippines. *Marine Policy*, *36*(4), 867–881. doi:10.1016/j.marpol.2011.12.003

Saluja, O. B., Singh, P., & Kumar, H. (2023). Barriers and interventions on the way to empower women through financial inclusion: A 2 decades systematic review (2000–2020). *Humanities & Social Sciences Communications*, *10*(1), 1–14. doi:10.105741599-023-01640-y

Sameer, K. (2009). Speeding Financial Inclusion. Academic Foundation in Association With Skoch Foundation.

Sanginga, N., & Bergvinson, D. (2014). *Oilseeds and Cowpeas*. Background Paper.

Santoso, D. B. (2016). *Credit Accessibility: The Impact of Microfinance on Rural Indonesian Households*. Lincoln University.

Sanusi, W., & Adedeji, I. (2010). A Probit Analysis of Accessibility of Small Scale Farmers to Formal Source of Credit in Ogbomoso Zone, Oyo State, Nigeria. *Agricultura Tropica et Subtropica*, *43*(1), 49–53.

Sapovadia, V. (2018). Financial inclusion, digital currency, and mobile technology. In Handbook of Blockchain, Digital Finance, and Inclusion, Volume 2 (pp. 361-385). Academic Press. doi:10.1016/B978-0-12-812282-2.00014-0

Saqib, N. (2016). Women empowerment and economic growth: Empirical evidence from Saudi Arabia. *Advances in Management & Applied Economics*.

Satı, Z. E., & Yılmaz, B. O. (2020). Endüstri 4.0 ortamında değişen iş ve mesleklerin Türkiye'de kadın istihdamına etkileri. *Strategic Public Management Journal*, *6*(11), 54–76. doi:10.25069pmj.701685

Schapper, A. (2017). Children's rights implementation as a multi-level governance process. *Human Rights Quarterly*, *39*(1), 104–129.

Schein, A. (2020). Female labor force participation in Israel, 1955-2017. *Israel Affairs*, *26*(5), 635–649. doi:10.1080/13537121.2020.1806515

Schindler, K. (2010). Credit for what? Informal credit as a coping strategy of market women in northern Ghana. *The Journal of Development Studies*, *46*(2), 234–253. doi:10.1080/00220380903002905

Schneider, H. (2018). Empowerment in HCI-A survey and framework. In *Proceedings of the 2018 CHI Conference on Human Factors in Computing Systems* (pp. 1-14). 10.1145/3173574.3173818

Schuler, S. R., Islam, F., & Rottach, E. (2010). Women's empowerment revisited: A case study from Bangladesh. *Development in Practice*, *20*(7), 840–854. doi:10.1080/09614524.2010.508108 PMID:20856695

Seenivasan, R. (2015). High Interest Rates Are an Amorality in Microfinance. *Economic and Political Weekly*, *50*(3), 75–77.

Seibel, H. D., Llanto, G. M., Garcia, E., & Callanta, R. (1997). *Microfinance in the Philippines: An assessment of viability, sustainability and outreach among Grameen replicators*. Working Paper/ University of Cologne, Development Research Center, No. 1997, 4. http://hdl.handle.net/10419/23667

Seibel, H. D. (1999, August). Banking with very poor women: Outreach and sustainability of CARD-Rural Bank, a Grameen Innovator in the Philippines. *The Journal of Microfinance*, *1*(1), 117–130.

Sekyi, S. (2017). Rural households' credit access and loan amount in Wa Municipality, Ghana. *International Journal of Economics and Financial Issues*, *7*(1), 506–514.

Selase, A. E., Xinhai, L., & Worlanyo, A. S. (2017). Combination Effects of Opportunity International Savings and Loans Credit Facility on Maize Production and Health: Evidence of Techiman Municipality in Ghana. *Agriculture Science Food Research Journal*, *8*, 196.

Şener, Ü. (2009). Kadın yoksulluğu. TEPAV (Türkiye Ekonomi Politikaları Araştırma Vakfı).

Serinikli, N. (2016). The importance of entrepreneurship in preventing the woman poverty: Woman cooperatives and micro-credit applications. *BJSS Balkan Journal of Social Sciences*, 598–609.

Servon, L. (2017). *The unbanking of America: How the new middle class survives*. Houghton Mifflin Harcourt.

Setiawan, B., Phan, T. D., Medina, J., Wieriks, M., Nathan, R. J., & Fekete-Farkas, M. (2023). Quest for financial inclusion via digital financial services (Fintech) during COVID-19 pandemic: Case study of women in Indonesia. *Journal of Financial Services Marketing*, 1–15. doi:10.105741264-023-00217-9

Seymen, S. (2011). *İl Özel İdaresi ve mikro kredi uygulamaları Kocaeli İl Özel İdaresi örneği* [Yüksek Lisans Tezi]. Kocaeli Üniversitesi Sosyal Bilimler Enstitüsü.

Shafique, O. & Siddique, N. (2020). The impact of microcredit financing on poverty alleviatıon and women empowerment: An empirical study on Akhuwat Islamıc microfinance. *PalArch's Journal of Archaeology of Egypt / Egyptology, 17*(8), 548-562.

Shah, H., & Saurabh, P. (2015). Women entrepreneurs in developing nations: Growth and replication strategies and their impact on poverty alleviation. *Technology Innovation Management Review*, *5*(8), 34–43. doi:10.22215/timreview/921

Shanthi & Padmaja. (2022). Financial Inclusion and Women Empowerment in India-An Overview. *International Journal of Creative Research Thoughts, 10*(2), d30-d33.

Sharma, A. D. (2019). Empowering Women through SHGs – Evidence from a Case Study of SHGs in Imphal East District, Manipur. *Economic Affairs*, *64*(1). Advance online publication. doi:10.30954/0424-2513.1.2019.3

Sharma, R., Mehta, K., Sidhu, N. K., & Vyas, V. (2023). Extending UTAUT2 Model With Sustainability and Psychological Factors in Adoption of Blockchain Technology for the Digital Transformation of Banks in India. In *Revolutionizing Financial Services and Markets Through FinTech and Blockchain* (pp. 27–43). IGI Global. doi:10.4018/978-1-6684-8624-5.ch003

Sharma, S. (2018). Emerging dimensions of women entrepreneurship: Developments & obstructions. *Economic Affairs*, *63*(2), 337–346. doi:10.30954/0424-2513.2.2018.7

Shaw, J. (2004). Microenterprise Occupation and Poverty Reduction in Microfinance Programs: Evidence from Sri Lanka. *World Development*, *32*(7), 1247–1264. doi:10.1016/j.worlddev.2004.01.009

Shema, A. (2022). Effects of increasing credit limit in digital microlending: A study of airtime lending in East Africa. *The Electronic Journal on Information Systems in Developing Countries*, *88*(3), e12199. doi:10.1002/isd2.12199

Singh, A., & Manisha, R. (2013). Women entrepreneurs in micro, small and medium enterprises. *International Journal of Management and Social Sciences Research*, *2*(8), 4–8.

Singh, S., & Singh, A. (2020). Women Empowerment in India: A Critical Analysis. *Tathapi*, *19*(44), 227–253.

Sinha, S. & UN.ESCAP. (2005). *Developing women entrepreneurs in South Asia: issues, initiatives and experiences*. Retrieved from: https://hdl.handle.net/20.500.12870/3557

Sinha, M., Mahapatra, S. S., Dutta, A., & Sengupta, P. P. (2023). Microfinance and women empowerment: An empirical analysis. In *Research Anthology on Microfinance Services and Roles in Social Progress* (pp. 1–13). IGI Global. https://www.igi-global.com/chapter/microfinance-and-women-empowerment-an-empirical-analysis/314741

Snyder, H. (2019). Literature review as a research methodology: A review and guidelines. *Journal of Business Research*, *104*, 333–339. doi:10.1016/j.jbusres.2019.07.039

Solotaroff, J. L., Kotikula, A., Lonnberg, T., Ali, S., & Jahan, F. (2019). *Voices to choices: Bangladesh's journey in women's economic empowerment.* World Bank Publications. doi:10.1596/978-1-4648-1374-0

Sörensson, A. & Ghannad, N. (2023). Entrepreneurial opportunities and difficulties under COVID-19 for women entrepreneurs in Asia and Europe. *Journal of Entrepreneurship in Emerging Economies.* doi:10.1108/JEEE-02-2023-0052

Soysal, A. (2010). Türkiye'de Kadın Girişimciler: Engeller ve Fırsatlar Bağlamında Bir Değerlendirme. *Ankara Üniversitesi SBF Dergisi, 65*(1), 83-114.

Statistics National Institute. (2016). *Demographics and Indicators.* INE. http//www.ine.gov.mz/estatisticas/estatisticas-demo

Strauss, A., & Corbin, J. (1990). *Basics of qualitative research: Grounded theory procedures and techniques.* SAGE Publications, Inc.

Stuart, S. (2018). Advancing the economic empowerment and autonomy of women in the Caribbean through the 2030 Agenda for Sustainable Development. *ECLAC-Studies and Perspective – The Caribbean, 60.*

Sultana, Y., Hazarika, P., Nu, F. R., V, A. F., & Javed, A. (2023). Women Empowerment Through Microfinance: Empirical Evidence from India (A Micro-Level Study). *Kepes, 21*(2), Article 2.

Sundari, S. (2020). Structural Changes and Quality of Women's Labour in India. *The Indian Journal of Labour Economics : the Quarterly Journal of the Indian Society of Labour Economics, 63*(3), 689–717. doi:10.100741027-020-00245-2 PMID:33046952

Sunstein, C. R. (2014). Nudging: A very short guide. *Journal of Consumer Policy, 37*(4), 583–588. doi:10.100710603-014-9273-1

Sürücü Bahar, H. (2015). *Yoksullukla mücadelede mikro kredi uygulamaları (Konya İli örneği) [Yüksek Lisans Tezi].* Selçuk Üniversitesi Sosyal Bilimler Enstitüsü.

Swain, R. B., & Wallentin, F. Y. (2009). Does microfinance empower women? Evidence from self-help groups in India. *International Review of Applied Economics, 23*(5), 541–556. doi:10.1080/02692170903007540

Tahir, I. M., & Tahrim, S. N. C. (2013, October) Efficiency analysis of microfinance institutions in ASEAN: A DEA approach. *Business Management Dynamics, 3*(4), 13-23. www.bmdynamics.com

Tambunan, T. (2009). Women entrepreneurship in Asian developing countries: Their development and main constraints. *Journal of Development and Agricultural Economics, 1*(2), 27–40.

Tang, S., Guan, Z., & Jin, S. (2010). Formal and Informal Credit Markets and Rural Credit Demand in China. *Agricultural & Applied Economics Association, CAES, & WAEA Joint Annual Meeting*, 1–26.

Tansel, A. (2002). İktisadi kalkınma ve kadınların işgücüne katılımı: Türkiye'den zaman-serisi kanıtları ve illere göre yatay kesit kestirimleri. *ERC Working Papers in Economics,* (01/05T), 1-31.

Tariq, S., & Sangmi, M.D. (2028). Microfinance and Women empowerment: A Brief Review of Literature. *Pacific Business Review International, 11*(3), 77–83.

Tchouassi, G. (2012). Can mobile phones really work to extend banking services to the unbanked? Empirical lessons from selected Sub-Saharan Africa countries. *International Journal of Developmental Science, 1*(2), 70–81.

Tewari, P., & Gakkhar, A. (2011). A study of opportunities extended to dairy women entrepreneurs under women's dairy development scheme. *Journal of Dairying, Foods & Home Sciences, 30*(3), 178–181.

TGMP. (2022). *Türkiye Grameen mikrofinans programı*. Available in: https://prezi.com/view/ApSSyoPAShK6RXBM-hDOG/

Thabethe, N., Vhumani, M., & Nyuswa, M. (2012). Micro-credit as a community development strategy: a South African Case Study. *Community Development Journal, 47*(3), 423-435. https://www.jstor.org/stable/pdf/26

Thakur, H., Gupta, A., & Johnson, L. T. (2021). *Women engaging with markets from positions of strength: An exploratory understanding of Kudumbashree women's food service enterprises*. Academic Press.

Thaler, R., & Sunstein, C. (2008). *Nudge: The Gentle Power of Choice Architecture*. Yale University Press.

Thapa, N. B. (2018). *Empowering citizen and community through social mobilisation* [Doctoral dissertation].

The UNCDF Report. (2023). https://www.uncdf.org/financial-inclusion-and-the-sdgs

TİSVA. (2013). *Girişimciliği Sağlayarak, Yoksulluğun Bir Başkasına İhtiyaç Olmadan Azaltılması Modeli: Türkiye Grameen Mikro Finans Programı, Sakarya Grameen Bankası Mikrofinans Şubesi'nden temin edilen broşür*. TISVA.

Todaro, M. P., & Smith, S. C. (2020). *Economic Development*. Pearson.

Toksöz, G. (2007). *Türkiye'de kadın istihdamının durumu*. Uluslararası Çalışma Örgütü.

Tran, T. K. V., Elahi, E., Zhang, L., Abid, M., Pham, Q. T., & Tran, T. D. (2018). Gender differences in formal credit approaches: Rural households in Vietnam. *Asian-Pacific Economic Literature, 32*(1), 131–138. doi:10.1111/apel.12220

TÜİK. (2022a). *Türkiye İstatistik Kurumu verileri*. https://data.tuik.gov.tr/Kategori/GetKategori?p=istihdam-issizlik-ve-ucret-108&dil=1

TÜİK. (2022b). *Türkiye İstatistik Kurumu verileri*. https://data.tuik.gov.tr/Kategori/GetKategori?p=Ulusal-Hesaplar-113

Turkish Statistical Institute. (2021). *İstatistiklerle Kadın*. https://data.tuik.gov.tr/Bulten/Index?p=Istatistiklerle-Kadin-2022-49668

Turkish Statistical Institute. (2022). *İstatistiklerle Kadın*. https://data.tuik.gov.tr/Bulten/Index?p=Istatistiklerle-Kadin-2022-49668

Turkish Statistical Institute. (2023). *İşgücü İstatistikleri*. https://data.tuik.gov.tr/Bulten/Index?p=Isgucu-Istatistikleri-Nisan-2023-49373

Türlüoğlu, E. (2018). Kadın İstihdam ve Büyüme İlişkisi: Var Modeli Analizi. *Avrasya Sosyal ve Ekonomi Araştırmaları Dergisi, 5*(9), 59–68.

Turvey, C. G., He, G., Ma, J., Kong, R., & Meagher, P. (2012). Farm credit and credit demand elasticities in Shaanxi and Gansu. *China Economic Review, 23*(4), 1020–1035. doi:10.1016/j.chieco.2012.05.004

Ufuk, H., & Özgen, Ö. (2001). Interaction between the business and family lives of women entrepreneurs in Turkey. *Journal of Business Ethics, 31*(2), 95–106. doi:10.1023/A:1010712023858

Ukoha, O., Mejeha, R., & Nte, I. (2007). Determinants of Farmers' Welfare in Ebonyi State, Nigeria. *Pakistan Journal of Social Sciences, 4*(3), 351–354.

Ulutaş, Ç. Ü. (2009). Yoksulluğun Kadınlaşması ve Görünmeyen Emek. *Çalışma ve Toplum, 2*, 25-40.

Uma, S. N., & Ramesh, H. N. (2018). A study on government support for promoting women entrepreneurs in Karnataka state. *Int J Econ Manage Sci, 7*, 521–525.

Umutlu, S., & Öztürk, M. (2020). İş Yaşamında Kadın ve Karşılaştığı Sorunlar. *Süleyman Demirel Üniversitesi İktisadi ve İdari Bilimler Fakültesi Dergisi*, *25*(3), 297–306.

UN. (2018). *Gender differences in poverty and household composition through the life cycle*. Available in: https://www.unwomen.org/sites/default/files/Headquarters/Attachments/Sections/Library/Publications/2018/SDG-report-Spotlight-01-Gender-differences-in-poverty-and-household-composition-en.pdf

UN. (2022). *UN Women*. Available in: https://data.unwomen.org/features/poverty-deepens-women-and-girls-according-latest-projections#:~:text=New%20projections%20of%20global%20poverty,372%20million%20men%20and%20boys)

UNFPA, I. (1994). Program of Action. *Paragraph*, 8.

United Nations Development Program (UNDP). (2020). *Gender Equality and Women's Empowerment*. Retrieved from https://www.undp.org/sustainable-development-goals/gender-equality

United Nations Educational, Scientific and Cultural Organization (UNESCO). (2020). *Why is Gender Equality Important for Sustainable Development?* Retrieved from https://en.unesco.org/gem-report/gender-and-education/why-gender-equality-important-sustainable-development

Unterhalter, E., North, A., Arnot, M., Lloyd, C., Moletsane, L., Murphy-Graham, E., Parkes, J., & Saito, M. (2014). *Interventions to enhance girls' education and gender equality. Education rigorous literature review*. Department of International Development.

Uruthirapathy, A., & Dyke, L. (2022). The influence of general causality orientations on self-esteem and perceived stress among undergraduate students in women-only colleges. *International Journal of Educational Management*, *36*(5), 766–783. doi:10.1108/IJEM-05-2021-0179

Uyanık, Ö. (2020). Türkiye'de Kadın Girişimciliğin Sosyal Hizmet Bağlamında İncelenmesi. *Toplumsal Politika Dergisi*, *1*(2), 134–154.

Vaessen, J. (2001). Accessibility of Rural Credit in Northern Nicaragua: The Importance of Networks of Information. *Journal of Microfinance/ESR Review*, *3*(2).

Vaish, S., & Tripathi, S. (2019). Empowering women dairy farmers through adoption of drudgery reducing technologies and availing government schemes. *Plant Archives*, *19*(1), 952–955.

Verdugo, G., & Allègre, G. (2020). Labour force participation and job polarization: Evidence from Europe during the Great Recession. *Labour Economics*, *66*, 101881. doi:10.1016/j.labeco.2020.101881

Vletter, F. (2006). *Micro-finance in Mozambique: Achievements, Prospects & Challenges*. Report of Mozambique Micro-Finance Facility. https://www.wvi.org/mozambique/about-us

Von Kotze, A. (2009). But what will we eat? Research questions and priorities for work and learning. In L. Cooper & S. Walters (Eds.), *Learning/Work: Turning Work and Lifelong Learning Inside Out* (pp. 16–29). HSRC Press.

Wang, F., Du, L., Tian, M., Liu, Y., & Zhang, Y. (2023). Sustainability of rural tourism in poverty reduction: Evidence from panel data of 15 underdeveloped counties in Anhui Province, China. *PLoS One*, *18*(3), e0283048. doi:10.1371/journal.pone.0283048 PMID:36913402

Warner, L. M., & French, D. P. (2018). Self-efficacy and its sources as determinants of physical activity among older people. In Palgrave handbook of ageing and physical activity promotion (pp. 231-250). Palgrave Macmillan. doi:10.1007/978-3-319-71291-8_12

Waterfield, C., & Duval, A. (1996). *Care savings and credit sourcebook*. CARE.

Weber, R., & Musshoff, O. (2012). *Microfinance for Agricultural Firms-Credit Access and Loan Repayment in Tanzania.* Paper presented at the EAAE Seminar, Dublin, Ireland. www.Nyu.edu/classes/nagler/quant1/Probit1-post.pdf

Wegren, S. K. (2021). Vulnerabilities in Russian Agriculture to Climate Change. *Sustainable Development Research, 3*(1), 2021. doi:10.30560dr.v3n1p1

Wellalage, N., & Locke, S. (2017). Access to credit by SMEs in South Asia: Do women entrepreneurs face discrimination. *Research in International Business and Finance, 41*, 336–346. doi:10.1016/j.ribaf.2017.04.053

Women's Enterprise Management Training Outreach Program for Asia (WEPTOP). (1992, August). *Pilot Project, Revised Draft Project Document for the Philippines*. Author.

Women, U. N. (2015). *Progress of the World's Women 2015-2016: Transforming Economies, Realizing Rights.* UN Women. doi:10.18356/2d5f74e3-en

Wooldridge, J. M. (2002). *Econometric Analysis of Cross Section and Panel Data.* MIT Press.

World Bank Group. (2018). *An Incomplete Transition: Overcoming the Legacy of Exclusion in South Africa.* World Bank Group.

World Bank. (2018). *Women's Financial Inclusion and the Law*. World Bank.

World Bank. (2019). *Toward Gender Equality in East Asia and the Pacific: A Companion to the World Development Report.* Retrieved from https://openknowledge.worldbank.org/handle/10986/31337

World Economic Forum. (2020). *The Global Gender Gap Report 2020.* Retrieved from https://www.weforum.org/reports/gender-gap-2020-report-100-years-pay-equality

World Vision. (2019). *Fostering productivity and innovation.* https://www.wvi.org/sites/default/files/2019-12/Microfinance%202019.pdf

Yadav, S. B., & Mittal, R. (2016). Poverty Alleviation through Micro Finance in India: Empirical Evidences. *Research Journal of Humanities and Social Sciences, 7*(4), 259–267.

Yadav, V., & Unni, J. (2016). Women entrepreneurship: Research review and future directions. *Journal of Global Entrepreneurship Research, 6*(1), 1–18. doi:10.118640497-016-0055-x

Yaman, M., & Sarihan, N. Ö. (2021). Kadınlara Yönelik Yapılan Uygulamalarda Kalkınma Ajanslarının Önemi: Doğu Karadeniz Kalkınma Ajansı (Doka) Örneği. *Eskişehir Osmangazi Üniversitesi Sosyal Bilimler Dergisi, 22*(1), 225–239. doi:10.17494/ogusbd.952814

Yan, Y., & Qi, S. (2021). Childhood matters: Family education and financial inclusion. *Pacific-Basin Finance Journal, 65*, 101489. doi:10.1016/j.pacfin.2020.101489

Yavuz Özgül, S. (2019). *Kamu desteklerinden yararlanan kadın girişimciler: Ankara ili örneği* (Publication Number 555502) [Master's thesis]. Ankara Yıldırım Beyazıt University, Ankara. tez.yok.gov.tr

Yıldırım, A., & Şimşek, H. (2018). *Sosyal bilimlerde nitel araştırma yöntemleri.* Seçkin Yayıncılık.

Yıldırım, P. D. (2020). Kırsal Kalkınmada Kadın Kooperatiflerinin Rolü: Ahatlı Kadın Kooperatifi Örneği. *Erzurum Teknik Üniversitesi Sosyal Bilimler Enstitüsü Dergisi*, (11), 159–170. doi:10.29157/etusbe.2020.58

Yılmaz, M., & Zoğal, Y. (2015). Kadının işgücüne katılımının tarihsel gelişimi ve kadın istihdamını etkileyen faktörler: Türkiye ve Avrupa örneği. *Econ World, 2015*, 1–25.

Yunus, M. (1992). *Grameen Bank Replication Project in Bangladesh: A Poverty Focused Rural Development Programme*. Grameen Bank.

Yunus, M. (1997). *Yoksulluğun bulunmadığı bir dünyaya doğru*. Doğan Kitapçılık.

Yunus, M. (1999). *Banker to the poor: The autobiography of Muhammad Yunus, founder of the Grameen Bank*. Oxford University Press.

Yunus, M. (2003). *Banker to the Poor: Micro-Lending and the Battle Against World Poverty*. Public Affairs.

Yur'evna, P. E., & Kristina, Y. (2022). Self-worth as a basis for the formation of self-esteem. *Modern Technologies and Scientific and Technological Progress*, *2022*(1), 361–362. doi:10.36629/2686-9896-2022-1-361-362

Zerai, B., & Rani, L. (2012). Is there a tradeoff between outreach and sustainability of microfinance institutions? Evidence from Indian Microfinance Institutions (MFIs). *European Journal of Business and Management*, *4*(2), 90–98.

Zins, A., & Weill, L. (2016). The determinants of financial inclusion in Africa. *Review of Development Finance*, *6*(1), 46-57.

About the Contributors

Yahaya Alhassan is a Principal Lecturer in Finance and Strategic Management at the University of Sunderland in London. He is also the Head of Academic Operations. He holds a PhD in Business Management from Anglia Ruskin University and MBA in Finance from the University of Sunderland. He is also a Senior Fellow of the Higher Education Academy (HEA). He has over 20 years' teaching and management experience developed during roles in the higher education sector and the consultancy industry.

* * *

Hamna Abdallah holds an MPhil in Agricultural Economics focusing on women credit access in Northern Ghana from the University for Development Studies (UDS). Her research interests are in the areas of gender, social inclusion, and agricultural finance.

Mamudu Abunga Akudugu is an Associate Professor of Agricultural Economics at the Institute for Interdisciplinary Research of the University for Development Studies (UDS), Ghana. He is currently the Director of Directorate of Research, Innovation and Partnerships Services of the UDS and also the Monitoring and Evaluation (M&E) Coordinator of WACWISA. Prof. Akudugu specializes in agricultural commodity value chains, climate change and livelihoods development. He is a distinguished academic, Commonwealth Scholar and a Fulbright Scholar-I- Residence at the Appalachian State University in Boone, North Carolina, United States of America.

Abdul-Razak Alhassan is a Senior Lecturer at the Surrey Business School, University of Surrey, UK. His research interests are in the areas of International Business, Management and Development with a focus on emerging markets, agrarian change, agribusiness and supply change management among others.

Arohi Anand is an experienced economist and educator currently serving as an Assistant Professor at Sarala Birla University in Ranchi since February 2021. She teaches a variety of courses in the Department of Economics, including Microeconomics, Macroeconomics, Indian Financial System, Mathematical Economics, and Statistics. Her expertise extends to teaching students in BA Economics, BCOM, BBA, and MBA programs. Prior to her current position, Dr. Anand held the position of Assistant Professor at St. Xavier's College in Patna from July 2014 to January 2021. In this role, she taught subjects such as Microeconomics, Macroeconomics, Indian Financial System, SageMath, and SPSS to students pursuing a Business Economics course. Before her academic appointments, Dr. Arohi Anand worked as a PGT Teacher at SDV Public School in Patna from March 2013 to April 2014. During this time, she taught Social Sciences and English to students. Dr. Anand's educational background includes a Ph.D. in Economics, which she completed in 2022 at Patna University. Her doctoral thesis, titled "Analyzing Financial Market Volatility (2000-2010): A Case Study of India," demonstrates her expertise in the field. She also obtained her Master of Arts (M.A.) degree in Economics from Patna University in 2013, specializing in Monetary Economics at Magadh Mahila College in Patna. In addition to her academic pursuits, Dr. Arohi Anand has made significant contributions to the field through her published works. She has authored several books, including "An Introduction to Applied Mathematics for Economics," "Decisions that Changed India," "Transforming Indian Economy," "Economics for Managers," "Principles of Business Economics," and "The Tech Side of Money: An Introduction to the World of FinTech." These publications have been released by renowned publishing houses such as Kindle Publishing, Notion Press, and Cogent Publishing, and they cover a wide range of economic topics. Dr. Anand has also contributed to scholarly journals, with notable papers such as "A Comparative Study of Select 'Beyond GDP' Measures" published in the IUJ Journal of Management (Volume 9, Issue 2, December 2021), "Review of Impact of Monetary Tightening" in the Journal of Advances and Scholarly Researches in Allied Education (Volume 16, Issue 6, May 2019), and "Poverty Alleviation through SHGs in Patna" in Explore, the Department of Economics Research Journal at Patna Women's College in 2011. With her extensive teaching experience, academic achievements, and valuable publications, Dr. Arohi Anand has established herself as a knowledgeable economist and dedicated educator in the field of economics.

Aykut Arslan retired from the Turkish Armed Forces, where he served as a teaching officer for many years, in 2011. In the same year, he was appointed as Assistant Professor of Management and Behavioral Science at Haliç University and subsequently started to work at Piri Reis University since 2013. In 2017, he was appointed as Associate Professor at his current university. He has several publications in journals such as Journal of Business Ethics, Review of Managerial Science, Journal of East European Management. The author's working areas are "Entrepreneurship", "Positive Psychology and Behavior", "Strategic Management". Currently He works as dean of Faculty of Economics and Administrative Sciences of Piri Reis University.

Osman Tahidu Damba is an Agricultural Economist and lecturer at the Department of Agricultural and Food Economics (AFE) at the University for Development Studies (UDS). His research is in the areas of Agricultural policy, climate change, food systems, and agricultural markets.

Gideon Danso-Abbeam is a Senior Lecturer at the University for Development Studies (UDS) with the Department of Agribusiness. He is an Agricultural Economist with research interests in impact assessment of agrarian technology adoption, food security and climate change economics.

Vijay Dubey is an educational professional with about three decades of blended experience in corporate and mid to large-sized educational institutions. Prof Dubey has successfully handled diverse multiple roles within Academics and Academic Administration, Marketing, Admission, Student Recruitment, Strategy and Planning, Budgeting, and Control functions and has played an active role in meeting institutional goals. Prof Dubey believes in creating a work environment based on trust and mutual respect with little need for supervision and control. In his spare time, Prof Dubey loves to read and dream.

Maybel Fernandez-Vallado was a Senior Lecturer 2 in the College of Arts and Sciences (September 2020 until June 2023), University of the Philippines Visayas. She completed her PhD in Communication from the College of Mass Communication, University of the Philippines, Diliman; finished her Master's in Education, English as a Second Language (MEd-ESL) from the University of the Philippines Visayas; and, her Bachelor's Degree in Communication (major in Broadcast Communication) from the University of the Philippines, Diliman. She worked as a Consultant and Module Writer for the Asian Institute for Distance Education (AIDE) from 2017-2020. She was also a Lecturer in the International Foundation Program (now English Department), Gulf College, Sultanate of Oman from 2008 to 2012. She was an Assistant Professor in the Division of Humanities, College of Arts and Sciences, University of the Philippines Visayas, from 1995 to 2010. She is a mother of 6 adult children, a loving wife to Emmanuel, and a follower of Jesus. She loves writing, crocheting and listening to praise music. She is a resident of Dubai, United Arab Emirates, since November 2013.

Animesh Karn is an Assistant Professor at Amity School of Economics, Amity University Jharkhand. He teaches mathematical economics, inferential statistics, and behavioral economics. With over 18 years of teaching experience, he has taught at various institutions including ICFAI School of Marketing Studies, Hyderabad, Usha Martin Academy, Chandigarh, and St. Xavier's College, Patna. An alumnus of the Banaras Hindu University, Varanasi, he has authored books on mathematical economics, managerial economics, and the Indian economy. Animesh is an expert in econometrics and quantitative techniques. He has extensive research experience in education economics, leadership management, and environmental economics. His research interests include institutional economics, public policy, behavioral finance, and contract laws. He advocates using technology in education and skilling students with open-source tech like R, Python, and LaTeX. Animesh is a respected and approachable teacher, known for his innovative teaching methods and dedication to providing the best education possible to his students.

Ayşegül Eda Kop, PhD has been working as Lecturer at Healthcare Management department in Sinop University since September 2021. She has a MSc degree in Marketing/Unv. Of Nottingham/UK and a PhD in Management Studies/University of Aberdeen/UK. Her PhD explored "social media" and "new product development" using qualitative methodology. Her research interests include social media, new product development, sustainable marketing, marketing research, consumer behaviour and SMEs. She has previously published in international academic journals, international book chapters and international conference proceedings (including presenting papers) on these mentioned topics. Besides academic experience, she has consultation experience in SMEs in the UK and Turkey as well.

Sunil Kumar is working as Associate Professor in the department of HRM, Mittal School of Business, He Had published in various national and international journals. His research areas are women entrepreneurship, leadership, training, diversity management, and workplace spirituality.

Richa Nangia has more than fourteen years of teaching, research and professional assignments experience with reputed institutions. Currently she is working as Associate Professor at K. R. Mangalam University, Gurgaon, India. She has earned her doctorate from University of Rajasthan on the topic Human Resource Development in Automobile Industry (A Comparative study on Tata Motors and General Motors). She has done Masters in Business Administration in HR & IT from Rajasthan Technical University. She has many publications in reputed refereed and peer-reviewed International journals and has presented many research papers in various International and National Conferences. She has authored a book, few articles and book reviews. She is the member of editorial board of various UGC approved journal. Currently Supervising six Ph.D students and three students have been awarded Ph.D under her supervision. Her areas of interest include Organization Behaviour, Training & Development and Human Resource Development.

Issahaku Salifu is a fellow of the Association of Chartered Certified Accountants (ACCA, UK) and the Institute of Chartered Accountants, Ghana and currently a Ph.D. candidate in Business at the Faculty of Business, Law and Social Sciences, Birmingham City University, UK.

Kshama Sharma is currently working as an Assistant Professor in the School of Management and Commerce Department of K.R Managalam University, Sohna, Gurgaon, Haryana. She has been awarded Ph.D (Eco), M. Phil (Eco.), M.A. (Eco.) and B.A. Economics (Hons.) degrees from Banasthali Vidyapith, Rajasthan. She has also done Diploma in Management from IGNOU. In addition to it, she has more than 7 years of teaching experience at U.G., P.G. and Post P.G. levels. In 2014, ICFAI Business School, Gurgaon awarded her the Certificate of Appreciation for the Best SIP Award during SIP (Summer Internship). Her areas of interest are Managerial Economics, International Business, Macro Economic Environment and Strategic Management. She has published 4 papers in National and International Journals. She has participated in various National, International Conferences, Workshops and Symposiums. She has guided several SIP (Summer Internship Program) Students in MBA Program and now guiding 3 Research Students. She feels very fortunate to have closely worked and interacted with a very large number of stalwarts and luminaries from various top institutions of the country in various disciplines -Management and Social Sciences.

Swati Shrivastava is currently an assistant professor at the School of Management and Commerce K.R Mangalam University. She is having a total experience of 11 years which Include 3 years of Industrial and 9 plus years of Academic experience. She received a bachelor's degree in Engineering (IT) University of Rajasthan. She received her Master's Degree in Management from (NIILM CMS) Delhi. She obtained her Ph.D. degree in Management Sciences from Banasthali University (Rajasthan). Her PhD (2022) focused on Domestic and Cross Border Mergers and Acquisitions. Her main research interests include Mergers, women entrepreneurship, Accounting and Finance. She's having Professional membership of AIMA and CMA. She is a certified Innovation ambassador from Institutions innovation council a body working under Ministry of education. Her teaching focuses on entrepreneurship, Finance, Accounts, Banking and Insurance and Portfolio Management.

Rashmi Singel is an Associate Professor at School of Leadership and Management, MRIIRS. Since 2004 she has taught many courses to under graduate (UG) and post graduate (PG) students of business administration programme at reputed institutions like K R Mangalam University, DAV Institute of Management, Rai Business School, Entrepreneur Business School and many others in Gurgaon, Delhi and Faridabad. She has been the member of Board of Studies, Academic Council, School Research Committee and her experience includes managing and coordinating courses, taking lectures, conducting seminars, International Conferences, Faculty developing Programme, extension activities, inter university and intra university events industrial collaborations. She has been teaching courses of finance and accounts such as Security Analysis and Portfolio Management, Financial Analytics, Corporate Finance, Management

Accounting, Cost Accounting,, Entrepreneurship, Financial Accounting, Tally Prime, Insurance and Risk Management, Project Planning, Analysis and Management, Management of Financial Services, Principles and practices of Banking and Insurance, Behavioural Finance. Her research interest are rural entrepreneurship, women empowerment, personal finance, Banking, Women Entrepreneurship, Micro-financing. She has also published several research articles in quality journals indexed in ABDC, Scopus, and SSCI-WoS listed and book chapters with reputed publishers. She has one international and 2 Indian patents to her credit. She has participated in various national and international workshops, FDP, seminars, conferences to keep herself updated and well equipped with latest innovations and changes in the field of Finance and Banking Industry.

Soni Subedi is currently an Assistant Professor at ICFAI University, Sikkim, Gangtok. She has teaching experience of more than 10 years in the areas of School of Management and Legal Studies. Law. She is currently pursuing Ph.d degree from Lovely Professional University, Jalandhar, India. Her areas of interests are Corporate Law, Labour Relations, Entrepreneurship, Consumer Protection and Legal Rights of the Women. She has also presented academic as well as research-based papers at national and international conferences.

Serdar Yener served as a unit commander, headquarters officer, project officer and peacekeeping officer in low and high intensity conflict zones such as Turkey, USA, Afghanistan and Lebanon in the Turkish Armed Forces, NATO and the United Nations following military training from July 1997 to March 2016. Serdar YENER, who holds a bachelor's degree in business administration at Anadolu University, a master's degree at Selçuk University and a doctorate at Haliç University, has been working as a head of International Business and Trade Dpt. at Sinop University Boyabat Faculty of Economics and Administrative Sciences since March 2016. He also graduated from Anadolu University, English Language Teaching Undergraduate Program. He graduated from 27 courses of the United Nations Institute of Education in 2009. Serdar YENER, who has studies in national and international indexes in the fields of "Entrepreneurship", "Gender", "Role Stress", "Positive Psychology and Behavior", Strategic Management, etc. in the field of business administration, has field projects on "Women's and children's education, employment, psychological processes, etc. in Afghanistan, Lebanon and Turkey with the funds of the European Union, United Nations and Sinop University". He is the author of the books "Woman at Work" with Aykut ARSLAN and "Positive Behavior at Work" with Dr. Bilal Çankir.

Index

G

I

K

L

M

N

P

Q

R

S

T

V

W

Recommended Reference Books

IGI Global's reference books are available in three unique pricing formats: Print Only, E-Book Only, or Print + E-Book.

Order direct through IGI Global's Online Bookstore at **www.igi-global.com** or through your preferred provider.

ISBN: 9781799887096
EISBN: 9781799887119
© 2022; 413 pp.
List Price: US$ **250**

ISBN: 9781799874157
EISBN: 9781799874164
© 2022; 334 pp.
List Price: US$ **240**

ISBN: 9781668440230
EISBN: 9781668440254
© 2022; 320 pp.
List Price: US$ **215**

ISBN: 9781799889502
EISBN: 9781799889526
© 2022; 263 pp.
List Price: US$ **240**

ISBN: 9781799885283
EISBN: 9781799885306
© 2022; 587 pp.
List Price: US$ **360**

ISBN: 9781668455906
EISBN: 9781668455913
© 2022; 2,235 pp.
List Price: US$ **1,865**

Do you want to stay current on the latest research trends, product announcements, news, and special offers?
Join IGI Global's mailing list to receive customized recommendations, exclusive discounts, and more.
Sign up at: **www.igi-global.com/newsletters.**

Publisher of Timely, Peer-Reviewed Inclusive Research Since 1988

IGI Global
PUBLISHER of TIMELY KNOWLEDGE

www.igi-global.com Sign up at www.igi-global.com/newsletters facebook.com/igiglobal twitter.com/igiglobal linkedin.com/igiglobal

www.ingramcontent.com/pod-product-compliance
Lightning Source LLC
LaVergne TN
LVHW080525300926
849162LV00007B/1541